P9-CEU-059

Women's Rights in the U.S.A.

Second Edition

Women's Rights in the U.S.A.

Policy Debates and Gender Roles

Second Edition

Dorothy McBride Stetson

Garland Publishing, Inc.
New York & London
1997

Copyright © 1997 by Dorothy McBride Stetson
All rights reserved

Library of Congress Cataloging-in-Publication Data

Stetson, Dorothy M.
    Women's rights in the U.S.A. : policy debates and gender roles /
Dorothy McBride Stetson. — 2nd ed.
      p. cm.
    Includes bibliographical references and index.
    ISBN 0-8153-2076-0 (hardcover) (alk. paper)
    ISBN 0-8153-2075-2 (paperback)
    1. Women's rights—United States. 2. Sex role—United States.
3. Women—Legal status, laws, etc.—United States. I. Title.
HQ1236.5.U6S74 1997
305.42'0973—dc21   97-25107

Paperback cover design by Karin Badger

Printed on acid-free, 250-year-life paper
Manufactured in the United States of America

Contents

Preface to the First Edition xi

Preface to the Second Edition xvii

Acknowledgments xxi

CHAPTER 1

Introduction 1

    The Policy-Making Process 2

        Box 1.1 Name an Issue and Make It Yours: The "Feminization of
        Poverty" 4

        Policy Communities 5

        Conceptual Frameworks 6

        Box 1.2 Gender Neutrality—An Oxymoron? 7

        Changing the Framework 7

        Historical Context 8

    Sex, Gender, Feminism, and Women's Rights 9

        Feminist Debate 11

        Women's Rights Agendas 13

    Themes in Policy Making on Women's Rights Issues 15

        Connections Among Institutions and Arenas of Policy Making 16

        Role of Political Parties 16

        Piggybacking on Other Issues 16

        Policy As a Process 17

        Social Differences and Feminist Politics 17

        Further Study of Women's Rights 17

CHAPTER 2

The U.S. Constitution 21

    The Equality-Difference Debate 21

        Box 2.1 The Equality-Difference Debate: What Makes Sense
        to You? 22

    The Fourteenth Amendment in the Courts: 1868 to 1963 24

Box 2.2 Women in the Law 26
Box 2.3 Pauli Murray: "On the Edge of History" 29
The Equal Rights Amendment 29
Bringing Women into the Constitution 33
Congress and the Courts: 1970 to 1973 33
Box 2.4 Do You Want to Be Famous? 35
Equal Protection and Sex Classification in the Courts: 1973 to 1982 37
Box 2.5 Who's Your Favorite Justice? 40
ERA Debate and Defeat: 1972 to 1982 44
State ERA Efforts 47
Feminist Debate on Constitutional Equality 48
Box 2.6 Is There a Feminist in the Court? 49
Conclusion 54

CHAPTER 3
Political Resources 59
The Vote 62
Inalienable Right to Elective Franchise 62
Box 3.1 The Arrest and Trial of Susan B. Anthony 63
Emancipation of Women 64
Woman's Special Role 65
Box 3.2 Getting Mr. Wilson's Attention 67
Access to Power 69
Box 3.3 Women in National Legislatures 70
Groups 70
Political Parties 72
Box 3.4 A Recurring Feminist Dream: A New Party 73
Appointments and Commissions 74
Box 3.5 Women in the Cabinet: 1932 to 1997 76
From Women's Bloc to Gender Gap 79
Box 3.6 The Gender Gap: Presidential Elections 82
Box 3.7 The Gender Gap: Senatorial Elections 83
Indirect Policies 84
Family Law 84
Jury Service 85
Election Laws 86
Conclusion 87

CHAPTER 4
Reproduction 95
Contraception 97
Obscene Materials 97
Prevention and Treatment of Disease 100
Family Planning 101
Women's Health Movement 105

Box 4.1 Methods of Contraception Used in the United States,
1982 to 1990 107
Sterilization 107
Abortion 109
Criminalization of Abortion 109
Reform/Repeal of Abortion Laws 110
Roe v. Wade 112
Clarifying Roe v. Wade: Restricting Public Assistance 114
From Roe to Casey: The Battle over Abortion Rights 116
The Pro-Choice/Pro-Life Debate 116
Box 4.2 Abortions Performed in the United States, 1973 to 1992 118
Restrictive Laws: Creating Administrative Hurdles 119
Roe or Not? Planned Parenthood v. Casey 121
The Debate over Abortion Services and Clinic Access 123
Box 4.3 Images of Women: Roe and Casey Compared 124
Contemporary Debate over Abortion Rights 125
Box 4.4 Public Opinion on Abortion 126
Surrogacy Contracts 127
Box 4.5 Feminist Views on New Reproductive Technology 129
New Reproductive Technology and Women's Rights 130
Conclusion 131

CHAPTER 5
Education 137
Women's Education: Why Educate Women? 139
Elementary School 140
Secondary School 140
Box 5.1 Coeducation and the Rights of Woman 141
Box 5.2 High School Education by Sex in the Nineties—
the 1890s 142
Higher Education 142
Not Separate, and Not Equal 143
Gender Equity in Education 145
Title IX 146
Title IX Regulations 148
Box 5.3 Some Indicators of Title IX's Impact on Women's Higher
Education 150
Box 5.4 Gender Equity in Athletics: Does One-Third Make Half? 153
Enforcement: A Continuing Controversy 155
Other Gender-Equity Policies 158
Box 5.5 The Gender Divide in Vocational Education: Can It Be
Bridged? 159
Single-Sex Schools 162
Women's Studies 167
Conclusion 168

CHAPTER 6

Family 173

    Box 6.1 Family and the Role of Women 176

    Marriage 178

        Gender-Role Relationships Within Marriage 178

        Box 6.2 The Debate on Coverture—New York, February 20, 1854 ... 180

        Marriage Regulations 183

        Interspousal Immunity 186

        The Marital-Support/Marital-Services Contract 187

        Box 6.3 Does Marital Support Include Indoor Plumbing? 189

        Box 6.4 Criminal Conversation: A Husband's Right to Sue for
        Damages to His Sexual Property 191

        Marital Property Systems 191

        Status of Women and the Feminist Response 193

    Divorce 194

        Legal Divorce 194

        Box 6.5 The South Carolina Paradox 196

        Alimony and Property Settlements 197

        Status of Women and the Feminist Response 198

        Box 6.6 Giving Women Credit: The Equal Credit Opportunity
        Act of 1974 200

    Parental Rights and Responsibilities 201

        From Common-Law Unity to Shared Partnership 201

        Who Gets Custody After Divorce? 202

        Child Support—and Nonsupport 203

        Box 6.7 Child-Support Awards to Mothers, 1978 to 1991 204

        Box 6.8 Child-Support Awards: Mothers and Fathers Compared,
        1991 205

        Status of Women and the Feminist Response 205

    Families Without Marriage 207

        Are Property Rights Recognized? 208

        Parental Rights and Responsibilities 208

        Status of Women and the Feminist Response 211

    Conclusion 212

CHAPTER 7

Work and Pay 217

    Box 7.1 Why Women Worked in the U.S. Meat-Packing Industry
    in 1932 219

    Protective Legislation 219

        The Test of Constitutionality: *Muller v. Oregon* 221

        Restricted Hours, but No Minimum Wage 221

        The Role of the Women's Bureau 222

    Equality for Working Women 224

        Box 7.2 Women Who Work; Women in the Work Force 226

Equal Pay Act of 1963: Equal Pay for Equal Work 226
Civil Rights Act of 1964, Title VII: Equal Employment Opportunity 229
Executive Orders 11246 and 11375: Affirmative Action 233
Implementation of Equal Employment Opportunity Laws 235
Sex As a BFOQ 236
Box 7.3 The Supreme Court Defines a BFOQ 237
Criteria for Proving Sex Discrimination 238
The Continuing Debate over Affirmative Action 240
Box 7.4 Qualifications of Teresa Joyce and Paul Johnson for
Promotion to Road Dispatcher 241
Equal Pay and Nondiscrimination in Compensation 242
Overcoming the Wage Gap 243
Box 7.5 The Wage Gap Between Men and Women 244
Moving Women into Better-Paying Jobs 244
Raising the Pay for Women's Jobs 245
Conclusion 248
Box 7.6 Job Opportunities for Women in the U.S. Military: A
Chronology 249
Box 7.7 The Pay Gap Is Closing . . . White Men Retain the
Advantage 251

CHAPTER 8
Work and Family 257
Box 8.1 Mothers in the Work Force: Then and Now 260
Pregnancy and Childbirth 260
Maternity Protection 261
Box 8.2 Sheppard-Towner: The "Red Menace" 263
Pregnancy As Disability 264
Maternity/Parental Leave 268
Box 8.3 New Definitions of Equality 270
Relief for the Sandwich Generation? 273
Child Care 275
Child Development Act of 1971 276
Box 8.4 Nine Reasons to Veto National Child Care 278
Child-Care Debates Continue 279
Box 8.5 Who's Caring for Preschool Kids While Mom Works? 281
Box 8.6 Tax Laws and Child Care 282
Conclusion 284

CHAPTER 9
Sexuality 289
Prostitution 292
Box 9.1 Contagious Diseases Acts in England: 1864 294
Criminalization of Prostitution 295
Reform Efforts and Effects 297

Pornography 300
  Pornography As Obscenity 301
    Box 9.2 Two Commissions, Two Conclusions 302
  The Feminist Debate 303
Rape 307
  Common-Law Definition of Rape 307
  Rape-Law Reform 309
    Box 9.3 The More Things Change, the More They Remain the
      Same 310
    Box 9.4 The Criminal Justice System's Two Percent Response
      to Rape 313
  Sexual Harassment 316
  Lesbian Issues 320
    Box 9.5 Domestic Partnership Laws: Prelude to Legal Marriage? 323
  Conclusion 326

CHAPTER 10

Economic Status 333
  The Feminization of Poverty 334
    Box 10.1 "Reprehensible Poverty of Our Sex": Indicators of
      Economic Status 335
  What Causes Women's Poverty 336
  Government Programs for Income Security 339
  Single Mothers and Welfare 339
    Aid to Families with Dependent Children (AFDC) 340
    Box 10.2 A Sampling of AFDC Payments: The Erosion of a
      Safety Net 342
    Welfare Reform 342
    Family Support Act and the Aftermath 344
  Welfare for Waged Workers: Women's Share 347
    Unemployment Insurance and Job Training 347
    Retirement, Social Security, and Insurance 350
    Box 10.3 Confused? Some Federal Programs and Their
      Acronyms 353
  Battered Women and Dependency 354
    Box 10.4 The Violence Gender Gap 359
  Conclusion 360

Index 369

Preface to the First Edition

Women's rights is an often-used expression whose meaning is difficult to pin down. It is an equal opportunity concept: everyone has an equal opportunity to offer a definition in hopes that her or his particular perception of the situation will prevail. *Women's Rights in the U.S.A.: Policy Debates and Gender Roles* is my offering.

Years of teaching a course on women and the law have taught me that the concept of *women's rights* embraces ideas and activities of broader scope than those covered by the concept of the *law* as conventionally understood. More than statutes, rules, and court cases, women's rights encompasses all the conflicts—the ongoing public debates—over what it means and should mean to be a female citizen, rather than a male citizen, in the United States of America. In turn, these debates give meaning to the laws, statutes, and court decisions they produce. Therefore, to study women and the law, women and policy, or women and politics, students must learn about the terms of the debates affecting women, as well as how those debates form and change. The purpose of this text is to help instructors and students explore women's rights in the wider context of these policy-making conflicts.

Since the 1950s, there have been changes in the laws and policies that affect gender roles and the status of women in nearly every aspect of life. The process continues, and public controversy about the proper relation between gender roles and public policy persists. It is a difficult subject to teach, and class materials rapidly become out of date. Still, the very features of the subject that make it difficult also make it fascinating. This

book can serve as a guide to many contemporary policy reforms, as well
as to ongoing controversies about new policies. I hope that focusing on
the public debates will encourage students to political action of some
type.

Many of the debates over women's roles and rights relate directly to
students' own lives. In studying the different ideas that swirl around in
public debates on divorce, sexuality, and abortion rights, for example,
students develop their own views on these issues. Often they join organizations that are active on the issues they study in class. By examining all
points of view on an issue, such as contraception, rape, or comparable
worth, students learn to gauge the effectiveness of some demands and
strategies in comparison with others.

This text is a resource for the inquiry into women's rights politics and
policies. It is a record of the changes in the major policy areas affecting
gender roles and the status of women: constitutional law, political resources, reproduction, family law, education, work and pay, work and
family, sexuality, and economic status. It is more than a recital of laws,
statutes, and court decisions. The chapters focus on the development of
and the changes in debates over these issues and on how the debates produce laws and provide the environment for their administration and interpretation. The text also highlights the role of feminists in the debates
and the impact of feminists on policies.

Audience

Instructors and students in undergraduate women's studies courses in
political science compose the major audience for this book. These days,
many political science departments offer one or two courses that involve
women specifically or gender roles more generally. Courses entitled
Women and the Law and Women and/in Politics are probably the most
common, but one can also find Sex, Gender, and Politics; Politics of
Equality; Sex and Power in American Politics; Women, War and Peace;
Gender Politics and Policy; Women and Power; Politics of Sex Roles; Politics of Gender; and others that show the vitality of the subject and the
diversity of approaches to it. *Women's Rights in the U.S.A.* will work as a
central text for Women and the Law courses or as a co-text in other
courses on women, gender, sex roles, and politics.

I hope this book will also help instructors who are interested in developing new courses. For conventional parts of the political science curriculum, such as Political Parties, American Foreign Policy, or Constitutional Law, texts are developed to serve an existing demand. This book is designed in part to stimulate a demand. It may give instructors ideas for developing courses on women's rights politics, laws, and policies. The book will also increase options for readings on women and politics and law beyond the case-laws or case-study approach found in most available texts.

Although this book focuses on policy debates and policy making, its readers are assumed to have a basic knowledge of American government and politics. In my experience, however, even though students have had a basic American Government course, they remain confused about many of the relationships among units of government. Therefore, instructors may find it necessary to explain such subjects as judicial review, federal-state relations, the federal and state court systems, and the role of administrative agencies or congressional committees. When students have real policy issues to follow through various governmental institutions, they often get a better knowledge of government than when they study institutions in isolation. They certainly begin to appreciate the complexity of relationships among Congress, the courts, interest groups, and the bureaucracy, as well as federal-level and state-level policies and policy debates.

Philosophy and Approach

The approach of this book is to understand the contemporary debates on policy in terms of their historical development. Knowing this context is essential to the analysis of current laws and debates. Sometimes, the media treat issues such as child care, abortion, affirmative action, or equal pay as though they were brand-new issues. A search for the origins of such issues usually points to previous debates, many dating back to the nineteenth century. Most contemporary controversies are shaped by the earlier discussions. By looking at the development of these issues, we see just how and why statutes have been written as they are and their effects. For example, the Pregnancy Discrimination Act of 1978 is a reaction to earlier definitions of *mothers and work*. Implementation of prohibition of sex discrimination in education ordered by Title IX in 1972 has been slowed by controversies over the meaning of equal educational opportunity. By tracing policy conflicts, the text also makes connections between policies and shows how *Roe v. Wade* led to *Webster v. Reproductive Health Services* and the path from Aid to Families with Dependent Children (AFDC) programs of 1950 to the Family Support Act of 1988.

A second theme in the text is the role of feminists and women's advocacy organizations in the debates, as well as their impact on policies. It is interesting to follow the changes in feminist views through the years and the effect of social and economic development on feminist perspectives. Sometimes, for example, in debates over women and work, ideas of difference and women's special needs predominate. At other times, nondiscrimination and gender neutrality take over as the dominant ideology among activists. Over time, women's advocacy organizations may move from the periphery to the center of debates, as in the case of the issues of rape and abortion. Students have the opportunity to see a range of impacts of women's advocacy organizations as well. In some cases, such as child care, women's groups are among many involved in seeking control of the debates and seem to have little independent effect. In others, such as sexual harassment, they gain control of the issue and shape policy directly to benefit women.

What is striking, however, is the extent to which feminists debate among themselves over the impact of particular laws on the status of women. These controversies arise from a central question: how can demands for equality be reconciled with sex differences? Debates revolve around the nature and effect of sex differences, definitions of equality, and ideas of what is in the best interest of women. As more women participate in politics, the legal system, bureaucracies, interest groups, and academic careers studying women, these controversies are likely to become more—rather than less—rich and varied. Sometimes, such conflicts limit the effectiveness of women's advocacy activities in the political arena. Disagreement over the Equal Rights Amendment (ERA), for example, handcuffed feminist groups in the 1940s and 1950s. Controversies over pornography and maternity leave found opposing feminist coalitions in the 1980s. In this text, instructors and students will be able to find many cases in which the basic tensions of this equality-difference conflict find expression in the policy-making process.

Reviewers of the book manuscript at once noticed a feminist bias on my part but at the same time suggested that in outlining the disagreements among feminists on various issues, I do not treat them fairly. I am an advocate of women's rights and women's studies. But for me, that fact requires that any study of policy increase understanding of the barriers to achieving women's rights. And, like many other feminist scholars, I have not set my mind firmly on one side of every policy issue. How can we, when we learn new information daily and eagerly anticipate new perspectives on and fresh analyses of central issues of equality and difference?

Framework

This book is organized according to general areas of policy. After the Introduction (Chapter 1), Chapter 2 on the Constitution presents the issues of equality and difference as framed by the Fourteenth Amendment, its interpretation by the courts, and efforts to pass the ERA. A description of political resources as affected by public policy follows in Chapter 3. Chapters 4 through 9 cover reproduction, education, family, work and pay, work and family, and sexuality. The final chapter traces a variety of areas that are primarily defined by their relation to women's economic status, as indicated by the policy area's effect on women's autonomy or dependency. Each chapter is a unit and so may be assigned in any sequence or to supplement other readings. For a Women and the Law course, an instructor might assign specific court cases as supplemental readings. For Women and/in Politics, readings on the participation of women in government and politics would be complementary.

Each chapter contains a list of references that may be used by students who wish to explore some areas in more depth. There are basic readings on the feminist debates, useful government publications, journal articles, and general studies of policy areas. The boxes in each chapter contain a variety of information, including data tables, excerpts from source materials, and elaborations of points made in the text. Many boxes suggest subjects for class discussion.

The book's framework permits exploration of public issues where, even though Congress has enacted a statute or the Supreme Court has made a ruling, conflicts persist. Issues affecting women's rights often remain conflictual. In the absence of social consensus on proper gender roles, many debates will persist, as amply demonstrated by the issues of abortion and education equity. Other subjects await some initial government response. The public regulation of new technologies of reproduction, pornography and its relation to sexual violence, lesbian rights, sexism in school textbooks, and the tension between work and family responsibilities are examples of policy conflicts that will not soon be resolved.

Preface to the Second Edition

Women's Rights in the U.S.A.: Policy Debates and Gender Roles was first published in 1991. The book approached the study of women and the law by emphasizing the framing of public debate on the relation between beliefs about gender roles and public policy. As such, it placed the "hardware" of government—laws, cases, regulations, constitutions—in the context of the political struggle that determines not only their content but also their applications and meaning to people's lives. This book was especially designed, therefore, for those interested in studying the political meaning of gender in American society.

The essential features that are the core of the book remain the same. As outlined in the Preface to the First Edition, these include: a comprehensive survey of laws, statutes, and regulations that affect the status of women in relation to men in American society; the commitment to tracing issues through a variety of public arenas—national, state, and local; the study of policy and policy debates in their historical context; and the analysis of the role of feminists and women's advocacy organizations in the debates.

In picking up the second edition of *Women's Rights in the U.S.A.*, the prospective reader wants to know what's new. The second edition incorporates changes in policy and public debates about constitutional law, political resources, reproductive rights, education, family, work and pay, work and family, sexuality, and economic status. In the 1990s, the Supreme Court has rendered opinions that bear significantly upon abortion rights, single-sex public education, claims under Title IX and Title VII, and equal protection. Federal legislation has brought family and medical leave for some workers, attention to child support enforcement for single mothers, and national remedies for crimes against women. Some issues have gained new currency in public debate, especially sexual harassment, lesbian rights, woman battery, and new reproductive technologies. Others have persisted; this has been true of debates over reproductive rights, welfare and poverty, affirmative action, and child custody.

A conflict as old as the United States itself—over the proper division of financial and policy responsibility between the federal government and the states—has once again come to the public agenda. This question promises to have an as-yet undetermined but no doubt important consequence for most issue areas discussed in this book. It has already brought about an overhaul of welfare policy that sends most of the responsibility, and the federal funds, to the states. This shift away from centralized policy alerts feminists and other advocates for women's rights that power in this large nation is becoming more decentralized, that policies vary from one state to another, and that interest groups must find ways of influencing the many state and local governments. The effect of this shift of resources is likely to be uneven, but we will have to turn our attention increasingly to the study of the grass-roots activities of millions of individuals and thousands of organizations throughout the country.

Both editions of this book are intended for use primarily by instructors and students in women's studies courses. Women's studies curricula continue to expand, and I am pleased to see that much of this expansion has been in courses in political science. The American Political Science Association has helped to distribute collections of syllabi. The breadth of content is evident from the range of subjects: from general women and politics to specialized offerings in reproductive rights; environment; leadership; world politics; feminist theory; feminist approaches in international relations; and comparative gender politics.

Questions in women's studies have become more complex as scholars have investigated diversity among women and the ways that different ethnic, class, and cultural groups relate to themes in feminist and gender studies. When describing policy debates in this edition, I have sought to include perspectives and interpretations by women who identify as members of minority groups. In this, I have benefited from a growing literature by African American feminists and the stirrings of feminist identity among women of Hispanic/Latina descent.

The first edition reported on the debates among feminists over many issues, such as pornography, prostitution, work and family, and constitutional equality. This discussion is now enhanced by attention to diversity among American women. The search for the meaning of gender within groups with racial, ethnic, religious, and other identities is just beginning, and there is little agreement on which questions are most important, let alone on what their answers will be. Terms to refer to members of groups are themselves a matter of choice, and the meanings are controversial. Is it Black or African American? Hispanic or Latina? White or European? Lower class or economically disadvantaged? Native American or Indian? Handicapped or Disabled? Lesbian or lesbian? Following the policy of the publisher of the first edition, I used *Black American* and *White American* and *Hispanic American.* In this text, again following the policy of the publisher, I use *African American* and *black* interchangeably; *Hispanic American* and *Hispanic/Latina* interchangeably; and *women of color* and other terms as they seem appropriate.

Finally, a word about sources. Notes and references are at the end of each chapter. In preparing this edition I found many electronic information resources useful, especially a number of those on the World Wide Web. Such sources are likely to replace many of the traditional library materials. The U.S. government is shifting publication of documents to electronic form, and many agencies have established comprehensive Web sites where data reports are available for individual use. Especially useful in preparing this book were the drafts of Supreme Court syllabi and opinions for recent cases; census data on income and marital status; and information about advocacy organizations. I urge students to use both the electronic resources and the lists of references at the end of each chapter for their own research on subjects of interest.

Acknowledgments

In nearly every aspect, this book has been a product of the growth of women's studies. The first edition of *Women's Rights in the U.S.A.* arose from a frustration that, after fifteen years of teaching Women and the Law, I could not find a suitable textbook. Now, nearly a decade after the publication of that first edition, I am still teaching this course, along with another in comparative gender politics. I have accumulated lots of ideas and a core of data on public policy affecting women and gender roles in America, but it is through teaching these courses that I am able to provide the up-to-date material and analysis included in this second edition.

Since 1969, the Women's Caucus for Political Science has fostered the growth of women's studies in the discipline of political science. Since 1990, the Women and Politics Research Section of the American Political Science Association has provided the institutional support for the growing number of scholars in the field. Even as recently as ten years ago, dissertation research on women and gender topics was rare in political science; thanks to these support groups, it is flourishing today. In addition, the establishment, flowering, and expansion of the Women's Studies Program at Florida Atlantic University (FAU) has enriched my studies with perspectives from many other disciplines. My participation in these organizations and activities has continued to stimulate my thinking about women's rights politics.

The result is that I want to thank them all: the several hundred students who have studied Women and the Law with me since 1976; my colleagues throughout the nation who study women and politics and who encouraged me to undertake the project; those, many unknown to me, who adopted the first edition in their classes, providing the evidence of a need for a second edition; and the faculty in the Women's Studies Program at FAU, who saved me from the isolation that innovation can produce. There are some special colleagues who have long given me encouragement and ideas: Sue Tollesin Rinehart of Texas Tech; Peggy Conway, University of Florida; Helen Bannan, West Virginia University; Laura Woliver, University of South Carolina; Marianne Githens, Goucher College; Robyne Turner, Florida Atlantic University; and Amy Mazur of Washington State University and co-director with me of the Research Network on Gender, Politics, and the State. Many thanks to Peggy Stone Walker and Rita Pellen, professional librarians at FAU, and to Anita Bluestein for her help in preparing the manuscript.

I am grateful to David Estrin of Garland Publishing for his enthusiastic interest in this book and to the editors and production staff who have brought about the finished product with competence and efficiency. Finally I thank my family: my mother, Louise Lilly Albertson, and my sister, Virginia McBride Altman, for their love and support; and my husband, Robert F. Stetson, for that stability which is the foundation of all my projects.

CHAPTER 1

Introduction

Public policies and political practice determine the rights of women in the United States. In learning about these rights, we discover what it means legally, politically, and governmentally to be female, rather than male, in American society. The concept of *rights* implies that the status of women has both legitimacy conferred by government action and value as a public good. With not only gender roles but also public values at stake, women's rights issues provoke controversy.

Consider the "football" issue. Budgets for college athletics have been drastically skewed in favor of men's sports, especially football. After Congress passed Title IX in 1972 to prohibit sex discrimination in federally financed educational institutions, the National Coalition for Women and Girls in Education demanded that colleges and universities be required to allocate funds equally to male and female athletes. Coaches and college presidents mobilized to protect football from pesky demands for gender equity. At stake were not only long-held beliefs about the inferiority of women as sports competitors but also a potential redistribution of economic resources that could revolutionize athletic competition. Final Title IX regulations adopted in 1978 seemed likely to shield the football culture from potential disturbances resulting from improvements in the status and rights of women in education.

Nearly 20 years later, it was time for the Friends of Football (FOF) to regroup. By 1991, strengthened enforcement of Title IX meant more and more resources were needed for women's teams. Even the National Collegiate Athletic Association (NCAA), once the major lobby for football, started to evaluate athletic programs in terms of their gender equity. When a federal court ruled in 1995 that Brown University could not cut women's programs to protect football-heavy budgets for men's teams, the FOFs in the Congress quickly convened hearings. Should football be exempt from Title IX? In the battle over equality for women, the very existence of college and even professional football seemed to hang in the balance. So far, football is not exempt from Title IX coverage, but the tension between demands for equity and sports tradition is likely to persist.

Gender differences and conflicts do not always pertain to all women competing with all men. On the contrary, there is enormous diversity represented by the term *American women*. Whatever we learn about the status of women vis-à-vis public policy, it is important to recognize that the meaning of government action varies from woman to woman and from group to group. For some, their ability to use their legal rights is limited by their poverty. For others, legacies of struggles against racism and a history of oppression have separated people from mainstream social and economic opportunity. Women of various religious, ethnic, and sexual identities often find themselves in conflict with each other over basic values and beliefs.

The politics of women's rights involves debate over what the status of women is, what it should be, and what actions by government will achieve it. At any time, the heterogeneous U.S. society harbors an extraordinary variety of beliefs about gender. The public debate, thus, is frequently a contest to determine the gender-role ideology that will be the basis for policies. *Women's Rights in the U.S.A.* describes the development and change in the public debate about the roles of women in several areas: constitutional law, political resources, reproduction, education, family, work and pay, work and family, sexuality, and economic status. This chapter introduces the vocabulary—concepts, terms, phrases—used throughout the book.

The Policy-Making Process

This global view of women's rights, encompassing political, governmental, and legal aspects, requires a global view of policy making. The goal of examining women's rights in the United States of America is ambitious, especially given the diversity of American society and the complexity of its federal system. Some studies of policy focus only on the national government or on the actions of Congress or the courts. Others attempt to describe lawmaking in the states, singly or as a group. Women's rights politics, however, has always involved interaction among all levels and institutions of government. Drawing boundaries around any one level or institution risks ignoring important actions that affect the status of women. Each woman in the U.S.A. is part of several overlapping political systems and cultures, from local municipalities through state governments to the national government. Her rights are affected by the policies and practices of a variety of public authorities and by her ability to use them. However we think about women's rights—as those of the individual, the group, or American women as a whole—we must consider policy activities of all levels of government.

The subjects of this book are the policies and public debates affecting women's rights in the U.S.A. The book is organized according to areas of policy activity. For each *area* of importance to women's lives, such as education, family, or work, there are questions, or *issues*, about the relation of gender to the subject and the actions that government should take. In the area of education, for example, one issue has been the purpose of public education for girls in comparison with that for boys. Some people believe schools should recognize that women have different adult roles in the family and at work than men and should educate them accordingly. Others argue there should be no recognition of gender differences in public education policy or practice. Some feminists want schools to take an active role in stamping out sexist stereotypes, gender bias, and discrimination.

The expression of these different points of view is the *public debate* on gender and education. The debate involves an argument over the *definition*, or meaning, of the issues of education and women's rights. The stakes in these debates are high. Participants seek to gain acceptance for their definition of the issue by government—the legislatures, courts, executives—and by political organizations, interest groups, the media, and political parties. If participants can persuade policy makers to see the issue as they do, then specific policy actions—statutes, rules, court decisions—are more likely to encourage schools and universities to treat girls either as a special group or as individuals, depending on which definition of gender and education prevails.

Before an issue can be a topic of public debate, it must be presented in some *public arena*. The concept of a public arena for policy making is general enough to encompass not only all levels of government but also other outlets of discussion, such as the media, interest groups, and political parties. There are national arenas, including the Congress, federal bu-

BOX 1.1

Name an Issue and It Is Yours: The "Feminization of Poverty"

Those who can put a new name on a problem and make it stick may claim not only the issue but also the political influence associated with it. The *feminization of poverty* was one such case. Many Americans seem to believe that the "poor are always with us" and that poverty is a product made up of 10 percent disability and 90 percent laziness. Although women and children have always been a majority of the poor, only since 1978 has poverty been defined as a women's issue, a product of sex discrimination. The feminization of poverty names a real problem: two of three adults living in poverty are women. Half of all families living below the poverty line are headed by women. Women dominate in jobs paying minimum wage, and women receive the lowest Social Security pensions. By giving these dismal statistics a new name, women's rights advocates of the 1980s made poverty their issue and added political resources to their demands for better pay, child care, and job training.

The history of this idea also shows the risk in claiming an issue on behalf of all women. Women of color are overrepresented among the poor, and yet they criticize this women's rights strategy for ignoring them. Policy solutions proposed to overcome the feminization of poverty will fail, they maintain, unless they consider such factors as race discrimination, capitalist labor markets, and restructuring of the economy.

In the debates that have taken place in the 1990s over questions of race, class, gender, and poverty, conservatives have mounted a renewed campaign to redefine poverty as a product of cultural flaws and immorality. They have added a gender twist to the old arguments, claiming that by helping a poor unmarried mother, the government subsidizes her immoral choices to continue to have children out of wedlock: "The best thing we can do for poor women, is stop giving them money; it just encourages them to stay poor."

reaucracies, and the national media, and there are state and local arenas. Some issues being considered in a state or locality may become part of a national debate, as did the Indianapolis antipornography ordinance and the Missouri abortion statute. The list of subjects that participants in the public arena, especially political and governmental leaders, agree to discuss and act on is the public agenda, and it is the goal of advocates to get their issues on this agenda. The processes that bring issues to the public arena and win them a place on the political agenda are complex. There is only so much room on the agenda, and many issues compete for attention. Time and energies are limited, so that some problems are debated for a while and then recede from view. Others disappear completely for decades. A few are never far from view and appear and reappear.

When a policy issue, such as education or child care, does come to the agenda for public debate, it is rarely a wholly new issue. The government has no need to reinvent the wheel because it has very likely considered the issue before and has resolved the debates, or similar debates, and has made policy. Judges can rely on precedents, and bureaucrats feel secure sticking to established rules and procedures. For each issue, therefore, there is a way things are discussed and done, based on the outcome of an even earlier debate. Everyone accepts a basic framework for looking at the issue. Groups, including feminists, that want to change policies must confront not only the content of the law, but a network of attitudes, relationships, and practices that resist change. This idea has four components:

1. For each area of women's rights policy, policy communities already exist.

2. Basic conceptual frameworks dominant in these communities rarely change, framing policy responses for decades.

3. When frameworks change, it is because of major social and economic shifts.

4. The study of policy making today must include the historical development and change in debate and government action.

Policy Communities

People in government and those trying to influence them get used to laws on the books and the way these laws work in practice. In Washington, D.C., networks of people in Congress, in the federal bureaucracies, and in interest groups agree on what issues are important and accept a framework for debate. They often establish connections with individuals and groups in state governments, municipalities, and universities and draw them into the *policy community*. People may disagree on the proposed policies, but they agree on what the debate is about, and they use the same concepts and language. Usually these communities are grounded in a government institution, such as a congressional committee or an administrative agency, and attract interest-group leaders, political-party activists, academic researchers, and journalists.

In the area of women and work, for example, a particular policy community dominated the political debate from 1920 to the 1950s. This community was centered in the Women's Bureau, a permanent agency of the Department of Labor. Bureau officials had close ties with women trade-union leaders and the women's section of the Democratic party (Sealander, 1983). Between the 1960s and the early 1990s, a new policy community on women's work issues took the place of the old. This one focused more on women members of Congress and congressional staffs, especially the House Labor and Education Committee, with close ties to a number of feminists and women's advocacy organizations, as well as unions and academics. This new community forged a conceptual approach to women-and-work issues that is quite different from the one dominated by the Women's Bureau. A number of factors suggest that we may be in the midst of yet another change in policy making about women and work; restructuring of the postindustrial economy, increases in families headed by females, chronic inequity in wages, and the shift of policy responsibilities to the state may result in a "framework shift" in the women and work issue.

Conceptual Frameworks

Once a set of values, definitions, and assumptions about an issue becomes officially accepted, it remains for a long time. Most of the people involved in the debate find that this *conceptual framework* helps them sort through proposals and structure the discussion of alternatives. In the area of women and work, for example, the dominant conceptual framework currently in force assumes that women are an integral part of the labor force and should be treated fairly. This perspective in turn is part of a larger civil rights issue framework. Thus, the policy debate is about what actions are permitted to achieve antidiscrimination, equality of opportunity, and individual rights. As long as this framework was dominant there has been little discussion within the policy community about whether ideas of equality and individual rights are the best way to frame the issue of the rights of women workers. If a new question, such as maternity leave or child care, is to have any credibility with this policy community, it must be framed as a gender-neutral issue.

Another policy area, sexuality, has been dominated by a framework that poses a dichotomy: preserving standards of morality versus guaranteeing freedom of speech and expression. Any issue that is classified as sexual, from prostitution to homosexuality, is drawn into this dichotomy,

BOX 1.2

Gender Neutrality—An Oxymoron?

A linguistic victory for the feminist movement of the 1970s was the substitution of gender-neutral names for jobs that, by their titles, excluded women: *fireman* changed to *firefighter; policeman* to *police officer; chairman* to *chairperson.* Did that mean that women would have equal opportunity to these occupations? Does it help women to ignore gender differences? It takes more than a change of title for women to join the fire department in any great numbers. To no one's surprise, such jobs, based on male standards of physical strength and traditional family roles, continue to be suitable for, attract, and select for men much more than women.

In legal discussions, gender neutrality refers to the language, specifically, the nouns and pronouns, used in statutes and regulations. Gender-specific nouns like *man, woman, father, mother, husband,* and *wife,* are replaced by words such as *person, parent,* and *spouse,* which could apply to either sex. But in a society where gender identity and sex differences are so basic to social roles, it is doubtful that neutral nouns are enough to achieve equality of opportunity. More important is the standard used to determine a policy of equality. A male standard will work against women whose lives, due to biological and family differences, are different from those of most men. Similarly, a white-female standard will perplex women of color as they combat both race/ethnic and sex discrimination.

and the moralists line up against libertarians to battle it out. (This struggle has been going on since the arrival of the Mayflower.) One side prevails for a time; then the other side pulls the debate back toward equilibrium.

Changing the Framework

These fundamental frameworks last a long time because they are familiar and comfortable. After a while, they take on a patina of eternal truth: it's the way things are and always have been. Fifty years ago, the women-and-work policy community clung to the fundamental assumption that motherhood made women as workers categorically different from men. They needed special help to improve their lot and to make them better mothers. This framework was institutionalized in government, expressed in state protective laws, and given constitutional authority by the Supreme Court. Generations of political actors accepted the assumption without question.

Then, in a remarkable transformation, this eternal truth changed. The framework and assumptions about women as workers shifted from a focus on fundamental differences to a focus on individualism and equality. Now, efforts to bring motherhood back into the official calculations are stymied by the widespread acceptance of this new truth. Without mentioning the term *mother*, policy makers scramble to answer the continuing needs of mothers in the work force.

Frameworks change as a result of politics in its widest sense. After a major social change, participants usually find that old assumptions simply don't work any more. Frameworks may also be upset in other ways, even by other issues or by shifts in political alliances. Since it's a political process, change in conceptual frameworks is complex.

Historical Context

All this points to the need to study policy debates on issues of women's rights in their historical contexts. Today's actions, in courts, Congress, and state governments, take their meaning for women's rights both from the framework that structures the debate and from the way that framework has changed. Knowing this, we can interpret a Supreme Court ruling on affirmative action or maternity leave in relation to the official definitions of the issue of equality and gender roles in the courts and legislatures. Is a specific decision part of a shift in the fundamental approach to a new issue, or is it a continuation of a long-standing debate?

Some conceptions of issues recede but do not disappear; they mix with new values in a variety of odd ways. This is especially true in family law. Eighteenth-century ideas of common-law unity of husband and wife have been winnowed out but not entirely eliminated from marriage laws in many states. An old law may be put in a new framework to gain acceptance for its continuation in a changed social environment. Until recently, for example, California had a sex-discriminatory statutory rape law: males could be prosecuted for having sexual relations with underage females. Such laws were enacted many years ago in most states on the assumption that females were unable to make responsible choices in sexual matters. When the case came up for the constitutional review by the U.S. Supreme Court in 1981, however, the attorney general of California convinced a majority of the justices that the purpose of the law was to prevent teen pregnancy (*Michael M. v. Superior Court*, 1981). In the mid-1990s, state legislators paid renewed attention to these laws, seeing them as a way to reduce welfare payments. Statistics showed that many teenage mothers become pregnant as a result of encounters with older men, and as a deterrant, some states threatened to prosecute these men either under existing statutory rape laws or by enacting special legislation. When tracing the development of policy through time, we can spot these inconsistencies and shifts in the meaning of laws.

This section has introduced some of the terms that will be used in describing the policy-making process related to women's rights issues. Such terms are useful only if they help the reader to understand the policy conflicts and to interpret their effects on women's rights. As you read the various chapters, you will find many examples of issues, issue definitions, public debates, policy communities, conceptual frameworks, and public arenas and agendas. The relationships among these aspects of the policy-making process vary with each subject treated. The particular configuration in each area determines the fortunes of feminists in their quest to improve the rights of women in the United States.

Sex, Gender, Feminism, and Women's Rights

Questions relating to what it means to be male or female in American society are of great interest to many people, including journalists, advertisers, teachers, social workers, and students. With all this attention, the terms *sex, gender, women, men* that we use to discuss these questions have taken on a variety of meanings. Some time ago, people used *sex* to refer to differences between men and women. Then, *gender* became more popular, and for some people it came to replace *sex* (as when a Supreme Court justice wrote about the two *genders*, or the LSAT application that asks applicants to identify their *gender*). Some people use *gender* to refer to anything that pertains to *women*. Others use *sex, gender,* and *women* interchangeably.

With all this confusion it is important for anyone using these terms, especially in academic or political writing, to make their meanings clear. In this book, *sex* will be used to refer to people in terms of their biological differences. In social science, such terms as *sex, race,* and *age* are useful for

describing the demographic composition of populations. *Gender* will refer to beliefs about people according to their sex—the cultural and social
meaning of being male or female in a particular context. *Gender roles* refers to expectations or prescriptions about behavior and characteristics of
men and women, especially in relation to, or in comparison with, each
other. The terms *women* and *men* can be used to refer to people according
to either their sex or gender differences. When political scientists study
how women vote, they are referring to the political choices made by female human beings—a sex classification. When people describe their beliefs about women—for example, by asserting that women can't play
football (implying some basic difference from men) or that women could
not perform adequately in military combat roles—they are referring to
women in gendered terms. Similarly, men can be discussed as a sex and as
a gender. Data about the percentage of men who are the heads of households counts men as a sex category, whereas assertions that men must
take more responsibility for their families is a gender prescription.

Feminism also has various definitions and uses. In one sense, the
word refers to a view of the social world that assumes that any social order is set up to ensure men's domination over women. But other definitions of *feminism* include any beliefs or action to promote the interests
and rights of women. Feminist advocates are an essential part of the
women's rights policy-making process. Although there are many other
participants in the debates, the feminists are the only ones whose primary
interest in any issue is how it will improve the status of women. The 134
million women in the United States are a diverse lot, and it is no easy
matter for feminists to agree on what specific goals are in the best interests of all American women. A variety of subcategories or adjectives have
appeared to account for the diversity: feminists may be liberal, socialist,
ecological, radical, conservative, and/or advocates specifically for women
of color. It is even more difficult to find agreement on who is or is not a
feminist. Phyllis Schlafly, leader of the Eagle Forum and the now-defunct
STOP-ERA coalition, has said she wants to help women by testifying
against abortion rights, child-care legislation, displaced homemaker services, and laws prohibiting sexual harassment. Leaders of the National
Organization for Women (NOW) find it impossible to include Schlafly
on a list of feminists. Advocates of women's rights rarely accept the notion that such an adversary truly wants to make things better for women.[1]

Most working definitions of *feminism* are likely to sweep up anybody
who claims to be promoting women's interests. Otherwise, someone
would have to rule that not all visions of women's rights are feminist. To

sift among the self-declared advocates for women and to separate those who are really going to improve the status of women from those who are not would inevitably require some judgment about what is in women's best interests, making the definition ideological. To avoid diverting the reader's attention to arguments over such definitions of *feminism,* this book uses an operational definition. *Feminists* include those who identify themselves as feminists and those who are in organizations that advocate women's rights *but not* those who are expressly antifeminist (such as Schlafly). *Feminist demands* are the definitions of issues and the policy proposals made by feminists. The term *feminism* was coined in the early 1900s but was not used widely by activists to identify themselves until the 1960s. Therefore, for earlier periods, the concept will be applied as it has been in women's history. If women's history scholars call a person, group, or proposal *feminist,* that's good enough.

Feminist Debate

The difficulties establishing a definition of *feminism* illustrate the widespread tendency of feminists to disagree over public policy.[2] Times of agreement on goals and strategies, especially on a national basis, are rare. When agreement has occurred, feminists have usually been successful in influencing policy debates and outcomes, especially when their proposals fit into existing conceptual frameworks and policy communities (Gelb and Palley, 1987). Even in times of unity, such as the drives for ERA and suffrage, various groups have supported the common goal for different reasons. In fact, disagreement among feminists over the goals themselves is far more common than unity. They disagree about the meaning of gender differences and their effects on women's lives. They disagree about the relative importance of race, ethnicity, class, and gender for the status of women. They also differ about which specific laws and statutes would promote women's rights. Sometimes, one position will prevail in public debate. At other times, ambivalence numbs controversy, making any clear proposal, even a minority view, difficult to articulate.

The diversity in feminism takes several forms. It may be a debate over a particular policy question, such as pornography. In the 1980s, a lively debate developed between antipornography feminists and free-speech feminists (see Chapter 9). These groups have confronted and confounded each other in arenas of debate over local pornography ordinances, diluting the clout that organized feminist groups might exert on the outcome.

A second form of conflict is ideological. One fundamental value dividing feminists is the importance of biological differences, both reproductive and sexual. In the early 1900s, this conflict produced two camps: the *social feminists*, who considered women to be fundamentally different from men and in need of special protection, and the *egalitarian feminists*, who ignored biology and wanted men and women to be treated identically. In the 1970s, *radical feminists* focused on sexual differences and analyzed patriarchy as the dominance of males over female sexuality. Liberation from male dominance required no less than a sexual revolution, with women gaining control of their sexuality. From this radical feminist viewpoint, laws would do little to help women in the absence of this major transformation. *Liberal feminists* (also known as *reform feminists*) focused on the similarities of women and men as human beings and citizens and sought removal of stereotypes and legal barriers that have kept women from reaching their full potential. Liberal feminists focused on issues of work and pay, educational opportunity, and reproduction, and they agreed that changes in laws would mean an improvement of women's rights.

Women, regardless of color, religion, or ethnicity, who live lives similar to those of white middle-class women can enter into the dominant feminist debate over reform and radical change and work with the agenda of women's rights organizations. However, those who have consciousness about race and class oppression, along with gender consciousness, are dissatisfied with the failure of these feminisms to consider their own racism and classism. Theorists and activists contemplate a women-of-color feminism, challenging the idea that feminism is exclusively about white middle-class women. They advocate a feminist theory and ideology grounded in the experience of women of color. When this is done, perspectives change on questions of gender. For example, reform feminists may seek economic autonomy for women through equal opportunity at work and shared responsibility at home. From the perspective of women whose immigrant status forces them to work in sweatshops, however, the life of a dependent wife with a breadwinner in the suburbs may seem to be an advance. The abortion issue is another example. Access to abortion rights has occupied energies of reform feminists as a top issue. But access to abortion pales in significance for women whose race and poverty have made them targets of forced sterilization. Similarly, for some radical feminists, the "personal is political," that is, the struggle for equality begins in the household relations between husband and wife. But for women who don't live with men who have the economic and political resources, the economic structure itself becomes the most important target.

The debate among radical, reform, and women-of-color feminists promises to produce new forms of feminist theory and practice, as for example, a "multi-racial" feminism (Zinn and Dill, 1994, p. 11). Evidence is strong that gender ideologies and relations are not universal; they are "constructed by and between races, classes and cultures" (Harding, 1991, p. 179). Thus it follows that to be effective, ideologies that challenge gender-based hierarchies must be grounded in their diverse cultural, racial, and class contexts.

Women's Rights Agendas

Despite these ideological and group differences in feminist politics, there are agendas for women's rights in the policy arena. They are especially important sources of information about the way feminists define issues and about their conceptions of which policies will promote women's rights. Where do these agendas come from? They have been developed in several ways. National conventions and federal government commissions have produced the clearest and most comprehensive lists of demands.

National women's rights conventions are rare. But events show that two of them—Seneca Falls in 1848 and Houston in 1977—produced the women's rights agenda for their time. The first attracted women and a few men who answered the call for the Woman's Rights Convention. The 1977 convention was supported by the U.S. government to develop an agenda for the International Women's Decade. Each produced a document: the Declaration of Sentiments (Stanton, Anthony, and Gage, 1881, pp. 67–74) and the National Plan of Action (Bird, 1979).

Activities on behalf of women in the international arena have stimulated the latest effort to develop a women's rights agenda. To prepare for the United Nations Fourth International Conference on Women in Beijing in September 1995, the Women's Bureau of the U.S. Department of Labor convened workshops in every region, drawing together representatives of interest groups and state and local commissions on the status of women to prepare the U.S. plan of action.[3] As a follow-up to the conference, the President's Interagency Council on Women has coordinated U.S. conferences to engage women's groups in working on the agenda (see Chapter 2).

Two major presidential commissions have also investigated women's issues. Presidents Kennedy and Nixon each assembled people from government, universities, unions, business, and interest groups to study the status of women and make policy recommendations. The 1963 report of the President's Commission on the Status of Women was a major review of education, work, family, and political issues, providing extensive recommendations (Mead and Kaplan, 1965). In 1970, *A Matter of Simple Justice* by the President's Task Force on Women's Rights and Responsibilities was much shorter and more specific, with recommendations for federal legislation in education, employment, public accommodations, pay, Social Security, and child care. The 1970 task force also endorsed the Equal Rights Amendment.

The configuration of feminists and women's organizations that are active at any time yields ideas about the women's rights agenda. Frequently, one organization becomes dominant because of its size and public support. In 1890, during the suffrage movement, two competing organizations formed the National American Women's Suffrage Association (NAWSA), which led the coalition to success in 1920. Since the 1970s, the National Organization for Women, formed in 1966, has been the largest women's rights organization. NOW often joins with other organizations to form coalitions to campaign for specific issues, such as pregnancy nondiscrimination, education equity, rape law reform, and violence against women. Finally, individual women—including Elizabeth Cady Stanton, Margaret Sanger, Esther Peterson, Betty Friedan, Catharine MacKinnon—have, through their writings and activities, become representatives of feminist agendas on specific issues and debates.

To explore public policy about women's rights, it is essential to study the participation and impact of feminists. Contrary to popular belief, feminists' political activity has never ceased: every generation has had advocates of women's rights who have sought influence in the political arena. What has distinguished one generation of feminists from another is the environment they have faced. Many have found they could have little impact because they encountered entrenched and immovable frameworks and policy communities incompatible with their demands. All these feminists could do was try to develop their proposals in such a way that they would fit into one of the existing frameworks. If they did not fit, or if the framework made it impossible that a policy would improve women's lot, there was little to be done.

A few feminists, however, have found themselves participating in times of major social and political change, times in which old frameworks have lost their support and new ones are taking their place. At those times, feminists have had the chance to try to get their definition of the issues accepted, to win the conflict over the definition of issues, and to shift policy direction fundamentally. In the area of policies affecting women's rights, there have been two such periods in the past one hundred and twenty years or so: 1870 to 1900, and 1960 to 1980.

The last three decades of the nineteenth century marked a period of major economic and social change. Circumstances produced movements for reform in many areas of life. Feminists participated in the development of conceptual frameworks of gender difference and women's place in society that were the basis for policy debates in areas of political rights, work, family, education, and sexuality. These led to a widespread acceptance of the separation of women and men into distinct roles with equal status.

The social and economic changes after World War II produced dislocations that broke down the old framework and built a new approach to women's rights. After 1960, the framework shifted away from gender difference and toward assumptions of equality and individual rights. Feminists on the scene played a major part in the changes that have had an important impact on women's status and opportunities. Many policies were affected by this shift, especially policies related to work, family, education, and constitutional law.

In neither period did the dominance of one framework drive other perspectives from the debate or deny them an occasional victory. What it did do, however, was to shift dramatically the bias in policy making.

Themes in Policy Making on Women's Rights Issues

The study of women and politics demonstrates how difficult it is to draw a boundary between the political and the nonpolitical. Potentially, everything has a political aspect, that is, a meaning that confers more power, legitimacy, and value to some people and ideas than to others. Because some subjects are more important than others, even the choice of chapter themes and titles in a textbook has a political dimension. Deciding which issues to include in each chapter involves other political choices, as well as the inevitable analysis and conclusions about the debates. The astute reader will be aware of the choices that the author has made and will consider their political meaning.

The subjects of the following chapters are the Constitution, political resources, reproduction, education, family, work and pay, work and family, sexuality, and economic status. Each chapter contains an elaboration of policy debates and government actions on specific issues and problems. Readers are invited to draw their own conclusions and connections about the politics of women's rights in the U.S.A. The following sections describe some of the themes to look for as you read this text.

Connections Among Institutions and Arenas of Policy Making

Policy debates are rarely played out in one institution. Congress may be discussing parental leave and child care or may be silent on these issues. Some states may also be actively passing laws on an issue, while others are ignoring the issue. In addition, state legislators are often in contact with congressional staffs. And the federal and state courts interpret statutes, thereby establishing a basis for further debate.

Role of Political Parties

Political parties' activities related to defining women's rights issues have been sporadic. For the most part, making a women's rights issue a partisan matter has increased the conflict, leading to the defeat of the feminist proposal. Campaigns, elections, and political parties, which have a central place in democratic theory, have usually not been important in the policy debates on women's issues.

Piggybacking on Other Issues

Feminists have sometimes increased the visibility of issues by piggybacking on debates launched by other movements, such as the social purity movement in the 1890s, the civil rights movement in the 1960s, and the labor movement in the 1980s. This strategy has pros and cons. Feminists gain strength from the larger, more successful movement. Women with loyalties in both camps are helped: religious women benefited in the 1890s and African American women in the 1960s and 1970s. But women can also lose control of the definition of *women's status* during these piggyback rides as happened during the social purity crusade. Or, they may discover that feminist policy solutions that deviate from or threaten a companion movement are eliminated, as occurred during the civil rights movement.

Policy As a Process

Although we describe policies as though they were separate things, a policy is in fact a process that involves continuing debate. Statutes enacted by legislatures and major court decisions are usually important milestones in the evolution of the debate. Statutes and court decisions are readable and quotable. Although the process of implementing and interpreting them is more difficult to observe and delineate than are the documents themselves, both implementation and interpretation must be described in order to define women's rights policy.

Social Differences and Feminist Politics

A study of public policy focuses on government action that governs a diverse population. Because people are different, an action's meaning to them will also vary. Feminist activists who believe their campaign will change laws to benefit women may be fully aware that not all women agree on the outcome. Throughout the book you will see instances where the dominant gender roles and the policy debates about them promote disagreement among advocates for women. Some of these occur when feminist perspectives on women, gender roles, and rights are limited by class, race, and other cultural divisions.

Further Study of Women's Rights

Policy conflict over the political meaning of *gender* and *women's rights* is the subject of the chapters that follow. Although the chapters are rich in detail, they are not complete descriptions and do not exhaust the information available on pertinent issues and roles. You may wish to explore connections across policy areas and issues, looking for similarities and differences in the policy debates and processes. You may also wish to examine issues or laws in more detail, especially in your own state and municipality, by consulting some of the materials in the list of references at the end of each chapter.

Notes

1. It is simpler to accept different views of women's rights from the perspective of history. Looking back, for example, both proponents and opponents of protective legislation for women workers seemed to be promoting what they considered to be the best plan to improve the status and fortunes of women. Many historians accept that both proponents and opponents were feminists, one side standing for social protection, the other for equality.

2. The conflicts and disagreements among feminists are neither pathological nor unique. As political representatives of a social movement, feminists have expressed in their debates the dynamism and complexity of the changes in gender roles in the last two hundred years. Controversy produces new discoveries and theories in feminist scholarship. At the same time, the disagreements sometimes dilute the political influence of women who, as a group, have the numbers, wealth, and education to dominate the political process.

3. The Beijing Conference represents the latest stage in the global campaign to improve the status of women waged by the United Nations Commission on the Status of Women (UNCSW). Beginning with International Women's Year in 1975, the UNCSW has convened conferences in Mexico City (1975), Copenhagen (1980), and Nairobi (1985). To date, little research has taken place on the effect of this global campaign on women's rights politics in the United States.

References

Bem, Sandra Lipsitz. *The Lenses of Gender: Transforming the Debate on Sexual Inequality*. New Haven: Yale University Press, 1993.

Bird, Caroline. *What Women Want*. New York: Simon & Schuster, 1979.

Collins, Patricia Hill. *Black Feminist Thought*. Boston: Unwin and Hyman, 1990.

Evans, Sara. *Born for Liberty: A History of Women in America*. New York: Free Press, 1989.

Gelb, Joyce, and Palley, Marion, eds. *Women and Public Policies*, rev. ed. Princeton: Princeton University Press, 1987.

Giddings, Paula. *When and Where I Enter: The Impact of Black Women on Race and Sex in America*. New York: Morrow, 1984.

Harding, Sandra. *The Science Question in Feminism*. Ithaca: Cornell University Press, 1986.

Harding, Sandra. *Whose Science? Whose Knowledge? Thinking from Women's Lives*. Ithaca: Cornell University Press, 1991.

hooks, bell. *Feminist Theory: From Margin to Center*. Boston: Southend Press, 1984.

Mead, Margaret, and Kaplan, Frances Balgley, eds. *American Women: The Report of the President's Commission on the Status of Women and Other Publications of the Commission*. New York: Scribner's, 1965.

Michael M. v. Superior Court of Sonoma County, Ca. 450 U.S. 464. 1981.

President's Task Force on Women's Rights and Responsibilities. *Task Force Report: A Matter of Simple Justice*. Washington, D.C.: GPO, April 1970.

Sealander, Judith. *As Minority Becomes Majority: Federal Reaction to the Phenomenon of Women in the Work Force, 1920–1963*. Westport, Conn.: Greenwood, 1983.

Stanton, Elizabeth Cady, Anthony, Susan B., and Gage, Matilda Joslyn, eds. *History of Woman Suffrage*, Volume I: *1848–1861*. Rochester, N.Y.: Charles Mann, 1881.
Zinn, Maxine Baca, and Dill, Bonnie Thornton. "Difference and Domination." In *Women of Color in U.S. Society*, edited by M. B. Zinn and B. T. Dill. Philadelphia: Temple University Press, 1994, pp. 3–12.

CHAPTER 2

The U.S. Constitution

The issue that links most of the policy debates described in this book is the proper balance between gender differences and legal equality. The equality-difference issue takes its most basic form in the controversy over the meaning of the U.S. Constitution and its guarantees of equality as they apply to gender and women's rights. This book begins with constitutional policy because it is the foundation for other policies of federal and state governments. It is also representative of the legal ideologies that inform debates over specific areas, such as education, work, family, and sexuality.

The Equality-Difference Debate

What sort of foundation does the Constitution provide? Are women equal to men or not? These questions seem simple enough. But, in fact, the answers are not simple, and the foundation is not solid. Since the Fourteenth Amendment's Equal Protection Clause is the only place in the document where the term *equal* is found, this controversy focuses on the meaning of this clause and the Supreme Court's interpretation of it.[1] Some say *equality under the law* means that no one should have a higher or lower status than another person because of sex—an accident of birth. Men and women are entitled to identical treatment by the government. Anything else would condemn women to certain inferiority. Others criticize this view as overly simple and unrealistic. Women and men are dif-

BOX 2.1

The Equality-Difference Debate: What Makes Sense to You?

To sort out your own views on the difficult questions raised by the equality-difference debate, complete the following sentence using phrases a, b, and c.

Under the law, women and men should be treated
   a.   the same.
   b.   similarly, except in matters relating to reproduction.
   c.   in ways that will empower women to achieve equality.

Which sentence makes the most sense to you?

ferent, they argue, at least with respect to reproductive biology, and, for most, different social roles follow from biological differences. Women and men must have equal status under law, but this standard should allow for their different lives. One way to accommodate equality with differences is to consider men and women as having complementary rather than identical roles. Finally, some feminist legal scholars have argued that equality or difference in the framing of policy is not the most important question. Rather, law should be assessed according to whether it helps women overcome subordination to men.

What the Constitution means or should mean for women's rights has divided feminists, judges, lawyers, and the public, and the controversy is likely to continue. As long as there is no agreement in society on gender roles, the legal establishment will be unable to forge a consensus.

All successive movements for women's rights in the United States have been concerned with efforts to change prevailing constitutional provisions on equality. This is understandable because the drafters of the U.S. Constitution were devoted to an ideology that either placed women in an inferior position, or, more often, ignored them altogether. State constitutions, adopted as each state was admitted to the Union, embraced English common law. Common law took note of women, all right, by inflicting legal disabilities and handicaps that kept them out of public life.

Debates over constitutional law are usually more complex, absorbing, and politically relevant in the United States than in other countries. Most governments have put guarantees of sex equality in their constitutions, many at the behest of the United Nations or other regional organizations. In the United States, however, there remains disagreement over the constitutional language of equality. During the campaign for the

Equal Rights Amendment (ERA), advocates often astonished audiences by pointing out that only in the United States, the greatest democracy, do women not have the guarantee of equality written into the Constitution. But it is important to keep in mind the role of the Constitution in the U.S. political system and especially the powers of the courts in judicial review. In many countries, constitutional guarantees of equality are symbolic and have little effect on policy debates and the drafting of laws and regulations. In the United States, constitutional language is only partly symbolic; it is also instrumental and crucial to policy powers, especially in the states, where many laws affecting gender are deliberated. With judicial review, the federal courts can strike down laws that are unconstitutional.

Although constitutional issues have been part of the women's rights movement, only rarely have feminists agreed on what they want the Constitution to mean and then worked together to achieve their goal. From 1912 to 1920, they united in a campaign to pass a constitutional amendment and thereby achieve the right to vote. And, from 1970 to 1982, they worked together for the ERA. Except for these brief episodes, feminists have disagreed over how to deal—constitutionally—with the issue of equality and difference.

Feminists were most divided on the issue after the Nineteenth Amendment was ratified in 1920. The proposal in the early 1920s for the ERA caused a rift that separated women into two schools of thought that belied their agreement on many other issues. This conflict was the main business of women's rights advocates until the 1960s. Both sides wanted to do what was best for women. One side saw a constitutional standard of equality as the only way. The other believed the ERA was too rigid to allow for the special needs of women as workers and mothers. The divide was so great that women activists could not unite on other issues, such as family law and equal pay. Finally in 1963, the President's Commission on the Status of Women (PCSW), called together by President Kennedy, proposed a compromise. It agreed that equality of rights under the law for all women and men is "so basic to democracy and its commitment to the ultimate value of the individual that it must be reflected in the fundamental law of the land" (Mead and Kaplan, 1965, p. 65). But the PCSW maintained that the Constitution already contained this principle in the Fifth and Fourteenth Amendments. There would be no need for an ERA; what was needed was "judicial clarification." Thus the PCSW urged interest groups to bring cases challenging laws that discriminate and to force the Supreme Court to confer constitutional equality on women.

This chapter takes this 1963 proposal as a starting point for examining the complex political debate over constitutional equality. Does the Fourteenth Amendment contain a sufficient guarantee of equality, or is the ERA necessary to achieve women's rights? Until 1963, the Fourteenth Amendment, ratified in 1868, had been interpreted to permit sex-discriminatory laws. The following section begins with a description of pertinent cases that shows the development of this litigation, including the period from 1923 to 1963 when the issue of the ERA hovered over women's rights politics. This is followed by a description of the ERA controversy and an analysis of why the PCSW preferred the Fourteenth Amendment. We then turn to the years after 1963, when most feminists worked together to get women into the Constitution through both strategies: the ERA and the Fourteenth Amendment. This section shows the interrelatedness of the debates over the two amendments and the outcome up to 1982. The chapter ends with a look at feminist activities since 1982. Feminists have once again begun to debate the issue of difference and equality, trying to develop for the first time a feminist legal ideology of constitutional equality.

The Fourteenth Amendment in the Courts: 1868 to 1963

After the Civil War, the Reconstruction Congress pushed through three amendments to the Constitution. The Thirteenth Amendment abolished slavery. The Fifteenth Amendment prohibited states from denying citizens the vote "on account of race, color, or previous condition of servitude." The Fourteenth Amendment set forth details for regulating the states' powers in the wake of the Civil War and the freeing of the slaves. Section 1 of that amendment has had the effect of extending to the states the limits on the national government's power to interfere with citizens' rights contained in the Bill of Rights. Three clauses in the Fourteenth Amendment are important in relation to women's rights:

- *Privileges and Immunities Clause:* No state shall make or enforce any law which shall abridge the privileges or immunities of citizens of the United States.

- *Due Process Clause:* Nor shall any state deprive any person of life, liberty, or property without due process of law.

- *Equal Protection Clause:* Nor deny to any person within its jurisdiction the equal protection of the laws.

With respect to equality, the key phrase for interpretation is in the Equal Protection Clause. While it is not possible to know fully the motives or intent of the framers of this language, they were closely related to the antislavery movement and were influenced more or less by the same theories of natural rights embodied in the clause "all men are created equal" in the Declaration of Independence.

At the time the Fourteenth Amendment was being considered, feminists were most concerned about Section 2, which determined the number of representatives a state had in Congress based on the number of *male* citizens allowed to vote. For the first time, gender-specific language was in the basic law of the land, denying women of all races their place in the political community. The framers told Susan B. Anthony and Elizabeth Cady Stanton that "this is the Negro's hour," dashing hopes that the emancipation of slaves would lead to the emancipation of women. These leaders of the Woman Movement saw little in the Fourteenth Amendment to help their cause. Thus, the political and ideological context in which the amendment was ratified limited its effect on women's rights, despite the gender-neutral language of the Equal Protection Clause. Two individuals brought cases to test the amendment's application to specific rights.[2] Virginia Minor claimed in 1875 that the right to vote for women was embodied in the Privileges and Immunities Clause (see Chapter 3). Counsel for Myra Bradwell argued in 1873 that the Privileges and Immunities Clause gave her the right to practice law in Illinois, which forbade married women from entering that profession (*Bradwell v. Illinois*, 1873).

Whereas the U.S. Supreme Court majority denied Bradwell's claim, basing its decision on a general restriction of the Fourteenth Amendment's coverage, one of the justices concurring in the decision elaborated on the *separate spheres* of men and women. Justice Bradley thus provided the classic and definitive statement of the nineteenth-century legal ideology of sex differences as reinforced by common law:

> [T]he civil law, as well as nature herself, has always recognized a wide difference in the respective spheres and destinies of man and woman. Man is, or should be, woman's protector and defender. The natural and proper timidity and delicacy which belong to the female sex evidently unfits it for many of the occupations of civil life. The constitution of the family organization, which is founded in the divine ordinance, as well as in the nature of things, indicates the domestic as that which properly belongs to the domain and functions of womanhood. The harmony, not to say identity, of interests and views which belong or should belong to the family institution, is repugnant to the idea of

BOX 2.2

Women in the Law

Myra Colby Bradwell (1831–1894) sought a career in law as a means of promoting women's rights. In 1868 she established and edited the *Chicago Legal News*, the first law journal printed in the West. "Myra Bradwell became a significant intellectual force in the development of law in her region" (Brownlee and Brownlee, 1976, p. 288). Nevertheless, when she applied for entrance to the state bar of Illinois she was refused on the grounds that she was a woman; the U.S. Supreme Court sustained the Illinois Court's decision. This meant that women had to fight a state-by-state battle for the right to practice law. From the first "first woman lawyer" (Belle Mansfield in Iowa in 1869) to the last (Mildred Herman in Alaska in 1950), each state produced a pioneer for the cause (Morello, 1986, pp. 37–38). The Illinois legislature admitted women to all professions in 1872, but Alta Hulett, not Myra Bradwell, was the first Illinois woman admitted to the bar.

As for Myra Bradwell, she continued her campaign for women's rights, but never sought admission to the bar again. The Illinois Supreme Court, acting on her 1869 petition, admitted her in 1890. In a symbolic gesture, the U.S. Supreme Court opened its doors to her two years before her death.

a woman adopting a distinct and independent career from that of her husband. (*Bradwell v. Illinois,* 1873, p. 141)

While Bradwell's case was being considered, the U.S. Supreme Court ruled that the Fourteenth Amendment's range would be strictly limited, and the Equal Protection Clause would apply only to state actions affecting race. Even when reviewing racial laws, the Supreme Court was willing to accept a state's argument that such laws would be *reasonable* if related to *legitimate ends*. Thus, from the 1870s on, the Equal Protection Clause of the Fourteenth Amendment did not have much effect on discriminatory state laws.[3] By 1896, in its ruling in *Plessy v. Ferguson*, the Supreme Court declared that the equal protection clause permitted separate treatment by race, reinforcing a wide array of racist laws.[4] Thus, even if the Fourteenth Amendment had been brought to bear on gender classifications, such as the Illinois law challenged by Bradwell, the outcome would have upheld separate treatment of women and men, so widespread was the belief in woman's essential difference.

Although, for the next hundred years, there was no political strategy to force the Supreme Court to add sex classifications to its review of the Fourteenth Amendment, it occasionally rendered opinions that tended to reinforce and build on Bradley's argument. In *Muller v. Oregon* (1908), the Supreme Court examined state protective labor legislation that limited the hours employers could require women to work (see Chapter 7 for a full discussion of the case). The Supreme Court sustained the legislation, and a majority ruled definitively that the Constitution permitted states to treat women differently because of their physical and social differences. "Differentiated by these matters from the other sex, she is properly placed in a class by herself, and legislation designed for her protection may be sustained, even when like legislation is not necessary for men, and could not be sustained" (p. 422).

One of the best cases to illustrate the Supreme Court's traditional approach to the Equal Protection Clause and sex discrimination is *Goesaert v. Cleary* (1948). At the time, the test of constitutionality in place for most discriminatory laws was quite weak.[5] The court would accept a state's power to separate people into groups and treat them differently as long as such unequal treatment was not arbitrary. In other words, what the Equal Protection Clause did was prohibit totally capricious laws. When a state's laws treated women differently, all the state government had to do was give some reason that sounded plausible. This was a little tricky in the *Goesaert* case because Michigan had a law that prohibited any woman from being employed as a bartender unless she were the wife or daughter of a male owner. Neither a female owner nor her daughter could tend bar. Thus, Michigan had to show why it made sense to keep most but not all women out of the bartending occupation. Justice Frankfurter's opinion applying the equal-protection test to Michigan's defense of its law shows that he was easily convinced. He stated that the "Constitution in enjoining the equal protection of the laws upon states precludes irrational discrimination as between persons and groups of persons." Bartending by women may give rise to social and moral problems (thus justifying banning women), but the legislature was rational in believing that a husband and father who owned the bar would be "sufficient protecting oversight" (p. 466). This is an example of a weak test of constitutionality. When justices use a weak test, they approach the case assuming that the law is constitutional, unless the challengers make a convincing case to the contrary.

Two years before the PCSW issued its 1963 report arguing that the Fourteenth Amendment embodied a basis for equal rights for women, the Supreme Court reviewed Florida's law on jury selection. While all male registered voters were in the jury-selection pool, only those women who specially registered could be selected. This discriminatory selection process was reviewed after Gwendolyn Hoyt was charged with the murder of her husband and was convicted by an all-male jury. She claimed that women would have been more likely to understand why, because of her husband's infidelity, she was driven to assault him with a baseball bat. However, in *Hoyt v. Florida* (1961), the Supreme Court was unanimous in upholding this absolute exemption for women but not for men. The Supreme Court agreed that the exemption was based on a reasonable classification: "Despite the enlightened emancipation of women from the restrictions and protections of bygone years, and their entry into many parts of community life formerly considered to be reserved to men, woman is still regarded as the center of home and family life" (pp. 61–62). The test the Supreme Court was using is called *ordinary scrutiny*, based on the expectation that the legislature has acted within its powers in establishing any classification as long as it is shown to be reasonable or, even weaker, "not unreasonable." Although the language had been updated, the Supreme Court's view of the special and unequal place of women vis-à-vis the Constitution had not changed much since Justice Bradley's day.

Many members of President Kennedy's PCSW, which had been established the same year the *Hoyt* case was decided, had reason to believe that the Supreme Court, faced with a concerted demand from women, might extend the equal protection of the Fourteenth Amendment. Pauli Murray, an attorney who headed a subcommittee on constitutional equality, was especially impressed by the success of civil rights groups. These groups had mounted a special campaign of litigation to push the Supreme Court to develop and apply a strict test of constitutionality in its review of race discrimination. After decades of such litigation, the Supreme Court added a second tier of strict scrutiny especially for racially based laws.[6] It called them *suspect* and would permit them only if the state could show such laws served a *compelling* state interest. Today, race-discriminatory statutes do not survive this test. Contrast the suspect-classification test with the ordinary-scrutiny test used for sex classifications: under ordinary scrutiny, laws that treated people unequally were acceptable if the laws were based on reasonable classifications related to legitimate interests. The PCSW agreed that if the Supreme Court would also change its treatment of sex discrimination and adopt the stricter test, women and men would be equal under the Constitution.

BOX 2.3

Pauli Murray: "On the Edge of History"

Pauli Murray's historic 1963 contribution to the development of women's rights was one episode in the remarkable life of a twentieth-century pioneer. Murray (1910–1985) fought race and sex barriers her entire life, from struggles to gain education in the 1930s to her ordination as one of the first women priests in the Episcopal Church in the 1970s. A comrade-in-arms of both civil rights and feminist leaders, she integrated restaurants in Washington, D.C., with Patricia Roberts Harris (later Secretary of Housing and Urban Development under President Jimmy Carter), prodded Eleanor Roosevelt on race issues, studied law at Yale along with Eleanor Holmes Norton (later head of the Equal Employment Opportunities Commission and the District of Columbia representative in Congress), and helped found the National Organization for Women with Betty Friedan. When Congress passed Title VII of the Civil Rights Act prohibiting both race and sex discrimination in employment, Murray said, "I was overjoyed to learn of the House action, particularly because as a Negro woman, I knew that in many instances it was difficult to determine whether I was being discriminated against because of race or sex and felt that the sex provision would close a gap in the employment rights of all Negro women" (Murray, 1987, p. 356).

The Equal Rights Amendment

Until the 1960s, few feminists believed that the Equal Protection Clause of the Fourteenth Amendment applied to women. Women's rights organizations and advocates were embroiled in another controversy over whether the Constitution *should* guarantee equal rights for women. This battle focused on the Equal Rights Amendment. The original ERA was drafted by Alice Paul and her National Woman's Party (NWP) and introduced in Congress in 1923 (see Chapter 3 for a discussion of the NWP). It was a straightforward statement of egalitarian feminism:

> Men and women shall have equal rights throughout the United States and in every place subject to its jurisdiction. Congress shall have power to enforce this article by appropriate legislation. (U.S. Senate. *Senate Journal*. Res. 21 68th Cong., 1st sess.)

After a brief debate, the NWP agreed that enactment of this amendment would end special benefits for women. This small but vocal group believed that equal rights would so improve the status of all women there would be no need for any special treatment. The majority of supporters of women's suffrage, however, opposed the ERA, considering it a threat to the interests of poor mothers and working women. They campaigned hard for protective laws, such as the one upheld in the *Muller* case, and demanded further help for mothers and children. The public's recognition of the special needs of women had justified giving them the vote. Thus, they believed the ERA threatened the very basis of women's political rights. Many historians consider this disagreement central to feminist politics in the 1920s and have labeled two separate factions: social feminists and egalitarian feminists (Becker, 1981; Chafe, 1977; Lemons, 1973).

The NWP saw to it that the ERA was introduced in every session of Congress, starting with 1923. Despite its centrality to the small group of activists in the 1920s, the proposal initially had little impact outside feminist circles. The NWP began to attract support for its cause in the 1930s. In 1937, the National Federation of Business and Professional Women's Clubs made the ERA a legislative priority. The Republican party adopted a plank supporting the amendment in the 1940 party platform, although labor-union opposition kept the Democratic party from endorsing it until four years later. Finally, during World War II, Congress held the first debate on the amendment. Some considered the ERA a way to encourage and reward women's work in the war effort. The House Judiciary Committee endorsed new wording, drafted with the assistance of Alice Paul and the NWP, to make the ERA more consistent with the Nineteenth Amendment and more specific to governmental, as opposed to private, action. The ERA language has remained the same ever since:

> *Section 1.* Equality of rights under the law shall not be denied or abridged by the United States or by any State on account of sex.

> *Section 2.* The Congress shall have the powers to enforce, by appropriate legislation, the provisions of this article.

> *Section 3.* This amendment shall take effect two years after the date of ratification.

In 1944, both the Democratic and Republican parties endorsed the ERA in their party platforms.

As support for the ERA grew, opposition to it also became more active. Labor unions, the Women's Bureau (at the Department of Labor), liberal Democrats—even the American Civil Liberties Union (ACLU)—expected the ERA to promote individual rights at the expense of the interests of workers and mothers. The Women's Bureau drafted a position paper in 1943 detailing the dangers inherent in the ERA: it would injure wives and mothers, unsettle the law for years, lead to changes in Social Security, require equal induction in the armed forces, threaten husbands' support of wives, and repeal protective labor laws. Frieda Miller, director of the Women's Bureau, labeled the ERA "radical, dangerous and irresponsible" (quoted in Harrison, 1988, p. 18). The NWP countered that it would take too long to chip away the inequalities, one law at a time. As for labor laws, laws that improved the conditions of women workers would be extended to men; those that restricted and paralyzed women would be eliminated.

These early debates on the ERA forecast arguments that reappeared in the 1970s and 1980s. Note which groups were on opposite sides of the issue. In the 1940s, liberal politicians and labor unions joined coalitions to defeat the ERA, while conservatives in the Republican and Democratic parties supported it. At that time, the main factor that defined the ERA was its effect on protective labor legislation. Both groups agreed the ERA would abolish such government regulations. Liberals wanted to retain them; conservatives wanted to be rid of them altogether. Thus, economic class and place in the labor force, rather than sex, separated the proponents and opponents. Race also played a part: some southern legislators saw the ERA as a measure to help white women in the face of all the demands for black people's rights. Black women were caught up in the struggle to launch the union and civil rights movements and did not weigh in on either side of the ERA.

The ERA made more progress in the Congress of 1945, passing the Senate by a majority, although not by the necessary two-thirds majority. Opponents stepped up their efforts, establishing the National Committee to Defeat the Unequal Rights Amendment (NCDURA), and tried to derail the ERA. The Equal Status Bill they insisted on provided that in "law and its administration no distinctions on the basis of sex shall be made except such as are reasonably justified by differences in physical structures, biological or social function" (Harrison, 1988, pp. 27–28). Most active women's organizations found the exceptions to this bill just too extensive to have any impact on many laws that they believed to be restrictive. Members of Congress were offered two choices on "the women's thing": The ERA or the Equal Status Bill. Neither piece of legislation was acceptable to both sides.

Finally, Senator Carl Hayden (D.-Ariz.) offered a compromise that brought Congress to a standstill on the ERA. Hayden's amendment was added to the ERA during debate in 1950: "The provision of this article shall not be construed to impair any rights, benefits, or exemptions conferred by law upon persons of the female sex" (Harrison, p. 31). Proponents rejected the ERA with the Hayden Amendment because they believed it would make the ERA essentially meaningless. Yet members of Congress, beleaguered on the issue, welcomed the compromise they had been waiting for. They could vote for equal rights and still not offend labor unions, liberal Democrats, and advocacy groups for mothers and children. Although the ERA remained in the platforms of both political parties, deadlock persisted in Congress. Nevertheless, the NWP and other women's groups supporting equality measures kept up the pressure.

The ERA became a contentious issue during the 1960 Democratic convention. Labor-union activist Esther Peterson led ERA opponents, with arguments similar to those the Women's Bureau had offered twenty years earlier:

- If there are unequal laws, fix them with "specific bills for specific ills" (Harrison, p. 116), not a blanket amendment.
- The ERA would nullify protective laws that benefit women.
- The ERA would threaten to bring confusion to family law.

The Democratic party softened its support for the ERA, and Peterson went on to head the Women's Bureau under President John F. Kennedy.

At the Women's Bureau, Peterson revived the long-standing demand for a national commission on women's status (see Chapter 3). Such a commission had been proposed in the United States regularly since 1945, when the United Nations had appointed a Commission on the Status of Women (CSW) to document women's social, economic, and political positions and to recommend policy. But the proposal had always foundered on the shoals of the ERA. The issue of constitutional equality so divided women's advocacy organizations and feminists that most people felt any commission representing women would be unable to act. Thus it came about that, in order to launch President Kennedy's newly authorized PCSW, which was charged with addressing basic economic and education issues, Esther Peterson in 1961 took up Pauli Murray's suggested compromise on the ERA. Not long afterwards, the PCSW endorsed the concept of equal rights in the Constitution but argued that these rights were already embodied in the Fifth and Fourteenth Amendments. They recommended that women's advocacy organizations use these amendments to challenge unequal laws and encourage the Supreme Court to make a judicial clarification of the constitutional status of women.

The effect of the PCSW's proposal was to shift the burden of reconciling equal rights with sex differences from Congress to the courts. Organizations began to bring lawsuits to extend coverage of the Equal Protection Clause of the Fourteenth Amendment to women. After the mid-1960s, however, the demand for equal constitutional rights took another turn. The issue of the ERA was redefined; feminists united to campaign for its ratification. These debates and campaigns were interrelated; as a result, although the Equal Rights Amendment was not added to the U.S. Constitution, constitutional law in the United States was changed.

Bringing Women into the Constitution

As the women's movement organized and grew after 1963, many feminists agreed to a theory of equal rights heavily influenced by civil rights ideology and consistent with ideas of American liberalism. The theory downplayed the importance of biology in determining people's lives. Just as race had little effect on individual talents, neither were there any sex differences relevant to abilities. It also ignored the relationship of economic status to the effective use of rights, a concern that had moved labor activists opposed to the ERA. Laws should be written to encourage individual choice *and not* to classify people according to sex, beliefs, or race. Women and men had many more human qualities in common than they had differences. As long as laws continued to separate them, women would be discriminated against according to outmoded stereotypes of woman's place. Sex should not be a permitted basis for writing laws. In 1970, many laws still classified people by sex, especially in family law, education policy, Social Security, and the military. Leaders of the new feminist movement set about to change the basic law to achieve equality of individual rights.

Congress and the Courts: 1970 to 1973

Dramatic events affecting constitutional rights occurred in the Supreme Court and Congress in the early 1970s. Following PCSW recommendations, women's rights organizations watched for court cases that might lead to a reinterpretation of the Fourteenth Amendment. Most of these organizations were not yet geared up to sustain long-term litigation projects. The ACLU, which had brought the Florida jury case *Hoyt v. Florida* in 1961, provided most of the resources. Finally, in 1971, a case challenging an Idaho statute made it to the Supreme Court. Idaho law gave automatic preference to males as executors of estates when there were two relatives of equal relation to a person who died without a will. *Reed v. Reed* (1971) became the first decision by the Supreme Court to rule that a law that discriminated on the basis of sex was in violation of the Equal Protection Clause. A unanimous Supreme Court, using ordinary scrutiny, clearly indicated that not all sex classifications were reasonable, stating that a classification

> must be reasonable, not arbitrary, and must rest upon some ground of difference having a fair and substantial relation to the object of the legislation, so that all persons similarly circumstanced must be treated alike. (*Reed v. Reed*, p. 76, quoting *Royster Guano Co. v. Virginia.* 253 U.S. 412. 415. 1920)

The state of Idaho had argued that giving automatic preference to the male as executor improved administrative convenience by avoiding costly and cumbersome hearings to determine competence. (They also mentioned that men would be more interested in and capable of handling finances than women would be.) The arguments did not move the Supreme Court, as Chief Justice Warren Burger wrote:

> To give mandatory preference to members of either sex over members of the other, merely to accomplish the elimination of hearings on the merits, is to make the very kind of arbitrary legislative choice forbidden by the Equal Protection Clause of the Fourteenth Amendment. (*Reed v. Reed*, p. 76)

Although the law was struck down, the feminists at the ACLU did not get what they wanted: to have the Supreme Court declare sex classifications suspect, thus making their constitutional status the same as those classifications based on race. It had taken six cases and two decades for the race standard to be established. The ACLU set up a section to press the Supreme Court to continue its clarification of women's status. Under the leadership of Ruth Bader Ginsburg, the Women's Rights Project (WRP) became the only organization to promote a strategy of systematic results-oriented litigation for constitutional rights (O'Connor, 1980).

Just two years after the *Reed* case, in *Frontiero v. Richardson* (1973), the WRP came as close as it ever has to achieving its goal. The WRP chal-

BOX 2.4

Do You Want to Be Famous?

One way to preserve your name for posterity is to bring a successful appeal to the U.S. Supreme Court. If your case sets a historic precedent, as Sally and Cecil Reed's case did, your name will be recorded in law journals and history books and will be memorized and cited by generations of law students, attorneys, and judges. But they will remember little of your life or the hardships that brought you to court. Certainly, little is mentioned of the Reeds' family saga. They divorced shortly after adopting their son Richard. The "tender years" doctrine (see Chapter 6) gave Sally custody at first, but moved Richard to live with his father when he reached adolescence. After that, Richard became depressed and committed suicide. Sally blamed her ex-husband for the tragedy, which ultimately brought them to be parties to a historic challenge of sex-discrimination law.

These facts give background only, however. What is important for the law is not the personal story, but the precedent the ruling sets. The Reeds' personal tragedy faded from view; the fact that the sex classification in the law they challenged was found unconstitutional remains a historic shift of legal precedent.

lenged a military regulation that provided dependents' benefits to all spouses of male officers but awarded benefits to husbands of female officers only if they could prove they depended on their wives for more than half of their support. Eight justices agreed this discrimination violated the Constitution. They differed, however, over what test of constitutionality to use. Justices Brennan, Douglas, White, and Marshall argued that sex should be a suspect classification: "Sex, like race or national origin, is an immutable characteristic determined solely by accident of birth. . . . [T]he sex characteristic frequently bears no relation to ability to perform or contribute to society" (pp. 686–687). But four justices does not make a Supreme Court majority. The other concurring justices (Burger, Stewart, Powell, and Blackmun) maintained it was unnecessary to use the stricter standard since the military regulation did not survive even under ordinary judicial scrutiny. They made it clear they were not ready on their own to take this far-reaching step of establishing a new constitutional principle.

> There is another . . . compelling reason for deferring a general categorizing of sex classifications as invoking the strictest test of judicial scrutiny. The Equal Rights Amendment, which if adopted will re-

solve the substance of this precise question, has been approved by the Congress and submitted for ratification to the States. If this Amendment is duly adopted it will represent the will of the people accomplished in the manner prescribed by the Constitution. (p. 692)

Although the Supreme Court is insulated from politics, the justices are aware of changes and relevant events outside the courts. Between 1961 and 1970, they strengthened their application of the Equal Protection Clause to sex-discrimination laws. In this they were undoubtedly affected by the enactment of the Civil Rights Act and the birth of a civil rights movement for women during the 1960s. In the early 1970s, they took notice of the efforts of the women's movement to amend the Constitution.

By 1973, the ERA had already passed Congress and seemed headed to early ratification in the states. Just ten years earlier, ERA advocates had been in a deadlock with opponents. But opposition to the amendment quickly evaporated after Title VII of the Civil Rights Act went into effect (see Chapter 7 for details of Title VII). Title VII prohibited sex discrimination in employment and preempted state protective laws. When NOW made the ERA part of its national platform in 1967, some labor-union supporters left the organization. By 1970, however, the United Auto Workers had endorsed the ERA, and other unions and liberal interest groups followed suit. (The AFL-CIO held out, however, until 1973.) With the protective-legislation obstacle out of the way, support, based on the simple principle of legal equality, grew. The heir of the PCSW—the Citizens' Advisory Council on the Status of Women (CACSW) in the Labor Department—also endorsed the ERA in 1970. Presidents Nixon and Johnson both favored the amendment. Nixon's Task Force on Women's Rights and Responsibilities recommended that the president urge passage: the ERA would "impose upon women as many responsibilities as it would confer rights. The task force views this objective as desirable" (President's Task Force on Women's Rights and Responsibilities, 1970, p. 4).

As these endorsements piled up, so did the pressure on Congress, where the amendment had long languished at the bottom of the agenda. Members of NOW—by making a surprise visit during the hearings on an amendment to secure voting rights for citizens ages 18 to 21—prodded Senator Birch Bayh's (D.-Ind.) Subcommittee on Constitutional Reform to act on the ERA. Bayh held extensive hearings in 1970, producing documentation of the many laws that still discriminated against women. In the House, where Emanuel Celler (D.-N.Y.) had for decades kept the ERA bottled up in committee (he saw it as conservative and antilabor), Martha Griffiths (D.-Mich.) got enough signatures on a discharge petition to bring the ERA to the floor. By 1972, the resources of the women's movement, both in numbers and in media attention, were impressive. Organization after organization—lawyers, veterans, nurses, churches and temples, unions, women's clubs—passed resolutions in support of the amendment. Few members of Congress opposed the symbolism embodied in an amendment that would finally give women equal legal status with men. The amendment passed—by a vote of 354 to 23 in the House and by an 84-to-8 vote in the Senate.

A few opponents did testify, however, and Phyllis Schlafly presented testimony that portended the battles to come. The ERA would, she noted, threaten the support that wives enjoyed from their husbands, make women subject to the draft, reduce retirement benefits for dependent wives, and eliminate separate physical education classes, separate prison cells, and separate bathrooms. She called the ERA a radical measure that would do little to help most women. Despite efforts by Senator Sam Ervin (D.-S.C.) and others to amend the ERA in the Hayden style, lobbyists showed that they had widespread popular and organized support from the revitalized and growing women's rights movement. Although opponents were unable to gain control of the issue in Congress, they were much more successful in the state legislatures. While the STOP-ERA campaign grew in the states, the Supreme Court considered more challenges to sex-discriminatory laws, and groups pushed for stiffer standards of constitutionality and judicial review.

At this point, women's rights activists were united on the goal of constitutional policy: to prohibit states from using sex classifications in constructing laws. They agreed that by furthering the ideology of individual rights and equality, discriminatory laws would be eliminated. In addition, the symbolic victory would be an impetus to improve women's status in the family and on the job.

Equal Protection and Sex Classification in the Courts: 1973 to 1982

The Supreme Court's nine justices were unanimous in *Reed v. Reed* in 1971, but unanimity has rarely prevailed in sex-discrimination cases since that time. After flirting with the suspect-classification standard in *Frontiero v. Richardson* (1973), the justices heard many cases over the next decade. Throughout, they disagreed about what standards to use, how broadly to define the issues, and whether specific laws favored men or women. The membership changed only slightly: Justice William Douglas resigned and was replaced by Justice Paul Stevens in 1975; Justice Sandra Day O'Connor—the first woman justice—replaced Justice Potter Stewart in 1982. O'Connor, however, took part only in the final case discussed in this section. Out of the decade's litigation, the Supreme Court set forth at least five standards to guide lawmakers in drawing up legislation that might treat men and women differently, that is, that classifies by sex. They have recently been reiterated in *U.S. v. Virginia* (1996). The Court seemed to agree on discarding old stereotypes, helping women overcome past discrimination, imposing a higher-than-ordinary test, assessing the potential adverse effects of a law, and acknowledging that for legal purposes women may be different from men.

Discarding Old Stereotypes

There was most agreement among justices when they ruled that laws based on the traditional assumptions of separate spheres enshrined in the *Bradwell* case are no longer rational under the Fourteenth Amendment. Two 8-to-1 decisions in 1975 made this clear. Absolute exemptions from jury duty for women based on their domestic duties were struck down in *Taylor v. Louisiana* (1975). The Supreme Court decided that the growing numbers of women, especially married women, in the labor force had "put to rest the suggestion that all women should be exempt from jury service based solely on their sex and the presumed role in the home" (p. 535).

Following trends already present in state legislatures, the Supreme Court removed the constitutional foundation from any laws that defined different ages of majority for males and females. *Stanton v. Stanton* (1975) addressed child-support laws that obligated parents to take care of male children until 21 but female children until age 18 only. The difference had been based on assumptions about the needs of males, rather than females, to earn a living to support a family. Justice Harry Blackmun, writing for the eight justices in the majority, provided a sentence that has been cited often by the Supreme Court and other writers, and that seemed to overrule the separate-spheres argument of *Bradwell* once and for all: "No longer is the female destined solely for the home and the rearing of the family, and only the male for the marketplace and the world of ideas" (pp. 14–15). Using this conclusion, the Supreme Court proceeded to invalidate federal policies and state laws that treated men and women differently based on the assumptions that women are economically dependent and men are independent: dependents' benefits under Social Security laws (*Weinberger v. Wiesenfeld* [1975]); widowers' benefits in Social Security (*Califano v. Goldfarb* [1977]); alimony (*Orr v. Orr* [1979]); and marital property rights (*Kirchberg v. Feenstra* [1981]).

Helping Women

The Supreme Court has occasionally been persuaded that compensating women for past discrimination may be a legitimate legislative goal. Thus it has upheld laws that discriminate in favor of women. With sex not considered a suspect classification, legislators have some leeway in permitting such positive discrimination. This argument was used to sustain a Florida law (which was later repealed by referendum in 1988) that gave widows and not widowers an extra homestead exemption on their property taxes (*Kahn v. Shevin* [1974]). Justice Douglas wrote that "cushioning the financial impact of spousal loss upon the sex for which that loss imposes a disproportionately heavy burden" was legitimate (p. 355). He cited evidence of sex inequalities in wages. He argued that if a widow is forced into the job market, she will suffer from these wage inequities, which are increased by the impact of former dependency as a wife. Thus she deserves special help to meet her financial burden. A similar argument was used in sustaining different time limits for promotion in the military (*Schlesinger v. Ballard* [1975]). The court is cautious in allowing such special treatment. In *U.S. v. Virginia*, Justice Ginsburg noted that "such classifications may not be used, as they once were . . . to create or perpetuate the legal, social, and economic inferiority of women" (p. 2276).[7]

Applying Middle-Level Scrutiny

In 1976, a Supreme Court majority signed on to what appeared to be a new standard of review in sex-discrimination cases, stiffer than the ordinary-scrutiny test traditionally used for sex but less stringent than the suspect-classification test used for race. In *Craig v. Boren* (1976), the Supreme Court examined an Oklahoma law that established a lower legal age to buy 3.2 beer for females (age 18) than for males (age 21). State authorities insisted that the goal of this statute was to promote traffic safety, and they presented evidence that young men are more likely to have accidents than are young women. Although drinking beer accounted for such a small percentage of deaths that the law would not have survived even low-level scrutiny, five members agreed to Justice Brennan's articulation of a higher standard: "To withstand constitutional challenge, previous

BOX 2.5

Who's Your Favorite Justice?

One way to study the Supreme Court's behavior is to examine voting patterns to find which justices are most consistent and which are the swing votes. Table A shows voting patterns for each justice for the major Equal Protection cases between 1971 and 1981. X indicates a vote in favor of eliminating all sex classifications; O represents a vote upholding the constitutionality of laws that treat men and women differently. Justice Stevens replaced Justice Douglas in 1975.

Table A. Voting Records of U.S. Supreme Court Justices, Equal Protection Cases (1971–1981)

Justice	Kirchberg	Taylor	Frontiero	Stanton	Weisenfield	Craig	Orr	Califano	Michael M.	Parham	Schlesinger	Rostker	Kahn	Feeney
Brennan	X	X	X	X	X	X	X	X	X	X	X	X	X	X
Marshall	X	X	X	X	X	X	X	X	X	X	X	X	X	X
White	X	X	X	X	X	X	X	X	X	X	X	X	X	O
Douglas		X	X	X							X		O	
Stevens	X					X	X	X	X	O		O		O
Blackmun	X	X	X	X	X	X	X	O	O	X	O	O	O	O
Powell	X	X	X	X	X	X	O	X	O	O	O	O	O	O
Stewart	X	X	X	X	X	X	X	O	O	O	O	O	O	O
Burger	X	X	X	X	X	O	O	O	O	O	O	O	O	O
Rehnquist	X	O	O	O	X	O	O	O	O	O	O	O	O	O

cases establish that classification by gender must serve important government objectives and must be substantially related to achievement of these objectives" (p. 197).

Just a few words make this a stiffer test than ordinary scrutiny, but in Supreme Court jurisprudence, much law can develop from just a few words. Compare the three tests of constitutionality, and note the change in one or two words in each:

• *Ordinary scrutiny:* Sex classification must bear a *rational* relationship to a *legitimate* state objective.

BOX 2.5 *(continued)*

Table B compares the votes for two cases, one in 1982 and the other in 1994. Five of the justices voting in 1994 are replacements (indicated by italic) for justices who voted in 1982. As in Table A, an X indicates a vote to eliminate sex classifications; an O indicates a vote upholding the constitutionality of laws treating men and women differently. A decade of appointments to the bench by Presidents Reagan and Bush has had little effect on the outcome of Equal Protection cases. Only Justice Thomas has turned against Justice Marshall's consistent pro-equality vote.

Table B. What Is the Effect of Replacements on Equality Cases?

Mississippi v. Hogan (1982)		*J.E.B. v. Alabama ex rel T.B.* (1994)	
Justice	**Vote**	**Justice**	**Vote**
Brennan	X	*Souter*	X
Marshall	X	*Thomas*	O
White	X	*Ginsburg*	X
Stevens	X	Stevens	X
Blackmun	O*	Blackmun	X
Powell	O*	*Kennedy*	X
O'Connor	X	O'Connor	X
Burger	O	*Scalia*	O
Rehnquist	O	Rehnquist	O

*Justices Blackmun and Powell have mixed records on equality. Here they see separate education for the sexes as potentially helpful to women and, contrary to their view of race segregation, not a "badge of inferiority" (*Brown v. Board of Education,* 1954).

• *Middle-level scrutiny:* Sex classification must bear a *substantial* relationship to an *important* state objective.

• *Strict (suspect) scrutiny:* Sex classification must bear a *necessary* relationship to a *compelling* state objective.

Each justice listens to the arguments of participants in a case, as well as those of colleagues, and must decide, based on previous cases, which test applies. If a majority uses ordinary scrutiny, then sex classifications may survive. If the majority agrees, on the other hand, to use the middle-level test of *Craig,* then states would find it difficult to defend sex discrimination. In 1982, the *Craig* test was used in *Mississippi v. Hogan* (1982) to require the Mississippi University for Women to admit men to its nursing program, and in 1996 in *U.S. v. Virginia* to admit women to Virginia Military Institute. The Court has clarified that it would not automatically accept a state's defense of its objectives. "A tenable justification must describe actual state purposes, not rationalizations for actions in fact differently grounded" (*U.S. v. Virginia*, p. 2276). If a majority would one day agree that sex is a suspect classification under the Equal Protection Clause, then nearly all laws would have to be gender neutral.

Assessing the Adverse Effects of a Law

Sometimes, despite gender-neutral language, statutes and regulations have the effect of discriminating because of other laws or practices. Feminist litigators have contended that the Supreme Court should apply the equal-protection tests to laws that have adverse effects on women. In *Personnel Adm. of Massachusetts v. Feeney* (1979), the Supreme Court used the middle-level test of *Craig* to examine a veterans' preference law. Veterans' preference laws give special help to veterans applying for public-sector employment in the federal government and most states. In Massachusetts, veterans who had served at least one day during wartime automatically were put at the top of lists ranking candidates who had passed the job-entrance examinations. Feminists challenged this statute, arguing that discrimination in armed forces recruitment, including female quotas and prohibitions on combat jobs, meant that women did not have an equal opportunity to achieve veteran status. The Supreme Court agreed that the law favored men, but it ruled that the law was constitutional since its intent was to help veterans, not to hurt women. The message in the *Feeney* case was that those who challenge gender-neutral laws that have an adverse effect on women must prove that the lawmakers intended to use the categories in the law as an excuse to exclude women or as a substitute for sex discrimination.

Acknowledging That Women Are Different from Men

Actually, what the justices say is that women and men are not "similarly situated," usually because of their biology but also because of their legal status and responsibilities. When a majority can be persuaded that reproductive and biological differences (rather than social stereotypes and gender roles) are the issue, then such laws often withstand judicial scrutiny. The most famous case applying this approach is *Michael M. v. Superior Court of Sonoma County, CA* (1981). Only males could violate the statutory rape law of California, which made it unlawful for males to have sexual intercourse with females under age 18.[8] California argued that the goal of the legislation was to prevent teenage pregnancy. The Supreme Court majority, represented by Justice William Rehnquist, admitted that the traditional ordinary-scrutiny test "takes on sharper focus" when gender is involved but also noted that the Supreme Court has upheld statutes "where gender classification is not invidious, but rather realistically reflects the fact that the sexes are not similarly situated in certain circumstances" (p. 469). Preventing teenage pregnancy is important, Rehnquist recognized, and "only women become pregnant, and they suffer disproportionately the profound physical, emotional, and psychological consequences of sexual activity" (p. 471). Thus since women and men are not "similarly situated" with respect to pregnancy, laws relating to pregnancy could treat them differently."[9]

The Supreme Court has found women and men "not similarly situated" with respect to other laws. It sustained a Georgia law that denied the father, but not the mother, of an illegitimate child the right to sue for wrongful death of the child. In Georgia, fathers are legally different from mothers: a father but not a mother can declare paternity and make the child born out of wedlock legitimate. The Supreme Court perceived that biological differences made identity of a father a potential problem, whereas the identity of the mother was rarely in doubt. Thus the implication was that fathers had to prove their biological relationship to the child, while the child was living, and then they would be entitled to rights as well as responsibility regarding their offspring. Mothers established their status by giving birth (*Parnham v. Hughes* [1979]).

It is also not unconstitutional for Congress to require that men but not women register for the draft. When the president and Congress reinstituted the draft registration for 18-year-old men in 1980, some men and women protested that equal rights for women must mean equal responsibilities, including being liable for military service. By challenging draft registration, they prodded the Supreme Court to make women equal with men in the military. Although opportunities for women had begun to open up in the military in the 1970s, Congress prohibited the armed forces from recruiting women into combat. Since the Supreme Court gives "great deference" to Congress in military matters, the justices declined to examine the constitutionality of this legislation. Draft legislation existence was crucial to the ruling in *Rostker v. Goldberg* (1981): "Men and women, because of combat restrictions on women, are simply not similarly situated for purposes of a draft or registration for a draft" (p. 78).

Thus, between 1973 and 1982, the U.S. Supreme Court delivered five messages on the constitutional status of women. As Justice Rehnquist noted (*Michael M. v. Superior Court of Sonoma County, CA* [1981]), the Court "has some difficulty agreeing on the proper approach and analysis in cases involving challenges to gender-based classification" (p. 468). This difficulty attests to the relative newness of the issue in the legal system and reflects disagreement in the society about gender roles. It also comes from the complexity of the issue of gender roles and the law in trying to accommodate the perennial tensions between equality and difference. Meanwhile, as the Supreme Court was grappling with the gender question, most politically active feminists united behind the campaign for the ERA, which they hoped would settle the issue of constitutional equality with a strict prohibition against sex classification in the law.

ERA Debate and Defeat: 1972 to 1982

"Ratification of the Equal Rights Amendment would give the Supreme Court a clear signal—a more secure handle for its rulings than the Fifth and Fourteenth Amendments" (Ginsburg, 1978, p. 174). At the time of that writing, Ruth Bader Ginsburg and others hoped the problems the Supreme Court was having in devising a certain standard for review of sex classifications were traceable to the ongoing ratification process of the ERA in the states. Once the ERA was ratified, the issue would be settled, they reasoned. However, the longer the ratification dragged on, the greater became the conflict over the amendment's fate.

Ratification of an amendment to the Constitution requires the support of three-fourths of the states, or thirty-eight states. When the ERA passed Congress in 1972, many states competed to be the first to ratify the amendment. (Hawaii won.) Twenty-two ratified in 1972, eight in 1973, three in 1974, one in 1975, and one in 1977. In fact, a reversal in the trend started when four states voted to rescind their previous ratifications. No state voted to ratify it after 1977, and in 1982, despite extensions of the Congress-imposed deadline, time ran out. Since 1982, scholars have examined the reasons for the defeat of the ERA in the states (Berry, 1986; Hoff-Wilson, 1986; Mansbridge, 1986; see also Boles, 1979). The reasons involve an interaction between the kind of political process surrounding constitutional amendments in the United States and the conflict over the meaning of the ERA.

The U.S. Constitution is very difficult to amend. It requires a supermajority: at least two-thirds of both houses of Congress, that is, up to 292 members of the House and 67 senators. Clearly, members of both major political parties must be supportive. Each state requires a simple majority (except Illinois, which requires 60 percent). An amendment must pass in thirty-eight different legislatures, all but one bicameral and each one influenced by a variety of political cultures from the Northeast to the South to the Midwest to the Far West. No compromise is possible: it's all or nothing, yes or no. A near-consensus is necessary, yet legislators must also see some need the amendment can answer that can't be satisfied by ordinary legislation or judicial interpretation. Opponents of an amendment thus need not get majority support to defeat it; all they need to do is create enough doubt and conflict to increase the costs of support by state legislators. They don't have to conduct a national campaign. Thirteen states can keep an amendment out of the Constitution.

When the ERA passed the Congress, the issue was a high-consensus, low-conflict, bipartisan issue. The ERA meant rectifying an error in the Constitution to make it clear that men and women have equal rights. It was symbolic. In 1977, the International Women's Year Conference convened in Houston endorsed the principle:

> Women have waited more than 200 years for the equality promised by the Declaration of Independence to all men. Two years after the United States of America celebrated its Bicentennial, it is time to extend democracy to all American citizens and to put women into the Constitution at last." (Bird, 1979, p. 123)

Opponents took their case to the unratified states. All they had to do was prevent ratification in thirteen states. Some states were already dead set against the amendment and required little attention. Others were more uncertain. During the struggle over ratification, the issue went from being noncontroversial on the national stage to confronting expanded conflict on diverse local stages. By shifting attention away from symbolic rights of equality, the opponents raised questions about the specific effects of the ERA. They charged that it would put mothers and daughters into combat and threaten the security of homemakers. They linked the ERA with abortion, homosexuality, and unisex bathrooms. To gain the support of those not frightened by these threats, the STOP-ERA group argued that Congress and the courts would be imposing a radical standard of justice on states. In southern state legislatures, this associated the ERA with unpleasant memories of recent federal civil rights laws.

Throughout the 1970s, ERA proponents rapidly lost evidence of the need for the ERA. Supreme Court decisions—starting with *Reed v. Reed*—encouraged states to remove outdated sex classifications. Most state legislatures started to make changes in family and criminal laws to reflect changes in gender roles. Federal laws abolished most of the blatant inequalities in employment and education. Even the military joined in, admitting women to the service academies and into many combat-related jobs. Success in such policies seemed to lessen the urgency for the ERA.

Lacking such specific laws to attack, ERA proponents found it difficult to tell state legislators—in a way that would counter intensely emotional opponents—why passing the ERA was so necessary. The STOP-ERA coalition included fundamentalist churches and New Right conservatives who took on the ERA as a crusade. They were willing to endure hardship and long days lobbying to defeat the evils they perceived in the ERA and feminism. Faced with such a lobby, many legislators saw little to be gained and some political risk to be taken by voting for the ERA. When opponents shouted that homemakers would lose their special privileges and be forced to work and send their daughters to war, feminists were hard-pressed to prove that homemakers would be better off with legal equality. When preachers warned that homosexual marriages would become legal and that young girls would be forced to share public bathrooms with men, how could feminists explain the intricacies of Supreme Court judicial review and levels of scrutiny? No one knew what the Supreme Court might do; even the legal experts would not give any guarantees.

When feminists lost control of the debate over the ERA in the states, they were placed on the defensive, having to prove that dire predictions of STOP-ERA would not come true. It is impossible, in politics, to prove that something won't happen. Proponents of STOP-ERA also turned the ERA into a partisan issue when the Republican party refused to endorse the ERA in 1980 (at the same convention that nominated that hero of the New Right—Ronald Reagan). This shift increased the costs to pro-ERA Republicans in state legislatures. The National Organization for Women (NOW), in leading the feminist campaign, was not able to shift attention to emphasize the need for ERA to help working women, especially women of color. Had the debate been framed differently, a coalition of predominantly white middle-class feminists in NOW and black women union and church activitists might have prevented the narrow losses in several key states such as Illinois (Giddings, 1984, pp. 344–348). In the end, the ERA lost because it became too controversial to achieve the supermajority required to amend the U.S. Constitution.

State ERA Efforts

In addition to the U.S. Constitution, each state has its own constitution, which it is free to change within limits set by the federal document. States are sometimes more innovative than the national government, and their constitutions reflect the particular social, cultural, and political environments within their own boundaries. Feminist campaigns since the early nineteenth century have usually sought changes in state laws and constitutions along with, and sometimes ahead of, the national effort. In the first ERA campaign, primary emphasis was on the U.S. Constitution. The National Woman's Party rejected state efforts as ineffective or too prolonged. In the early 1970s, however, feminists in some states were successful in adding equal rights provisions to their state constitutions; these remain in spite of the foundering of the national campaign.

Eighteen states have ERAs. There are three types:

- Two states—Utah and Wyoming—have constitutions that gave women the right to vote plus equal legal rights when the states first joined the union in the late nineteenth century.[10]

- Nine states—Colorado, Hawaii, Illinois, Maryland, Massachusetts, New Mexico, Pennsylvania, Texas, and Washington—have amendments similar to the proposed federal amendment.

- Seven other states—Alaska, Connecticut, Louisiana, Michigan, Montana, New Hampshire, and Virginia—have adopted amendments that contain language that resembles the Equal Protection Clause of the Fourteenth Amendment.

Between 1977 and 1997, no state adopted an ERA, and four such amendments were rejected by voters: in Florida (1978), Iowa (1980), Maine (1984), and Vermont (1986).

The effects of state ERAs suggest what might happen if the federal amendment should pass. State provisions have led to a range of legislative and judicial responses. The most active legislatures appointed special commissions to review the law codes and make recommendations to bring the laws into compliance by eliminating sex classifications and segregation in favor of gender-neutral language. In states such as Pennsylvania, Alaska, Colorado, and Montana, ERAs have provoked extensive changes in labor laws; marriage, divorce, and child support laws; education policies; and rape and prostitution statutes. Washington, Pennsylvania, and Maryland also have state courts that use strict tests in determining which state laws are constitutional.

A more lenient pattern developed in other states. Legislators were not aggressive in rooting out sex classifications, and the courts tended to use ordinary rationality tests when examining claims of sex discrimination. The language used in equal rights amendments seems to be important in determining which will be active and which more restrained in changing statutes. Most of the active states had ERAs that copied the federal amendment. The more lenient states tended to have general equal-protection provisions.

The range of women's legal status found in the state constitutions only adds to the complexity of constitutional policy and women's rights in the United States. Clearly, the constitutional rights of American women vary according to the state—its courts, its legislature, and the type of law involved—as well as to the choice of federal judges in using strict, middle-level, or low-level tests of constitutionality in interpreting the Fourteenth Amendment.

Feminist Debate on Constitutional Equality

The defeat of the ERA gave feminist legal scholars some room to resume their debate over the constitutional standard that would be most effective in promoting women's rights. These debates on constitutional equality and legal doctrine are important because they provide a basis for debate in all substantive areas of policy: reproduction, sexuality, family, work, and education.

By the early 1980s, several points about women's status under the Constitution had become manifest. The campaign for the ERA—and with it the hopes of a clear, simple standard prohibiting sex classifications in federal and state law—had foundered. The ERA failed to get the necessary thirty-eight states by the ratification deadline. An immediate effort at resuscitation in the House of Representatives failed when the amendment received 278 votes, 6 short of the necessary two-thirds of those present.[11] The litigation of sex-discrimination cases slowed down at the same time, leaving lawyers to make some sense of the standards of review coming from all the cases since 1971 and *Reed v. Reed*.[12]

BOX 2.6

Is There a Feminist in the Court?

When she enrolled as one of eight women in the Harvard Law School in 1956, Ruth Bader Ginsburg—wife and mother—was not a feminist, even when the dean of the Law School asked the new women students how they felt about filling a class slot that was supposed to be for a man. Like many of her generation, it was working in the field of law, as a volunteer for the American Civil Liberties Union (ACLU) in the 1960s, that "raised her consciousness" (Markowitz, 1992). Ginsburg assumed leadership of the national ACLU Women's Rights Project (WRP) in 1971, in time to make the winning argument in *Reed v. Reed*. As head of the WRP, she helped build a body of precedent giving the individual the right to equal treatment by government regardless of sex. Ginsburg led or participated in all the major equal protection cases of the 1970s: *Frontiero v. Richardson*, *Weinberger v. Wiesenfeld*, and *Edwards v. Healy* (a companion case to *Taylor v. Louisiana*). Her brief in *Craig v. Boren* was the source of the assertion by Brennan that the Court's test in sex-discrimination cases constituted "heightened scrutiny."

On October 2, 1993, Ruth Bader Ginsburg took the oath as associate justice of the U.S. Supreme Court, becoming the first feminist on the High Court.

The ruling in *Mississippi v. Hogan* in 1982 used the standard of middle-level or heightened scrutiny to send the message that despite the acceptance of sex classifications in the *Michael M.* and *Rostker* cases, the Court would impose on states the responsibility of providing "exceedingly persuasive justification" to defend their discriminatory laws (p. 724). Between 1982 and 1994, when the Court made its next equal protection ruling on sex classifications, the membership of the court changed. After appointments by Presidents Reagan, Bush, and Clinton, only three justices from the 1970s era remained—Blackmun, Stevens, and Rehnquist. O'Connor was Reagan's first appointment to the Court in 1982. With the arrival of Justice Ginsburg in 1993, there were two women amongst the "brethren." In 1994, this new court, in *J.E.B. v. Alabama ex rel T.B.*, invalidated the use of preemptory challenges by lawyers during jury selection if challenges are based solely on the gender of the prospective juror. The ruling reinforced the use of the middle-level scrutiny test as set forth in the *Craig* and *Hogan* cases. The opinion also reaffirmed the message from the mid-1970s that old stereotypes are dead: "Today we reaf-firm what, by now, should be axiomatic: Intentional discrimination on the basis of gender by state actors violates the Equal Protection Clause, particularly where, as here, the discrimination serves to ratify and per-petuate invidious, archaic, and overbroad stereotypes about the relative abilities of men and women" (p. 1422).

The doctrine that seems to be the foundation of equal protection is that, where people are alike, as in their capacity for education or to serve on juries, they should be treated alike. But the precedent established in the *Michael M.*, *Rostker*, and *Parnham* cases stands: that where the sexes are unlike—for example, relating to pregnancy or sexuality or because of legal status—the law can treat them differently.

Feminist legal scholars, in analyzing the Court's equal protection doctrine relating to sex and gender differences, agree that the Court is al-most certain to interpret the clause to mean that government may not, without substantial justification, deny to one sex a privilege that is en-joyed by the other. While many writers recognize the value of a gender-neutral standard in challenging blatant gender stereotypes and the separate-spheres doctrine, both of which limit individual choice, many are critical of gender neutrality as a blanket standard (Baron, 1987; Law, 1984; MacKinnon, 1983; Wolgast, 1980).

Gender neutrality in the law requires the acceptance of the analogy between sex discrimination and race discrimination. This analogy as-sumes that race differences and sex differences are *wholly irrelevant* to purposes of governmental policy. While there are similarities in the way race and sex have been used unfairly to limit individuals, there remain important biological and social differences between the sexes that have no counterparts between the races. It is possible to contemplate a color-blind society; few can contemplate a gender-blind society.

In addition, critics ask, which group has been helped by this equality standard in practice, women or men? The major equal protection cases since *Frontiero* in 1972—*Craig v. Boren*, *Weinberger v. Wiesenfeld*, *Orr v. Orr*, *Michael M.*, *Rostker*, *Mississippi v. Hogan*—were initiated by men, ei-ther to secure for themselves a right enjoyed by women or to relieve themselves of a responsibility placed only on men. To argue that equal protection rules in these cases help women assumes that sex classifica-tions and sex discrimination are equally hurtful to men and women. In practice, it appears the Court considers the sexes interchangeable as far as their legal status under the Constitution is concerned. Many feminist scholars challenge this assumption.

The problem with the gender-neutral standard is that it is based on a vision of equal rights that has women assuming all the rights and responsibilities of men. Using a male standard of equality helps women only in those areas where they are like men. In areas where women are different, because of biology and socialization, equality results in more burdens on women. For example, gender-neutral equality in the work force means real equality only for those women who, like men, do not allow family responsibilities to interfere with work responsibilities.

This criticism asserts that contemplating gender differences involves more than just taking biological differences into account; such analysis must also recognize the social and cultural differences between women and men. Research has shown that as a result of early infant and childhood experiences, women are different from men in this society (Chodorow, 1978; Dinnerstein, 1976; Gilligan, 1982).

Feminist proponents of equal rights, called liberal feminists, respond to these critics by asserting that there are more differences among women than between women and men. While many women have family obligations, some men have them as well. Gender-neutral solutions can accommodate gender-based differences. For example, special maternity policies are not necessary to accommodate the disabilities related to pregnancy; they can be classified along with other conditions as medical matters. After childbirth, leave for family care responsibilities can pertain either to mothers or to fathers. Therefore, laws accommodate the needs of parents, not just of mothers.

Critics counter that making allowances for such differences in gender-neutral terms does not solve the problem, that the new categories it creates are also gendered, in that the effects fall disproportionately and adversely on women more often than on men. For example, efforts made by employers to accommodate parental needs have created two categories: workers on the "parent track"whose family obligations interfere with work, and workers whose family obligations do not interfere with work. The first group will be made up overwhelmingly of women, while the family-free workers will be mostly men. Another example could be drawn from athletics. If schools are prohibited from maintaining separate tennis teams for girls and boys, then because of differences in training and physical ability, fewer girls will have the chance to make *any* team. While this solution gives individual girls who can compete with boys a chance to do their best, it deprives many girls of the opportunity to compete at all. The gender-neutral solution would be to establish teams based on ability, not sex. The A cross-country team would have the best players, based on skill and speed, the B team the next-level players, and so on. Chances are that most girls would not qualify for the A team, but some would. Although integrated, the teams would still be gendered, with the slower B team associated with its majority female makeup.

The Supreme Court, of course, has not closed the door to different treatment when the sexes are "not similarly situated." But feminist critics of the gender-neutral standards do not find this to be a solution to the problem, either. Thus far the power in the hands of the Court to accept laws that treat women differently has been used to reinforce traditional norms about women's abilities and sexuality in relation to men. Critics argue that the goal of a feminist approach to law should be to free women from the subordination reinforced by gender hierarchies, not give government the tools to reinforce them. They are thus reluctant to pursue a course that would give the male-dominated judiciary additional ammunition to determine when sex and gender differences can be taken into account through legislation, without major changes in gender ideology in the legal culture.

Thus the feminist debate on equality reveals the dilemma that has stymied efforts to establish a feminist standard for assessing women's constitutional status in relation to men's. If the equality standard is used to ignore the differences through gender-neutral language, it leaves the social gender hierarchies intact. Yet, if law sets women apart for special consideration, even with the motive of helping them overcome obstacles to be able to compete with men on an even field, negative stereotypes of women's abilities are reinforced. In other words, to ignore gender differences perpetuates them; to notice gender differences perpetuates them (Minow, 1987, pp. 11–17).

Some feminist legal theorists suggest that activists should give up the campaign for a formal constitutional standard of equality in the Constitution, either through litigation or amendment, and return to crafting policies made by legislatures and the bureaucracy. "Rather than attempt to find one abstract standard to solve women's problems, we should identify objectionable aspects of particular situations and argue for particular changes in the appropriate forum, which will often be the legislature" (Becker, 1993, p. 221).

For a guide in assessing whether policies meet feminist goals, attention could shift away from analyzing the language of laws and turn toward looking at their effects on perpetuating gender inequality in society. This approach would combine consideration of difference with the power to change one's life. With respect to gender hierarchies at work or in the family, the important question is the law's effect on the ability of those at the bottom of the ladder to climb up and improve their lives. Colker (1993) calls this the "anti-subordination principle," stating, "The issue is how the action contributes to or perpetuates the existing subordination of women" (p. 290). Rather than using the biological standard of sex differences, attention would be given to the way laws affect people who live their lives according to gendered patterns. Such a gendered pattern, for example, is the place of the family in relation to work.

This approach might open a dialogue with legal scholars dissatisfied with "single axis" frameworks for determining equality (Crenshaw, 1989). Studies of the special situation of women of color, especially black women, show that their subordinate status is the function of the intersection of race and gender hierarchies. Courts, however, treat sex and race discrimination as two distinct questions. Discrimination based on race is suspect; that based on sex deserves special scrutiny. There is no principle to analyze race and sex together. The result is that removing sex classifications aids white middle-class women; removing race classifications aids African- and Asian-American middle-class men. Critics of such single-axis approaches call for multiple consciousness of identities as the foundation of constitutional jurisprudence (Harris, 1990; Matsuda, 1989).

Critics of an equality standard based on gender neutrality advocate the search for a feminist jurisprudence that will produce a constitutional policy to promote women's rights directly and to improve their status in all aspects of society. Thus, these advocates want judges to evaluate a law according to its effect on women, not to analyze its language or decide whether the law seems "rational." They want courts to ask whether, given biological differences of women and men, a law as written works to harm women or perpetuate their disadvantages.

Feminist legal scholars, however, are especially skeptical of the Supreme Court's ability to take gender differences into account in a way that will promote women's rights. The tendency of judges is still to accept stereotypical views of differences in relation to sexuality and motherhood. Thus far, the effect of the Supreme Court's "judicial notice" of the differences between men and women has tended not to challenge but rather to reinforce traditional stereotypes about women's economic dependency (*Kahn v. Shevin*), sexual behavior (*Michael M. v. Superior Court of Sonoma County, CA*), and parental roles (*Parnham v. Hughes*). The problem is that these differences are defined by male judges from a traditional male, legal perspective.

There is no agreement yet among feminists about the proper legal doctrine to pursue; the debate will continue. Many believe that a standard that will truly overcome subordination of women must await major changes in the participation of women, especially feminists, in the drafting and review of constitutional policy:

> To use law as an effective strategy in the feminist struggle for gender equality requires changing the male perspective embedded in law; and, in turn, this requires women's voices. But women's voices are barely audible against the backdrop of patriarchal legal traditions, institutions, processes, and statutes. Adding women to a male legal process makes little difference unless it is connected to broader feminist struggles for social change. (Baron, 1987, p. 493)

Conclusion

The U.S. Constitution has both a symbolic function and an instrumental function. As a symbol, the Constitution has had little effect on furthering women's rights. Those who support the ERA have come to view its defeat as evidence that the Constitution is bereft of meaning for women and, with the exception of the Nineteenth Amendment, is unchanged since its eighteenth-century origins. As a legal instrument interpreted by the Supreme Court, the Constitution limits the powers of state and federal governments to discriminate against women based on traditional patriarchal stereotypes. Gender-neutral laws, however, may not change women's inferior status in many areas of life. At the same time, the Supreme Court guidelines leave room for legislation that treats men and women differently, with the potential for unequal treatment. The equality dilemma remains unresolved.

When constitutional law is considered in terms of the political debate about the meaning of concepts like equality and difference, we see that the question of women's constitutional status is part of a continuing controversy played out in various institutions of the federal system and affected by social, economic, and political changes. Constitutional policy takes place in the courts in the interpretation of various provisions, and in national and state legislatures in the consideration of amendments.

The debate in the Supreme Court has undergone a major shift. Before 1971, the Supreme Court accepted nearly all laws that classified the sexes, based on its acceptance of the doctrine of separate spheres. In 1971, the Supreme Court rejected such a law and ever since has been searching for a balance between the doctrines of equal rights and sex differences.

Since the 1920s, the ERA has periodically been the focus of debate on constitutional policy in the legislatures. The story of this issue reveals three major shifts in the definition of the ERA and its effects. In the first phase, the ERA was a conservative middle-class issue opposed by most liberals and feminists. A major switch occurred in the 1960s, and the ERA became a civil rights issue, a simple matter of equal justice, supported by liberals and conservatives and pushed by a united feminist movement. Finally, opponents took control of the ERA, and it became a symbol of radical change, especially in state legislatures, where battles for ratification were staged. The trends in debate on the ERA show how the meaning of policy proposals can change (even without changing a single word in the amendment) in response to changes in laws and campaigns by interest groups. It also reveals the importance of federalism to constitutional policy. An issue successfully defined to promote feminist interests in Congress did not travel well to all the states, especially in the South.

The way an issue like the ERA is defined and is related to other policy questions, such as protective labor laws, sets boundaries for the formation of opposing coalitions. Changes in the definition or the importance of other policies may cause politicians to change their positions on the issue or leave the arena of debate altogether.

Finally, the story of constitutional policy reveals disagreement among feminists over the balance between equality and sex differences that will further women's rights. The idea of equality as gender neutrality has been a consistent liberal feminist position, probably because of analogies with liberal ideals of individual rights. At times, this egalitarianism has been dominant; at other times, it has been the minority position. Some feminists have also periodically extolled, or at least recognized, sex and gender differences and feared that, in practice, gender neutrality would hurt women.[13] In the past, feminists sought to recognize women's traditional place in the family. The current feminist debate shows that advocates of taking gender-based differences into account need not adhere to traditional roles, but can use women's special position to challenge a patriarchal legal culture and assert women's independence and autonomy.

Notes

1. The assumption that "all men are created equal and endowed by their Creator with certain inalienable rights" is stated in the Declaration of Independence.
2. They used the Privileges and Immunities Clause, rather than the Equal Protection Clause, to argue that they were being denied rights as citizens.
3. Most laws affecting sex roles are in the policy areas for which states have primary constitutional responsibility: laws related to the family, criminal acts, education, and labor policy.
4. Today, opponents of affirmative action refer to the *Plessy* decision as analogous to affirmative action and often quote Justice Harlan's dissent: "Our Constitution is color-blind, and neither knows nor tolerates classes among its citizens. In respect of civil rights, all citizens are equal before the law" (p. 559).
5. At this time, the Supreme Court was well into the development of a stricter test for reviewing race discrimination.
6. As with most Supreme Court doctrine, the suspect classification test developed through several cases: From *Korematsu v. U.S.* (323 U.S. 214 1944): "[A]ll legal restrictions which curtail the civil rights of a single racial group are immediately suspect" (p. 216). From *Bolling v. Sharpe* (347 U.S. 497 1954): "Classifications based solely on race must be scrutinized with particular care, since they are contrary to our tradition and hence constitutionally suspect" (p. 499).
7. A comment by Justice Brennan in the majority opinion in *Orr v. Orr* (1979) also foresees heightened scrutiny of such positive discrimination: "Legislative classifications which distribute benefits and burdens on the basis of gender carry the inherent risk of reinforcing stereotypes about the 'proper place' of women and their need for special protection. Thus, even statutes purportedly designed to compensate for and ameliorate the effects of past discrimination must be carefully tailored" (p. 238).
8. According to Oberman (1994), only fifteen states still have gender-specific statutory rape laws in which perpetrators are referred to as males. The states are Alabama, Arkansas, Delaware, Georgia, Idaho, Kentucky, Louisiana, Missouri, New Hampshire, Nevada, New Jersey, North Carolina, North Dakota, Pennsylvania, and Texas; California is not one of them.
9. For another example of the Court looking at pregnancy under the Fourteenth Amendment, see the discussion of *Geduldig v. Aiello* (417 U.S. 484. 1974) in Chapter 8.
10. Wyoming's constitution, for example, includes Article VI, Section 1: "The rights of citizens of the State of Wyoming to vote and hold office shall not be denied or abridged on account of sex. Both male and female citizens of this state shall equally enjoy all civil, political, and religious rights and privileges."
11. ERA advocates agreed not to bring the amendment to Congress again until the required two-thirds majority was guaranteed. Unlike the period from 1923 to 1972, when the NWP saw to it that the ERA was on the formal agenda every year, the issue has disappeared from the congressional calendar.
12. There were other sex-discrimination cases—related to reproduction, work and family, and education—not discussed in this chapter because their content is important to policy areas treated in other chapters.
13. Recognizing the important role social and pro-labor feminists played from 1920 to 1960 may require a reconsideration of Phyllis Schlafly and her STOP-ERA coalition. No one on either side of the ERA debate would be likely to call Schlafly a feminist, least of all Schlafly herself. Yet her assertion that the constitutional policy best for women would be one that recognizes women's special role as wife, mother, and homemaker places her in the tradition of social feminists of that earlier period.

References

Baer, Judith. *Equality Under the Constitution*. Ithaca: Cornell University Press, 1983.

Baron, Ava. "Feminist Legal Strategies: The Powers of Difference." In *Analyzing Gender: A Handbook of Social Science Research*, edited by Beth B. Hess and Myra Marx Ferree, pp. 474–503. Newbury Park, Calif.: Sage, 1987.

Bartlett, Katharine T., and Kennedy, Rosanne, eds. *Feminist Legal Theory: Readings in Law and Gender*. Boulder: Westview Press, 1991.

Becker, Susan. *The Origins of the Equal Rights Amendment: American Feminism Between the Wars*. Westport, Conn.: Greenwood Press, 1981.

Becker, Mary E. "Prince Charming: Abstract Equality." In *Feminist Legal Theory: Foundations*, edited by D. Kelly Weisburg. Philadelphia: Temple University Press, 1993, pp. 221–236.

Berry, Mary Frances. *Why ERA Failed*. Bloomington: Indiana University Press, 1986.

Bird, Caroline, ed. *What Women Want*. New York: Simon & Schuster, 1979.

Boles, Janet. *The Politics of the Equal Rights Amendment*. New York: Longman, 1979.

Bradwell v. Illinois. 83 U.S. [16 Wall] 130, 1873.

Brown v. Board of Education. 347 U.S. 483. 1954.

Brownlee, W. Elliot, and Brownlee, Mary M. *Women in the American Economy: A Documentary History, 1675–1929*. New Haven: Yale University Press, 1976.

Califano v. Goldfarb. 430 U.S. 199. 1977.

Chafe, William. *Women and Equality: Changing Patterns in American Culture*. New York: Oxford University Press, 1977.

Chodorow, Nancy. *The Reproduction of Mothering*. Berkeley: University of California Press, 1978.

Colker, Ruth. "The Anti-Subordination Principle: Applications." In *Feminist Legal Theory: Foundations*, edited by D. Kelly Weisberg. Philadelphia: Temple University Press, 1993, pp. 288–300.

Craig v. Boren. 429 U.S. 190. 1976.

Crenshaw, Kimberle. "Demarginalizing the Intersection of Race and Sex: A Black Feminist Critique of Anti-Discrimination Doctrine, Feminist Theory, and Anti-Racial Politics." Originally published in 1989; reprinted in *Feminist Legal Theory*, Volume I, edited by Frances Olsen. New York: New York University Press, 1995, pp. 443–471.

Dinnerstein, Dorothy. *The Mermaid and the Minotaur*. New York: Harper & Row, 1976.

Frontiero v. Richardson. 411 U.S. 677. 1973.

Frug, Mary Joe. "Progressive Feminist Legal Scholarship: Can We Claim 'A Different Voice'?" *Harvard Women's Law Journal* 15 (1992): 37–64.

Giddings, Paula. *When and Where I Enter*. New York: William Morrow, 1984.

Gilligan, Carol. *In a Different Voice*. Cambridge: Harvard University Press, 1982.

Ginsburg, Ruth Bader. "Sex Equality and the Constitution: The State of the Art." *Women's Rights Law Reporter* (Spring 1978): 143–147.

Goesaert v. Cleary. 335 U.S. 464. 1948.

Harris, Angela. "Race and Essentialism in Feminist Legal Theory." *Stanford Law Review* 42 (February 1990): 581–616.

Harrison, Cynthia. *On Account of Sex*. Berkeley: University of California Press, 1988.

Hoff-Wilson, Joan, ed. *Rights of Passage: The Past and Future of ERA*. Bloomington: Indiana University Press, 1986.

Hoyt v. Florida. 368 U.S. 57. 1961.

J.E.B. v. Alabama ex rel T.B. 114 S.Ct. 1419. 1994.

Kahn v. Shevin. 416 U.S. 351. 1974.

Kirchberg v. Feenstra. 450 U.S. 455. 1981.

Kirp, David L., Yudof, Marck G., and Franks, Marlene Strong. *Gender Justice.*
Chicago: University of Chicago Press, 1986.

Law, Sylvia A. "Rethinking Sex and the Constitution." *University of Pennsylvania Law Review* 132 (1984): 955–1040.

Lemons, J. Stanley. *The Woman Citizen: Social Feminism in the 1920s.* Urbana: University of Illinois Press, 1973.

McGlen, Nancy, and O'Connor, Karen. *Women's Rights: The Struggle for Equality in the Nineteenth and Twentieth Centuries.* New York: Praeger, 1983.

MacKinnon, Catharine A. "Feminism, Marxism, Method, and the State: Toward Feminist Jurisprudence." *Signs* 8 (1983): 635–658.

Mansbridge, Jane. *Why We Lost the ERA.* Chicago: University of Chicago Press, 1986.

Markowitz, Deborah L. "In Pursuit of Equality: One Woman's Work to Change the Law." *Women's Rights Law Reporter* 14 (Spring/Fall 1992): 335–360.

Matsuda, Mari. "When the First Quail Calls: Multiple Consciousness as Jurisprudential Method." *Women's Rights Law Reporter* 11 (Spring 1989): 7–10.

Mead, Margaret, and Kaplan, Frances Balgley, eds. *American Women: The Report of the President's Commission on the Status of Women and Other Publications of the Commission.* New York: Scribner's, 1965.

Michael M. v. Superior Court of Sonoma County, CA. 450 U.S. 464. 1981.

Minow, Martha. "The Supreme Court 1986 Term, Foreword: Justice Engendered." *Harvard Law Review* 101 (November 1987): 10–95

Mississippi v. Hogan. 458 U.S. 718. 1982.

Morello, Karen Berger. *The Invisible War: The Woman Lawyer in America, 1638 to the Present.* New York: Random House, 1986.

Muller v. Oregon. 208 U.S. 412. 1908.

Murray, Pauli. *The Autobiography of a Black Activist, Feminist, Lawyer, Priest, and Poet.* Knoxville: University of Tennessee Press, 1987.

Oberman, Michelle. "Turning Girls into Women: Reevaluating Modern Statutory Rape Law." *The Journal of Criminal Law & Criminology* 81 (1994): 15–79

O'Connor, Karen. *Women's Organizations' Use of the Courts.* Lexington, Mass.: Lexington Books, 1980.

Orr v. Orr. 440 U.S. 268. 1979.

Parnham v. Hughes. 441 U.S. 347. 1979.

Personnel Adm. of Massachusetts v. Feeney. 442. U.S. 256. 1979.

Plessy v. Ferguson. 163 U.S. 537. 1896.

President's Task Force on Women's Rights and Responsibilities. *Task Force Report: A Matter of Simple Justice.* Washington, D.C.: GPO, April 1970.

Reed v. Reed. 404 U.S. 71. 1971.

Rostker v. Goldberg. 453 U.S. 57. 1981.

Schlesinger v. Ballard. 419 U.S. 498. 1975.

Stanton v. Stanton. 421 U.S. 7. 1975.

Taylor v. Louisiana. 419 U.S. 522, 1975.

U.S. Senate. *Senate Journals.* Res. 21 68th Cong., 1st sess.

U.S. v. Virginia. 116 S.Ct. 2264. 1996.

Weinberger v. Wiesenfeld. 420 U.S. 636. 1975.

Weisberg, D. Kelly, ed. *Feminist Legal Theory: Foundations.* Philadelphia: Temple University Press, 1993.

Williams, Wendy. "The Equality Crisis: Some Reflections on Culture, Courts and Feminism." *Women's Rights Law Reporter* 4 (Spring/Fall 1992): 151–174.

Wolgast, Elizabeth. *Equality and the Rights of Women.* Ithaca: Cornell University Press, 1980.

CHAPTER 3

Political Resources

Women have had equal voting rights for seventy-five years, yet men hold formal political power. Apparently, women and political power don't mix. It's not that women don't participate—they outnumber men in the electorate by a good 10 million votes. In every election since 1964—over thirty years—more women than men have voted. Yet women remain a minority of policy makers: 9 percent of U.S. senators; 11.7 percent (51 members) of U.S. representatives; 4 percent of governors; 25.9 percent of statewide elective officers; 21 percent of state legislators; 18.2 percent of municipal officers; 9 percent of county officers.[1]

This outcome certainly would not be predicted by dominant ideologies in the United States. Americans value democracy; the political environment is rich with concepts of majority rule, equality, individual rights, and popular sovereignty. The conventional explanation for this inconsistency between the theories of democracy and the low representation of women runs something like this: women have had the right to vote only since 1920. It has taken several generations for women to acquire the culture and resources for political action, that is, to develop the interest, knowledge, and economic base to become serious players on the political scene. Women's family roles continue to be a major barrier to their participation.

Accurate explanations of the political inequality of women depend on accurate information on the extent of women's political achievements. Sometimes the conventional accounts are based on narrow definitions of political action. These accounts focus on two types of action: voting, which their authors assume women began in 1920, and the percentage of women in elective offices. In fact, women have participated in politics since the colonial days. (Women's historians continue to document their activity.) For example, in some of the colonies, women voted when voting rights were tied to property ownership. After independence, New Jersey's new state constitution formally enfranchised women between 1787 and 1807.[2] In 1838, Louisville, Kentucky, enfranchised women in school elections. In fact, the thirty-year period between 1807 and 1838 was the only time in U.S. history that no woman had the right to vote. After 1838, the number of jurisdictions enfranchising women grew steadily until 1920, when the Nineteenth Amendment to the Constitution prohibited states from using sex as a disqualification. Since 1920, the proportion and number of women voters have continued to grow, with the result that women are a majority of the electorate. Since 1980, the proportion of eligible women who vote has surpassed the proportion of men who vote (45.3 to 44.7 percent in 1994).[3]

In addition, women have found ways other than voting or holding office to influence the powerful. Focusing only on the percentage of women in elective office has tended to discount the importance of womanpower in community activities, interest groups and lobbying, political parties, and government agencies. Much research on politics has tended to ignore gender. Now, however, when scholars studying political events ask questions about the role of women, and specifically about the role of feminists, they produce evidence of diverse and influential political activities by women. In this chapter, we look at women's participation in a variety of influential roles.

Conventional explanations of women's low rates of political activity have also tended to focus on the incompatibility of women's interests and responsibilities with the requirements of political action. Questions are rarely asked, except by feminist scholars, about the ways the political system and public policies affect women's political fate. Research now shows that electoral laws restrict claims to legislative office. At the same time, the federal structure of the U.S. government encompasses several arenas for the play of political influence: local governments, state laws, and national institutions. For women seeking power, this structure provides a variety of points of access, and if one is blocked, others may open. At the same time, the relations among the various government levels complicate efforts to resolve conflicts. The story of women in American politics shows patterns of intense interaction between women seeking influence and the authoritative policy actions that limit or enhance their opportunities.

This chapter focuses on that interaction between women and the political system.

Another theme is the relation of issues of women's political participation to dominant ideologies of democracy. Conventional theories assume a dichotomy between public and private spheres and assign women to the private sector. This dichotomy alone serves to isolate women from the political arena. Ideas of what would constitute equal and fair political participation for women depend on ideas of participation in general. When the vote is limited to people with property, demands for the suffrage of all women are not likely to have much credibility. At times, democratic movements arise in several groups at the same time. The demands of women to share in political life have often been caught up in the demands of blacks, although not always in harmony. Even when one barrier—gender or race—has lifted, the other remains. Class issues also affect women's rights. The limited rights that middle-class women might desire could be opposed by workers.

The extent to which the political debate limits women's access to power will be central to the discussion in this chapter. Some themes recur in the various conflicts over suffrage, interest groups, political parties, appointments, and the gender gap. Most striking in looking at women's political fortunes over the long view of history is the way the conflict between equality and difference has divided advocates of women's rights and limited the opportunity of the many women who have wanted to participate in political activities. These women have found themselves having to choose between two views of women in politics. One view is that women have interests in common that transcend partisan differences and party labels. Women must act as a separate group in government, essentially *of the women, by the women, and for the women.* The other side argues for equality by emphasizing the human interests that women and men share. Women should not be treated as a special group; rather, they should get into the male-dominated institutions and act *of the people, by the people, and for the people.* Gender should be irrelevant.

This dichotomy has divided women and placed them in an impossible position: either they choose equality leading to invisibility, or they choose difference leading to inferiority. Neither solution will achieve equality in power without major changes in gender roles in the family, economy, and culture. As you read through the description of the fate of the issues and demands of women for access to power, note how often this conflict between equality and difference has arisen and what effects it has had. At the end of the chapter, we will return to the question. The conclusion will take a look at the efforts of feminist theorists to break down (to deconstruct) this dichotomy and to expose the way such frameworks themselves constitute barriers to political power for women.

The Vote

Central to the lore of women's struggle for political rights is the quest for the vote. The suffrage movement's official day of birth is July 20, 1848—the day the Declaration of Sentiments was signed at Seneca Falls, New York, during the first meeting for women's rights. Political action for suffrage continued for the next seventy years, during times of dramatic economic growth, social change, and political development in the United States. During those years, the issue of votes for women bounced around in various public arenas. By 1920, just about every possible argument for and against women's suffrage had been heard and reheard. The specific goal—the right to vote for women—never changed. But the meaning of the vote, as well as the tactics, alliances, and strategies in the suffrage movement proved to be very dynamic. As with any public issue, a major part of the debate on suffrage was over the definition of the issue—why votes for women was a desirable policy. Answers to the question varied, but the definition that prevailed in 1920 when the Nineteenth Amendment was finally ratified has had an important impact on women's political power ever since. As a central issue of women's rights, probably the most famous of all, the fate of women's suffrage illustrates many aspects of contemporary feminist politics. Lessons learned through the study of this subject have influenced feminist strategies in the 1980s and 1990s.

Inalienable Right to Elective Franchise

One of the first and most famous arguments for women's suffrage came when the founding fathers were drafting documents for the independence of the American republic. Abigail Adams's letter to her husband, John, to "remember the ladies" set forth the notion that policies such as taxation without representation might be as unjust for women as they were for men: "If particular care and attention is not paid to the ladies, we are determined to foment a rebellion, and will not hold ourselves bound by any laws in which we have no voice or representation" (quoted in Flexner, 1975, p. 15). Adams's request for attention to women's political

BOX 3.1

The Arrest and Trial of Susan B. Anthony

Some feminists maintain that suffragists were the first activists to use civil disobedience and militancy as political tactics. Certainly Susan B. Anthony set a precedent by managing to be arrested and convicted for "illegal voting." As U.S. District Attorney Richard Crowley stated at her trial:

> The defendant, Miss Susan B. Anthony . . . upon the 5th day of November, 1872, . . . voted for a representative in the Congress of the United States, to represent the 29th Congressional District of this State, and also for a representative at large for the State of New York, to represent the State in the Congress. At that time she was a woman. I suppose there will be no question about that.

Miss Anthony took the opportunity of her conviction to make a public case for the cause:

> Yes, your honor, I have many things to say; for in your ordered verdict of guilty, you have trampled underfoot every vital principle of our government. My natural rights, my civil rights, my political rights, are all alike ignored. Robbed of the fundamental privilege of citizenship, I am degraded from the status of citizen to that of a subject; and not only myself individually, but all of my sex, are, by your honor's verdict, doomed to political subjection under this so-called Republican government. (quoted in Buhle and Buhle, 1978, pp. 293–294)

rights was made in a context of limited political rights for men. Despite the concepts of equality that inspired the Declaration of Independence, during the early years of the United States of America, state electoral laws retained property qualifications.

The first formal demands for women's suffrage did not arise until theories of natural rights and popular sovereignty had yielded widespread democratization and universal white-male suffrage in the early 1800s. In outlining demands for women, the Seneca Falls Declaration of Sentiments paraphrased the language of the Declaration of Independence. The Seneca Falls declaration was a general plea for equality of rights between women and men and was a political document through and through. Both the complaints and remedies were charged to the power of mankind over women:

The history of mankind is a history of repeated injuries and usurpa-
tions on the part of man toward women, having its direct object the
establishment of an absolute tyranny over her. . . .
He has never permitted her to exercise her inalienable right to the
elective franchise.
He has compelled her to submit to laws, in the formation of which
she has had no voice . . .
Having deprived her of this first right of a citizen, the elective franchise, thereby leaving her without representation in the halls of legislation, he has oppressed her on all sides. (Buhle and Buhle, 1978,
p. 94)

Based on the assumption that women had the same inalienable rights as
men, the declaration demanded the remedy: "Resolved, That it is the duty
of the women of this country to secure to themselves their sacred right to
the elective franchise" (Buhle and Buhle, 1978, p. 96).

From a contemporary perspective, it is difficult to imagine how controversial this simple argument was. The argument over the franchise was
so intense that it was the only resolution not passed unanimously at Seneca Falls. Many feared it was so radical it would make the entire Woman
Movement look ridiculous. These hesitations by many people who were
committed to improve women's lot in other areas show the depth of the
conflict over political rights. Ideas of equality, liberty, and inalienable
rights were competing in American culture with common-law and religious traditions of the unity of husband and wife. The husband acted for
and ruled the wife—the stability of the family and society depended on it.
To separate men and women, which a doctrine of individual rights required, would threaten social peace.

Once these arguments and definitions were introduced into the debate, they remained. The argument for the vote as an inalienable right
continued, as did the opposing view that saw individual rights for women
as a threat to the family. What changed was the dominance of each view
in the various policy debates.

Emancipation of Women

The demands for women's suffrage were influenced by the ideas and
rhetoric of the crusade to abolish slavery. The Woman Movement leaders
first began their political activity in the abolitionist movement. They bor-
rowed the language, seeking "emancipation" for women from the "slavery" of marriage and the assumption of their full rights as citizens. But

their effort to keep the issues together failed after the Civil War. The Thirteenth, Fourteenth, and Fifteenth Amendments were victories for abolitionists but crushing blows to the Woman Movement. Section 2 of the Fourteenth Amendment reduced the number of Congressional representatives in any state that denied voting rights to male citizens, thereby implying that states had unlimited power to deny the right to vote to females. When Susan B. Anthony and Elizabeth Cady Stanton protested the insertion of these "male-only" rights in the Constitution, they were told that their issue of women's rights was too controversial. Reconstructionists wanted nothing to interfere with their efforts at signing up what they expected would be compliant and grateful former slaves as voters.

The Fourteenth Amendment was especially important as a policy that shaped political rights of women. It clearly and formally established—for the first time—two separate constitutional categories of citizens: male and female. To this day, that differentiation has not been totally overcome. In addition, the amendment defined the franchise as a federal issue. This was the beginning of the gradual increase in the federal government's supervision of state policies. The Southern white establishment resented the growing power of the national Constitution over the states' power in establishing voting rights. Any attempt to extend civil rights through a constitutional amendment was considered suspect. The opposition has continued until the present, explaining, in part, the nearly solid Southern opposition to the Equal Rights Amendment (ERA).

Suffrage activists adhered to their belief that the franchise was an inalienable right that signified freedom and equality. In the 1870s, they tried to make a specific association between *voting* and *citizenship* as defined in the Constitution. In *Minor v. Happersett* (1875), the Supreme Court considered the argument that the Privileges and Immunities Clause already enfranchised women; all the Supreme Court had to do was recognize it.[4] The Supreme Court did not, saying that citizenship did not include the right to vote. "For nearly ninety years the people have acted upon the idea that the Constitution, when it conferred citizenship, did not necessarily confer the right of suffrage" (p. 178).

Woman's Special Role

After the Civil War, the suffrage issue was caught up in the social changes that swept the nation. Part of this was a growing conservatism among the privileged and powerful in response to economic change, immigration, and westward expansion. The suffrage movement split, and many women sought new arguments to push their cause in the changing environment. Some concentrated on state-by-state campaigns; others sought national attention to votes for women (Flexner, 1975; Scott and Scott, 1975). By the 1890s, a new definition became dominant. Before, the suffragists had argued that women deserved the vote because they were human beings first and women second. By the 1890s, a new argument prevailed: that women could contribute to political life because they were women. Their experience as wives and mothers gave them expertise in those areas where government was weakest—in social policy and morality in public life. The suffragists became natural allies of the progressive leaders seeking to clean up corruption, promote sobriety, and care for the poor and unfortunate who suffered from social and economic abuses in factories and cities.

This new definition of the franchise for women prompted another set of opponents with new arguments: people with liquor interests, who feared prohibition of alcohol; textile manufacturers, who feared prohibition of child labor; politicians, who feared reform; and white supremicists, who feared race-conscious black women voters. All of these groups saw their interests threatened by the policies women claimed to promote. The political process was changing, and suffrage politics was changing along with it. Increasingly, the ballot became not only an individual right but a tool of group interests. This change coincided with the growth of interest-group politics. Voluntary organizations proliferated, and lobbying started to change legislative deliberations. Women presented themselves as a group who could act in politics to promote a particular agenda if only they had the vote.

The demand for women's suffrage became a mass movement after 1910 (Morgan, 1972). Energies focused on getting congressional support for an amendment to the Constitution, while continuing drives for referenda in the states. A wide variety of groups supported the plan, but the vote had different meanings to each group. Black American women joined suffrage organizations so they could use the vote to fight against oppression by white men. Working women wanted to vote to help them get better wages and conditions. Some upper-class women thought the vote would ensure their supremacy over growing numbers of immigrants. (The suffrage movement was not immune to racism and ethnocentrism in the culture.) Militant suffragettes considered absolute equality of the sexes an essential part of democracy. Woodrow Wilson eventually supported the Nineteenth Amendment, linking votes for women to his own credibility as a democratic leader in world politics. But

BOX 3.2

Getting Mr. Wilson's Attention

With the suffrage amendment stalled in Congress in January 1917, suffragists implored President Woodrow Wilson to lead his party to support votes for women. He refused, saying, "As the leader of my party, my commands come from that party and not from private personal convictions." The next day, January 10, the picketing of the White House began, as Doris Stevens (1920, pp. 65, 66) recalled.

> The beginning of our fight did indeed seem tiny and frail by the side of the big game of war, and so the senators were at first scarcely aware of our presence. But the intrepid women stood their long vigils, day by day, at the White House gates, through biting wind and driving rain, through sleet and snow as well as sunshine, waiting for the President to act. Above all the challenges of their banners rang this simple, but insistent one:
>
> Mr. President!
> How long must women wait for liberty?

Finally after six months, Wilson's patience ran out. As he marshaled national support for America's entrance into World War I to save democracy, women's continued picketing of the White House and their demands for the vote led to their arrest, prison, and, for some, hunger strikes and forced feeding.

the dominant definition of the women's vote in 1920, held by the leadership of the movement in the National Women's Suffrage Association (NAWSA), was that women would use the vote to transform politics and bring their agenda of good government and social welfare into national and state legislatures. They did not expect to achieve their goal by electing women to office, but rather by using their voting bloc of women as a lever in lobbying the men elected to office.

The Nineteenth Amendment was passed by Congress and ratified in 1920.[5] What would women do with their hard-won voting rights? The answer was anxiously awaited by politicians and feminists. In fact, a women's voting bloc did not appear at the national level, at least not in the calculations of politicians in the 1920s. And the initial interpretations of those first elections in the 1920s created a myth about women as political actors that affected their influence for decades. The myth went something like this: feminists promised a powerful voting bloc of women. Among other things, they pledged revenge against antisuffrage senators and rewards for those who adopted the feminist agenda. Politicians who expected a voting bloc were ready to consider reform proposals from the leaders of these new voters. After two presidential elections, however, no bloc seemed to materialize. Far fewer women than men voted, and they voted as their husbands did. Few promises of revenge came true, and suffrage opponents were reelected. Most women were not interested in voting and politics because it was foreign to their primary domestic role in the family. In fact, once women got the vote, overall voter participation dropped precipitously.

This myth persists but is now subject to feminist analysis by women's studies scholars (Alpern and Baum, 1985; Kleppner, 1982). The final verdict on the voting behavior of women during the 1920s may never be known for sure. There were no polls to compare the turnout or the choices of men and women. (Only one state, Illinois, had separate ballot boxes for men and women.) But a number of facts alter the credibility of the conventional wisdom about women's political behavior. As voters, women were diverse. Turnout varied from group to group, state to state. The costs of voting the first time are relatively high, and women may have had many educational and cultural barriers to surmount. In many Southern states, white leaders prevented newly enfranchised black women from registering. But not all women were first-time voters in the 1920s. Women were already voting in some states. Wyoming was the first state to enfranchise women (in 1869),[6] and by 1917, women voted in sixteen states. Little is known about patterns of turnout in those states. While women probably turned out in smaller percentages than men, a number of other factors contributed to an overall decrease in voting in the 1920s. A decline in party competition had already brought about a decline in turnout, beginning with the 1890s. There was also widespread disillusionment with political issues in the post–World War I period.

As for the way women voted, again diversity seems to be important. We know little about what having the vote meant to individual women. Several factors might have discouraged women from following would-be leaders of the women's bloc. Many active women believed the vote made them equal citizens with men. They might have shied away, as they still do, from topics defined as "women's issues." Voting for an agenda defined by one women's group like the League of Women's Voters (LWV) may have seemed to reinforce differences and thereby a sense of inferiority. After 1920, the LWV itself tended to downplay its role in influencing voter choice and did not endorse candidates, focusing instead on voter education. Finally, political leaders, especially in the parties, were very hostile to women's nonpartisan organizations. Any woman active in one of the major parties had to place party loyalty above feminist loyalty.

The campaign for the suffrage spanned seventy years of major social and political changes in America. Throughout, the concept of votes for women assumed several meanings, from simple notions of equality of citizenship to ideas of the value of women's special nature (the dual roles of wife and mother) to public life. As the debate became more intricate, the organization, strategies, and tactics of suffragists changed in response to the growing complexity of the political system. Between 1910 and 1920, the mass suffrage movement that emerged sheltered many diverse groups that held various goals and conceptions of the issue. Few of these groups considered the vote as a means of putting women in political office. Rather, they saw it as a resource to enhance the influence of women as a group on the nation's policy makers.

Access to Power

According to ideologies of democratization, the next step after winning the right to vote is to use the vote to gain access to political power. It took seventy years for women to gain the vote; more than seventy-five years later, equality seems a long way off.

It is important to remember that women can gain access to power in a number of ways. Traditionally, women have had influence through their personal relationships with powerful men. Political scientists have not usually been interested in searching for general theories of the role of wives and mistresses, but historians have found examples of their importance (Gutin, 1989).

Representation of women and their interests includes more than looking at the percentage of women in Congress or in the Cabinet. Judging the success of women in politics requires attention to their participation in pressure politics and through campaigns and appointments. In the 1920s, women's rights leaders thought issues and policies were more important than being elected to office. Ever since, the means to power has been through interest groups, political parties, and personal influence with presidents and Congress. Representation of women in elective office is still low. However, it is important to keep in mind that only since the 1970s have feminists made a concerted effort to seek elective office.

BOX 3.3

Women in National Legislatures

The legislative elections of the 1980s and 1990s show that representation of women has increased in most Western democratic countries, reaching near-parity in the Nordic countries. In the following
table, an asterisk (*) marks the countries in which political parties
(usually those on the left) have some form of quota system for
bringing more women into parliament. Iceland, marked with a
double asterisk, has an all-woman party represented in parliament.

| | Percentage of Women in Lower House | | |
Nation	1975	1984–87	1994–95
Australia	0.0	6.1	9.5
Denmark	15.6	29.0	33.0*
Finland	23.0	31.5	33.5
France	1.6	6.4	6.4*
Germany	5.6	15.4	26.2*
Greece	2.0	4.3	6.0
Iceland	2.0	8.4	25.4**
Italy	3.0	12.8	15.1*
Japan	1.4	1.4	2.7
Luxembourg	5.1	14.6	20.0
The Netherlands	9.3	20.0	31.3*
Norway	15.5	35.4	39.4*
Portugal	8.0	7.6	8.7
Spain	–	6.4	16.0
Sweden	21.4	30.9	40.4*
Switzerland	7.5	14.0	18.0*
United Kingdom	4.2	6.3	9.5
United States	3.6	5.3	10.8

Sources: United Nations, Center for Social Development and Humanitarian
Affairs. *1989 World Survey on the Role of Women in Development.* New York:
United Nations, 1989, pp. 337–341; Intraparliamentary Union. *Women in
Parliament 1945–1995.* Geneva: Intraparliamentary Union, 1995; Kelber, Mim.
Women in Government: New Ways to Political Power. Westport, Conn.: Praeger,
1994.

Groups

In the United States today, demands for women's rights are the business
of a strong and permanent network of national feminist and women's advocacy organizations. The foundation of this network was built during

countless campaigns for equality and liberation conducted since the 1970s (Costain, 1988). The diversity and expertise of the groups in the network has grown as their members have toted up impressive successes in policy reforms (Hartman, 1989; Spalter-Roth and Schreiber, 1995). The solidarity weathered the difficult environment brought on by the administrations of Presidents Ronald Reagan and George Bush. Every chapter in this book describes the groups' activities in areas such as reproductive rights, health, education, labor, social welfare, and criminal justice.[7] The network of groups, with strong support in state and local organizations, is built on a long tradition of lobbying by women. This tradition resulted from the chronic refusal of most states to give women the vote. Without the franchise, women were driven to petitioning legislatures, testifying before committees, and lobbying. Sophonisba Breckinridge, a political scientist who wrote one of the first studies of women and politics, termed lobbying a "natural" channel for women. She claimed it has been such a channel ever since 1837 when "John Quincy Adams introduced their antislavery petition in the House of Representatives as a part of his campaign to establish the right of petition for all, a right which had been hitherto believed to belong only to electors" (Breckinridge, 1933, p. 257). Women's right to associate and to address legislatures came to them as part of the general trend toward democratization in the young republic.

In the late nineteenth century, the women's club movement brought both black and white American women into local politics.[8] Women honed their lobbying skills in reform, temperance, and suffrage organizations. After 1920, old organizations attracted more members, and new organizations formed as channels for the participation by educated women and those in business and professions. Ten national groups formed the Women's Joint Congressional Committee to coordinate lobbying efforts. Since then, the lobbies have been ready to adapt to any changes in the context of politics that affect their access to power. In the 1960s, they focused on developing mass membership. They mastered media and mass-mailing techniques and other aspects of the increasingly sophisticated lobbying profession. When the feminist lobby, preoccupied with ERA and abortion rights, seemed to overlook needs of minority poor and working-class women, specialized groups such as the Congress of Labor Union Women (CLUW), Mexican American Women's Association, and the National Alliance of Black Feminists organized.

In the contemporary era, when weakened party control has led to interest-group organizations within Congress itself, one of the first interest groups to arise was the Congressional Caucus on Women's Issues. This caucus assembled all the women in the House and Senate as well as other members of the House of Representatives with a staff to work for the women's rights agenda. When the Republican party majority came into power in the House in 1995, it eliminated support for all such internal caucuses, forcing support staff to work informally from outside the walls of the Capitol building.

Political Parties

Once a feminist becomes active in one of the two major political parties, she will soon face a conflict between support for a women's rights agenda and loyalty to her party, whose goal is to elect its candidates to office. Such conflict may arise when she must choose between voting for a man of her party or a woman candidate of the opposite party. The party committee may consider her proposal in favor of reproductive choice or making violence against women a top priority too controversial and a threat to party candidates. Or she may run into old-fashioned sexism from men in higher party positions. Then she is forced to choose: political party or women's rights?

Many suffrage leaders were not interested in political parties and preferred to work on feminist issues through lobbying organizations. Some egalitarian feminists formed their own party, the National Woman's Party (NWP) (Becker, 1981; Lunardini, 1986). Since it did not run candidates for office, the NWP was a party in name only. Rather, it was a single-issue feminist organization whose major goal was, first, the vote, and then the ERA. It had sixty thousand members in 1920, but that number steadily declined. The NWP attracted a community of educated feminists, mostly white professional women, under the tight direction of a small elite.

Still, seeking a leadership position in the Republican or Democratic party has appealed to many women as a way to participate and as a path to power. Parties have traditionally been the route to many political jobs and government appointments, and, of course, they play an important role in the electoral process. Recognizing the place of political parties in mainstream American politics, the LWV campaigned in the 1920s for state laws requiring equal participation of women and men in party organizations. Political parties have been interested in women, too, ever since women became voters. A means to satisfy this common interest was through establishing quotas for women in party organizations. The LWV's quota idea caught on. Both parties set up rules for equal male-female representation from each state on their national committees. Campaigns in the 1920s and 1930s led to state laws requiring equal male-

BOX 3.4

A Recurring Feminist Dream: A New Party

Laws and traditions have not allowed any new parties to compete with Republicans and Democrats. Nevertheless, feminists past and present dream about a party that would put their agenda first.

> "The Republican party is petrifying rapidly and is nearly in the same fossil state as the Whig party. . . . The Democratic party is in a state of decomposition. . . . The way is therefore clear and the need imminent for a third party composed of the men and women of the future."
>
> *Susan B. Anthony, May 1872* (quoted in DuBois, 1981, p. 167)

> "We are locked out of the real power circles of both parties. The Democrats take us for granted; the Republicans often lead the fight against us. We need a new party. . . . Nothing will put more feminists on the ballot quicker—*and* push the Democrats and Republicans harder."
>
> *Eleanor Smeal, 1992* (quoted in Alh, February 1993, p. 13)

female representation on state and local committees.[9] Parties also sought to attract women's support through the establishment of women's divisions within the national organizations. The women's division was a means for individual leaders to gain access to top politicians, from Franklin Roosevelt to Dwight Eisenhower. Through their close contacts with Eleanor Roosevelt, Democratic women were especially influential on policies of the New Deal (Ware, 1982).

The idea of quotas surfaced again in party reforms of the late 1960s. Women in both parties worked to increase their representation at the national conventions. Through indirect means, women's representation at the last several Republican national conventions has ranged from 30 percent to 45 percent of the delegates. The Democrats have taken the more direct approach through requiring numerical representation. Since 1980, women have comprised 50 percent of the representation in state delegations. Feminists' influence in national Democratic party politics reached its height in 1984, when they had near-veto power over the platform and pressured presidential candidate Walter Mondale to select the first woman vice-presidential candidate, Geraldine Ferraro.

Although women's participation in political-party organizations has increased at all levels, this has not resulted in much increase in their representation in office. Political-party activity has not been a step toward sharing power for women. The story of women's access to power in political parties suggests an irony, if not a law, of feminist power: women's participation and access to leadership roles in the parties has approached equality at a time of steady decline of the influence of the party organizations in national and state electoral politics. Quotas put women on boards and committees in the parties, but candidates need resources beyond political parties to get elected. It sometimes seems that women and other groups outside the powerful networks of electoral politics struggle to acquire necessary resources, only to find that, once acquired, the value of these resources has diminished.

Elections in the 1990s have produced some gains for women in their efforts to win electoral office through support networks and political action committees (PACs). Leading the way has been EMILY's (Early Money Is Like Yeast) List, which, using a nationwide fundraising effort, provides resources to Democrat pro-choice candidates. The Republican counterpart, WISH (Women in the Senate and House), provides financial support to Republican candidates. The Center for the American Woman and Politics counted 42 PACs that have a female donor base and/or gave money to women candidates (CAWP 1993). This bipartisan attention to the common goal of electing more women meant that, despite the defeat of many Democrats in the 1994 election, the gains made by women in the House of Representatives in 1992 (the so-called Year of the Woman) stayed steady in 1994.[10]

Appointments and Commissions

Women's rights groups have, since World War II, taken a direct approach to increasing the political influence of women. They have demanded that the president appoint women to high-level policy positions. The practice of politicians rewarding faithful supporters with cushy public appointments is at least as old as the ancient Greeks and is still pervasive. Through visibility and access to contacts, appointive office is often a route to elective office. Feminists want the rewards, of course, but they also agree it is desirable to appoint women for several other reasons: to represent women's point of view and balance the male perspective; to exercise leadership; to represent women's interests in issues; to show that women are as capable as men; to serve as an example to other employers;

to give women resources for elective campaigns; to build women's self-esteem; and because it is fair.

There has been a mixed record in this effort. At first, in the administrations of Presidents Harry S. Truman and Dwight D. Eisenhower, prominent women in each president's political party secured some attention to female patronage. Women were beginning to infiltrate the smoke-filled rooms. But when John F. Kennedy became president in 1961, he decided to make top-level appointments on merit. He wanted to attract the most-talented people in the country to help him conquer the New Frontier. Kennedy began to draw less from cronies in the party organization and more from national networks in universities, business, and financial circles. At that time, women had made more progress in interest groups and political parties than they had in getting access to the intellectual and financial elite. For the next fifteen years, presidents seemed to forget about women; none joined the Cabinet until President Gerald Ford appointed Carla Hills as Secretary of Housing and Urban Development in 1975. President Jimmy Carter appointed more women to top positions than had any other president before him, because of the strong pressure from Rosalyn Carter and a number of feminists on the White House staff. Even so, women made up barely 15 percent of his highest appointments. Carter, Reagan, and Bush each appointed four women as Cabinet members. During President Bill Clinton's administration, however, five have served simultaneously, making up one-third of the top executive body. At the urging of Hillary Rodham Clinton, this administration appointed the second woman to the Supreme Court and several other women as "first" in their office: attorney general; communication director; director of the Office of Management and Budget; and chair of the Council of Economic Advisors. In 1997, the "first" continued with the appointment of Madeleine K. Albright as Secretary of State. Even with these gains, there remain many agencies where women hold token top policy positions.

Even when women are appointed to high offices, feminists are not always pleased with the results. The old problem of conflicting party and feminist loyalties reappears, this time as tension over loyalty to the president. How outspoken an advocate of abortion rights can a Cabinet secretary be when the boss is trying to please conservative pro-life factions? How can she direct budget cuts away from programs that benefit poor women and children? Should she resign rather than compromise? Many appointments suffer the worst effects of tokenism: high visibility but little support. Tokens can be manipulated by powerful men or isolated and ignored. Should feminists support successful women in top political offices

BOX 3.5

Women in the Cabinet: 1932 to 1997

Nineteen women have held twenty-two offices under seven presidents in sixty-five years. The following table shows the offices these women have held and the presidents who appointed them.

Secretary	President	Term	Department
Frances Perkins	Roosevelt	1933–1945	Labor
Oveta Culp Hobby	Eisenhower	1953–1955	Health, Education, and Welfare
Carla A. Hills	Ford	1975–1977	Housing and Urban Development (HUD)
Juanita M. Kreps	Carter	1977–1978	Commerce
Patricia Roberts Harris	Carter	1977–1979	HUD
Patricia Roberts Harris	Carter	1979–1980	Health and Human Services (HHS)
Shirley Hufstedler	Carter	1979–1980	Education
Jean J. Kirkpatrick	Reagan	1981–1985	United Nations
Elizabeth H. Dole	Reagan	1983–1987	Transportation
Margaret M. Heckler	Reagan	1983–1985	HHS
Ann Dore McLaughlin	Reagan	1987–1988	Labor
Elizabeth H. Dole	Bush	1989–1990	Labor
Carla A. Hills	Bush	1989–1990	Trade Representative
Lynn Martin	Bush	1991–1992	Labor
Barbara Franklin	Bush	1992	Commerce
Hazel Rollins O'Leary	Clinton	1993–1996	Energy
Donna Shalala	Clinton	1993–	HHS
Carol Browner	Clinton	1993–	Environment
Janet Reno	Clinton	1993–	Attorney General
Madeleine K. Albright	Clinton	1993–1996	U.N. Ambassador
Madeleine K. Albright	Clinton	1997–	State
Alexis Herman	Clinton	1997–	Labor
Charlene Borshevsky	Clinton	1997–	Trade Representative

Sources: Sue Tollesin Rinehart. "Madam Secretary: The Careers of Women in the United States Cabinet." Paper presented at the Southern Political Science Association, November 3–5, 1988; *Congressional Quarterly*, 1990–1997.

despite disagreements on specific actions? Is *any* woman better than any man? And, finally, how can politically active women overcome the self-satisfaction that comes with tokenism, and how can they help other women to the top?

The idea of establishing gender quotas in government appointments appeals to some. Several states already require fifty-fifty representation in party organizations. Some are considering laws requiring gender balance on state boards and commissions. Iowa passed such a law in 1987, followed by North Dakota (Baruch, 1988). Other states—such as Montana, Illinois, Pennsylvania, Rhode Island, and Florida—have laws urging governors to seek balance (Kelber, 1994). But quotas raise the specter of reverse discrimination and are likely to be highly controversial. The most effective solution is to treat the problem as one of employment opportunity and to combine continued pressure for recruitment of women to government positions with additional efforts to increase the pool of qualified women candidates and applicants.

Parallel to the demands for more appointments have been proposals for the establishment of permanent boards and commissions to promote women's policy concerns.[11] The model was the United Nations Commission on the Status of Women (CSW) established in 1946. Such institutions are permanent, have independent budgets, and are charged with the responsibility of collecting information on the status of women in all aspects of social, economic, political, and cultural life. Many make recommendations for policy to executives and legislative bodies. Women's associations requested that the United States follow this international example, but it wasn't until the Kennedy administration that a commission was established. The President's Commission on the Status of Women (PCSW) seemed to compensate for the president's failure to appoint women to his Cabinet (Harrison, 1988). In fact, the PCSW became the catalyst for the development of the contemporary feminist movement. The PCSW's report recommended the establishment of a permanent body in the Department of Labor, the Citizens' Advisory Council on the Status of Women (CACSW), which, in turn, led the drive from within the government for equal opportunity in employment. The CACSW and the Department of Labor encouraged the appointment of CSWs in every state and in many local governments. It was at the meeting of the state CSWs in 1966 that the National Organization for Women (NOW) was formed (see Chapter 7).

As new issues arise or old issues are redefined, the demand for presidential-level commissions has recurred: in 1970, President Richard Nixon appointed the President's Task Force on Women's Rights and Responsibilities; in 1975, President Ford assembled a bipartisan commission to direct U.S. observance of International Women's Year (IWY); and in 1978, President Carter established the National Advisory Committee for

Women (NACW). Becoming a member of one of these commissions can place a woman in a very strategic position for influencing the political process. Although commissions don't have the decision-making power of legislatures, commission members are free to concentrate exclusively on a women's rights agenda, whereas elected officials have to balance a number of competing demands. Commissions can be like strong interest groups *inside* the government. Of course, to be effective they have to mobilize political resources, just as any other political actor must.

The experiences of the Nixon and Carter women's commissions demonstrate the problems: if commissions advocate the feminist agenda, they may become too controversial and threaten the political status of the president. He and his staff will then ignore or reconstruct them. The President's Task Force on Women's Rights and Responsibilities (1970) recommended passage of the ERA despite growing opposition in the Republican party. The task force's report also recommended that the president establish a permanent Office of Women's Rights and Responsibilities in the White House to take positive steps to bring more women into power: to "coordinate recruitment and urge consideration of qualified women for policy-level Federal positions; seek to inform leaders of business, labor, education and religion, State and local governments and the communications media on the nature and the scope of the problem of sex discrimination, striving to enlist their support in working toward improvement" (p. 1). After receiving the report, President Nixon's White House staff refused to publish and distribute it. They relented only after Marie Anderson of the *Miami Herald* published a purloined copy in the women's section of that newspaper.

President Ford's commission received funding from Congress to convene a national meeting for International Women's Year. Assembling delegates from every state, the 1977 IWY meeting in Houston showcased many issues and enacted the wide-ranging National Plan (Bird, 1979). This commission presented its report with a recommendation that a new commission on women's issues be established. Thus, Carter appointed the National Advisory Committee for Women (NACW) in June 1978. The NACW saw its role as an advocate for the IWY Commission's National Plan and to evaluate the effect of all policies on the status of women. When the NACW's evaluation turned into criticism of Carter's economic and budgetary policies, Carter fired the chair, Bella Abzug, and reconstituted the committee with restricted functions as the President's Advisory Committee for Women.

President Reagan showed little interest in reconstituting a national commission, but he did appoint a Task Force on Legal Equality, which reviewed federal laws and regulations for gender bias. Special advisory committees connected to administrative offices—such as the National Advisory Council on Women's Educational Programs and the Task Force on Women, Minorities, and the Handicapped in Science and Technology—come and go. The Defense Advisory Committee on Women in the Service (DACOWITS), established in 1951, has lasted longest. In 1991, Congress created the Glass Ceiling Commission to review the means of removing barriers to employment in top jobs; that commission issued its report in 1995.

Some women's rights groups continue to seek the establishment of a national commission or council with cross-policy-sector responsibilities, such as are found in many other countries, to make politicians and bureaucrats more sensitive to the effect of policies on women and to push an agenda to advance their status. One proposal is that Congress establish a Federal Council on Women (FCW) as an advisory body to Congress, not to the president. With the power to hold hearings, seek information from executive agencies, and recommend policies, especially on economic issues, the FCW would avoid the political problems associated with patronage appointments by the president.

When the Clinton administration took office in 1993, activists proposed that a national commission be reestablished along with an Interagency Task Force to provide administrative support. The first order of business would be to prepare needed reports for the Fourth United Nations Conference on Women in Beijing in 1995. Instead of creating new machineries, the administration placed the responsibility in the State Department, which in turn enlisted the assistance of the Women's Bureau at the Department of Labor to convene regional meetings and prepare the report for the conference. As a follow-up to the Beijing Conference, the President's Interagency Council on Women was set up to coordinate federal implementation of the United Nations plan of action in the United States.

From Women's Bloc to Gender Gap

According to American democratic theory, the ballot is a citizen's means of political action. In a collective sense, voting by groups with common interests is the way to get interests heard by elected officials. In turn, political leaders try to win votes by attending to the needs and demands of voters. They often think of the electorate as composed of blocs: black

Americans, labor, senior citizens, or "angry white men." Political activists try to increase their clout with politicians by claiming to speak for a voting bloc. Being able to deliver votes is a valuable political resource.

In the 1920s, women's rights advocates rapidly lost influence with Congress when the expected bloc of new women voters failed to materialize. In fact, politicians had no way of knowing if women voted as a group or not; these elections took place before the development and widespread use of polling techniques. In politics, however, it matters less how women actually vote than what people believe about their voting behavior. After the ratification of the Nineteenth Amendment, political actors did not want to confront a voting bloc of women. Fearing the development of a new political game they could not control, politicians offered women opportunities in regular political-party organizations only if the women would renounce one of the goals of women's suffrage, that is, to bring the woman's perspective to public life. That meant sacrificing issues specially aimed toward women in favor of achieving success for male candidates and issues.

Women activists were divided. Many wanted to share political life with men and did not want to maintain a separate bloc. They preferred to work for reform of the government and the betterment of society rather than for a specific feminist agenda. While they believed that women would bring a different perspective to politics, it would not be on behalf of their own rights. The League of Women Voters, successor to the dominant suffragist organization, consciously chose to become an organization on behalf of good government, not of women's rights or feminism. Ironically, only the egalitarians of the National Woman's Party, whose ideology suggested an identity of interests between men and women, opted for a separatist strategy. But they were not interested in mobilizing voters, instead preferring to promote their personal influence on national leaders.

Without a women's voting bloc to back them up, nonpartisan women's groups found it difficult to prevail in political debate. During the first fifty years of women's suffrage, success in policy debates was due to individual women, acting alone and in networks inside political parties, legislatures, and the administration—what Jo Freeman (1975) has called the "woodwork feminists."

In the 1980s, the concept of a women's voting bloc finally caught on in the political discourse as the *gender gap*. The gender gap is both an objective observation of differences in voting choices and attitudes of women and men *and* a partisan tool of feminist political influence. Technology and politics have combined to produce, at long last, a women's voting bloc. Since the 1950s, the federal government has funded regular election polls, the National Election Studies (NES), by the University of Michigan. Effective social science polling techniques yield evidence of many types of group-based voting. The NES polls revealed sex differences in voting behavior since the beginning. In the first polls, women's turnout lagged behind men's by about 10 percent; the difference narrowed until 1976, when it was even. Since 1976, more women than men have voted. In the 1950s, women voted differently, favoring Dwight Eisenhower and Richard Nixon over their Democratic opponents. Women seemed to be more conservative than men, favoring traditional values of home, religion, family, and peace. Since the 1970s, however, women have voted more often for Democrats than for Republicans in presidential elections and in several state races as well. In 1986, a number of newly elected Democratic senators owed their victory to the support by women. In the 1980s, women seemed to be more worried about the economy and more in favor of government action on family, social, and education policies than men.

Before 1980, feminists wanted to focus on common concerns of women in both political parties. Groundwork was laid in the early 1970s with the organization of the National Women's Political Caucus (NWPC), a bipartisan group to elect women to office and to support women's issues and candidates across party lines. Emphasizing women's preferences for one party over the other would have contradicted this strategy.

The hope for bipartisanship faded, however, after the ERA and other women's rights goals became partisan issues and antifeminists began to dominate the Republican party. Beginning in 1980, feminists cautiously created the gender-gap concept by interpreting the differences in turnout, candidate selection, and attitudes to mean opposition to the antifeminist policies of the Reagan and Bush administrations and the Republican party's right wing. The willingness of feminist leaders to accept and promote the idea of a gender gap in voting behavior communicated the strength of this potential voting bloc in a way that the voting data alone could not. Labeling the gender gap also indicated the willingness of feminist leaders to recognize that women have special interests that are different from those of men. This has not meant a return to the old ideas that women, because they are mothers, are gentler and more moral than men, although some feminists believe that women have a more socially conscious and accommodative morality (see Carol Gilligan, 1982). But most

BOX 3.6

The Gender Gap: Presidential Elections

Between 1952 and 1980, men and women voters differed in their support of the winning presidential candidates. The extent of this gender difference was less than 6 percent:

Year	Winner	Percentage of Votes Cast by Women	Percentage of Votes Cast by Men	Gender Gap
1952	Eisenhower	58%	53%	5%
1956	Eisenhower	61	55	6
1960	Kennedy	49	52	3
1964	Johnson	62	60	2
1968	Nixon	43	43	0
1972	Nixon	62	63	1
1976	Carter	48	53	5

After 1980, the difference grew to 8 percent, constituting a gender gap, with women giving less support to Reagan and Bush and more to Clinton:

Year	Winner	Percentage of Votes Cast by Women	Percentage of Votes Cast by Men	Gender Gap
1984	Reagan	54%	62%	8%
1988	Bush	50	57	7
1992	Clinton	45	41	4*
1996	Clinton	54	43	11

*There was no difference between men and women in support for Bush. In the 1992 election, male voters favored third-party candidate Ross Perot more than female voters by 21 percent to 17 percent.

Source: CAWP, National Information Bank on Women in Public Office, Eagleton Institute of Politics, Rutgers University; Jackman, 1996–97, pp. 1, 4.

activists explain the gap in terms of the lower economic status of women and the problems of reconciling work and family responsibilities. "Issues, particularly the economy, provide the roots of the gender gap. Women and men do not have different issue agendas, but they do see the world and their own economic lives through different lenses. Women also have different priorities for government action than men and want a more active role for government in domestic and family policies" (Celinda Lake, quoted in Baruch, 1988, p. 8).

BOX 3.7

The Gender Gap: Senatorial Elections

From 1992 to 1994, four senators (all Democrats) owed their election victories to women.

Year	State	Winner	Percentage of Votes Cast by Women	Percentage of Votes Cast by Men
1992	California	Barbara Boxer	57%	43%
1994	California	Dianne Feinstein	52	41
1994	New Jersey	Frank Lautenberg	55	44
1994	Virginia	Charles Robb	50	40
1996	Massachusetts	John Kerry	56	47
1996	Minnesota	Paul Wellstone	55	46
1996	Louisiana	Mary Landrieu	54	45
1996	Iowa	Tom Harkin	55	49

During the same period, seven senators (all Republicans) owed their election victories to men:

Year	State	Winner		
1992	North Carolina	Lauch Faircloth	49	56
1992	New York	Alfonse D'Amato	47	56
1992	Oregon	Bob Packwood	44	60
1992	Pennsylvania	Arlen Specter	46	56
1994	Michigan	Spencer Abraham	46	57
1994	Minnesota	Rod Grams	45	54
1994	Washington	Slade Gorton	48	60

Source: CAWP News & Notes: 9 and 10 (Winter 1993 and Winter 1994): 9–11. Jackman, 1996–97, p. 8.

Feminists have used the gender gap to increase their influence in the political parties and in policy making. Since Democrats seem to be the chief beneficiaries of the gender gap, they were expected to act to promote feminist issues and women candidates. They complied in 1984, a high point of feminist influence, with the nomination of Geraldine Ferraro for vice president on the ticket headed by Walter Mondale. Republicans countered by pronouncing the Democrats in the grip of "special interests," citing NOW's close relation to Mondale as evidence.

Republicans were not immune to the influence of the gender gap. During the 1980 election campaign, Ronald Reagan promised to appoint a woman to the Supreme Court. Throughout his administration, his staff contended with the women's lobby, usually responding with highly visible appointments of women rather than policy adjustments. Republicans also tried to enter the debate by making the gender gap an issue itself. Pronouncements by politicians that the polls are not accurate is one such effort. Statements denouncing voting blocs as evidence of lack of independence or as proof of selfish special interests and reiterating the politician's belief in the independence of the voter are similar efforts.

In the 1990s, the gender gap has benefited Republican candidates as well as Democratic, signifying the beginnings of a "men's vote" in opposition to the women's vote. In the Senate races in 1992 and 1994, seven Senators, all Republicans, owed their victory to men, whereas four Democrats would not have been elected in those years without strong majority support from women. In 1996, five Democrats from Massachusetts, Minnesota, Georgia, Louisiana, and Iowa owed their election to the U.S. Senate to majority support from women. In all races, more men favored their opponents. Data such as these, along with the polarizing of the two parties over issues of gender and feminism evident at the 1992 and 1996 presidential nominating conventions, have led some observers to question whether the gender gap in voting reflects more than just a difference over policy preferences. They suggest it is the foundation of "two different and conflicting visions of how Americans should engage in everyday life" (Freeman, 1993, p. 21).

Indirect Policies

The democratic ideology of equal individual political rights is so strong that government would not enforce any policies that directly limit them. But some government policies can indirectly limit political opportunities for women. Such policies continue to impede equal participation because they are not defined in the political debate as issues affecting citizenship and goals of equal representation. Feminists, with a full agenda of demands, also overlook the limitations that government policies may impose indirectly in their effect on family law, jury service, and election laws.

Family Law

The dominant tradition in American family law has been the doctrine of common law that set forth the legal unity of husband and wife. Upon marriage, a woman traditionally lost her separate legal status, and her husband acted for her and for the family unit. Opponents of suffrage often used this concept of common-law unity to limit participation of women outside the home.

Before 1907, the loss of married women's identity had never extended to citizenship, which a woman retained separate from the legal unity of husband and wife. In 1907, however, the laws changed to threaten the citizenship rights of married women. According to the new law, a woman born in the United States lost her citizenship—and with it her right to vote (in those states where she had that right), to hold public office, or to serve in civil service—if she married a foreigner. The motive behind this policy was surely xenophobic. Some people wanted to penalize women for "mixing their blood" and that of immigrants. The law led to severe problems for individual women who, eventually, found themselves deprived of all rights and property during World War I. An early postsuffrage victory for the women's lobby was the Cable Act of 1922, which partially restored rights to the wives of foreigners, although these women were not declared fully equal with other citizens until the 1930s.

Many of the worst legal disabilities stemming from common law have been removed from state laws (see Chapter 4). However, most jurisdictions still retain the common law of domicile: a husband and wife must have the same legal residence—that of the husband. A woman who has lived her whole life in Kentucky may marry someone whose residence is Kansas and lose her voting registration and her eligibility to run for office where she lives. This could be extremely awkward for a woman already active in public life in her county or state government. The remedy is either for the state to enact a blanket exclusion of domicile law for political functions or for the woman to establish a separate domicile through a court order.

Jury Service

That the Nineteenth Amendment did not confer any blanket civil or political rights should be evident by now. Even after 1920, state laws restricting women from serving on juries remained untouched unless a state court or legislature removed the restrictions by special action. The debate on jury service for women followed two directions. The first debate was based on the assumption that jury duty is a burden that most people would rather avoid (as is compulsory military service). Initially, the opponents of women on juries emphasized that the unpleasant nature of the courtroom was not suitable for feminine sensibilities. Later, when the double moral standard had less credibility, the opponents argued that women should be relieved of the burden because of their more important duties at home, such as caring for small children. The second debate focused on the rights of the defendants to a fair trial "by a jury of their peers." Proponents of equality argued that women could not be guaranteed fairness if they had to submit to all-male juries.

The debates on jury service for women recurred in various states until the Supreme Court in 1975 prohibited sex discrimination in the obligation for jury duty. Rarely, by the way, was the argument made that jury service was an obligation of citizenship and represented equal responsibility for women with men in civil life. Finally, in *J.E.B. v. Alabama ex rel T.B.* (1994), the Court linked exclusion from juries to sex discrimination more generally: "Striking individual jurors on the assumption that they hold particular views simply because of their gender is 'practically a brand upon them, affixed by law, an assertion of their inferiority (*Stauder v. West Virginia*, 100 U.S. 303, 308, 1880).' . . . [I]t denigrates the dignity of the excluded juror, and for a women reinvokes a history of exclusion from political participation" (p. 1428).

Election Laws

Laws barring women from seeking public office disappeared after 1920, although special action by courts and states was needed to remove that legal barrier. Nevertheless, particular election rules still in effect may more subtly affect women's political fortunes. To what extent have electoral districts, primary laws, poll taxes, and literacy tests discouraged women and minority men from participating? Soon after women got the right to vote, Southern states took action to keep African American women from registering. The all-white primaries left them with little say in these one-party states (Prestage, 1991). Despite all the rhetoric in the United States about the virtues of democracy, candidate choice, and multiparty elections, it is strikingly difficult for new political parties and candidates to gain access to the ballot in this country. Even registering to vote has been a difficult procedure, constituting a challenge to citizens' rights in many states (Piven and Cloward, 1988). The original intent of many of these laws was to maintain the power base of a particular elite. Since women are challengers to this dominance, many election regulations probably operate as barriers to women.

Political science research has begun to assemble evidence linking particular election arrangements to increased or decreased opportunities for women seeking elective office at local, state, and national levels. Due to the strength of incumbency, opportunity is limited for any newcomers. The U.S. Congressional elections are single-member contests where the candidate with the most votes wins, even with less than a majority. These arrangements favor Anglo, Hispanic, and African American men (Rule 1989; Darcy, Welch, and Clark, 1994). Multimember electoral districts, which are found in some state and local elections, are most favorable to both African American and Anglo women (Darcy, Hadley, and Kirksey, 1993; Rule, 1992). There, several representatives are chosen at once from a district, and those who come in second or third are able to win as well as the frontrunner.

Periodically, efforts arise to unlock the hold the political elite has on power. The successful campaign for the Voting Rights Act of 1965 brought federal authority against restrictive practices in districting and registration, and that law was "significant empowering legislation for African American women" (Prestage, 1991, p. 97). The so-called motor voter laws, which enable citizens to register to vote when they register for their driver's license, are expected to increase election rolls and turnout (Knack, 1995). Campaigns for mandatory term limits for state and elective offices have sought to loosen the grip of incumbents and cause more turnover. Rule changes like these have the potential to give outgroups, such as women, a greater opportunity for election.

For many women, clustered at the margins of the economy, political rights are limited by class influences. When issues of access to elections are raised in public debate, however, they are usually issues of civil rights for African Americans rather than gender or class issues. For example, incumbency is a barrier to women; campaign finance arrangements work against poor women. Yet proposals for term limits and campaign reform in the 1990s are rarely discussed in terms of their effect on women. When the constitutionality of California's term limits law was challenged in court, no women's rights group filed a brief. (Darcy, Welch, and Clark, 1994, p. 194). The gender effects of motor-voter laws are not yet clear. So far, the debate on electoral reform has not been defined in terms of the effects on women as a minority group seeking representation.

Conclusion

In considering politics as a problem of women's rights, it is important to distinguish between several different rights. These are the rights to (1) participate as citizens; (2) have influence in decision-making bodies; (3)

share in the benefits of political office; and (4) govern. Despite progress in the areas of participation and influence, feminists despair at the chronic inequalities they face as they try to share governing power and the benefits of office with men. The problem is much more serious than indicated merely by the data on the percentage of women holding political office. It is a cultural problem. It's not just that women do not hold office; there is no cultural or philosophical foundation for women sharing power with men.

Artists and writers have been inspired by the battle of the sexes. The literary tradition contains some fantasies about powerful women, but not as equals with men. In the legends of the Greeks, Amazon women were more manly than men and ruled them, and Lysistrata and her sisters exerted their influence by withholding sex from their husbands. In European cultures, stories recur of communities of women who enslave or banish men.[12] Yet there are no popular legends that declare peace in the battle of the sexes and allow women and men to share power.

American political theorists offer few examples of circumstances where men and women could achieve parity in government. Many theorists have found it difficult enough to wrestle with ideas allowing women to participate as citizens, let alone to contemplate shared governance. The debate over women's political role has been greatly affected by dominant ideologies of democracy and by contemporary movements for political power. An apparently simple concept such as votes for women has ranged in meaning from an inalienable human right to a requirement of emancipation to an instrument of political reform. Finally, in the form of the gender gap, the vote is seen as a means of promoting women's rights.

Feminists have been handicapped by the continued tension between demands based on equality and demands based on difference. The contradiction plagued the suffragists, separating the movement into two organizations; it divided social and egalitarian feminists in the 1920s over the ERA and forced women to choose between tokenism and isolation. It may have prevented a clear recognition of a women's voting bloc. Also limiting the development of a single women's constituency is multiple consciousness. Although many women voters identify with other women, they have other loyalties as well, based on ethnicity, race, religion, neighborhood, and place in the work force. These differences have stymied feminist efforts to establish permanent government institutions for the advocacy of women's interests. These differences have isolated Republican women advocates from leaders of their party and from their counterparts in Democratic circles, and they have divided liberal feminists from feminists of color.

Some feminist theorists are seeking to deal with this crippling inconsistency by challenging the equality-difference dichotomy itself (Scott, 1988). This involves breaking down the separation of the two concepts by pointing out that equality is possible only among people who differ. In other words, equality does not mean identity; rather, it means ignoring difference in a particular context, as when determining eligibility for public office. At the same time, differences between the sexes and among women are not fundamental and general but are specific to time, social location, and culture. Being a mother may handicap a woman in seeking public office only because of the prevailing social definitions of politics and motherhood. Among African American women, for example, family roles have enhanced their participation in activist community organizations. There is nothing inherent in human biology that separates all women from all political activity. According to this view, focusing on gender differences in public debate reinforces values of women's incapacity without challenging masculinist views of power. Unless challenged, socially constructed gender differences will continue to reinforce a pattern of formal male authority in the United States.

Another approach is to focus on the inadequacies of democratic theory itself, pointing to the need for more, not less, attention to sex and gender differences. Over the centuries of dialogues over democracy, conversations have taken place as though women did not exist. To overcome this situation of democracy *without women*, we must think of democracy—both in theory and in practice—as deliberately, constructing space *for women*. In a practical sense, this would mean policies, like quotas, would be needed to achieve parity. This may be seen as a sort of transitional shock therapy for democracy. The debate among feminists over equality and difference thus persists and has become international (Kelber, 1994; Lovenduski and Norris, 1993; Phillips, 1991). Although quotas are unpopular in the United States, debates for promoting women framed in terms of parity may gain some support given the slow increases in gains in office since 1920 and the increased gender consciousness in the electorate (Rinehart, 1993).

Notes

1. Data in this chapter come from the Center for the American Woman and Politics and the National Information Bank on Women in Public Office. Both are with the Eagleton Institute of Politics at Rutgers University, and both collect data on women's participation in politics and publish fact sheets periodically.

2. "It was a distinction briefly held, however, for in 1807 a chastened legislature terminated their enjoyment of the franchise. The candid explanation was that although women had used the ballot quite generally, they had failed to support the proper candidates in the election!" (Breckinridge, 1933, p. 246, fn. 3).

3. In 1992, 53 percent of registered voters were women. Since then, the federal "motor voter" law has gone into effect linking voter registration to the issuance of automobile licenses. It is expected to have an impact on both voter registration and turnout. Watch for any shift in sex distribution in voting.

4. The Privileges and Immunities Clause found in Section 1 of the Fourteenth Amendment reads as follows: "No State shall make or enforce any law which shall abridge the privileges or immunities of citizens of the United States."

5. One of the lesser-known stories of the suffrage concerns Harry T. Burn, the man who broke the tie in the Tennessee legislature to put ratification over the top on August 26, 1920. "I want to state I changed my vote in favor of ratification, first, because I believe in full suffrage as a right; second, I believe we had a moral and legal right to ratify; third, I knew that a mother's advice is always safest for her boy to follow and my mother wanted me to vote for ratification; fourth, I appreciated the fact that an opportunity such as seldom comes to mortal man to free . . . women from political slavery was mine" (Cahn, 1970, p. 63). The letter from Burn's mother, a poor farm wife who nonetheless read the newspaper was: "Dear Son. Hurrah and vote for suffrage! Don't keep them in doubt . . . Don't forget to be a good boy and help Mrs. Catt put the 'rat' in ratification."

6. New Jersey's enfranchisement of women (1787–1804) had been brief and short-lived. Wyoming was the first state to grant women the vote after the beginning of the suffrage movement. Women there have had the right ever since.

7. For descriptions of several recent policy issues, see Gelb and Palley (1987), Boneparth (1988), and Ferree and Martin (1995).

8. Both Angela Davis (1981) and Paula Giddings (1984) devote a chapter to the club movement of black American women. For a fictional account of white American women's local political participation between 1870 and 1900, see Helen Hooven Santmyer (1984).

9. At least sixteen states now have laws mandating fifty-fifty representation of men and women.

10. Compare party affiliations of women in the House of Representatives over four elections:

Election	Democrats	Republican
1988	20	9
1992	36	12
1994	30	17
1996	35	16

11. The United Nations classifies such commissions under the general term *women's policy machinery*. This also includes permanent agencies charged with a women's policy agenda, such as the Women's Bureau of the Department of Labor (see Chapter 7). For information on other countries, see Stetson and Mazur (1995).

12. Nineteenth-century England produced two popular versions of the tale: Tennyson's poem "The Princess" and Gilbert and Sullivan's "Princess Ida." Italian composer Giacomo Puccini was also fascinated by the princess who shunned men, and he featured one in his opera *Turandot*. Resolution of the

conflict between female independence and romantic love defied Puccini, and he died leaving that opera unfinished.

References

Abzug, Bella, with Mim Kelber. *Gender Gap.* Boston: Houghton Mifflin, 1984.

Ackelsberg, Martha, and Diamond, Irene. "Gender and Political Life: New Directions in Political Science." In *Analyzing Gender,* edited by Beth B. Hess and Myra Marx Ferree, pp. 504–525. Newbury Park, Calif.: Sage, 1987.

Alh. "The Formation of a New Political Party." *Off Our Backs* (February 1993): 12–13.

Alpern, Sara, and Baum, Dale. "Female Ballots: The Impact of the Nineteenth Amendment." *Journal of Interdisciplinary History* 16 (Summer 1985): 43–67.

Baruch, Lucy, ed. "News & Notes About Women Public Officials." *Center for the American Woman and Politics* 6 (Winter 1988, entire issue).

Becker, Susan. *The Origins of the Equal Rights Amendment: American Feminism Between the Wars.* Westport, Conn.: Greenwood Press, 1981.

Bird, Caroline, ed. *What Women Want.* New York: Simon & Schuster, 1979.

Boneparth, Ellen, and Stoper, Emily. *Women, Power, and Policy: Toward the Year 2000,* 2nd ed. New York: Pergamon Press, 1988.

Breckinridge, Sophonisba. *Women in the Twentieth Century.* New York: McGraw-Hill, 1933.

Buhle, Marijo, and Buhle, Paul, eds. *The Concise History of Woman Suffrage.* Urbana: University of Illinois Press, 1978.

Cahn, William. "The Man Whose Vote Gave Women the Vote." *Look Magazine* (August 25, 1970): 60–63.

Center for the American Woman and Politics. *CAWP News & Notes* 9 (Winter, 1993).

Cook, Elizabeth Adell, Thomas, Sue, and Wilcox, Clyde, eds. *The Year of the Woman: Myths and Realities.* Boulder: Westview Press, 1994.

Costain, Anne N. "Representing Women: The Transition from Social Movement to Interest Group." In *Women, Power, and Policy: Toward the Year 2000,* 2nd ed., edited by Ellen Boneparth and Emily Stoper. (New York: Pergamon Press, 1988) pp. 26–47.

Cott, Nancy F. *The Grounding of Modern Feminism.* New Haven: Yale University Press, 1987.

Darcy, R., Hadley, Charles D., and Kirksey, Jason F. "Election Systems and the Representation of Black Women in American State Legislatures." *Women and Politics* 13 (1993): 73–89.

Darcy, R., Welch, Susan, and Clark, Janet. *Women, Elections, and Representation,* 2nd ed., New York: Longman, 1994.

Davis, Angela. *Woman, Race, and Class.* New York: Random House, 1981.

DuBois, Ellen Carol, ed. *Elizabeth Cady Stanton, Susan B. Anthony: Correspondence, Writings, Speeches.* New York: Schocken Books, 1981.

Elshtain, Jean Bethke. *Public Man, Private Woman.* Princeton: Princeton University Press, 1981.

Ferree, Myra Marx, and Martin, Patricia Yancey, eds. *Feminist Organizations.* Philadelphia: Temple University Press, 1995.

Flexner, Eleanor. *Century of Struggle,* rev. ed. Cambridge: Belknap, 1975.

Freeman, Jo. *The Politics of Women's Liberation.* New York: McKay, 1975.

Freeman, Jo. "Feminism vs. Family Values: Women at the 1992 Democratic and Republican Conventions." *PS: Political Science and Politics* 26 (March 1993): 21–27.

Gelb, Joyce, and Palley, Marian Lief. *Women and Public Policies,* rev. ed. Princeton: Princeton University Press, 1987.

Giddings, Paula. *When and Where I Enter.* New York: William Morrow, 1984.

Gilligan, Carol. *In a Different Voice.* Cambridge: Harvard University Press, 1982.

Gutin, Myra G. *The President's Partner: The First Lady in the Twentieth Century.* Westport, Conn.: Greenwood Press, 1989.

Harrison, Cynthia. *On Account of Sex.* Berkeley: University of California Press, 1988.

Hartman, Susan M. *From Margin to Mainstream: American Women and Politics Since 1960.* New York: Knopf, 1989.

Intraparliamentary Union. *Women in Parliament 1945–1995.* Geneva: Intraparliamentary Union, 1995.

Jackman, Jennifer. "Gender Gap Decisive—Women Elect President, Men Elect Gingrich Congress." *Feminist Majority Report* 8 (Winter 1996–1997): 1.

J.E.B. v. Alabama. 114 S. CT. 1419. 1994.

Kelber, Mim. *Women in Government: New Ways to Political Power.* Westport, Conn.: Praeger, 1994.

Kendrigan, Mary Lou. *Political Equality in a Democratic Society: Women in the United States.* Westport, Conn.: Greenwood Press, 1984.

Kleppner, Paul. "Were Women to Blame? Female Suffrage and Voter Turnout." *Journal of Interdisciplinary History* 12 (Spring 1982): 621–643.

Knack, Stephen. "Does 'Motor Voter' Work? Evidence from State-Level Data." *The Journal of Politics* 57 (August 1995): 796–811.

Lemons, J. Stanley. *The Woman Citizen: Social Feminism in the 1920s.* Urbana: University of Illinois Press, 1973.

Lovenduski, Joni, and Norris, Pippa, eds. *Gender and Party Politics.* London: Sage Publications, 1993.

Lunardini, Christine A. *From Equal Suffrage to Equal Rights: Alice Paul and the National Woman's Party 1920–1928.* New York: New York University Press, 1986.

Mead, Margaret, and Kaplan, Frances Balgley, eds. *American Women: The Report of the President's Commission on the Status of Women and Other Publications of the Commission.* New York: Scribner's, 1965.

Minkoff, Debra C. *Organizing for Equality: The Evolution of Women's and Racial-Ethnic Organizations in America 1955–85.* New Brunswick, N.J.: Rutgers University Press, 1995.

Minor v. Happersett. 88 U.S. 162. 1875.

Morgan, David. *Suffragists and Democrats: The Politics of Woman Suffrage in America.* East Lansing: Michigan State University Press, 1972.

Mueller, Carol M., ed. *The Politics of the Gender Gap: The Social Construction of Political Influence.* Newbury Park, Calif.: Sage, 1988.

Phillips, Anne. *Engendering Democracy.* University Park: University of Pennsylvania Press, 1991.

Piven, Frances Fox, and Cloward, Richard A. *Why Americans Don't Vote.* New York. Pantheon, 1988.

Prestage, Jewel L. "In Quest of African American Political Woman." *Annals of the American Academy of Political and Social Sciences* 515 (May 1991): 88–103.

President's Task Force on Women's Rights and Responsibilities. *Task Force Report: A Matter of Simple Justice.* Washington, D.C.: GPO, April 1970.

Rinehart, Sue Tolleson. *Gender Consciousness and Politics.* New York: Routledge, 1993.

Rule, Wilma. "Multimember Legislative Districts: Minority and Anglo Women's and Men's Recruitment Opportunity." In *United States Electoral System: Their Impact on Women and Minorities,* edited by Wilma Rule and Joseph F. Zimmerman, pp. 57–72. New York: Greenwood Press, 1992.

Rupp, Leila, and Taylor, Verta. *Survival in the Doldrums: The American Women's Rights Movement, 1945 to the 1960s.* New York: Oxford University Press, 1987.

Santmyer, Helen Hooven. ". . . And Ladies of the Club." New York: Putnam's, 1984.

Scott, Anne, and Scott, Andrew. *One Half the People: The Fight for Woman Suffrage.* Philadelphia: Lippincott, 1975.

Scott, Joan W. "Deconstructing Equality Versus Difference, or, The Uses of Post Structural Theory for Feminism." *Feminist Studies* 14 (Spring 1988): 33–50.

Spalter-Roth, Roberta, and Schreiber, Ronnie. "Outsider Issues and Insider Tactics: Strategic Tensions in the Women's Policy Network During the 1980s." In *Feminist Organizations*, edited by Myra Marx Ferree and Patricia Yancey Martin, pp. 105–127. Philadelphia: Temple University Press, 1995.

Stetson, Dorothy McBride, and Mazur, Amy, eds. *Comparative State Feminism*. Thousand Oaks, Calif.: Sage Publications, 1995.

Stevens, Doris. *Jailed for Freedom*. New York: Boni and Liveright, 1920.

Stewart, Debra. *The Women's Movement in Community Politics in the U.S.: The Role of Local Commissions on the Status of Women*. New York: Pergamon, 1980.

United Nations, Center for Social Development and Humanitarian Affairs. *1989 World Survey on the Role of Women in Development*. New York: United Nations, 1989.

Ware, Susan. *Beyond Suffrage: Women in the New Deal*. Cambridge: Harvard University Press, 1981.

Ware, Susan. *Holding Their Own: American Women in the 1930s*. Boston: Twayne, 1982.

Welch, Susan. "A Gender Gap Among Hispanics? A Comparison with Blacks and Anglos." *Western Political Quarterly* 45 (March,1992): 181–199.

CHAPTER 4

Reproduction

Contemporary feminists consider the issues and policies relating to reproduction central to the status and opportunities of women. The effects of different physical demands on women and men in conceiving and bearing a child are at the root of most social conceptions of gender roles. It seems elementary to feminists that only through control of her biology can a woman make choices about other areas of her life. Surprisingly, concentrated efforts to shape a public policy that will safeguard and enhance women's choices in reproduction are relatively recent, even among feminists. Although reproductive issues have been in the public-policy arena for nearly two hundred years, they have usually been peripheral to other, more central feminist demands, and feminists have been on the periphery of the public debate. The abortion issue, especially, has changed that.

This chapter traces the evolution of the public debate about reproduction and the impact that debate has had on the two central issues of reproductive policy: access to contraceptives and access to abortion. What is striking about the debate's evolution is that all of the various definitions that have arisen since the beginning of the nineteenth century have accumulated in the contemporary debate. A combination of social, economic, and technological changes, including changes in the status of women, have brought new perspectives and demands to the controversy. Although old definitions may retreat from time to time, they do not fade away. This review of the history of the debate about reproduction will also serve to explore aspects of the contemporary and, probably, the future debate.

Contraception and abortion have not been in the policy arena continuously. In fact, legislators have acted infrequently on these subjects. Perhaps they avoid them. After all, these subjects are difficult issues for politicians—what some political scientists call *emotive-symbolic issues* (Smith, 1975). Most legislative business involves the distribution of funds and opportunities to a variety of competing interests. With emotive-symbolic issues, the demands of interest groups are not for money or contracts but for values: these demands force legislators to decide between strong but conflicting convictions of right and wrong. Legislators, who are used to seeking compromises on policy that will please a majority yet offend few, must side with one group over all others. Compromise of absolute values is not acceptable to participants, yet picking one side over the others may serve only to increase the conflict.

Not only are policy choices with respect to reproduction difficult, they have little effect. Rules and regulations about such intimate matters as conception and termination of pregnancy are remote from the circumstances surrounding the personal behavior of millions of women and men. Reproduction is intimately bound up with psychological, social, cultural, and religious attitudes and practices. Whether to have a baby, or the next baby, has been a choice faced by women and their families in all societies since prehistoric times. Any particular public policy can have only a small impact among these other influences. Faced with intense and emotional conflict among interest groups and with the likely ineffectiveness of policy, American legislators have found it easier to pass symbolic restrictions on access to contraception and abortion than either to remove restrictions and use state power to expand access or to try to regulate family size. By leaving economic, social, and educational barriers to reproductive choice undisturbed, U.S. policy on reproduction tends to be pro-natalist, in effect if not by design.[1]

There is one refuge for legislators caught up in periodic religious wars over reproduction policy: medicine. Medical issues can be turned over to doctors to resolve. Politicians can allow doctors to regulate access to contraception and abortion as deemed medically necessary without facing the wrath of the religious fundamentalists and antifeminists. When contraception and abortion can be defined as medical issues—rather than sexual, religious, moral, social, or feminist issues—then some liberalization of government regulation is possible. As doctors gain more and more control over all aspects of the fertility process, this growing medicalization threatens every woman's right of choice.

Contraception

Since the early 1800s, the debate over the regulation of contraception has yielded three distinct phases of policy, reflecting three definitions of contraceptives as:

- obscene materials
- prevention and treatment of disease
- an aid in family planning

The policies that emerged during each phase of the debate are the product of three forces: (1) the way the contraception issues came to public discussion, (2) the development of the debate in relation to social and economic change, and (3) changes in technology. Feminists have participated in each phase of the debate but have not yet managed to gain control. Thus, access to contraceptive information and services is not yet officially defined as a matter of women's rights. As a consequence, the women's health movement remains vigilant in alerting feminists to the impact of contemporary governmental rules and regulations on reproductive choice.

Obscene Materials

The subject of contraception, which had been practiced privately for generations, came to the public attention of nineteenth-century U.S. political leaders through books. In the 1830s, a period of much discussion of utopias and revolution in Europe, tracts advocating birth control as a means of social reform began to appear in the United States. The perfect society would be fully planned, down to the size of the population. These views were inspired by the writings of Malthus, who in the late 1700s had linked overpopulation to poverty and alerted government to the need for balance between people and resources. Whereas earlier Malthusians had advocated sexual restraint as a means of preventing the ravages of overpopulation, the neo-Malthusians favored informing people of methods of contraception and also improving contraceptive techniques.

Beginning in 1832 with *The Fruits of Philosophy* by Charles Knowlton, books on birth control ran into obscenity laws. Most of these laws were part of common-law practices transferred from England rather than specific statutes enacted by state legislatures in the United States. Enforced by the courts, these laws depended on the activism of religious reform groups for their effectiveness. Although every state had laws about obscenity, patterns of repression of birth-control materials varied with the politics and culture of each state and community.

Unlike our contemporary culture, nineteenth-century culture did not separate reproduction from sexuality. (If this book had been written then, it would not have separate chapters on reproduction and sexuality.) Many considered topics such as birth control and conception to be as intimate as intercourse and orgasms. Thus, at the same time the demand for information about birth control was growing, so was a counter reaction based on religious and moral grounds, which became part of a movement for moral regeneration and social purity after the Civil War. Among the leaders of this movement was Anthony Comstock, who feared that corruption and debauchery threatened youth and who believed that law could eliminate immoral practices. Backed by evangelical reformers such as the Young Men's Christian Association (YMCA), churches, and anti-vice societies, Comstock lobbied in Washington for federal legislation to keep what he saw as an avalanche of smut out of the United States, its postal system, and its interstate commerce. Comstock and his allies considered contraceptives immoral and obscene, much as many people today consider hard-core pornographic movies. For Comstock and his allies, contraception meant vile interference with the divine scheme for procreation. It involved unnatural acts such as withdrawal or intercourse without ejaculation or chemicals such as douches or devices such as condoms, with vulgar names such as "French letter" or "English riding coat" (Gordon, 1976). These political leaders charged that contraceptive practices encouraged premarital and extramarital sex, which they classified along with rape, prostitution, and pornography as part of the general moral corruption and decay of society.

Comstock was remarkably successful in lobbying. In 1873, less than one month after his bill was introduced, the Act for the Suppression of Trade in and Circulation of Obscene Literature and Articles of Immoral Use passed both the houses of Congress, with no opposition and only fifteen minutes of debate. The so-called Comstock Act defined contraceptives and materials written about them as "articles of immoral use," and it prohibited mailing or importing these materials or buying or selling them across state lines. Success at the federal level was followed by a state-by-state campaign. By the beginning of the 1900s, half of the states had little Comstock Acts, and all but two defined contraceptive sale and distribution as already prohibited by anti-obscenity laws. Contraceptives were officially defined as obscene and thus were illegal commerce—at least in the law books.

Any movement as fervent and religious as the moral-regeneration and social-purity movement is bound to provoke opposition, but rarely are the opponents as intensely committed as are the crusaders fighting evil. Although no one stopped the Comstock Act while it was in Congress, attempts to enforce it—by banning books, restricting mail, and arresting people for giving out information—stirred to action some advocates of free speech. Free speech is often a minority issue, and this time was no exception. All attempts to gain repeal of the Comstock Acts by labeling them violations of free speech failed. To this day, the First Amendment permits legislatures to regulate obscene materials (see Chapter 9). Apparently, free-speech advocates did not try to change the rhetoric that classified contraceptives as obscene. There was, however, an early effort to exclude "information given by medical men from operation of the statute" (Dienes, 1972, p. 58).

Feminists in the last quarter of the nineteenth century were affected by the controversy over contraceptives and morality but chose a course separate from it. Many began to advocate "voluntary motherhood" to promote the status of women. *Voluntary motherhood* meant that women should have the right to decide when to bear a child. Feminists presented the argument not that women were enslaved by biology and their bodies but that women were enslaved by the lust of men. Thus, the way for women to gain control over their childbearing was not by using contraceptives but by abstaining altogether from sexual intercourse that would lead to conception. Advocates of voluntary motherhood were often involved with social-purity and other reform groups and accepted the separate-sphere arguments. For them, purity was power. By controlling their childbearing, women could limit male control over them. They could also bring the values of motherhood into public life and displace male-produced vulgarity and corruption. Contraception did not figure in this scheme for women's rights. Even the radical feminists of the time who espoused free love and sexual expression for women were not much interested in contraceptives. They saw contraceptives as artificially inhibiting the free and natural expression of sexual pleasure. Thus, until 1900, feminists either were little interested in the Comstock Acts or accepted them by default.

Prevention and Treatment of Disease

Margaret Sanger changed that. In 1912, when the Post Office refused to mail her article "What Every Girl Should Know," Sanger began a lifelong commitment to the legalization of contraceptives and contraceptive information. Dubbing the project the "birth control" campaign, she defined the issue as a question of women's rights—to free women from dependency on frequent pregnancies and to improve social conditions among the poor. At first, her method was direct confrontation with the guardians of the so-called Comstockery at the Post Office. She was arrested several times, escaped to England, returned to face prosecution, and served time in prison. These activities drew some publicity (but little legislative notice) to the issue. And the conservative churches, especially the Roman Catholic church, remained stalwart in their opposition (Sanger, 1938).

After World War I, however, Sanger's goals and methods changed, as did the debate. At her trial in 1917, the court alerted her to a possible "medical loophole" in the Comstock Acts. Judges pointed out that if doctors needed contraceptive materials to prevent disease or save lives threatened by pregnancy, the doctors should not be prohibited from importing or distributing the materials they needed. Sanger organized the American Birth Control League (ABCL) and, in alliance with a growing number of sympathetic medical people, opened clinics in states where medical exemptions seemed likely. She no longer emphasized the basic rights of women to be free from too-frequent childbearing, but instead focused on the right of doctors to treat patients. Introduction of the medical loophole proposed a distinction between the moral and immoral use of contraceptives.

The birth-control debate became more complex. Not only did the health issue undermine the simple and absolute morality of Comstockery, but concerns about fertility rates among the poor stirred conservatives. Fears of "race suicide"—the decline in the proportion of native-born white Americans in the face of massive immigration from southern and eastern Europe—had been voiced for decades. While at first that seemed to be a reason to oppose contraception, the desire to have "inferior orders" of the population produce fewer children meant that some means of birth control would be necessary. By the 1920s, eugenics groups also realized that birth control very likely would be part of the solution to the cost to society of "excessive breeding" among the "unfit." For many ethnic groups, however, the campaign for birth control became suspect—a thinly disguised effort to retain white European supremecy. Feminists in the suffrage movement and its aftermath kept some distance from this debate. Although individuals in the movement had joined in Sanger's early campaign, the birth-control issue was not prominent on the women's rights agenda.

Meanwhile, into the 1930s, contraceptive information, use, and distribution grew, at the same time that technologies improved and demand increased. Sanger organized a national lobbying effort to repeal the federal Comstock Act. But most legislators, in the face of stalwart religious opposition, continued to evade the issue. The solution to this impasse was left to the courts. After a series of court decisions in the 1930s, prosecution for the import and sale of contraceptives under federal law ceased.[2] The Supreme Court simply defined contraceptives as "presumed not to be obscene." State courts eased the effects of the little Comstock Acts as well. Some states, motivated by racial and eugenics considerations, even offered birth control in state clinics (Gordon, 1976, p. 30).

Thus, contraceptives became available in the United States, not by conscious policy but through exceptions. Contraception was not an acceptable means of exercising reproductive choice or women's rights, but it was tolerated for treatment or prevention of disease and, occasionally, for eugenics purposes. Women's lot shifted from having to persuade husbands to use withdrawal, intercourse without ejaculation, or condoms, to having to persuade their doctors to give them diaphragms. It was part of the unwritten agreement between the courts and the medical profession that such devices would be used only for moral purposes, that is, within marriage. Not all doctors, not even all states, approved of birth control. The Comstock Acts remained on the books, if not enforced. The issue was not settled.

Family Planning

In the early 1940s, *birth control* died and *family planning* was born. The ABCL became the Planned Parenthood Federation of America (PPFA), as part of a conscious effort to change, once again, the terms of debate on contraception. Family planning had meaning on two levels: (1) as the personal choice of families in determining the number and spacing of children; and (2) as social planning to provide social services to limit population-growth rates.

Personal Choice

The new concept of family planning benefited from social changes in the 1940s and 1950s. The arguments about smaller families alleviating the effects of poverty and promoting health had been around since the time of Malthus. But this time, having only the children one can afford to rear did not mean sexual abstinence, restraint, and deprivation. New knowledge about human sexuality from psychologists and sociologists coincided with new attitudes about sexual needs. Sex manuals were being published to teach couples how to expand their sexual expression as part of general physical and mental health. The Kinsey reports in 1948 and 1953 showed a sexually active public. Clearly, responsible parenthood had to be congruent with increasing sexual liberalization. Family planners began to argue that, by eliminating worries about having too many children, contraception could enhance sexual expression in marriage and lead to happier families. In the 1950s, the PPFA acquired new allies and resources in Protestant and Jewish Reform congregations and the medical community. Alarm in social and intellectual organizations over the population explosion brought additional support. Although opposition forces, especially Catholics, retreated from the national stage, they remained entrenched in certain state legislatures.

Despite growing public attention to family planning, there was little government action. President Dwight D. Eisenhower considered the subject a private matter. Legally, contraception was still considered prophylactic or therapeutic, not a way of preventing unwanted pregnancies. In 1961, the PPFA took the fight to the state with the most reactionary law—Connecticut (Garrow, 1994). The law in Connecticut not only considered the manufacture, distribution, and advertisement of birth-control devices illegal but even forbade their use by married couples. By opening a clinic and advertising services especially for married persons, the PPFA was able to provoke Connecticut authorities to arrest the clinic director, giving her grounds for a constitutional challenge of the Connecticut statute. Thus, still unable to influence legislators, the PPFA continued to use litigation to wear away Anthony Comstock's legacy.

Griswold v. Connecticut (1965) is one of the most important of the Supreme Court decisions of the past forty years. It is controversial because of its wide sweep and because it set up a new policy definition of contraception. In a 6-to-2 decision, the Supreme Court declared Connecticut's law unconstitutional because it interfered with the *right of privacy* of married couples. The right of privacy is not explicitly set forth in the Bill of Rights, or anywhere else in the Constitution. For decades, however, the Supreme Court has asserted that families have a right to make certain decisions without interference by the government. In *Griswold*, Justice Douglas argued that various guarantees, such as due process and protection from illegal search and seizure, create "zones of privacy." He placed marital sexual behavior squarely in such a zone:

> We deal with a right of privacy older than the Bill of Rights—older than our political parties, older than our school system. Marriage is a coming together, for better or worse, hopefully enduring, and intimate to the degree of being sacred. It is an association that promotes a way of life, not causes; a harmony of living, not political faith; a bilateral loyalty not commercial or social projects. (p. 486)

But what of unmarried people? Do they too, have a right to sexual privacy? Can states allow access to contraceptives to married couples but deny it to the unmarried? A few years after *Griswold*, PPFA officials challenged a Massachusetts law that made such a distinction. In doing so, they were confronting the concept of immoral uses for contraceptives, enshrined by the Comstock Act. In 1972, the U.S. Supreme Court struck down the Massachusetts law but stopped short of placing extramarital sexual behavior in a "zone of privacy" outside government interference. *Eisenstadt v. Baird* (1972) relied on the Equal Protection Clause to invalidate the law. Because of *Griswold*, Massachusetts had to allow married people access to contraceptive services, even while continuing to deny them to the unmarried. Fresh from its decision in *Reed v. Reed* (see Chapter 2), the Supreme Court applied the rationality test: "whether there is some ground of difference that rationally explains the different treatment accorded married and unmarried persons under Massachusetts laws" (p. 447). Massachusetts officials offered some grounds for the legislation, but the Supreme Court did not accept any of them:

Massachusetts: The purpose of the law is to discourage premarital intercourse.

Supreme Court: It is not rational to punish unmarried people with unwanted children.

Massachusetts: The purpose of the law is to regulate the distribution of harmful articles.

Supreme Court: It is not rational that only unmarried people should be protected from harmful substances.

The Supreme Court ruled that the married and the unmarried are similarly situated with respect to contraception. Any personal ideas of morality do not apply. So, the Supreme Court said, unmarried people have an equal right to privacy as it relates to conception: "If the right of privacy means anything, it is the right of the *individual,* married or single, to be free from unwarranted governmental intrusion into matters so fundamentally affecting a person as the decision whether to bear or beget a child" (p. 453).[3]

Finally, with *Carey v. Population Services International* (1977), the Supreme Court cleared up the remnants of state Comstock Acts. *Carey* invalidated laws that prohibit distribution of contraceptives to minors, that limit distribution and sale of nonprescription contraceptives, and that prohibit advertisement.

Social Policy

Litigation proved successful in promoting individual rights by challenging state laws, but advocates wanted a more positive national policy encouraging the use of contraception and family planning, and that required legislative action. Congress finally repealed the Comstock Act in the 1970–1971 session, but this action was overshadowed by debate on a major federal program for family-planning services and research. Congress had begun discussing family planning in the early 1960s as part of foreign-aid programs. Then the issue became part of the program for families proposed by President Johnson's Great Society legislation. His Commission on Population and Family Planning advocated a federal policy of services and research. The Family Planning Services and Population Research Act of 1970 is the statutory basis for the federal government's aid to help public-health and planned-parenthood clinics dispense contraceptive information and services. It also authorizes funds for research on all aspects of family planning and population through the National Institutes of Health. Funding levels remain a matter of controversy and are affected by shifts in the debate over contraception, and by pressure from two groups: first, from antiabortion campaigners who associate contraception with promiscuity and abortion, and, second, from conservatives who seek to reduce social spending.

Where were the women's rights organizations during the debate over family planning? They were not prominent in the events leading to the decriminalization of the Comstock Acts. The PPFA took the lead, and it was solidly for ideas of family planning, not women's rights. By 1970, the feminist organizations, which had remained on the sidelines of the contraceptive debate for one hundred years, began to participate. This came about as part of the growth of the *women's health movement*. This movement provided, for the first time, an ideology of women's health rights that gave direction to a feminist definition of contraception use, as well as a platform for attacking a wide range of social and medical practices. The women's health movement would politicize legislators' traditional refuge from moral controversy, the doctor's office.

Women's Health Movement

The women's health movement of today takes up many issues that had their origins in the nineteenth century. The professionalization of medicine at that time meant that formally trained medical doctors, called *regulars*, drove out all other practitioners, many of whom were women. These doctors successfully pushed for laws requiring formal training and licenses and limited access to the training institutions. Only a few women were admitted to medical school after these laws were passed. Women who had turned to midwives and wisewomen to help them with many aspects of their reproductive lives—menstruation, contraception, childbirth, abortion, menopause—then had to consult male doctors. These normal conditions—along with complications related to them—became medicalized, that is, placed in medical categories of disease and dysfunction requiring not comfort but cures, through medication and surgery. Women protested these changes and formed self-help groups rather than submit to medical men with their speculums. But the regulars prevailed, and generations of women thereafter obeyed the directives of male gynecologists and obstetricians.

Looking back, contemporary feminists see the political overtones to these events. Quite simply, under the guise of professionalization and raising standards, men went beyond improving health care to establish hegemony over women's bodies. For African American women, it meant replacing the black female midwife with a white male doctor. The women's health movement that began in the 1970s has challenged this patriarchal dominance. Women in the health-care professions sought higher status and responsibilities. Feminists intend this rebellion to proceed by empowering women to take charge of their own bodies and their health care, especially as related to reproduction. To achieve empowerment and female autonomy they reason, access to contraception and abortion is essential. With knowledge of their own health, women can attack the medicalization of reproduction by rejecting forceps deliveries, induced labor, anesthetized delivery, and excessive hysterectomies and cesarean births. The methods of the movement range from informal self-help groups and clinics to lobbying and litigation.

In the area of contraception, women's health workers advocate the distribution of information, access to services, and choice. But they have become especially active over the issue of the safety of contraceptives and other drugs and devices used on women. They have charged that the real motive behind international family-planning organizations is the exploitation of Third World populations abroad and at home. Some feminists claimed that family planners in the 1960s, in their often-racist enthusiasm to get their new devices to Third World women of color, failed to conduct adequate tests on the side effects of the pill and the intrauterine device (IUD). Senate hearings in 1970 brought testimony about side effects from overdoses of potentially lethal hormones and from using an IUD. Not only did IUDs cause excessive bleeding, but some of them, such as the Dalkon shield, also were linked to cancer. Yet, in 1970, the Food and Drug Administration (FDA) had little power over the use of such devices (as opposed to drugs).[4] Therefore, women's health advocates provoked Congress and the FDA to include warnings of the health dangers of the pill with every prescription. And, in 1976, President Ford signed legislation that required the FDA to regulate devices such as IUDs to avoid tragedies like those associated with the Dalkon shield.

Health movement activists remain vigilant in assessing the potential use and misuse of new contraceptive methods. They set up warning flags, for example, when family-planning policy makers heralded hormonal implants, such as Norplant, as the solution to problems of education and reliability associated with self-administered modes. Norplant is embedded in the skin of the upper arm and slowly releases hormones: one implant provides five years of protection from pregnancy. It requires a medical practitioner to implant it and remove it. The temptation to use Norplant as an implement of social policy for dealing with welfare mothers is great. Feminist movement activists warn against efforts to force implants on poor and minority women.

BOX 4.1

Methods of Contraception Used in the United States, 1982 to 1990

Method	Percentage Distribution Among Women 15–44 in:		
	1982	1988	1990
Sterilization*	27.1	29.6	32.1
Pill	15.6	18.5	16.9
IUD	4	1.2	.8
Diaphragm	4.5	3.5	1.7
Condom	6.7	8.8	10.5
Abstinence**	2.1	1.4	1.6
	N=54.0 million	N=57.9 million	N=58.3 million

*either woman or partner

**includes natural family planning and other types of periodic abstinence

Source: Linda S. Peterson. "Contraceptive Use in the United States: 1982–90." Advance Data, No. 260. Washington, D.C.: National Center for Health Statistics, Centers for Disease Control and Prevention, February 14, 1995.

In the 1990s, the women's health movement can count on a small number of women in top government positions, including the Senate and the administration, to support their expanded campaign for gender equity in all aspects of health, especially in funded medical and social research. Important agenda items include questions about menopause, breast cancer, heart disease, estrogen replacement therapy, nutrition, and exercise (Howes and Allina, 1994). Aware of the continuing controversy over women's access to both contraceptives and abortion services, health-movement activists stress the essential connection between women's reproductive rights and their overall health.

Sterilization

Researchers report that the most popular contraceptive method in the United States is not the pill, the IUD, or even the condom; it is sterilization (see Box 4.1). Since sterilization is a form of surgery, it remains under the control of physicians. Nonetheless, public debate has arisen over two aspects of the procedure: the right to be sterilized and the right not to be sterilized.

Although no state prohibits voluntary sterilization, some have enacted regulations that include age requirements, a waiting period, consent of spouse, or obtaining a second opinion. In addition, doctors and hospitals may set up their own restrictions (Blank and Merrick, 1995). A woman cannot have her "tubes tied" or a tubal ligation, without a physician willing to perform the surgery. In making the decision, doctors are influenced by two factors in addition to ordinary health considerations: (1) their own values about reproduction and (2) fear of lawsuits. Doctors may refuse to perform sterilization if they think the patient is too young to make a definitive decision (in most cases they draw the line at 21, but some could make it 35) or the patient has not had enough children in the doctors' estimation, or the patient is single. Fear of lawsuits may require patients to obtain spousal consent for the procedure, although such consent is not usually required for other forms of surgery.

The right not to be sterilized is far more controversial. The problem arose in reaction to laws enacted years ago giving governments the power to order the sterilization of persons deemed unfit to reproduce. At first, these laws were enforced with the mentally ill. But the idea that some groups should not reproduce at will has lingered. In the early 1970s, sterilization rates were higher among minority women than among nonminority women (Shapiro, 1985, p. 100). Practices of welfare officials in coercing poor women to be sterilized as a condition for receipt of welfare payments came to light. Not all coercion was as crude as the Georgia case where an illiterate woman signed consent forms with an X for her teenage daughters in order to continue receiving welfare checks. Civil rights activists and feminists defined government policies and practices in this regard as class-based and racist. For many African American and Hispanic American women, the issue of forced sterilization is a more important women's rights issue than abortion is (Petchesky, 1984).

In 1978, the federal government issued regulations with respect to the administration of any surgical sterilization. These regulations prohibit the use of federal funds for the procedure on persons under age twenty-one and set up safeguards to ensure informed consent. There are sanctions against practices such as failing to inform patients that the procedure is irreversible, threatening to withhold welfare in order to obtain consent, and failing to provide information about alternatives such as contraception and abortion.[5]

Abortion

The origins of policy affecting abortion are in common law, which was more explicit about the termination of pregnancy than about its prevention. Policy related to abortion has undergone two periods of major debate and reform: from 1840 to 1880 and from 1960 to the present. Today, the abortion issue is, for many feminists, central to women's rights. In this view, they differ from their predecessors. The linchpin of the debate has been the Supreme Court's ruling in *Roe v. Wade* (1973). In 1992, the Supreme Court sought to settle the constitutional debate over abortion. The debate has shifted to a contest over access to services. In this section, we examine the history of the abortion debates in America as they led to *Roe*, as well as the aftermath of that ruling and recent efforts to achieve a compromise in this emotive-symbolic issue.

Criminalization of Abortion

Common law rules that prevailed in the American colonies divided pregnancy into two parts: before quickening (animation) and after.[6] Abortion was a criminal act only after quickening. From colonial times on, American women went about securing abortions from practitioners. The common law in regard to abortions was rarely enforced. For one thing, it was almost impossible to determine by independent authority whether the aborted fetus was "quick." For another, there was popular acceptance of the inevitability of abortion in the absence of effective ways of preventing pregnancy.

In the early 1800s, regular physicians condemned abortion as symptomatic of "demoralization." When abortion rates increased in mid-century and the practice spread from poorer to more prosperous classes, the physicians took more direct action to prevent it. In 1859, the American Medical Association (AMA) passed a formal resolution declaring the fetus a "living being" and pledged to work for laws "against unwarrantable destruction of human life" (Mohr, 1978, p. 157). As early as 1821, states had already begun to enact statutes against abortion, but after the Civil War, the criminalization of abortion spread. By 1880, abortion was illegal nearly everywhere in the United States. Yet most laws permitted legal abortion for therapeutic reasons, usually to save the life of the mother. Thus, the first conceptual shift in abortion policy had occurred: from delineation of phases of pregnancy—quickened/unquickened—to classification according to the purpose of abortion—therapeutic/criminal. Whereas the pregnant woman had been the one to determine whether her unborn child was quick, the policy shift in the 1880s left it up to regular doctors, duly licensed by state examining boards, to determine whether abortion was medically necessary.

This major shift in policy had several causes. It was certainly a product of the campaign of regulars to gain control and drive nonregulars from the practice of medicine. There were also concerns about increases in death from abortion, unsafe procedures, incompetent practitioners, and other threats to women's health. For these reasons, laws prosecuted the person performing the abortion, not the woman who sought the abortion. Given the popular acceptance of abortion, lawmakers had few illusions that these new laws would be any more enforceable than the common law had been. To cut down on the trade, most statutes, therefore, included special penalties for advertising. Laws prohibiting abortion were effective only at removing the subject from public notice: no more advertisements for certain "relief to ladies in trouble with or without medicine" (quoted in Gordon, 1976, p. 58). The practice of abortion went underground for eighty years.

In the nineteenth century, feminists generally opposed abortion. They envisioned women as victims of men twice over: first, by the man who made them pregnant and, then, by the abortionist who butchered them for profit. Desperate women were pushed to abortion because men took little responsibility for preventing too-frequent pregnancies. Many feminists recommended sexual abstinence as the way of making choices about motherhood.

Reform/Repeal of Abortion Laws

Doctors and lawyers brought abortion back to the public agenda in the 1950s. Doctors wanted to reduce state regulations and to secure the right to order abortion when they considered it medically necessary. These same motives were behind the loosening of control on contraceptives. Lawyers launched a reform of many nineteenth-century laws that had been outmoded by social change. They worried that when laws are inconsistent with widely held attitudes, they will be disregarded, leading to general disrespect for legal institutions. Together, doctors and lawyers promoted reforms to expand the number of conditions of pregnancy whereby a doctor could order an abortion.

In the late 1950s, the American Law Institute (ALI) drafted a model statute allowing abortion under several conditions, not only to save the life of the mother:

> A licensed physician is justified in terminating a pregnancy if he believes that there is substantial risk that continuance of the pregnancy would gravely impair the physical and mental health of the mother or that the child would be born with grave physical or mental defects or that pregnancy resulted from rape, incest, or other felonious intercourse. (quoted in Davis, 1985, Appendix B)

Public attention to abortion came first over the question of fetal deformity. When thalidomide, a tranquilizer, caused grave deformity of fetuses in the 1960s, demands for abortion arose. In 1962, Sherri Finkbine brought the issue to the U.S. press when, after having taken the drug in Europe, she was unable to obtain an abortion in the United States. Soon after the publications of the thalidomide-induced deformities, an epidemic of rubella (German measles) further dramatized the tragic implications of the ban on legal abortions. Women continued to have abortions, and it became increasingly clear that the main effect of American laws was to restrict the choices of law-abiding physicians rather than to stop abortions. Beginning with Colorado, California, and North Carolina, twelve states, under pressure from doctors and lawyers, adopted the ALI reform in 1967.

About this time, women's rights organizations were attracting support from the revival of feminism. These groups expanded the debate on abortion to include a different perspective. In 1967, when the first laws based on the ALI model were passed, the National Organization for Women (NOW) included women's "right to control their reproduction" in its first bill of rights. Radical feminist groups insisted that women must take control over their bodies and sexuality from men—from their lovers, doctors, and legislators. They wanted abortion on demand, which the ALI reforms did not provide. Instead of freedom and control, these laws required a woman to submit her request for abortion either to a medical doctor (or often to teams of doctors) who would determine her mental state or to police who would affirm or deny her claim of rape or incest. Beyond that, the conditions written into these laws addressed only a small percentage of the reasons women seek abortions. Even with the reform, most women would still have to seek back-street practitioners.

What feminists demanded was the repeal of abortion laws. They also wanted to bring abortion practice back under the control of women.

(With modern techniques of vacuum aspiration, abortion in the first twelve weeks had become an outpatient clinical procedure.) Thus, not only did feminist organizations lobby state legislatures for repeal, but they took direct action by establishing abortion clinics in defiance of laws. Four states, beginning with New York in 1970, responded by repealing abortion laws together.[7]

Efforts at repeal through state legislatures were complemented by litigation. Advocates of reform asked state and federal courts to invalidate outdated and overly restrictive state laws and to force legislators to consider reforms. (Then, as now, most legislators prefer not to have to consider such a difficult, divisive, and emotional issue.) Such cases were effective, and the policy debate on abortion spread. The momentum was with the forces for change: feminists, doctors, and lawyers were joined by family planners and leaders concerned with "the population bomb."[8] Leaders of the Catholic church and conservatives still opposed to abortion testified at legislative hearings and presented briefs in lawsuits. The conflict expanded into widespread public discussion; positions strengthened, and legislatures faced difficult battles in finding a way of framing the issue that would permit compromise. At that point, the Supreme Court stepped in to help establish a viable framework for state policy making.

Roe v. Wade

Roe v. Wade (1973) began as a challenge to a nineteenth-century Texas abortion law that prohibited abortions except to preserve the life of the mother. Jane Roe was the anonymous name used by Norma McCorvey, who had sought an abortion because she could not afford to raise a child.[9] (At the time, she claimed she was gang-raped, but she later denied the rape.) Seeking to overturn the law, two feminist attorneys brought suit. This case presented the Supreme Court with all the arguments of the contemporary abortion debate. Sifting through the briefs, the Court outlined the problem as the need to reconcile four competing demands: (1) the right of the woman to privacy to decide if and when to bear a child, a privacy right outlined in the Griswold and Eisenstadt contraceptive cases; (2) the right of physicians to make judgments in treating pregnant patients without unnecessary government interference; (3) the interest of the state governments in protecting the health of pregnant women; and

(4) the state's responsibility to protect the life of the unborn, what the Supreme Court termed as "potential life."[10]

Justice Harry Blackmun wrote the opinion for the 7-to-2 majority. (There were three concurring opinions.) The majority opinion achieved what fifty state legislatures had found impossible: a compromise amid the clash of absolute values and rights. The means of compromise was a conceptual framework that divided pregnancy into trimesters, three roughly equal time periods. This is a variation on the age-old common-law framework that set up two phases of pregnancy: before quickening and after quickening. To justify the tripartite division, Justice Blackmun cited changes in the fetus and the complexity of abortion techniques: simple out-patient procedures in the first trimester, serious but safe hospital procedures in the second, and potentially life-threatening procedures in the third. The fetus is so well-developed during the third trimester that, at some time, it becomes viable—able to live outside the uterus. During the third trimester, the state's responsibility to protect potential life would then become compelling, and the Constitution would permit government to prohibit abortion. Note that this is stated as a permissive power. Under *Roe*, a state may prevent or permit abortion; it is not required to prohibit it.

In the second trimester, abortion procedures may constitute increased health risks to the pregnant woman and may require hospitalization. Thus, the state's interest in safeguarding women's health would allow some regulation of abortion procedures. These regulations would be in the context of the privacy of an abortion choice, and states could not prohibit abortions before the third trimester.

Here, then, is a summary of states' constitutional powers to make policy with respect to abortion according to *Roe:*

1. In the first trimester, the state may not regulate or otherwise interfere with the decisions of the doctor and the patient to terminate her pregnancy.

2. In the second trimester, the state may regulate the medical conditions under which abortions are performed but may not restrict the practice.

3. In the third trimester, the state may prohibit abortion except to save the life of the mother.

After the decision in *Roe*, most states had to revise their statutes.[11] In some states, galvanized opposition forces sought to restrict access to abortion wherever possible. An early victory was in the area of public assistance.

Clarifying *Roe v. Wade*: Restricting Public Assistance

"*Roe v. Wade* sets forth our conclusion that a pregnant woman does not have an absolute constitutional right to an abortion on demand" (*Doe v. Bolton* [1973], p. 189). Despite this language in the companion case to *Roe*, feminists interpreted the court action as giving women some government-protected rights. Thus, when opponents of legal abortion, who called their cause "pro-life" and "right to life," worked to exclude abortion from all forms of public support, feminists argued that poor women were being unconstitutionally stripped of their rights.

Pro-life organizations grew in strength and commitment during the 1970s. They lobbied Congress to remove every shred of federal support for abortion: limiting funds for fetal research, allowing federally funded hospitals to refuse to perform abortions, and eliminating abortion services from military hospitals. They attached restrictions on any proposal remotely related to pregnancy or children, such as the Pregnancy Discrimination Act of 1978 (see Chapter 8). Most controversial was the successful campaign to deny the states Medicaid funds for abortion.[12]

Also at the national level, a provision was introduced in Congress by Representative Hyde (R.-Ill.) in 1976, as an amendment to an annual appropriations bill; it has been attached every year since. Essentially, the so-called Hyde Amendment blocks the use of federal money for all nontherapeutic abortions—that is, those in which the primary intent is not that of saving the life of the mother. In its more liberal forms, the amendment has also allowed payment in some budgets for abortions resulting from rape or incest or for pregnancies posing a grave threat to health. Pro-life forces also took their cause to state legislatures and succeeded in cutting state funds for abortion assistance there as well.

Abortion-rights groups immediately challenged these actions in court, and a series of cases relating to public support for abortion services reached the U.S. Supreme Court between 1977 and 1980.[13] Together, these cases clearly fixed the constitutional status of abortion rights for women. Feminists' questions about abortion laws were answered as follows:

1. Do states have a constitutional responsibility to provide health service, including abortion, to poor people? Doesn't refusal to

fund abortions for poor women, while rich women can get them, constitute a denial of equal protection?

Court: Indigent women are not a protected class under the Equal Protection Clause of the Fourteenth Amendment. "The Constitution imposes no obligation on the states to pay the pregnancy-related medical expenses of indigent women or indeed to pay any of the medical expenses of the indigent" (*Maher v. Roe* [1977], p. 469). The choice is up to the legislature.

2. Does denial of funds for abortions to poor women interfere with their constitutional right to abortion?

Court: There is no constitutional right to abortion. Rather, the Constitution does protect "women from an unduly burdensome interference with her freedom to decide whether to terminate her pregnancy. It implies no limitation on the authority of a state to make a value judgment favoring childbirth over abortion, or to implement that judgment by allocation of public funds" (*Maher* [1977], pp. 473–474).

3. Medicaid is a federal program, part of the Social Security Act. It funds the costs of childbirth, but not abortion. Doesn't the federal government have a responsibility to provide assistance to poor women to make their choice meaningful?

Court: The federal government, like the states, has the authority to use its funds to encourage women to choose childbirth over abortion. "Whether freedom of choice that is constitutionally protected warrants federal subsidization is a question for Congress to answer, not a matter of constitutional entitlement" (*Harris v. McRae* [1980], p. 318).[14]

These cases constitute a conservative shift from the decision in *Roe.* The status of a woman's right to abortion did not change; it was still described as a right to be free of governmentally imposed barriers and restrictions. What *did* change was the court's definition of abortion as a medical procedure. In *Roe,* it was the physician's right to prescribe abortion to patients. If abortion is defined as an ordinary medical procedure, it would follow that government health programs can not exclude coverage any more than they could exclude coverage for a tonsillectomy or biopsy or a dilation and curettage. But these cases seem to reintroduce the old dichotomy between therapeutic (medically necessary) and nontherapeutic (medically unnecessary) abortion. Most abortions are "unnecessary" (not necessary to save the life of the woman) and therefore are something other than health care. This definition allows the moral conflict between fetal rights and woman's rights to unfold.

From *Roe* to *Casey:* The Battle over Abortion Rights

The Pro-Choice/Pro-Life Debate

At the center of the contemporary policy debate is a bitter battle between feminists and conservatives over the control of reproduction. On questions of contraception and abortion, feminist goals have remained fairly consistent. Feminists believe that women must have effective choice in deciding when and if to bear a child. To them, choice means not only the removal of legal barriers to contraception and abortion but also full access to information and services from public and private agencies regardless of their economic circumstances. They believe women must be full participants in making decisions about their health care. To play this role, women require complete and accurate information. Feminists also believe there should be continuing research for safe contraceptive and abortion methods; only with such a policy can women exercise their civil rights, have legal equality, and take advantage of opportunities for achievement in all aspects of life. Feminists see reproductive choice as the substance of independence and freedom for women in family and sexual relations. It is crucial to empowerment in all social relations.

Since the early 1980s, however, feminists have not had the resources or energy to promote their vision of feminist reproductive policy. Instead, they have had to concentrate on repelling attacks by opponents of legal abortion and family planning against the gains they themselves made in the 1970s.

Pro-life activists have joined in a small but energetic coalition of religious fundamentalists and Far Right conservatives to promote a policy that restricts choice and reinstates their view of traditional family life.[15] Pro-life groups have three major goals in the area of reproduction: restricting access by teenagers to contraceptive information and services, preventing abortions from being performed, and making abortion illegal.

The conservatives see contraceptive services for teenagers as the cause of high levels of teenage pregnancy and abortion, in turn produced by a general undermining of parental authority over conduct. They believe that ready access by teens to contraceptive services and talk about the need to be "protected" pushes teens into premature sexual activity that results in pregnancy. Availability of abortion as a "backup" eliminates all restraint. Conservatives have fought the establishment of contraceptive services in health clinics in high schools, and they have campaigned to require parental consent for contraception and abortion. In 1981, they were successful in enacting the federal Adolescent Family Life Act, which authorized federal funds for programs, dubbed "chastity clinics," that discourage sexual behavior in teens.

Pro-life tactics to prevent abortions have ranged from the bureaucratic and legislative to the militant. Pro-life bureaucrats have sought to place several restrictions on the use of family-planning funds for abortion counseling, often requiring separate accounting procedures to ensure that family-planning programs receiving federal financial assistance are untainted by the mention of the "A-word." Foreign-aid administrators have promoted natural family planning methods in less-developed countries and have denied assistance to some governments, such as China's, that encourage abortions. Pro-life lobbyists tack abortion amendments onto every possible bill going through Congress to restrict the bill's application to abortion. They held up the Civil Rights Restoration Act for four years over the abortion issue (see Chapter 5). They also seek to ban specific abortion procedures.

Opponents of abortion have picketed doctors' offices. Some have broken into clinics and destroyed equipment there. Doctors who performed abortions have been murdered and several clinics have been bombed. Pro-life activists threaten boycotts and litigation for any pharmaceutical firm that considers the development of abortion-inducing pills. Squadrons of committed pro-lifers have lain down on the sidewalks in front of clinics, requiring brigades of police to remove them by force.

The emotional fervor that energizes these people to such unconventional behavior has at its base the pro-life definition of the issue of abortion: saving fetal life. In a way, the issue is similar to the AMA concerns in the 1850s, but medical research on reproduction has now provided extensive information about fetal development and made the fetus more accessible and more knowable.[16] Pro-lifers view this information as incontrovertible evidence that a fetus is a human being, like all human beings who have been born. But it is a special human: a baby, innocent, just starting out. They attribute all these qualities to the fetus and equate abortion to murder of babies. They liken the number of abortions performed since 1973 to the Nazi policy of extermination of millions during the Holo-

BOX 4.2

Abortions Performed in the United States, 1973 to 1992

After an initial increase in abortions reported after *Roe v. Wade*, the numbers and rates have remained steady.

Date	Number*	Rate**	Ratio***
1973	744.6	16.3	19.3
1978	1,409.6	27.7	29.2
1982	1,573.9	28.8	30.0
1988	1,590.8	27.3	28.6
1992	1,528.9	25.9	27.5

*in thousands

** per 1,000 women, ages 15 to 44

***per 100 pregnancies

Source: Stanley Henshaw and Jennifer Van Vort. "Abortion Services in the United States, 1991 and 1992." *Family Planning Perspectives* 26 (May/June 1994): 100–106, 112.

caust in Europe.[17] Many pro-life activists also connect abortion with a deterioration of family values and social stability. They see reproductive choice as a threat to religious values supporting the traditional patriarchal family.

Armed with their definition of fetal rights, pro-life groups attacked their main target: *Roe v. Wade.* There are two ways to overcome judicial review by the Supreme Court: (1) amend the Constitution or (2) get the Supreme Court to change its mind. In the early 1980s, with a sympathetic administration in the White House and a Republican majority in the Senate, pro-life activists had their best shot at an amendment to the Constitution. A Senate subcommittee held hearings on the Human Life Amendment and reported it favorably, but it died in the full committee.[18] At the same time, state legislators were considering memorials calling for a constitutional convention, an as-yet-unused method of amending the Constitution. There was little enthusiasm in Congress for either the amendment or the convention, especially given the intensity of potential conflict on such moral and religious issues.

Between 1980 and 1992, Presidents Reagan and Bush made five appointments and replaced four retiring justices on the Supreme Court. (The fifth appointment was Rehnquist, an associate justice, as Chief Justice.) By the end of the 1980s, only two members of the *Roe* majority remained. Pro-life activists fought hard on each of these nominations to ensure that new justices would oppose abortion and would oppose and vote to overturn the *Roe* decision. They learned, as have many activists before them, that how justices vote when enjoying a life-tenure appointment on the Court is not always predictable during the confirmation process in the Senate. Still, the changes in the Court during the 1980s justified the pro-life litigation strategy: lobbying state legislatures to enact laws restricting abortion services, defending these laws against pro-choice challenges in court; and providing ample opportunities for newly appointed justices to push the Court to change its ruling and overturn *Roe v. Wade*. The rest of this section describes the outcome of the pro-life litigation strategy as it confronted both the pro-choice opposition and the U.S. legal system.

Restrictive Laws: Creating Administrative Hurdles

One goal of the pro-life strategy was to test the application of the trimester framework in *Roe v. Wade* by placing a variety of restrictions on a woman's effort to obtain a legal abortion in the first and second trimesters. A state might establish elaborate formal procedures requiring certified consent forms to be signed by the woman and by medical personnel. Policies could impose requirements that a woman obtain consent from or notify others: her spouse, her parents, the biological father. The government could order physicians to provide information on fetal development to convince the woman not to have an abortion. The government could impose a waiting period between the request and the procedure. These restrictions, if enacted in various states, could pose administrative hurdles that must be surmounted before women can legally obtain abortion services. As a result, abortion would remain legal but difficult to get.

Immediately after the decision in *Roe v. Wade*, opposition forces lobbied to obtain state laws limiting access, and challenges to such laws were reviewed by the Supreme Court. In the first case, *Planned Parenthood v. Danforth* (1976), the Court set forth several important details on the type of abortion laws states could enact. The decision defined viability of the fetus as "that stage in fetal development when the life of the unborn child may be continued indefinitely by natural or artificial support systems."

This was a guide to states in determining the point at which abortions could be prohibited. The decision also denied states the right to require the husband's or parents' consent to terminate a pregnancy. The state could not "delegate to a spouse a veto power which the state itself is absolutely and totally prohibited from exercising during the first trimester of pregnancy" (p. 69).

The question of parental consent reappeared before the Court in 1979. In *Belotti v. Baird*, the Court indicated that requiring parental consent before a doctor performed an abortion on a minor was not an unconstitutional violation of privacy. At the same time, the special nature of pregnancy and abortion meant that the government could not impose an absolute requirement on a minor woman, thus giving parents an unlimited veto power over her no matter what her family circumstances. Government had to provide a procedure whereby some official, probably a judge, could also give consent (called a judicial bypass). "We therefore conclude that if a State decides to require a pregnant minor to obtain one or both parents' consent to an abortion, it also must provide an alternative procedure whereby authorization for the abortion can be obtained" (p. 643).

Into the 1980s, the restrictive laws kept coming. For the first half of the decade, the court followed the precedent in *Planned Parenthood v. Danforth* and ruled that most hurdles were an unconstitutional interference with the right to privacy protected in *Roe*. But as the Reagan appointments took hold, the majorities became smaller and the dissenting justices increasingly cast doubt on the reasoning in *Roe*. In 1983, by a 6-to-3 vote, the Court invalidated an Akron, Ohio, ordinance that required informed consent, a twenty-four-hour waiting period, notification and consent of the father, and the provision to the woman of information about fetal development (*Akron v. Akron Center for Reproductive Health* 462 U.S. 416). In 1986, the majority had slipped again, in a 5-to-4 ruling that several Pennsylvania statutes with similar administrative hurdles were unconstitutional (*Thornburgh v. American College of Obstetricians and Gynecologists* 476 U.S. 747).

Before *Thornburgh*, Reagan had made only one addition to the Court, Sandra Day O'Connor, in 1982. After *Thornburgh*, two new Reagan justices were in place: Antonin Scalia (1986) and Anthony M. Kennedy (1988). The first case to feel the impact of the changed Court was *Webster v. Reproductive Health Services* in 1989. The justices considered the constitutionality of four aspects of a Missouri law: (a) the preamble, which stated that "the life of each human being begins at conception"; (b) the prohibition on the use of public facilities or employees to perform abortions; (c) the prohibition of public funding of abortion counseling; and (d) a requirement that physicians conduct viability tests on fetuses of twenty weeks or more prior to performing abortions.

The Court upheld the constitutionality of each section. The justices noted that the preamble did not appear to have any legal effect on access to abortion services. Bans on the use of public facilities and funds for counseling were consistent with the Court's previous decisions on the use of Medicaid funds. The requirement of viability tests did not conflict with the intent of *Roe v. Wade*. The justices voted on two levels. On the level of the legal validity of the Missouri law, there was a 5-to-4 majority. On the second vote—whether to overturn *Roe v. Wade*—pro-life won only four justices. But these four—Rehnquist, Scalia, Kennedy, and White—invited state legislatures to enact laws to restrict abortion that would directly challenge *Roe*.

The *Webster* case appeared to be a legal victory for the pro-life strategy, yet the effect was to galvanize pro-choice sentiment. Membership in the National Abortion Rights Action League (NARAL) and NOW soared. Massive public demonstrations supported choice. Opinion polls showed not only that voters preferred legal abortion, but that more were inclined to vote against pro-life candidates than in favor (Media General–Associated Press Survey, July 1989). As the Court's conservative justices wished, the abortion debate began to shift away from the Court to the various state legislatures.

Roe or Not? *Planned Parenthood v. Casey*

The stage for the showdown over the validity of *Roe* was not a state law prohibiting abortion in the first trimester of pregnancy—such a law would have been a direct attack, but no state enacted one. Rather, it was a law from Pennsylvania that tried again (after failure in *Thornburgh*) to enact constitutional administrative hurdles to the abortion procedure. These included informed consent, a twenty-four-hour waiting period, parental consent with judicial bypass, spousal notification, and elaborate reporting requirements. How, then, did this case become the arena for a reconsideration of *Roe v. Wade*?

The reaction to *Webster* had increased political resources of the pro-choice lobby substantially, despite the fact that Reagan's successor, pro-life supporter George Bush, had appointed yet another conservative to the Court. (Bush replaced Justice Brennan, one of *Roe*'s strongest supporters, with David Souter in 1991.) Membership in pro-choice organizations had increased, and evidence from 1990 elections indicated that taking the pro-life anti-*Roe* position made politicians vulnerable. Pro-choice activists introduced a Freedom of Choice Act in Congress, which, if enacted as law, would require states to ensure a woman's right to choose abortion before viability with no obstacles. They expected President Bush to veto this act.

They thus announced their intention to ask the Court to rule on the question of women's fundamental right to abortion. By so doing, they laid down a dramatic challenge to President Bush just prior to the 1992 presidential elections. Their logic was that if the conservative Court declared that *Roe* is no longer in effect, they had the votes to pass the Freedom of Choice Act. Bush would veto it, as demanded by the strong pro-life lobby in the Republican party (whose voice is especially effective during presidential elections). This would galvanize pro-choice activists behind Bush's opponent in 1992. Taking this challenge seriously, the pro-life strategists in the Bush administration tried to lower the stakes in the next abortion case before the Court.

Thus, *Planned Parenthood v. Casey* presented an unusual conflict: although the law did not directly challenge legalized abortion, the pro-choice briefs urged the Court to rule on the question of legalized abortion as a fundamental right. The defenders of the Pennsylvania law argued that *Roe* was not at issue, but only the question of administrative hurdles.

The Court's ruling and opinions in *Casey* are complicated. There is no majority opinion, for example. But the bottom line is as follows:

1. A majority of justices agreed that the fundamental guarantee in *Roe v. Wade* is still in force: "A recognition of the right of the woman to choose to have an abortion before viability and to obtain it without undue interference from the State" (p. 2804).

2. A plurality of the justices agreed that the trimester framework is no longer in force. In the future, a state might draw a line between legal and restricted abortion at viability, when the state's interest in protecting potential human life becomes compelling.

3. A plurality of justices agreed that prior to viability, a state may enact administrative hurdles that a woman must overcome as long as the hurdles do not constitute an "undue burden" on the woman's liberty: "A finding of an undue burden is a shorthand for the conclusion that a state regulation has the purpose or effect of placing a substantial obstacle in the path of a woman seeking an abortion of a nonviable fetus" (p. 2820).

With respect to the specific features of the Pennsylvania law under review, all provisions were found to be valid except the spousal notification requirement: "A husband has no enforceable right to advise him before she exercises her personal choice" (p. 2831).

Who won the showdown over *Roe?* Well, it is telling that both pro-life and pro-choice activists immediately condemned the decision. Pro-choice activists, stymied in their strategy to put President Bush's feet to the fire, attacked the undue-burden test as effectively denying women, especially low-income women, their rights. Pro-life activists found that the *Casey* decision, along with the election of pro-choice Bill Clinton as president in 1992, very likely doomed their strategy to get rid of *Roe* altogether through a reversal by the Court. The reactions and the shifts in the abortion debate that have occurred since 1992 indicate that *Casey* may constitute the long-awaited legal compromise over the constitutional foundation of abortion legislation.

The Debate over Abortion Services and Clinic Access

Throughout the national confrontation between pro-choice and pro-life advocates at the Supreme Court, a daily confrontation was acted out at many abortion clinics. Zealots, determined to use any means to protect what they regarded as sacred unborn life, followed their leaders to block entrance of patients to abortion clinics by any means possible: picketing, heckling, lying prostrate in the street. Pro-choice activists and clinic administrators sought laws to keep these campaigns, which are often costly to both clinics and to municipalities that must contend with the violations and violence, away from their businesses.

By bringing pro-life organizations like Operation Rescue to court, pro-choice activists and administrators were able to obtain injunctions in some states restricting the demonstrators from the walkways around the clinics. To strengthen the legal resources available, pro-choice activists, with the support of the Clinton administration, successfully lobbied for passage of the Freedom of Access to Clinic Entrances (FACE) Act through Congress in 1994. FACE makes it a federal crime to use force or threats of force against any organization that provides reproductive services or counseling, and the act provides for penalties, including fines and terms in federal prisons. Many pro-life organizations have decried this law, as well as similar restrictions enacted in several states and cities, as unconstitutional violations of the right of free speech. Thus far, however, these defendants have been unsuccessful in challenging such laws in Court.

BOX 4.3

Images of Women: Roe *and* Casey *Compared*

Roe v. Wade extended the right to privacy to include access to abortion. But whose privacy did the Court guarantee—the women's right to choose abortion or the physician's right to prescribe abortion?

The Physician's Right to Prescribe?

A careful reading of Justice Blackmun's decision indicates it is the doctor's right that was upheld, not the woman's right. At first, it looked like it might be a feminist-inspired outcome:

> The right of privacy, whether it is founded on the Fourteenth Amendment's concept of personal liberty and restrictions upon the state action, as we feel it is, or as the district court determined, in the Ninth Amendment's reservation of rights to the people, is broad enough to encompass a woman's decision whether or not to terminate her pregnancy. (p. 153)

But as the opinion unfolded, reference to the woman's rights receded in favor of the physician's rights:

> This means that, on the other hand, for the period of pregnancy prior to this "compelling" point, the attending physician in consultation with his patient, is free to determine, without regulation by the state, that in his medical judgment, the patient's pregnancy should be terminated. (p. 163)

> For the stage prior to approximately the end of the first trimester, the abortion decision and its effectuation must be left to the medical judgment of the pregnant woman's attending physician. (p. 164)

Finally, mention of the woman disappears altogether:

> The decision vindicates the right of the physician to administer medical treatment according to his professional judgment up to a point where important state interests provide compelling justifications for intervention. (p. 166)

The Woman's Right to Choose?

In comparison, Justices Souter, O'Connor, and Kennedy placed the image of individual rights at the center of the ruling in *Planned Parenthood v. Casey*:

> At the heart of liberty is the right to define one's own concept of existence, of meaning, of the universe, and of the

BOX 4.3 *(continued)*

mystery of human life. Beliefs about these matters could not define the attributes of personhood were they formed under compulsion of the State. (p. 2807)

The justices go on to make it clear that these rights are the woman's alone:

> Though abortion is conduct, it does not follow that the State is entitled to proscribe it in all instances. That is because the liberty of the woman is at stake in a sense unique to the human condition and so unique to the law. The mother who carries a child to full term is subject to anxieties, to physical constraints, to pain that only she must bear. That these sacrifices have from the beginning of the human race been endured by woman with a pride that ennobles her in the eyes of others and gives to the infant a bond of love cannot alone be grounds for the State to insist she make the sacrifice. Her suffering is too intimate and personal for the State to insist, without more, upon its own vision of the woman's role, however dominant that vision has been in the course of our history and our culture. The destiny of the woman must be shaped to a large extent on her own conception of her spiritual imperatives and her place in society. (p. 2807)

Finally, in rejecting the state's requirement that she notify her husband of her intention to end her pregnancy, the justices add their view of the effect of marriage on woman's status:

> Women do not lose their constitutionally protected liberty when they marry. The Constitution protects all individuals, male or female, married or unmarried, from the abuse of government power, even where that power is employed for the supposed benefit of a member of the individual's family. (p. 2831)

Contemporary Debate over Abortion Rights

Over the past forty years, courts and legislatures have developed a hands-off doctrine on reproductive rights; the basic premise is that the government should leave the individual woman or couple alone in making the fundamental decision about whether to conceive and bear a child. Women who have the means may seek reproductive services without government interference. But this hands-off approach offers little help to

BOX 4.4

Public Opinion on Abortion

Americans tend to separate the moral issue of abortion from the legal issue of choice. When the *Webster* case was being argued in 1989, a *Miami Herald* national poll reported the following results:

Do you agree or disagree with this statement: Abortion is murder?

Abortion is murder	38%
Abortion is not murder	62

Do you agree or disagree with this statement? "I personally feel that abortion is morally wrong. But I also feel that whether or not to have an abortion is a decision that has to be made by every woman herself."

Agree	78%
Disagree	22

In 1994, the National Opinion Research Center again reported a wide range of opinion, when survey respondents were asked to consider the legality of abortion in various circumstances:

Legal abortion is acceptable if:

The woman's health is endangered	91%
There is a fetal defect	82
Pregnancy is result of rape	84
The woman is low income and cannot afford more children	50
The woman is married and does not want more children	48
The woman is not married and does not want to marry father	40
For any reason	46

Source: Miami Herald, June 29, 1989, p. 15A; "How the Public Views Abortion." *Family Planning Perspectives* 26 (November–December 1994): 245.

women without means. Freedom of choice is of little comfort to those whose poverty and ill health make it impossible to care for a new baby. Public funds for services are limited and subject to annual budget fights. Native American women on reservations are totally dependent on federal support, which is often uncertain due to pro-life pressures on Congress.

Women with low income and little education are also more vulnerable to abuse of reproductive services—misuse of pills and IUD, forced sterilizations and hysterectomies. Twenty-four-hour waiting periods prior to abortion, not considered an undue burden on liberty by the justices of the Supreme Court, could be an enormous hurdle for poor mothers in rural areas. Few voices in the public debate over reproductive rights deplore this inequity in access to safe reproductive services that results from social and economic circumstances.

In the doctrine of rights, human reproduction is considered in its conventional biological sense: for each child there is one female parent who produces the egg and gestates the fetus, one male who produces the sperm. While the courts and law makers debated this legal doctrine, technologies of artificial and assisted reproduction were changing the basic assumptions underlying these rights. Since the 1940s, artificial insemination has allowed a third party to assist a couple in forming a family. More recent techniques of assisted reproduction have included in vitro fertilization, egg donation, and embryo transfer. New reproductive technology (NRT) enables physicians to accept a growing fetus as a separate patient for fetal diagnosis, treatment, and even surgery.

Two issues are particularly notable for the public discussion they have generated: surrogacy contracts and concerns that NRT will present serious threats to women's reproductive freedom and that the government will be unable to address these threats adequately.

Surrogacy Contracts

Surrogate motherhood or parenthood—the practice of family formation with the assistance of a third person—is in fact ancient. Genesis 16 tells the story of Sarah and Abraham having children with the assistance of Sarah's maid. Chinese parents often reproduced with the participation of concubines. The advent of legal adoption in the twentieth century established a means for making such practices more orderly: a wife could become the legal mother of her husband's child born to another woman. And artificial insemination techniques have made conception impersonal and unthreatening to wedding vows.

What has brought the practice of surrogacy to public discussion are the formal contracts to plan the conception of a baby and secure the guarantee of adoption before the birth in exchange for some financial payment to the mother. Many contracts are drawn up and honored in private.[19] The question for government policy arises when one party reneges on the contract. Should the courts enforce surrogate contracts the same way they enforce other contracts? The issue raises ethical and moral questions related to intense emotions surrounding such concepts as procreation, children, and motherhood. Opponents of surrogacy contracts raise two major objections. First, they define surrogacy contracts as a form of baby selling. A couple pays a woman to produce a baby for them. Treating human beings as commodities reeks of practices like slavery and prostitution and degrades people, especially mothers and innocent, vulnerable infants. Second, objections flow from the commercial aspect of the transactions. Since surrogacy costs money—$10,000 and up—only the rich can afford to pay, and the poor are tempted to offer the service. Poor women may be exploited to produce babies for the rich.

Those who defend surrogacy contracts counter this powerful rhetoric with language about the need for surrogacy. First, they call the financial transaction a payment for services a woman is freely giving. As such, the transaction is a service contract, not a production agreement. Second, they shift the issue to the realm of constitutional law, which guarantees privacy to married couples in reproductive matters. They reason that surely this guarantee applies to infertile couples as well as fertile; the government should not interfere with a couple's legitimate efforts to have a biologically related child through a surrogacy contract.

Feminists are divided on the issue. Opponents of surrogacy consider the commercialization of motherhood to be especially degrading to women. They believe it casts women into the role of impersonal incubator, with her uterus for rent to the highest bidder. For a growing number of feminists, biological mothering is more than donating an egg and gestating a fetus. It is a process that extends beyond birth. They insist that a woman's right to decide not to deliver her child up for adoption should be paramount, regardless of any contracts she may have signed prior to birth (Chesler, 1988, pp. 95–96).

Other feminists argue that a woman's right to reproduce should be equal to a man's. A man can donate sperm for money; a woman should have the right to contract and use her body to provide a service for another person. They say that a woman who is unable to have her own baby should also have the right to hire another woman to do it for her as long as all parties make free choices and there is no coercion. These feminists are reluctant to attribute special emotions and rights to women based on biological functions and differences from men. Such assumptions have inevitably led to sex discrimination and paternalistic protection, denying women choice and control.

BOX 4.5

Feminist Views on New Reproductive Technology

"Artificial reproduction is not inherently dehumanizing. At the very least, development of the option should make possible an honest re-examination of the ancient value of motherhood. At the present time, for a woman to come out openly against motherhood on prin-ciple is physically dangerous. She can get away with it only if she adds that she is neurotic, abnormal, child-hating, and therefore 'un-fit.' ('Perhaps later . . . when I'm better prepared.') This is hardly a free atmosphere of inquiry. At least until the taboo is lifted, until the decision not to have children or to have them by artificial means is as legitimate as traditional child-bearing, women are as good as forced into their female roles."

Shulamith Firestone, *The Dialectic of Sex*, 1970, pp. 189–190.

"Because all these technologies, drugs, and procedures violate the integrity of a woman's body in ways that are dangerous, destructive, debilitating, and demeaning, they are a form of medical violence against women" (p. viii).

"The right to privacy has moved from the sexual to the repro-ductive sphere, from the bedrooms of supposedly consenting adults to the boardrooms of surrogate brokerage agencies and medical en-trepreneurs who now demand contractual 'consent' of women used as surrogates. From a man's private entitlement to a woman's body in prostitution and pornography, the right of privacy includes yet another private male entitlement—his access to her reproductive capacities" (p. 83).

Janice Raymond, *Women As Wombs: Reproductive Technologies and the Battle over Women's Freedom,* 1993

"What do radical feminists tell women who choose to 'medicalize' the birth process by using such devices as electronic fetal monitors? Or the many women who seek out new technologies in order to have a child? Or the women who choose to be surrogate mothers? Would radical feminists deny these women the right to exercise medical choice over their own bodies?

In a word: Yes."

Wendy McElroy, "Breeder Reactionaries: The 'Feminist' War on Reproductive Technologies," 1994

The issue of surrogacy was a hot topic in the late 1980s when several cases, especially that of Baby "M," came to national attention. Despite the attention surrounding such cases, most states still have no legislation regarding surrogacy. Those that have passed laws have tended to outlaw surrogacy contracts for money. Some state courts have ruled that private surrogacy contracts are unenforceable (Blank and Merrick, 1995).

New Reproductive Technology and Women's Rights

The effectiveness of medical means for helping infertile couples bear children has been growing dramatically. Perhaps this has reduced the demand for surrogacy, but it has raised concerns about the effects NRT will have on women's rights. The technology places into the hands of the doctors new tools for making the essential decisions about conceiving and bearing a child. At the same time, the technology enhances the status of the fetus and separates it, conceptually, from the mother.

Many feminists warn that NRT constitutes a severe threat to women from a male-dominated medical and scientific establishment. As on the issue of surrogacy, however, feminists are not in full agreement on the effect of these changes in reproductive technology. Some argue that they have increased, not decreased, women's choices. Women are no longer necessarily bound by their biological timeclocks since better medical treatment has increased the chances of healthy births for women well into their forties. Some technologies hold the promise that women may be able to postpone childbirth until after menopause.

Technology has enhanced the "medicalization" of pregnancy (Woliver, 1989), and it has led to doctors treating a fetus as a patient separate from the mother. Once the fetus reached this status, many began to think that it had rights to health and well-being. Inevitably, the health of the fetus has become the responsibility of the mother. If the fetus is injured due to the actions of the mother, can she be held legally responsible? Not yet, in most states. However, the number of cases charging mothers with crimes, including child abuse and even attempted murder, for injuring their children before birth has been growing; so far, most have been dismissed on appeal. An example is *Johnson v. State of Florida* (1992), where a trial court convicted Jennifer Johnson, whose babies were born with an addiction to cocaine, with the crime of illegally delivering a controlled substance to her child during birth, and the appeals court dismissed the case due to inadequate legal foundation. In 1996, however, the South Carolina Supreme Court became the first high court to condone such suits, ruling that a pregnant woman can be criminally liable for endangering the health of a viable fetus (*Cornelia Whitner v. State of South Carolina*). Most experts agree that use of existing criminal statutes is not the most effective way to help both women and children to healthy lives. Threatening pregnant women with prosecution for their failure to behave in ways that will ensure the health of their babies is unlikely to accomplish the goal; it is more likely to drive women away from prenatal treatment altogether.

Conclusion

The debate over reproductive policy illustrates the importance of ideologies and systems of belief to the influence of feminists in defining the issue. Despite the importance of the debates on contraceptives and abortion to women, feminists were not major players in the policy game until the mid-1970s. Then, however, through the women's health movement, feminists developed an ideological framework and language that linked access to contraceptives and abortion to women's rights, especially the right to autonomy and self-determination. The ideology of empowering women to control their reproductive health has yielded feminist definitions of such issues as sex education, research on contraceptives and abortion pills, and the legalization of abortion. But, to date, reproduction policy has been formulated to serve goals other than women's rights.

The effectiveness of pro-choice ideology in coalition with doctors and family-planning groups has provoked opposition based primarily on fundamentalist religious ideology. The opponents try to push back achievements of the reproductive-rights coalition. To do that, they have had to expand the conflict to widen their pro-life coalition, redefine the issue in their terms, and increase their political resources. They have done this primarily by a battle over the use of words—what to call various aspects of the reproductive process. Here are some examples of emotional terms pro-life factions substitute for the more neutral medical ones: for *fetus, unborn child;* for *uterus, cradle;* for *termination of pregnancy, baby killing.*

How important are mere words? If people begin to see analogies between abortion and killing children or murder, it will be very difficult to argue that this practice should not be illegal. Pro-choice feminists have offered some emotional language to counter the pro-life manipulation of the issue. While pro-life advocates talk about saving babies, protecting the unborn, and safe-guarding the rights of citizens from the time of conception, pro-choice feminists respond that if abortion is made illegal women will be butchered by "back street" abortionists wielding coat hangers or will be condemned by the state to compulsory pregnancy. These issues demonstrate that the most important part of policy making is often the power to select the language that will be used to talk about an issue in the public arena.

The importance of the language used to frame issues of public interest explains the threat that new reproductive technology represents to women's reproductive rights. The medicalization of pregnancy has led to referring to the fetus as *patient*, separating it conceptually, but not physically, from its mother. The rhetoric is thus in place for use by a future court that might wish to rule that the fetus is a *patient* deserving of equal medical treatment with all other patients. And, the pregnant body of the woman fades as doctors, who have a major role in defining the debate, refer to women by their body parts—eggs, ovaries, uteruses—and to their role in the reproductive process as that of "alternative reproductive vehicles," "maternal environments," and "human incubators" (Raymond, 1993). For some feminists, the reintegration of a woman's body is the most pressing challenge of reproductive rights.

Notes

1. Political debates on contraceptive and abortion policy have appeared to be more directly influenced by pro-natalist interest groups in France and Sweden than in the United States. Nevertheless, the effect of policies in encouraging childbirth by putting up barriers to effective birth control are quite similar (Stetson, 1987).

2. The main case in this series was *United States v. One Package*, 13 F. Supp. 334, aff'd 86 F2d 737 (2d Cir. 1936). See Dienes (1972) for a discussion of this case and others related to it.

3. It is important to note that the Supreme Court drew this decision to give unmarried persons privacy in one area—contraception—based on arguments of equal protection. Thus states are still permitted to have laws limiting other forms of nonmarital sexual behavior, such as homosexuality, fornication, and adultery. See Chapter 9.

4. The company that made the Dalkon shield eventually took the product off the market, prodded by lawsuits from families of victims.

5. These federal guidelines apply only to the use of federal funds for the procedure. Several states still permit sterilization without consent of the patient, usually aimed at mentally retarded or mentally ill persons. Interest in sterilization as a punishment for criminals, especially for repeat sex offenders, periodically surfaces.

6. *Quickening*, or *animation*, refers to the point where the woman feels the fetus move. This occurs at different times in different pregnancies but typically around the end of the fourth month. Classical Catholic theories divided pregnancy according to ensoulment: the soul entered a male fetus at forty days' gestation, the female at eighty days.

7. The other states were Alaska, Hawaii, and Washington.

8. This term is from Paul Ehrlich's book *The Population Bomb,* published in 1968. Worries that population growth would outstrip resources had promoted extensive funding of family-planning services and population research.

9. Norma McCorvey's life since *Roe v. Wade* has been marked by her public shifts of ideology: from abortion rights to lesbian rights and, in 1995, a conversion to a pro-life anti-abortion religion. Her autobiography, *I am Roe* (New York: HarperCollins) appeared in 1994.

10. The Court refused to determine when human life begins: "When those trained in the respective disciplines of medicine, philosophy, and theology are unable to arrive at any consensus, the judiciary, at this point in the development of man's knowledge, is not in a position to speculate as to the answer" (*Roe v. Wade*, p. 154).

11. The companion case, *Doe v. Bolton*, 410 U.S. 179 (1973), invalidated ALI-inspired statutes.

12. Medicaid is the government-funded health-care program primarily for families on welfare and for the destitute. It is funded by both federal and state governments and is subject to regulations and restrictions at both levels.

13. The four cases were *Beal v. Doe*, 432 U.S. 438 (1977); *Maher v. Roe*, 432 U.S. 464 (1977); *Poelker v. Doe*, 432 U.S. 519 (1977); and *Harris v. McRae*, 488 U.S. 297 (1980).

14. Note that the coalitions on the Supreme Court have shifted between *Roe v. Wade* and the later cases. Justice Blackmun, considered the architect of *Roe*, dissented on these cases that accepted restrictions on funding. Justices Burger, Stewart, and Powell were the "swing" votes:

Comparison of Votes of Supreme Court Justices on *Roe v. Wade* and Medicaid Funding Cases

Justice	*Roe*	*Maher*	*Harris*
Blackmun	Yes	No	No
Burger	Yes	Yes	Yes
Douglas/Stevens	Yes	Yes[a]	No[a]
Brennan	Yes	No	No
Stewart	Yes	Yes	Yes
Marshall	Yes	No	No
Powell	Yes	Yes	Yes
White	No	Yes	Yes
Rehnquist	No	Yes	Yes

[a]Vote by Stevens.
Note: a Yes vote signifies a vote with the majority.

15. For a description of their overall vision, see the Family Protection Act ("Weekly Report." *Congressional Quarterly* 39, no. 40 [October 3, 1981]: 1916), a bill introduced by conservative senators in 1981.

16. In the 1980s, the pro-life advocates produced and distributed a film, purporting to show a sonar picture of a fetus undergoing abortion. Called *The*

Silent Scream, it relied on scientific data from fetology to make the moral case that the fetus is a human being.

17. Pro-choice advocates respond with their own analogies to the Nazi regime, stating that restricting access to abortion is the same as the compulsory pregnancy Nazis required of women of Aryan descent.

18. There have, in fact, been several versions of the Human Life Amendment. Some versions extend the definition of *personhood* to begin with the moment of conception. Other versions return to the states the power to regulate abortion.

19. Why not surrogate fathers? There have been surrogate fathers in the form of sperm donors to banks or individuals for artificial insemination. Common law assumed husbands were fathers of children born of their wives. Contracts have been used increasingly to ensure not only the husband's consent to artificial insemination of his wife but also his acceptance of parental responsibility for the child.

References

Akron v. Akron Center for Reproductive Health. 462 U.S. 416. 1983.

Beal v. Doe. 432 U.S. 438. 1977.

Belotti v. Baird. 443 U.S. 622. 1979.

Blank, Robert, and Merrick, Janna C. *Human Reproduction, Emerging Technologies, and Conflicting Rights.* Washington, D.C.: CQ Press, 1995.

Butler, J. Douglas, and Walbert, David F., eds. *Abortion, Medicine, and the Law,* 3rd ed. New York: Facts on File Publications, 1986.

Carey v. Population Services International. 431 U.S. 678. 1977.

Chesler, Phyllis. *Sacred Bond: The Legacy of Baby M.* New York: Times Books, 1988.

Commission to Explore Possible Third Party. *National NOW Times,* 22 (Oct./Nov./Dec. 1989): 3.

Cornelia Whitner v. State of South Carolina. 65 *U.S. Law Week* 2066. 1996.

Davis, Nanette J. *From Crime to Choice: The Transformation of Abortion in America.* Westport, Conn.: Greenwood Press, 1985.

Dienes, C. Thomas. *Law, Politics, and Birth Control.* Urbana: University of Illinois Press, 1972.

Doe v. Bolton. 410 U.S. 179. 1973.

Ehrlich, Paul. *The Population Bomb.* New York: Ballantine, 1968.

Eisenstadt v. Baird. 405 U.S. 438. 1972.

Eisenstein, Zillah. *The Female Body and the Law.* Berkeley: University of California Press, 1988.

Firestone, Shulamith. *The Dialectic of Sex: The Case for Feminist Revolution.* 1970. Reprint. London: Women's Press, 1979.

Freedom of Access to Clinic Entrances Act of 1994. PL 103–259. May 26, 1994.

Gallagher, Janet. "Fetal Personhood and Women's Policy." In *Women, Biology and Public Policy,* edited by Virginia Sapiro, pp. 91–116. Newbury Park, Calif.: Sage, 1985.

Garrow, David J. *Liberty and Sexuality: The Right to Privacy and the Making of Roe v. Wade.* New York: Macmillan, 1994.

Ginsburg, Faye, and Rapp, Rayna, eds. *Conceiving the New World Order: The Global Politics of Reproduction.* Berkeley: University of California Press, 1995.

Glendon, Mary Ann. *Abortion and Divorce in Western Law.* Cambridge: Harvard University Press, 1987.

Gordon, Linda. *Woman's Body, Woman's Right: A Social History of Birth Control in America.* New York: Grossman, 1976.

Griswold v. Connecticut. 381 U.S. 479. 1965.

Harris v. McRae. 448 U.S. 297. 1980.

Howes, Joanne, and Allina, Amy. "Women's Health Movements." *Social Policy* 24 (Summer 1994): 6–14.

Johnson v. State of Florida. 602 So 2d 1288. 1992.

Kinsey, Alfred C., Pomeroy, Wardell, and Martin, Clyde S. *Sexual Behavior in the Human Male.* Philadelphia: Saunders, 1948.

Kinsey, Alfred C., et al. *Sexual Behavior in the Human Female.* Philadelphia: Saunders, 1953.

Knowlton, Charles. *The Fruits of Philosophy, or, the Private Companion of Young Married People,* 2nd ed. London: Watson, 1832. Reprinted from the American Edition.

Luker, Kristin. *Abortion and the Politics of Motherhood.* Berkeley: University of California Press, 1984.

Maher v. Roe. 432 U.S. 464. 1977.

McCorvey, Norma. *I Am Roe: My Life, Roe v. Wade and Freedom of Choice.* New York: HarperCollins, 1994.

McElroy, Wendy. "Breeder Reactionaries: The 'Feminist' War on Reproductive Technologies." *Reason* 26 (December 1994): 18–24.

Mohr, James C. *Abortion in America: The Origins and Evolution of National Policy, 1800–1900.* New York: Oxford University Press, 1978.

Nsiah-Jefferson, Laurie. "Reproductive Laws, Women of Color, and Low Income Women." *Women's Rights Law Reporter* 10 (Spring 1989): 15–38.

Petchesky, Rosalind P. *Abortion and Woman's Choice.* Boston: Northeastern University Press, 1984.

Planned Parenthood of Southeastern Pennsylvania v. Casey 112 S Ct 2791. 1992.

Planned Parenthood v. Danforth. 428 U.S. 52. 1976.

Poelker v. Doe. 432 U.S. 519. 1977.

Raymond, Janice. *Women as Wombs: Reproductive Technologies and the Battle over Women's Freedom.* San Francisco: Harper San Francisco, 1993.

Rhode, Deborah L. *Justice and Gender.* Cambridge: Harvard University Press, 1989.

Roe v. Wade. 410 U.S. 113. 1973.

Rothman, Barbara K. "Reproduction." In *Analyzing Gender: A Handbook of Social Science Research,* edited by Beth B. Hess and Myra Marx Ferree, pp. 155–170. Newbury Park, Calif.: Sage, 1987.

Rubin, Eva R. *Abortion, Politics, and the Courts: Roe v. Wade and Its Aftermath.* Westport, Conn.: Greenwood Press, 1987.

Ruzek, Sheryl Burt. *The Women's Health Movement: Feminist Alternatives to Medical Control.* New York: Praeger, 1978.

Sanger, Margaret. *Margaret Sanger: An Autobiography.* New York: Norton, 1938.

Shapiro, Thomas M. *Population Control Politics: Women, Sterilization, and Reproductive Choice.* Philadelphia: Temple University Press, 1985.

Smith, T. Alexander. *The Comparative Policy Process.* Santa Barbara: ABC Clio, 1975.

Stetson, Dorothy McBride. *Women's Rights in France.* Westport, Conn.: Greenwood Press, 1987.

Thornburgh v. American College of Obstetricians and Gynecologists. 476 U.S. 747. 1986.

Webster v. Reproductive Health Services. 57 U.S.L.W. 5023. 1989.

Woliver, Laura R. "New Reproductive Technologies: Challenges to Women's Control of Gestation and Birth." In *Biomedical Technology and Public Policy,* edited by Robert H. Blank and Mirriam K. Mills, pp. 43–46. Westport, Conn.: Greenwood Press, 1989.

CHAPTER 5

Education

Even before there was a women's movement, women had begun to plead for and demand education (Wollstonecraft, 1972). In fact, early efforts to educate women in the United States became a foundation for the first organization that met at Seneca Falls in 1848 (Flexner, 1959; Kraditor, 1968). Since then, articulate American women have continued to claim equal rights to education. This issue has remained so important partly because the ideas about the purpose of education for women have continued to change.

When education is a scarce resource, the powerful keep it for themselves or ration it to groups, according to their own needs. The powerful have usually agreed that women have needed only enough education to permit them to perform their special roles in the family and the society. For white, middle-class women, this meant education to be wives and mothers. For Native American women or women who were slaves or immigrants, this meant no education at all. As social perceptions of women's roles have changed and minorities have demanded equality, women's access to educational resources has changed. All along, women's rights advocates have tried to exert their vision of women's roles and then relate education policy to that vision. Throughout the years, these feminists have sought equality. What has varied is their definition of what constitutes equality in education: equal access for men and women to fill separate roles; equal access to the same educational content; equal access in order to promote racial and ethnic culture; or separate education for the empowerment of women and women's culture. Only in the last thirty-five years has education been linked to women's economic status and their employment opportunities.

Public policy for education in the United States originated in the desire of communities of families, often centered around a church, to share the expense of educating their children. There has never been enough money for any educational enterprise. Excessive costs have perennially plagued group efforts to sponsor schools, driving administrators to seek financial help from ever-larger communities. Neighborhoods petitioned cities, which established school districts; cities requested state subsidies; state departments of education sought federal financial assistance. Thus was built a layer cake of public-education administration and institutions, guided, although not operated by, a national policy.

There is chronic tension and frequent conflict as the various government entities supplying money try to achieve their diverse goals. The battle is often fought over how much control the next-higher level of government should be permitted to exert over education practices in return for its financial assistance. The amount of federal control over state and local school administrations is especially contentious. The Constitution gives no power to Congress to regulate education; this is a power *reserved* to the states. Yet states, and even private schools, have come to depend on federal financial assistance. Efforts to direct education practices through the regulation of federal money often encounter fierce resistance aimed at protecting local prerogatives. What education policy means for women's rights is affected by this complex organization.

Since educating the children of a society is expensive, education policy is usually defined in a way that will justify to taxpayers the cost of educating the next generation. In the United States, the goals are economic, civic, and social. Schools will prepare young people as workers to keep the economy strong and prosperous, taking on the challenge of shaping skills to meet rapidly changing technologies. Educators will also teach civic values to all citizens so that the democratic government can function. In addition, education will be the means of solving social problems, from alcoholism to AIDS.

Another way to look at education is as a resource for individuals and groups seeking to better themselves. Knowledge is power, and when knowledge is available to a few, the many are powerless. Groups of people who consider themselves controlled by others usually see education as the primary means of overcoming their disadvantages and controlling their own lives. Such a goal has motivated indigent women, African Americans, Native Americans, various groups of immigrants, and the poor. Their efforts have not always met with success, for sometimes those in power want to protect their position, and they sometimes try to do so by denying others access to the resources of educational institutions.

A final way of looking at education is as the main social vehicle for maintaining and transmitting a political culture from one generation to another. As policy, education can be constructed to limit or expand citizens' views of the world or to shape a particular set of values, attitudes, and beliefs. Legislators and administrators may reinforce or change cultural attitudes by regulating books and courses on subjects such as creationism and evolution, Americanism and communism, and multiculturalism and classism. Control over the content of most courses is more diffuse, traced through the professional-education establishment to the scholarly base in various disciplines in colleges and universities. Thus, education is political in that it distributes important political resources by instilling in young people basic values that will affect their lives and fortunes and those of society for decades.

Education policy, as it relates to gender roles and women's rights, is affected by the conflicts over control of the policy, over the various justifications of education as a public good, over the demands of groups for access to education as a resource for advancement, and over the place of education in shaping basic cultural values, attitudes, and beliefs. This chapter traces the elaboration of public debate, beginning with the justifications for educating women. The major public-policy story is the shift from focusing on education for women so they can fulfill their special roles to recognizing sex discrimination as a problem and linking education policy to the economic status of women. The advances made in *women's studies*, however, hold the greater promise for women's rights. Resources for women's studies enhance the power to create knowledge.

Women's Education: Why Educate Women?

Why educate women? Since the beginning of the American republic, this has been the main problem of education policy as it relates to women's rights. When people were first taxed to support public education, they asked this same question about men, too: why educate them? But once answers were settled on, the reasons for educating men justified the establishment of public education itself: to prepare workers, to foster citizenship, and to improve society. But Americans kept asking about the reasons for spending money on girls, and the answers kept changing. Way back in colonial times, learning to read the Bible was necessary for both boys and girls. But early educators had no illusions about equal capacities: their belief in the smaller size of the female brain made it quite clear that women's potential must be inferior to men's.

Elementary School

The creation of a new nation with a growing democracy coincided with the expansion of *common*, or public, elementary schools. Boys who would one day be voting citizens needed education to sustain the democracy. But women could not vote, so why educate girls? Most educators admitted that the female brain could cope with the three Rs. Many realized the important role mothers had in bringing up their children (some of whom would be male). As mothers, women would have to instruct their sons in democratic ideals and civic responsibility. Then there was the moral angle. Mothers were the moral pillars of the family, and on them depended the maintenance of a strong moral order in society.

If money had been abundant, public-school officials probably would have preferred to follow the European model and establish separate schools for these separate educational needs. But few communities could afford separate systems, so elementary schools were coeducational from the start.[1] Their purposes for boys and girls were separate. Money was spent to educate girls to live their roles as adults separate from the roles of men. The growth of public education coincided with the expansion of the domestic role into a cult of womanhood, at least in the dominant ideology (Rothman, 1978). Homemaking took on the status of a profession. As such, it warranted one way of thinking about equality for women in education: to prepare them for separate but equally valued adult occupations.

Secondary School

Why send girls to high school? Most boys did not need to go to high school; all they needed to be voters and workers they learned in grade school. Secondary school was necessary only to prepare for professions such as law, medicine, banking, and engineering. Women would not be going into these male jobs, and so they would not need a secondary-level education. But the excessive cost of education intervened to affect women's fortunes.

BOX 5.1

Coeducation and the Rights of Woman

Mary Wollstonecraft (1759–1797) was the first English writer to present a public case for women's equality. Inspired by liberal ideas of inalienable human rights, Wollstonecraft published *A Vindication of the Rights of Woman* in 1792. In it she placed the blame for the "state of degradation to which women are reduced" on the men who deprived women of education. Coeducation would improve both sexes and society as a whole:

> If marriage be the cement of society, mankind should all be educated after the same model, or the intercourse of the sexes will never deserve the name of fellowship, nor will women ever fulfill the peculiar duties of their sex, till they become enlightened citizens, till they become free by being enabled to earn their own subsistence, independent of men; in the same manner, I mean, to prevent misconstruction, as one man is independent of another. Nay, marriage will never be held sacred till women, by being brought up with men, are prepared to be their companions rather than their mistresses; for the mean doublings of cunning will ever render them contemptible, whilst oppression renders them timid. So convinced am I of this truth, that I will venture to predict that virtue will never prevail in society till the virtues of both sexes are founded on reason; and till the affections of both sexes are founded on reason; and till the affections common to both are allowed to gain their due strength by the discharge of mutual duties. (p. 283)

Public elementary schools sprang up in every village, and they needed teachers. Salaries that would attract men with a high school education would be too costly. It was cheaper to train and hire women, especially if they worked for only a few years between school and marriage. Thus elementary school teaching rapidly became a woman's occupation. Since woman was considered the teacher in the home, being a teacher in elementary school was thought to suit her temperament and abilities. Then, too, well-educated women would be appropriate mates for well-educated men. As John Irving said at the opening of the girls' high school in New York City in 1826: "How important is the female character, how great its influence upon the wellbeing and the operations of man" (quoted in Woody, 1929, 1, p. 527). Thus, other reasons associated with the cult of womanhood accumulated to encourage the establishment of

BOX 5.2

High School Education by Sex in the Nineties—the 1890s

By the 1890s, women outnumbered men in high schools. But men were more likely to be on track to college.

Number of Schools, Instructors, and Students, 1889 to 1890	Public	Private
Schools	2,526	1,632
Instructors		
Male	3,597	3,272
Female	5,280	3,937
Students		
Male	84,451	47,534
Female	116,351	47,397
Students preparing for college		
Male	7,984	11,220
Female	6,915	5,421

Source: Sara A. Burstall, *The Education of Girls in the United States,* 1894, p. 196.

secondary schools for girls. At first, these schools were segregated extensions of the private female *seminaries,* secondary-level academies for girls. Later, public high schools set up courses suitable for girls. The woman educated in domestic arts and sciences would profoundly influence society through her husband and children, or so the experts believed. Clearly, secondary education would not be wasted on women.

After the Civil War, demographic changes boosted attention to vocations for women. Women outnumbered men, and basic arithmetic showed there were not enough husbands—a necessary component for a career as homemaker—to go around. Schools would have to pay attention to training girls in vocations "suitable" to their sex. Therefore, courses were added in commercial studies, including bookkeeping and clerical skills, and in nursing.

Higher Education

More education for women? Providing secondary education for anyone, male or female, strained the resources of local school systems. If there were to be postsecondary education, state governments or religious institutions would have to bear the cost. The pattern of state investment in postsecondary education for women was at first limited to state support of *normal schools*, special teacher-training schools usually attached to elementary schools. Started in the 1830s, state normal schools expanded until, by 1918, there were over two hundred publicly supported teacher-training schools, their student body 85 percent women. In the twentieth century, the normal schools disappeared. Many have evolved into state colleges and state universities. In nearly every state, at least one of the branches of the state university system began as a normal school and thus was the first institution in the state to welcome women to higher education.

Leaders of the Woman Movement, especially Elizabeth Cady Stanton and Susan B. Anthony, wanted more than special schools. They demanded coeducation. Their demand for equal education was similar to their demand for the vote. They argued that women and men were both endowed with the same inalienable rights and that girls were as capable of learning and reasoning as boys. Stanton and Anthony were not enamored of the cult of womanhood. Instead, they cheered on individual women who broke down barriers to the traditionally male professions of medicine, law, and physics.

After 1870, there was a boom in the building of state universities to fuel economic expansion and the growth of the union. To encourage this, the federal government helped fund *land-grant colleges*, many of which were coeducational from the start. Western states joining the union also established state universities, some of them coeducational. The first state to admit women to its public university was Utah. The curricula and the degree programs of these state universities and land-grant colleges were diverse and accommodated the different interests of men and women. Gaining access to the elite professions—medicine, engineering, law, and theology—was still a challenge. Nevertheless, by 1900, many state professional schools had also begun to admit women.[2]

Not Separate, and Not Equal

As many historians assert, the nineteenth century was a time for the expansion of women's education. Females shared in opportunities resulting from the growth of the public school system. Many barriers were lowered in secondary and higher education. The number of schools increased dramatically. Despite this growth, the definition of women's education changed little. Why educate women? The official answer was the same in 1900 as it had been in 1800: educate women to prepare them for their special separate female roles in the family—as wives, mothers, and home-makers—and in useful occupations suitable for their sex. The more en-lightened leaders accepted the fact that exceptional women might tackle the elite professions, but for the vast majority of American women, family roles were the end of education. Most leaders did not challenge the idea that female brains were biologically inferior to males. In the 1880s, no less an authority than Edward H. Clarke of the Harvard Medical School fac-ulty asserted that too much education would put such a strain on women's physical strength as to endanger their childbearing functions. (A similar argument was used to oppose political equality for women.) De-spite the growth of coeducational state universities, there was still deep opposition in many states to mixing the sexes. The opponents argued not only that exposure to men's education would coarsen and cheapen deli-cate female sensibilities but also that the presence of females would im-pair men's education by "feminizing" institutions of learning.

Parallel to the dominant nineteenth-century view that the goal of public education differed for the two sexes was a counter demand for identical education for women and men. Inspired by Mary Wollstone-craft's assertion that woman is man's potential intellectual equal, women's rights leaders linked the right to education closely to the overall emanci-pation of women. At Seneca Falls in 1848, conference participants agreed that women and men are "invested by the creator with the same capabili-ties" and charged man with depriving woman of "the facilities for obtain-ing a thorough education, all colleges being closed against her." Later, suf-frage leaders based their claim for identical education on their belief that there were no intellectual differences between men and women. Such egalitarian feminism inspired people to found private women's colleges after the Civil War. These colleges were not to be normal schools or to provide a special curriculum in domestic science. Vassar, Wellesley, and Smith Colleges copied the curriculum at the elite men's colleges.

By the turn of the century, psychologists had challenged the dogma that associated intelligence with brain size (Rosenberg, 1982). They found far more variation within each sex than between them. This research un-dermined the credibility of arguments based on the inherent inferiority of women rooted in biology and, instead, supported feminist claims. At the same time, girls were streaming into secondary schools, where they outnumbered boys, and women could be found in nearly all disciplines and professions (see Box 5.2). Nonetheless, the idea of identical educa-tion for women and men never triumphed in public debate. Public-school policy in the nineteenth century established the pattern of educa-tion that would endure until the 1970s. Boys and girls by and large attended school together, but once there, they simply received different educations.

After 1930, women's educational participation declined, and by 1960, women made up a smaller percentage in the elite professions than they had in the 1920s. In 1961, President Kennedy's Commission on the Status of Women approached its study of education policy in the spirit that had been dominant since the early 1800s. Why educate women? "To prepare women both to realize their intellectual and vocational potentialities and to fulfill their responsibilities to family, home, and community" (Mead and Kaplan, 1965, p. 101). In discussing the mature woman's education, the commission reported that she "also needs to continue her education in one form or another in order to provide the assistanceship, companionship, and stimulation needed by her husband and by her children as they develop" (p. 26). Even the most ardent advocate of the cult of womanhood of the 1880s would not be uncomfortable with this answer.

Gender Equity in Education

After 1960, the definition of education policy shifted away from the framework that accepted separate roles for women and men toward a framework that assumed equality of the sexes. This shift in debate took place in the context of several political changes: the civil rights movement leading to the Civil Rights Act of 1964; the appearance of feminist organizations, especially the National Organization for Women (NOW) and the Women's Equity Action League (WEAL); and the formation of women's liberation groups on college campuses and of women's caucuses in various disciplines.

The civil rights movement made some of its most dramatic gains toward equality in the area of education. In particular, *Brown v. Board of Education* (1954) banned segregated public schools. And access to education continued to be seen as an essential condition for the overall improvement of the status of black Americans. In the early 1960s, however, women's rights activists had not yet made education an issue. Gaining access to schools did not appear to be an immediate problem because they were not obviously segregated by sex. Employment status and unequal pay seemed to be much more important aspects of sex discrimination. Several antidiscrimination laws enacted in the 1960s banned sex and race discrimination. None, however, covered the admission of women to and the treatment of women in educational institutions. The education section (Title VI) of the Civil Rights Act of 1964 banned race, but not sex, discrimination. The only section of the act to include sex discrimination was Title VII, which covered employment but not state or professional employment (see Chapter 7).

President Lyndon B. Johnson's Executive Order of 1968 required federal contractors to adopt affirmative-action employment policies. This order opened the way for an attack on the practices that traditionally had excluded women from many elite colleges and universities. As WEAL's president Bernice Sandler reasoned, many higher-education institutions, both public and private, had contracts for research, buildings, and other projects, and so at least their employment practices were subject to compliance with antidiscrimination and affirmative-action policies. Her organization filed a massive suit against universities throughout the country, thus launching the first feminist campaign for equality in higher education. NOW followed this lead, with support from feminist and women's caucuses on campuses and in professional disciplines. Although demands for contract compliance were beginning to challenge many exclusionary practices in the "old-boy" academic network, feminists still had no legal tools to challenge discriminatory admissions policies or the deeply entrenched system of sex-linked tracking throughout education—from kindergarten on.

Title IX

In the early 1970s, several events converged, fortuitously, to produce a federal statute for sex equity in education. In April 1970, President Nixon's Task Force on Women's Rights and Responsibilities linked sex discrimination in education to a denial of employment opportunity: "Discrimination in education is one of the most damaging injustices women suffer. It denies them equal education and equal employment opportunity, contributing to a second-class self-image" (p. 7). Many of the federal education subsidies that had been enacted in the 1950s and 1960s were due to expire. Edith Green (D.-Oreg.), who chaired a special subcommittee of the House Education and Labor Committee, proposed a renewal of federal education funding that included many of the recommendations of the Nixon task force. Green's bill would have removed exemptions to education coverage in Title VII and in the Equal Pay Act of 1963 (see Chapter 7), and it would also have amended Title VI to ban sex discrimination in all federally funded education programs. The committee's five days of hearings produced public documentation of widespread sex discrimination at all levels of the educational system. These hearings still remain an excellent source of information about the status of women's education and employment.

It was not until 1972 that Congress acted on Green's proposal, which became Title IX of the Higher Education Amendments:

> No person in the United States shall, on the basis of sex, be excluded from participation in, be denied the benefits of, or be subjected to discrimination under any educational program or activity receiving federal financial assistance. (20 U.S.C. Sec. 1681, p. 15)

The wording of Title IX is exactly like that of Title VI of the Civil Rights Act, except that *sex* is substituted for *race*. Any educational institution receiving federal financial assistance must comply. Coverage is extended beyond higher education to preschool, primary, secondary, and vocational schools and from public education to private schools. Few school systems or colleges exist without some form of federal financial help, if only guaranteed student loans and work-study programs. Of course, many educational institutions have large grants and contracts for research, teacher training, and special programs for students. Despite the effort of a variety of feminist groups to publicize the discrimination inherent in American education, Title IX attracted little attention. The major controversy in congressional debate surrounding the Higher Education Amendments was the issue of court-ordered busing for racial integration. Green did not request testimony from feminists and was content that debate focused on other aspects of the bill.

Nevertheless, the differences in political debates on race discrimination and sex discrimination in education became apparent immediately. Racial integration was synonymous with equality, and racial segregation with inferiority. Total integration of the sexes in all aspects of education was not as compelling an issue for many people. Traditional women's and men's schools and colleges had substantial support, even from feminists. Congress addressed their concerns by exempting most such single-sex educational institutions from Title IX's open-admissions requirement. Military schools and some religious schools were also completely exempted from Title IX coverage. Only vocational, professional, and graduate schools, and public undergraduate colleges that were not traditionally single-sex were prevented from restricting admissions to one sex. Most types of schools, from preschool through high school, may be single-sex. Once they admit both sexes, however, they must use equal admissions requirements. Therefore, Title IX bans gender quotas altogether.

A second issue on which sex integration differed from race integration was the issue of privacy. Title IX specifies that educational institutions may retain separate living facilities on the basis of sex.

Title IX was debated and enacted at a time of widespread support for individual rights and equal opportunity. Even during this supportive period, however, exceptions to gender neutrality in Title IX demonstrated the depth of attachment to gender-role differences and was a harbinger of the chronic controversies over equality and sex differences that were to arise in the 1980s in other areas of policy.

After the Higher Education Amendments passed the Congress in 1972, the conflict intensified. It centered on the Department of Health, Education, and Welfare's (DHEW) development of specific regulations for schools and colleges, and on Congress, which had the power to amend both the statute and—after 1974—the administrative regulations. The controversies became so intense that it was not until 1975 that the initial regulations were published.[3] The conflicts focused on how completely a school system must integrate the sexes to achieve the statutory goal of nondiscrimination. But Title IX also attracted attention from defenders of limited government, who were opposed in principle to the involvement of the federal government in private schools and districts operated by local governments. Attempts to eliminate gender identity as a factor in teaching and learning and to seek shared participation in all aspects of education still provoke opposition from many who believe that the federal government should not interfere in the schools. Out of the battle over regulation emerged a strong feminist coalition of many groups and organizations well versed in legislative and administrative processes: the National Coalition for Women and Girls in Education.

Title IX Regulations

Least controversial of the Title IX regulations written by the DHEW were those affecting admissions standards and curriculum matters. Guidelines prohibiting any discrimination in recruitment or admissions qualifications of students in coeducational schools provoked little opposition. Thus, quotas that had limited some medical and engineering school classes to 10 percent women were no longer to be legal in institutions receiving federal assistance. Now no recipient coeducational schools may use different admissions standards for females and males. Once a school becomes coeducational, it must treat all students equally.

Generally the regulations sought to eliminate tracking in coed schools and to shake up traditional discriminatory practices. The separate-spheres ideology had led to separate vocational classes: girls took home economics and boys took carpentry. Physical education classes had been segregated by sex since the days when it was thought such activity was dangerous and unfeminine. Title IX now requires that all classes be open to both males and females. Physical education classes in high school are exempt when contact sports are played. A class may be separated by sex to discuss human sexuality. Grouping students in physical education classes according to ability is also permitted, even though this may result in sex segregation.

Even though classes are technically open to both sexes, girls and boys still tend to segregate on their own. In selecting classes and majors students often rely on advice of academic, career, and psychological counselors. Counseling had been an important concern of President Kennedy's Commission on the Status of Women, which urged counselors to get special training in order to help women and girls to overcome effects of separate spheres ideology. In contrast, the Title IX regulations showed little sympathy for the special needs of women, and the regulations ordered gender-neutral counseling. Thus, although there are no formal barriers to girls to sign up for math, carpentry, or auto mechanics, there is no special effort to help eliminate cultural constraints and stereotypes.

Another point of potential stress was financial aid programs. Some scholarships in these programs were gender-specific—the donor or legacy had designated that they could be awarded only to a boy or only to a girl. A compromise in the Title IX regulations allowed schools to keep such scholarships by pooling all financial aid and simply ensuring that no student would be denied a scholarship solely because of sex.

As part of their agenda to overhaul the sex-biased education system, feminists argued that a key aspect of discrimination was the content of the materials used in the classroom. They asked the DHEW to ban sexist textbooks. Publishers protested that their freedom of the press would be compromised. This issue went all the way to DHEW Secretary Caspar Weinberger, who pleaded the First Amendment and agreed with the publishers. As a result, textbooks and educational materials were removed from Title IX jurisdiction.[4]

As the focus of regulation moved out of the classroom and into extracurricular matters, conflicts intensified. The initial DHEW regulations prohibited any support for extracurricular organizations that limited membership by sex. Social fraternities and sororities, the Young Men's

BOX 5.3

Some Indicators of Title IX's Impact on Women's Higher Education

A. Women have become a majority of all college students. In the 1950s, 35% of students enrolled in institutions of higher education were women. Removing formal sex discrimination through Title IX regulation has reinforced steady gains until, in the 1990s, women have become a majority.

Year	Men	Women	Women as Percentage of Total
1957	2,170,765	1,153,018	35.6
1963	2,961,540	1,818,069	38.0
1966	3,856,216	2,533,656	39.7
1969	4,746,201	3,258,459	40.7
1972	5,238,757	3,976,103	43.1
1975	6,148,997	5,035,862	45.0
1978	5,640,998	5,619,094	49.7
1981	5,975,056	6,396,616	51.7
1984	5,863,574	6,378,366	52.1
1987	5,932,056	6,834,586	53.1
1990	6,283,909	7,534,728	54.5
1993	6,427,716	7,877,942	55.1

Christian Association (YMCA) and the Young Women's Christian Association (YWCA), and even the Girl Scouts and Boy Scouts bombarded Congress with pleas to retain their traditionally sex-segregated membership. Congress amended the guidelines to exempt these organizations, along with social-service organizations. And the DHEW developed a test: any organization that has academic or professional achievement as its goal must admit both sexes as members in order to receive support from a school or college accepting federal assistance. Those organizations that are primarily social, however, may remain single-sex within the school's or college's activities program.

Despite the lively discussion of admissions, curriculum, textbooks, and organizations, nothing was as controversial as the regulations relating to athletics. The feminists wanted women to share equally in the resources of college and high school athletics. The National Collegiate Athletic Association (NCAA), objecting to federal interference, lined up against NOW, WEAL, and the National Coalition for Women and Girls in

BOX 5.3 *(continued)*

B. Women have made steady gains in dentistry, medicine, and law.
Title IX has had a dramatic effect on sex distribution of students earning degrees in many professional programs such as dentistry, medicine, and law, programs previously dominated by men.

Year	Men	Women	Total	Women as Percentage of Total
Degrees Conferred in Dentistry				
1963–1964	3,168	12	3,180	.3
1973–1974	4,355	85	4,440	1.9
1983–1984	4,302	1,051	5,353	19.6
1992–1993	2,383	1,222	3,605	33.8
Degrees Conferred in Medicine				
1963–1964	7,303	425	7,303	5.8
1973–1974	11,356	1,263	11,356	11.1
1983–1984	11,359	4,454	15,813	28.1
1992–1993	9,679	5,852	15,531	37.6
Degrees Conferred in Law				
1963–1964	10,372	307	10,670	2.8
1973–1974	25,986	3,340	29,326	11.5
1983–1984	23,382	13,630	37,012	36.8
1992–1993	23,182	17,120	40,302	42.5

C. Women have made smaller gains in engineering.

Bachelor's Degrees Conferred in Engineering				
1963–4	35,067	159	35,226	.4
1973–1974	49,490	796	50,286	1.5
1983–1984	82,092	12,093	94,185	12.8
1992–1993	66,836	11,215	78,051	14.3

D. The gender distribution in some areas is unchanged. Women still take home two-thirds of the Bachelor's degrees in English literature.

Degrees Conferred in English literature				
1967–8	15,700	32,277	47,977	67.3
1973–1974	20,214	34,376	54,590	62.9
1983–1984	11,170	21,664	32,834	65.9
1992–1993	19,247	36,886	56,133	65.7

Source: U.S. Department of Education. *Digest of Education Statistics, 1995.* Washington, D.C.: Government Printing Office, 1995, pp. 176, 228, 279, 299.

Education. At stake was a potential redistribution of financial resources from males to females. Redistributive issues usually provoke intense political conflict (Smith, 1975). At one point, an NCAA ally, Senator John Tower (D.-Tex.), introduced a bill to exempt revenue-producing sports from coverage of Title IX. The DHEW's 1975 guidelines permitted high schools and colleges to retain football and basketball and other all-male teams in contact sports, but they did not settle the issue of funding.

What constitutes equal opportunity in athletics? The problem reflects the usual disagreements over the meaning of equality. Feminists looked at the enormous imbalance of resources—in the forms of scholarships, coaching staff, facilities, and supplies—between men's and women's teams. They wanted equal spending. The DHEW agreed and submitted proposed regulations in 1978 to establish "equal per capita spending" as a test of nondiscrimination. All deviations from the standard would have to be explained. The regulations went on to require the institution to work actively to develop women's athletic programs. Major universities and the NCAA wanted to exclude the big-ticket men's sports. They argued there was no equivalent interest or need among the women's sports.

The final regulations adopted in 1979 retreated substantially from the activist stance first proposed. Instead of equal spending, "institutions must provide reasonable opportunities for award [of financial assistance] for members of each sex in proportion to the number of students of each sex participating in . . . inter-collegiate athletics" (*Federal Register* 44, no. 239 [December 11, 1979]: 71415). The schools are to provide teams with "equivalence" of support in categories such as travel and per diem expenses, coaching staff, coaches' salaries, locker rooms and facilities, and publicity. Instead of affirmative action to increase opportunities, institutions need to "accommodate effectively the interests and abilities of students to the extent necessary to provide equal opportunity in the selection of sports and levels of competition available to members of both sexes" (p. 71417). They could retain separate teams by sex when "selection for such teams is based on competitive skill or the activity involved is a contact sport."[5] If the sport was noncontact and the institution provided only one team, members of the excluded sex, if their opportunities have been limited, must be allowed to try out for the available team.

The conflict over equity in athletics and Title IX appeared to be settled. The regulations left big-ticket men's sports untouched while also providing a basis for improved support for women's athletics and opportunities for individual athletes to win scholarships. It may also be the case that the controversy over coverage and enforcement of Title IX itself,

BOX 5.4

Gender Equity in Athletics: Does One-Third Make Half?

A. Percentage of athletes in intercollegiate sports who are women

1970–1971	7%
1972–1973	17
1976–1977	23
1980–1981	35
1993–1994	35

B. Colleges awarding athletic scholarships to women

In 1973, 60 colleges offered athletic scholarships to women.
In 1981, 500 colleges offered athletic scholarships to women.

C. Percentage of all athletic scholarships awarded to women

1972	1%
1981	22
1991	31

D. Division I ratio of women to men

For every female athlete, there are 2.24 male athletes.

For every woman receiving a scholarship, 2.28 men receive scholarships.

For every dollar spent recruiting women, $4.82 are spent recruiting men.

For every dollar spent on women's sports, $3.42 are spent on men's.

Source: U.S. Department of Education, National Advisory Council on Women's Education Programs. *Title IX: Half Full, Half Empty.* Washington, D.C.: GPO, Fall, 1981, pp. 41, 44–45; NCAA. *Gender Equity Study.* Overland Park, Kans., 1992.

which unfolded during the 1980s (see next section), provided a mask for many college sports programs to accommodate both football and more women's sports teams. In the 1990s, a combination of improved enforcement and declining revenues brought the issue of gender equity in athletics back to the public agenda.

An example of stronger enforcement is the federal court's ruling in *Cohen v. Brown University.* Brown University had cut two women's teams and two men's teams from its athletic program, a cut the university viewed as scrupulously equal. In 1993, a federal district judge ruled that Brown was out of compliance with Title IX regulations because it was no longer accommodating the interests and abilities of its women students or providing equal opportunity to them. In making this ruling, the court applied guidelines issued by the Office of Civil Rights (OCR) of the Education Department in 1979 for assessing compliance with the Interests and Abilities Requirement in a school where members of one sex have been underrepresented. According to OCR, one of the following alone will do: (1) if levels of sports participation are proportionate to the numbers of women and men in the student body; (2) if the school has a history of expanding opportunities for the underrepresented sex; and (3) if the school is fully and effectively accommodating the interests and abilities of the underrepresented sex. Because the effect of cutting two women's teams left the interests and abilities of women athletes comparatively less accommodated than those of men, Brown was found to be out of compliance.

The initial injunction in 1993 and the 1995 appeal served as catalysts to bring representatives of men's athletics to Congress to complain that Title IX was threatening men's athletic opportunities. While unanimously professing their support for gender equity and women's sports, they presented testimony before a House subcommittee hearing that the *Cohen v. Brown* decision and the OCR regulations required *proportionality*—a quota—as the only indicator of equality. With total budgets for athletic programs finite, men's sports other than football and basketball were suffering because the government was forcing them to play "numbers games." To comply with the law, schools were dropping low-profile men's teams: men's gymnastics had disappeared and wrestling was threatened. Surely, they pleaded, Congress did not intend that equity in athletics would mean fewer opportunities for men. Some coaches asked that Congress exclude football from Title IX coverage altogether.

Defenders of OCR and Title IX enforcement countered that the real problem was huge budgets for men's football and basketball (73 percent of the entire budget for men's athletic programs). When sex-equity guidelines were finally enforced and schools could no longer sacrifice women's participation to these ravenous programs, other men's sports suffered. Advocates for equity proposed a solution to the problem that would protect both men's participation and gender equity: cut back on football expenses. Countering the myth that football is a revenue producer (most operate in deficit), advocates for women's sports cautioned against blaming women for the problems of men's sports.

The debate over athletics is a difficult one for Congress to settle. It has the features of what political scientists call *redistributive* policy. Such policies require that for some groups to get resources others must be deprived of them. Thus, for women to gain opportunity, in the absence of infinite funding, money must be redirected from men's sports. The question is, which men's sports will take the hit? Will football and basketball be protected while other men's sports suffer? Or will the solution be to cut back on opportunity for women? In the 104th Congress, with its new Republican majority, football advocates saw an opportunity to weaken Title IX; proposals circulated to require the Department of Education to issue new "specific" guidelines on meeting the "interests and abilities" requirement. Conflicts over redistributive policies are often intense and protracted. As such, the battle over Title IX and athletics represents one of the more heated skirmishes in the political battle of the sexes.

Enforcement: A Continuing Controversy

If the conflict over enforcement of Title IX is an indication, even the narrow definitions of sex equity used within the Department of Education regulations don't sit well.[6] The enforcement task is enormous. There are thousands of colleges and universities and sixteen thousand school districts to oversee. Most of the responsibilities for enforcement lie with the recipients of federal aid themselves. Some critics have likened the enforcement role of these recipients to that of the proverbial fox guarding the chickens. The Office of Civil Rights (OCR) of the Department of Education receives and investigates complaints from students and teachers. The OCR's main weapon for enforcing compliance is the threat of cutting federal financial aid. The zeal with which OCR undertakes its enforcement responsibilities is bound to vary with the priorities of particular administrations.

In 1979, the Supreme Court ruled that those who believe they have been victims of discrimination do not have to wait for OCR to investigate; they can sue the school directly in court (*Cannon v. University of Chicago*). Such lawsuits gained considerable clout in 1991 when the Court concluded that "a damages remedy is available for an action brought to enforce Title IX" (*Franklin v. Gwinnett Cty. Public Schools*, p. 76). There is nothing like making administrators liable for monetary penalties to cause school districts and universities to pay heed to Title IX regulations.

With these added tools, enforcement of Title IX has been strengthened. This is remarkable in light of the uneven record of the first twenty years. During that period, implementation of Title IX was delayed by a combination of opposition to federal control of education policy plus the irritation of educators who found long-standing traditions and practices suddenly labeled "sex discrimination." After 1972, school officials tried everything to delay: private colleges refused to supply salary information; thousands of school districts resisted filing necessary compliance reports; and supervisors harassed faculty members who brought complaints.

Controversy over the content of regulations, especially those related to athletics, also slowed enforcement during the 1970s. Litigation cut it back in the 1980s. The first Supreme Court challenge came in *North Haven v. Bell* (1982) over whether Title IX banned discrimination in the employment of teachers and administrators. Although the statute's language was ambiguous with respect to the coverage of employment, the DHEW's 1975 regulations went ahead and included detailed responsibilities of recipient institutions for nondiscrimination in hiring, promotions, pay, and terminations. Challenged by the North Haven School District, the OCR held up more than two hundred complaints until the Supreme Court ruled that Title IX did indeed include a ban on discrimination in education employment. This was an important ruling, especially in light of the evidence presented during 1970 congressional hearings on the subject of underrepresentation of women in decision-making positions throughout the education hierarchy. However, the *North Haven v. Bell* decision occurred when leadership at the Department of Education was especially unenthusiastic about Title IX enforcement. Part of Ronald Reagan's campaign for the presidency in 1980 had been a pledge to reduce government bureaucracy by eliminating the Department of Education altogether. Even if the president had supported an activist Office of Civil Rights, it would have been only two years until the Supreme Court would have taken away the bulk of Title IX's effectiveness in its decision in *Grove City College v. Bell* (1984).

The motive behind *Grove City College* was to challenge the federal government's use of its own spending power to determine the policies throughout an educational institution. Grove City College was proud to be independent of federal subsidies, but it did allow federal financial aid for its students. However, the college objected to the federal government's control over the college's employment, admissions, organizations, and athletics—activities not remotely related, in its administrators' opinion, to student aid. After hearing this case, the Supreme Court agreed to a narrow interpretation of Title IX's language, concluding that Congress intended to prohibit discrimination only in the specific program or activity receiving the federal money, not in the entire institution or school district.

This decision sank hopeful hearts not only among women's rights groups but also in the entire civil rights community. Title IX language, which was copied directly from Title VI of the Civil Rights Act of 1964 banning race discrimination, was also used in statutes protecting against age and disability discrimination. A coalition was formed, including advocates from all affected interests and groups. The coalition promoted the Civil Rights Restoration Act, which defined *program or activity* to include all the policies and practices of a recipient institution. The issue quickly lost its identity as a gender-equity issue and became a test of the federal government's authority in all aspects of civil rights. The conservatives, including President Reagan's administration, labeled the bill a "power grab," raising the specter of federal intrusion into businesses of all sizes. Most agreed that they had little trouble with Title IX itself, and some feminists were frustrated that their issue had been converted into something much more controversial. As the coalition grew, so did the conflict. When conservatives offered to amend Title IX without accepting the demands of the other groups, some feminists were tempted to accept that offer. Their coalition partners made it clear, however, that *they* would work actively to defeat any bill limited to Title IX and sex discrimination.

The Civil Rights Restoration Act eventually passed in 1988 over President Reagan's veto. Finally, the issue of Title IX coverage was settled—sixteen years after the law's enactment. Although it is hard to tell how much damage was done to the campaign for equality in education for women in the four years the *Grove City College* precedent was in force, two other points are clear: the policy to achieve sex equity in education is uneven, and there have been recurring conflicts limiting enforcement. Sometimes, the most important effect of the federal education law seems to be that it is a resource for women working with local schools and universities to promote equal opportunity and women's rights. For example, untold numbers of school districts have complied with Title IX regulations because of pressure from local interest groups. And the threat of a lawsuit can encourage university presidents to respond to complaints from faculty members and students. But patterns of compliance are likely to be uneven, depending not only on the disagreements in the education and feminist communities over the definitions and goals of equity but also on the recurring controversy over the role and powers of the federal government in achieving them. Education reforms are difficult to sustain, and their effects are known only decades after they have been put in place.

Other Gender-Equity Policies

Women's Educational Equity Act of 1974

"A program with no director, with a staff of one and one-quarter persons located in two different offices of the Department of Education and operating under threat of extinction for a decade. . . ." (U.S.G.A.O., 1994, p. 6) Such was the General Accounting Office's assessment of the Women's Education Equity Act (WEEA) in 1994. WEEA was enacted in 1974 in the wake of Title IX. Whereas Title IX was primarily a regulatory law—setting forth requirements and prohibitions to end sex discrimination— WEEA was its substantive counterpart. It authorized funds to assist educators in developing nonsexist materials and textbooks, in changing programs of teacher training, in supporting research, and in developing bias-free counseling materials. WEEA also established a women's policy office—the National Advisory Council on Women's Education Programs—at the Department of Education and made that office responsible for overseeing the gender-equity policy.

The Reagan and Bush administrations put forth no effort to fund WEEA, and it survived into the 1990s only by token funding from Congress. The National Advisory Council was abolished in 1988. Always puny by federal budget standards, WEEA's appropriation dwindled from a high of $10 million in 1980 to less than $2 million by 1992. The feminist education lobby, the National Coalition for Women and Girls in Education (NCWGE), began a new campaign for gender equity in education, using the findings of an influential report by the American Association of University Women (AAUW)—*How Schools Shortchange Girls* (1992). Part of the campaign included the reinvigoration of WEEA and increased funding. In 1995, the appropriation was up to $5 million and WEEA became part of the omnibus education policy enacted by the 103rd Congress. In the 1996 budget battles, however, WEEA funding went to zero.

Carl D. Perkins Vocational Education Act of 1984

The 1976 amendments to the Vocational Education Act of 1963 required states that receive funds for vocational education programs to include efforts to integrate vocational classes and reduce barriers caused by sex ste-

BOX 5.5

The Gender Divide in Vocational Education: Can It Be Bridged?

Despite federal legislation in 1969 to bridge the gap, the gender divide in vocational education persists. The figures are percentages of high school graduates completing one or more courses in programs aimed toward specific labor markets in agriculture, business, marketing, health, home economics, trade and industry, and technical and communications fields. Only in marketing is there equal participation of women and men.

Year	Agric.	Bus.	Market	Health	Hom/Ec.	T&I	T&C
1969							
Male	5.4	31.0	3.8	0.0	1.2	63	.3
Female	1.8	60.5	5.2	.6	4.4	6.2	.3
1979–82							
Male	16.7	34.6	9.0	.6	4.0	69.2	15.0
Female	5.8	65.5	11.4	5.8	15.0	17.1	11.6
1987							
Male	12.5	42.5	7.4	2.7	5.2	61.3	28.2
Female	3.8	64.6	9.9	6.9	15.6	15.2	21.4
1992							
Male	14.0	48.1	8.5	2.5	5.4	54.1	25.3
Female	5.3	63.5	8.5	5.5	16.6	15.8	21.2

Agric.: Includes courses preparing students for employment in farming, horticulture, fishing, or forestry.

Bus.: Offers training in business support and business management, including data processing, accounting, shorthand, stenography, advanced typing, and recordkeeping, as well as finance, investments, personnel and other aspects of management, library science, and security services.

Market: Includes courses related to the selling and distribution of goods and services, teaching skills ranging from cash register operation to marketing and management research.

Health: Courses for careers in health professions, such as nurses, dental assistants, lab technicians, and ambulance operators.

Hom/Ec.: Occupational home economics, including child care, food preparation, cleaning services, plant maintenance, and protection services.

T&I: Trade and industry area, including construction, mechanics, and precision production, such as woodworking, graphic design, printing, sheet metal, and architecture.

T&C: Technical and communication, including courses related to skills used in television and radio, as well as computer courses such as programming.

Source: U.S. Department of Education. *Vocational Education in the United States: 1969–1990.* Washington, D.C.: GPO, 1992, p. 35; U.S. Department of Education. *Vocational Education in the United States: The Early 1990s.* Washington, D.C.: GPO, 1995, p. 147.

reotyping and sex bias. To oversee this goal, each state was required to designate a sex-equity coordinator. To ensure the states' attention to sex equity, the Carl D. Perkins Vocational Education Act of 1984 established set-asides: a percentage of a state's federal funds for vocational education would be earmarked for programs aimed at developing marketable skills and support services for single parents and displaced homemakers. The act was reauthorized in 1990, increasing the percentage set aside and strengthening the ability of the sex-equity coordinators to be more assertive in eliminating sex stereotyping and discrimination in vocational education programs, especially in elementary and secondary schools.

Elementary and Secondary Education Act of 1994

The 1992 AAUW study had documented the persistence of gender bias and a "chilly climate" inhibiting full educational opportunity for girls and women. Inspired by that study, the National Coalition for Women and Girls in Education launched a campaign to integrate gender-equity provisions into this major educational initiative early in President Clinton's first term. They were successful in inserting into the final bill several goals drawn from their action agenda. For the most part, however, the Elementary and Secondary Education Act (ESEA) of 1994 relies on the voluntary cooperation of school districts in working toward those goals. The ESEA expanded WEEA and encouraged teacher training to overcome persistent gender bias in classroom treatment of boys and girls. It set priorities on ways of bringing more girls and women into math and science programs and placed a special emphasis on education programs to deter sexual harassment and abuse. The act also created a special assistant for gender equity in the Department of Education to advise the secretary and coordinate efforts of other agencies and departments.

Contract with America, 1994

The 1994 elections not only changed the majority party in Congress but also brought in a Republican party leadership with an agenda that included enacting programs to change the relationship between the federal government and the states as well as cutting spending and balancing the budget. Slogans about ending "federal mandates" provided a way to put a halt to trends toward national education funding and standards that had been building for over thirty years. The policy mechanism for the major change would be replacing individually funded programs, like WEEA or the Perkins Act, with block grants: Congress would develop a formula for distributing funds to the states to use as they saw fit, within general funding categories. If successful, this approach would end policies outlined in WEEA, the Perkins Act, and ESEA. Advocates for gender equity in education would thus have to shift attention to the state level and campaign within each state and locality to develop substantive programs for ending gender bias. The outcome of such a shift is bound to be spotty.

Title IX is not an appropriations act, and it would therefore not be directly affected by the block-grant approach unless federal aid to education were entirely eliminated. Nevertheless, the ideology of a more conservative Republican majority is likely to undermine support for aggressive enforcement of the act by the administration. And, as we have seen in the area of athletics regulations, if school administrators lose many court cases, they are going to be strongly tempted to ask the conservatives to amend Title IX to eliminate its bite into business as usual.

Policies in the States

Federal policies provide uniformity in national standards of equal educational opportunity. By setting national goals and regulations that apply to all recipients of federal aid, these policies can shape activities of private schools and colleges, which possess some of the most valued educational resources in the United States. Despite fluctuations in federal attention to education, most of the funding and direction of education resides with states and local school boards. All states are covered by Title IX, yet they comply at different levels. The extent to which education authorities go beyond the limits of Title IX compliance is affected by the culture of the state and the political debate as it unfolds. For example, states with a more active stance on civil rights are also likely to be more active in eliminating sex discrimination in education and in improving educational opportunities for girls. State laws on sex equity in education can be classified into three types:

1. Comprehensive laws banning sex discrimination in all areas at all public institutions. Some of these laws reach beyond Title IX, to include training counselors, designing curricula, and eliminating sexist educational materials. Others are patterned after the federal legislation.

2. General human rights laws, public-accommodations statutes, or equal-rights amendments to state constitutions that cover sex

discrimination in education as part of an equal rights amendment. Although states within this category have statutes or amendments prohibiting such discrimination, they have no comprehensive statute or special enforcement mechanism.

3. No statutes or constitutional provisions have been passed.

It is risky to give exact numbers, since state statutes may change or be modified in any legislative session, but roughly one-third of the states comprise each of these three groups.

Single-Sex Schools

If gender equity in education is defined as a policy modeled after race equity, then U.S. education policy falls short of equity. The race model envisions the integration of all educational programs and activities. However, Title IX does not require integration of all schools; single-sex schools remain. Men and women seeking entrance to single-sex schools have challenged their constitutionality under the Equal Protection Clause. Feminists remain ambivalent about integration of the sexes in schools. Males and females have associated together in schools for a long time, evidence that coeducation does not necessarily mean equality of benefits for all. Some feminists, in fact, want to retain the right to have separate schools for girls under specific circumstances.

Feminists' and educators' acceptance of single-sex schools accounts for the different constitutional status of sex segregation and race segregation. *Brown v. Board of Education* (1954) banished the constitutional concept that education for black Americans and white Americans could be separate but not equal. Single-sex public schools, however, are not absolutely prohibited by the Constitution. How can segregation of the sexes be reconciled with bans on sex discrimination under Title IX and the Equal Protection Clause of the Fourteenth Amendment?

Most civil rights advocates agree that race-specific schools put a badge of inferiority on the minority race. Women's rights advocates, however, do not agree that a women's college or an all-girl high school will automatically be inferior and consequently stereotype women to inferior jobs and social roles. In fact, many contend that single-sex schools can actually help women because the absence of males requires women or girls to take all the various leadership roles. All-female sports teams do not automatically have the second-class status they do in mixed schools. These women's rights advocates point out that, in integrated classes, women are often intimidated by the presence of males but that, in women's colleges, women take an active part in all discussions. In contrast, these feminists contend, girls who go to school with boys often adapt to a male culture and power structure, which defines women as inferior. And professors in coeducational colleges often treat females differently, refusing to accept them as serious students (Hall and Sandler, 1982, p. 293). Under such conditions, learning to "get along" with boys may mean either competing with them according to male rules or gaining acceptance according to male-defined values of female achievement. In girls' schools, these advocates point out, there are no male-dominated fields. The curriculum encourages women to go into nontraditional disciplines; there are no informal sex-role barriers to the study of science and mathematics.

Other feminists oppose sex segregation, pointing out that even the best women's colleges have less prestige than the best traditionally all-men's colleges (most of which are now coed). The badge of inferiority is evident, they say. Does being class president in a women's college mean the same thing as being elected president in a coed school? These women's rights advocates suggest that only through competition with men in classrooms will women develop assertive skills to enable them to succeed in the business world and politics. They also point out that both women and men need to learn to work together to prepare them for the increasingly diversified workplace.

Another consideration for the critics of a policy that permits single-sex schools is that it could perpetuate all-male schools—assisted by public funds. Military schools, especially, offer a type of training and prestige not available at any other schools. Thus to retain the all-female environment for some, other women would be denied access to these publicly supported institutions because of their sex.

The division among women's rights advocates helps sustain in admissions policies the balanced definition of sex equity that exists in the federal law. Admissions bans or quotas denying women access to job training and professions have no support and are prohibited because policy makers see a clear relationship between the single-sex policy and the denial of equal employment opportunities. Traditional justification of these practices—that it is a waste of resources to prepare women for the professions of law, business, and medicine because women will just get married and quit—disappeared from the public debate of the 1970s. However, Title IX expressly requires open admissions *only* in professional and graduate schools, vocational schools, and public undergraduate colleges that are not traditionally single-sex. (Military schools, which are most likely to be single sex, are excluded from complying.) Otherwise, where there are a variety of choices among schools and universities, a particular institution could remain single-sex. Policy makers reason that an individual would not be deprived of educational opportunity and would be able to find another place to achieve educational goals. Thus, Title IX left untouched such schools as the Virginia Military Institute, the Citadel, Texas Woman's University, and Wellesley College, along with a variety of other schools from preschool through high school. Prep schools can receive public funds and still restrict admissions to one sex. Fewer than one-third of the states explicitly prohibit single-sex public schools. Of course, for historical reasons, nearly all public schools and universities are coeducational, but not because the law prohibits segregation in admissions. Other pressures may force the few remaining single sex schools to open their doors to both males and females, but Title IX will not be the reason.

Judicial interpretation of sex segregation under the Fourteenth Amendment's Equal Protection Clause may end government's role in operating segregated institutions. The first round of litigation, in the 1970s, established the principle that single-sex schools were not inherently a violation of the Constitution; they were prohibited only if plaintiffs demonstrated that they were denied an educational opportunity not available in any other institution in the system. The second round, at the Supreme Court, has abolished the few remaining traditionally single-sex state schools—the all-male military academies.

In *Kirstein v. University of Virginia* (1970) a federal district court ruled that the undergraduate college of the University of Virginia had to admit women as well as men because it offered a quality of educational opportunity not available at other public institutions in the state. The all-male policy denied women plaintiffs "their constitutional right to an education equal with that offered men at Charlottesville" (p. 187). Presumably, if Mary Washington, the women's college, had at that time offered an equal course with equal prestige, the Court would have been satisfied with keeping both schools segregated. Such was the reasoning by a district court in *Williams v. McNair,* also decided in 1970. In that case, men sought admission to South Carolina's then all-female Winthrop College.

The court ruled and the Supreme Court affirmed, however, that in South Carolina there were coeducational colleges offering courses similar to those offered by Winthrop. Men's opportunity for education was not being denied by the legislature's decision to keep one of its colleges female.[7]

In 1977, the Supreme Court affirmed a lower court's decision sustaining single-sex high schools in Philadelphia. The Court ruled in *Vorchheimer v. School District of Philadelphia* that two schools, which were established for a small percentage of exceptional students, provided equal quality. The Court was satisfied that students in Philadelphia, depending on their ability, had a full range of choices in schools. The Court reviewed arguments from educators showing that separating sexes in adolescence encouraged a better educational experience. So segregation could benefit both girls and boys; it was not a denial of any opportunity. To rule against the Philadelphia schools would have abolished all public single-sex high schools. "It follows too," the judge concluded, "those students who prefer an education in a public, single-sex school would be denied their freedom of choice" (*Vorchheimer v. School District of Philadelphia*, p. 888; 832 F. 2d 880, affirmed by an equally divided Court in 430 U.S. 730, 1977).[8]

The Supreme Court issued its first opinion on this subject in *Mississippi v. Hogan* (1982). The Court applied the *middle-level scrutiny test* to a policy of single-sex schools, in this case the all-female nursing program at Mississippi University for Women (MUW). Still, the Court refused to consider the constitutionality of single-sex schools in general. Instead, it ruled very narrowly, saying that the state failed to show that barring men from the nursing program was related to an important governmental objective. The state's argument—that its policy constituted affirmative action for women—was rejected: "Rather than compensate for discriminatory barriers faced by women, MUW's policy of excluding males from admission to the School of Nursing tends to perpetuate the stereotyped view of nursing as an exclusively woman's job" (p. 729). The Court refused to consider the larger issue of "separate but equal" or whether the university had to admit males to programs other than nursing.[9]

In 1996, the Supreme Court finally took on the question of whether a state may maintain programs or schools separated by sex. This issue was presented to the Court by the U.S. government's suit against the state of Virginia for operating the all-male Virginia Military Institute (VMI). The federal attorney general argued that the state violates the Equal Protection Clause of the Fourteenth Amendment by restricting admission to

VMI to men. Virginia's defense tried to link its desire to maintain the all-male student body at VMI to an important state objective—training citizen soldiers. This training, called "adversative" involved "physical rigor, mental stress, absolute equality of treatment, absence of privacy, minute regulation of behavior, and indoctrination of values" (*U.S. v. Virginia* [1992], p. 893). Such training, Virginia argued, could not occur if the student body included both men and women.

The district and circuit courts agreed that "it is the homogeneity of gender in the process, regardless of which sex is considered, that has been shown to be related to the essence of the education and training at VMI" (p. 897). At the same time, they ruled that Virginia violated the constitution by denying women the opportunity to receive such military training. Virginia was given three options: admit women to VMI; establish a separate but equal training program for women; or convert VMI to a private institution outside the reach of the Constitution's Equal Protection Clause. VMI opted to establish the Virginia Military Institute for Leadership (VMIL) for women at Mary Baldwin College.

The Supreme Court found VMI's VMIL program to be unequal in all respects and thus found that it denied the women of Virginia equal protection. The Court did not go so far as to issue a blanket prohibition on single-sex educational institutions (as they have done for race), but it is clear that such programs are not acceptable when they are based on traditional views of gender differences. In her opinion, Justice Ruth Bader Ginsburg clarified the test for determining the constitutionality of gender-based state laws:[10]

1. The state must demonstrate an "exceedingly persuasive" justification that, as in *Hogan*, the gender-based program has a substantial relationship to important government objectives. The burden for this demonstration rests with the state. (p. 2274)

2. The state "must describe actual purposes, not rationalizations for the actions in fact differently grounded." (p. 2267)

To summarize, the public policy for equality in education is a moderate one and demonstrates the limits of using the race analogy as a model for women's rights policy. Equity for females and males does not necessarily mean integration of the sexes. Rather, it is measured by the access individuals have to educational facilities and opportunities. Title IX mandates that barriers to education clearly related to professions and jobs be lowered. When a school does integrate the sexes, it must retain no internal barriers that reflect different treatment. When single-sex schools are permitted under the Fourteenth Amendment and Title IX in the context of "separate but equal," the schools that decide to admit some girls or women may not treat them differently through quotas or different admissions standards. So far, some separation is permitted, but inequality is not. Even in the area of individual rights, federal regulations permit exceptions that recognize traditions of gender-role separation, especially in organizations and athletics. The United States does not, by and large, have an activist education policy to secure equality-of-education results for persons regardless of sex.

Women's Studies

The gender-equity policies on the books go only part way toward achieving a feminist vision of equal opportunity in education. Except for a few state laws and the weak Women's Education Equity Act, gender-equity policies deal only with administrative procedures, not with the content of education. These policies conform to the liberal ideology of the individual's right to an opportunity to secure the benefits of education resources; these policies do not change the substance of education or empower women to create knowledge and shape the values that make up the culture. Knowledge of the origins of our male-dominated society and the support it receives from social and cultural structures has been a crucial component of the contemporary women's movement and the contribution most likely to sustain a transformation of gender roles. Women's studies has been called "the educational arm of the women's *liberation* movement" (Kramarae and Spender, 1992, p. 3).

Women's rights advocates have long recognized that education has political value. Knowing the history of suffrage, for example, can inspire women to join the fight for equality. Women's studies goes beyond the patriarchal system to discover and cultivate the culture of women themselves. Thus it challenges the way things are and places the conventional theories and frameworks of all disciplines under critical examination. A product of such criticism is new knowledge about women and gender relations that may replace, or at least greatly alter, the intellectual underpinnings of patriarchy. By developing women's own culture—including values, history, art, literature, and politics—women can seek equality without copying male culture. Women's studies also provides space for women with diverse racial, ethnic, religious, and cultural identities to explore gender relations within these groups.

Scattered courses in women's history appeared in universities as early as the late 1940s (Rupp and Taylor, 1987, pp. 70–71). Thus it was to be expected that a part of the contemporary feminist movement would focus on the development of new courses in colleges and universities. There is still a debate over which college had the first course that used a critical feminist perspective to study women. What is certain, however, is that such courses have proliferated, with the result that women's studies has become a part of most colleges and universities in undergraduate certificate or degree programs and a growing number of master's and doctoral offerings.

Feminists in the 1970s who were seeking federal funds for the study of women at all levels of education proposed a Women's Studies Act. As groups met to prepare a campaign for the act, the focus of the proposal changed from studying women to developing new educational materials to combat sexism and sex stereotyping. The groups agreed that eliminating sexism was a way to achieve gender equity, and they decided to cast their proposal in egalitarian, rather than pro-woman, language. With these changes, their proposal, which they presented as a companion to Title IX, also underwent a change in name. It became the Women's Educational Equity Act. (See earlier discussion in this chapter.)

That women's studies programs have grown enormously in the past thirty years is the result of the widespread interest of women in various academic disciplines. Women's studies programs have secured support from the administrations of universities and colleges and from the private sector. The networks of libraries, women's studies programs, publishers, and journals that foster scholarship in women's studies are growing in the absence of any conscious public policy to develop them. The changes in the content of education and culture that develop from the growth of research and teaching in women's studies will have the most far-reaching effect on educational opportunities for women.

Conclusion

For most of U.S. history, policy debates about education have focused on the purpose of education for girls and women. In some ways, they still do.

Concepts of equality have not produced a national policy of gender neutrality and sex integration that would officially obliterate notions of gender differences in education. Feminists are among those least committed to neutrality while they devote their energies to developing women's studies.

Policy debates on education are very complex, and issues of women's rights—even in areas where advocates agree—confront other obstacles. National policies get tied up in the battles over states' rights and resentment over federal regulations. Title IX enforcement was delayed for years as Grove City College and then conservatives fought against federal interference. Now national education programs are caught up in the struggle between Republicans and Democrats over finding ways to balance the budget. A basic issue is the choice of the programs—and the people these programs benefit—that will bear the cost of reducing the deficit. Adding to this complexity is the fact that U.S. education takes place in both public and private institutions, and policies affect them differently. The private ones often have the most valuable benefits, yet, as compared with public institutions, private institutions by their nature limit access. Policy makers have been reluctant to force all private and public schools and colleges to open their doors completely to both sexes. There is a national commitment now to the concept of equal access to educational opportunity and to an education policy that does not discriminate against members of one sex. However, what is meant by women's right to equal opportunity in education remains a matter for continuing debate.

Florence Howe (1984), founding editor of the Feminist Press and pioneer in women's studies, has outlined three great phases in women's education. The first phase separated woman into her sphere as virtuous wife and mother. Public-education policy valued the female role and turned it into a profession, bringing women into the classroom as moral leaders, teachers of the young, and transmitters of civic virtue to the society. The second phase emphasized the equal capacity of women to benefit from the educational opportunities enjoyed by men. Sex equity meant the right of women to seek education and professions identical to those of men. In the third phase, women have asserted their right to develop new knowledge by applying a framework of gender roles and a feminist lens to discovering and analyzing information. In this phase, women will challenge and change forever the intellectual tradition they receive, and for the first time they will exert control over the content of education for both men and women.[11]

Notes

1. Later, when schools were established for former slaves, many communities willingly bore the cost of race-segregated schools at all levels.

2. The policy of admitting women was often a token gesture. For example, the Montana School of Mines had three women in its second graduating class in 1904. Its next female student to receive a degree in engineering graduated in the 1970s.

3. The regulations were published in the *Federal Register* 40, no. 108 (June 4, 1975): 24128–24145.

4. The content of textbooks is a complex problem and requires a number of approaches. State and local school administrators usually select public school textbooks, and some have guidelines requiring a balance in presentation and the use of nonsexist language. Publishers in turn instruct authors to conform to these rules. Women's caucuses in various disciplines may monitor college-level textbooks. The attitudes of the faculty members selecting textbooks gradually change, both in response to efforts by publishers and women's caucuses, and in response to social change and awareness. In this process, the more blatantly sexist materials are retired.

5. Title IX regulations defined contact sports as "boxing, wrestling, rugby, ice hockey, football, basketball and other sports the purpose or major activity of which involves bodily contact" (*Federal Register* 40, no. 108, [June 4, 1975]: 24142–24143).

6. In 1978, Congress separated the education administration from the Department of Health, Education, and Welfare to create a new cabinet department, the Department of Education, charged with enforcing Title IX.

7. In 1974, Winthrop College changed its females only policy, and in 1992 it became Winthrop University. There are no longer any publicly run, all-female colleges in the United States.

8. In 1983, a state court in Pennsylvania declared that the two high schools in Philadelphia were unequal and violated the Fourteenth Amendment. The court used the middle-level scrutiny test and cited *Mississippi v. Hogan* (1982). It called the theory of single-gender schools "vague and unsubstantiated" (*Newbury v. Board of Public Education*, 26 Pa D & C. 682 [1983]).

9. "Mississippi maintains no other single-sex public university or college. Thus we are not faced with the question of whether the states can provide separate but equal undergraduate institutions for males and females" (*Mississippi v. Hogan*, 1982, p. 720, fn.1) The Court further stated, "Because Hogan's claim is limited . . . we decline to address the question of whether MUW's admissions policies, as applied to males seeking admission to schools other than the School of Nursing, violate the Fourteenth Amendment" (p. 723; fn. 7).

10. Virginia failed this test when it argued that diversity was the goal for maintaining an all-male VMI. Ginsburg pointed out that in 1839, when VMI was established, the goal was expulsion of women from all higher education.

11. For information on the changes that women's studies have brought about in research and teaching in a variety of disciplines, and for an analysis of the barriers that remain, see Kramarae and Spender (1992).

References

American Association of University Women. *How Schools Shortchange Girls.* Washington, D.C.: AAUW, 1992.

Boxer, Marilyn. "For and About Women: The Theory and Practice of Women's Studies in the United States." *Signs* 7, no. 3 (1982): 661–695.

Brown v. Board of Education. 347 U.S. 483. 1954.

Burge, Penny L., and Culver, Steven M. "Sexism, Legislative Power, and Vocational Education." In *Gender in the Classroom: Power and Pedagogy,* edited by Susan L. Gabriel and Isaiah Smithson, pp. 160–175. Urbana: University of Illinois Press, 1990.

Burstall, Sara A. *The Education of Girls in the United States.* London: Swan Sonnenschein, 1894. Reprint. New York: Arno, 1971.

Cannon v. University of Chicago. 441 U.S. 677. 1979.

Cohen v. Brown University. 991 F.2d 888. 1993; 897 F.Supp. 185 (D.R.I. 1995).

Fishel, Andrew, and Pottker, Janice, eds. *National Politics and Sex Discrimination in Education.* Lexington, Ky.: Lexington Books, 1977.

Flexner, Eleanor. *Century of Struggle.* 1959. Reprint. Cambridge: Belknap Press, 1975.

Franklin v. Guinnett Cty. Public Schools. 503 U.S. 60. 1992.

Grove City College v. Bell. 465 U.S. 555. 1984.

Hall, Roberta M., and Sandler, Bernice. "The Classroom Climate: A Chilly One for Women." 1982. In *The Law of Sex Discrimination,* edited by J. Ralph Lindgren and Nadine Taub, pp. 293–296. St. Paul: West Publishing Co., 1988.

Hole, Judith, and Levine, Ellen. *Rebirth of Feminism.* New York: Quadrangle Books, 1972.

Howe, Florence. *Myths of Coeducation.* Bloomington: Indiana University Press, 1984.

Kirstein v. University of Virginia. 309 F. Supp. 184. 1970.

Kraditor, Aileen. *Up from the Pedestal.* New York: Quadrangle Books, 1968.

Kramarae, Cheris, and Spender, Dale, eds. *The Knowledge Explosion: Generations of Feminist Scholarship.* New York: Teachers College Press, 1992.

Mead, Margaret, and Kaplan, Frances Balgley. *American Women.* New York: Scribner's, 1965.

Mississippi v. Hogan. 458 U.S. 718. 1982.

Newbury v. Board of Public Education. 26 Pa D&C. 682. 1983.

North Haven v. Bell. 456 U.S. 512. 1982.

President's Task Force on Women's Rights and Responsibilities. *Task Force Report: A Matter of Simple Justice.* Washington, D.C.: GPO, April 1970.

Rosenberg, Rosalind. *Beyond Separate Spheres.* New Haven: Yale University Press, 1982.

Rothman, Sheila. *A Woman's Proper Place.* New York: Basic Books, 1978.

Rupp, Leila J., and Taylor, Verta. *Survival in the Doldrums: The American Women's Rights Movement, 1945 to the 1960s.* New York: Oxford University Press, 1987.

Salamone, Rosemary. *Equal Education Under Law.* New York: St. Martin's Press, 1986.

Smith, T. Alexander. *The Comparative Policy Process.* Santa Barbara: ABC-Clio, 1975.

U.S. Congress. House. Committee on Economic and Educational Opportunities. Subcommittee on Postsecondary Education, Training, and Life-Long Learning. *Hearing on Title IX of the Education Amendments of 1972.* 104th Cong., 1st sess., 1995.

U.S. Congress. House. Committee on Education and Labor. Subcommittee on Elementary, Secondary, and Vocational Education. *Hearing on Women's Educational Equity Act.* 98th Cong., 2nd sess., 1984.

U.S. Department of Education. *Vocational Education in the United States: 1969–1990.* Washington, D.C.: GPO, 1992.

U.S. General Accounting Office. *Women's Educational Equity Act Program.* Washington, D.C.: GPO, 1994.

U.S. "Nondiscrimination on the Basis of Sex [under] Federally Assisted Education Programs and Activities." *Federal Register* 40, no. 8 (June 4, 1975): 24137–24144.

U.S. "Title IX of the Education Amendment of 1972; a Policy Interpretation; Title IX and Intercollegiate Athletics." *Federal Register* 44, no. 239 (December 11, 1979): 71413–71423.

U.S. v. Virginia. 976 F. 2d. 890. 1992; 52 F. 3d. 90. 1995; 116 SCt 2264. 1996.

Vetter, Louise. "The Vocational Education Option for Women." In *Job Training for Women: The Promise and Limits of Public Policies,* edited by Sharon L. Harlan and Ronnie J. Steinberg, pp. 91–113. Philadelphia: Temple University Press, 1989.

Vorcheimer v. School District of Philadelphia. 832 F. 2d. 880.; affirmed 430 U.S. 730. 1977.

Wandersee, Winifred D. *On the Move: American Women in the 1970s.* Boston: Twayne Publishers, 1988.

Williams v. McNair. 316 F. Supp. 134. 1970.

Wollstonecraft, Mary. *Vindication of the Rights of Woman.* London: Johnson, 1792. Reprint: London: Penguin, 1975.

Woody, Thomas. *A History of Women's Education in the United States,* vols. 1 and 2. Science Press, 1929. Reprint. New York: Octagon Books, 1966.

CHAPTER 6

Family

Of all areas of U.S. public policy, family law appears to be one of the most central to the status and rights of women. The women who in 1848 met in Seneca Falls, New York, for the first women's rights convention placed the issue of women's place in the family high on their agenda. Their Declaration of Sentiments recognized that law had rendered married women "civilly dead" (Stanton, Anthony, and Gage, 1881, p. 70). Men had set up all the rules of marriage and divorce "wholly regardless of the happiness of women . . . going upon a false supposition of the supremacy of man, and giving all power into his hands" (p. 71). Ever since Seneca Falls, women have sought political rights to gain parity in, if not control over, family law. The problem of women's status in the family has not always been cast as such a direct confrontation of male power as in the 1848 declaration. But women's special relation to reproduction and their social role in family formation produces inevitable conflict with men, singly and collectively. The war between men and women is waged, primarily and most directly, in the family.

There are two problems in interpreting women's rights in the family: difficulties in determining what the rules of family law are and difficulties in determining which rules will promote women's rights. The U.S. Constitution places responsibility for family law primarily with the states, through laws on marriage, divorce, and parent-child relationships. The federal government is involved only when constitutional issues are at stake, through Supreme Court decisions, or when Congress stumbles into family matters through its money-spending powers, usually affecting child support. Otherwise, the rights and responsibilities of men and women in marriage, in divorce, and as parents are determined by state governments. This means there are more than fifty different systems of family law—counting the District of Columbia, Puerto Rico, and U.S. territories.[1]

It might be possible to keep up with family law in the fifty states if Americans had a code-law system or if each state had a coherent set of statutes that clearly outlined the state's legal rules and was kept up-to-date as amendments were made. But state family-law regimes are composed not only of many statutes and amendments but also of court interpretations and guidelines. Statutes are usually drafted to be broad guidelines with general language, empowering local courts to reach decisions for each family on a case-by-case basis. Judges, lawyers, and family members themselves vary in their view of the proper rights and responsibilities within the family. Some are feminists; others respect old-fashioned ideals based on patriarchy. What the law is at any time must therefore also include every family's experience in court. Nowhere are the complex implications of our judge-made common-law traditions more evident than in family law.

Patterns of change in family law also reflect this complexity. Some reforms occur through legislative action. For these, it is possible to locate the various definitions of issues at stake in the debate and the role of feminists in the resolution of that conflict. In general, reform issues appear simultaneously in various states. The National Conference of Commissioners on Uniform State Laws, composed of legal experts in many fields, develops model statutes to help state legislators respond to social change. Such legislative direction of law reform is a relatively recent phenomenon. Reforms also continue to come through court decisions and their incremental erosion of precedent. Such change develops from the real grass roots: the pressure represented by contradictions between traditional concepts in the law and actual behavior of individuals in families. At this level, it is possible to glean only a general idea of trends reinforced by reports in legal reference works and law journals.[2]

For the most part, families and family behavior are not of government concern. Family relationships are private, and the pattern of gender-role rights and responsibilities is developed by family members for themselves. These rights and responsibilities need not conform to the official or dominant views. Laws may require husbands to support their wives and may give them sole control over their own salaries and property. In practice, a husband may give his biweekly check to his wife or keep it for himself; he may give her total responsibility or a meager allowance. In two-earner families, where both husband and wife work outside the home, decisions about how these earnings are spent—jointly, separately, or by one spouse alone—are entirely up to the couple. Law may define marriage as between a man and a woman, but it does not prevent two men or two women from establishing a marriagelike bond (see Chapter 9). A couple, even several persons, could form a household with family relationships without any government registration whatsoever. What family law does is grant rights and responsibilities, many of which come into force when conflicts arise (either within families or between families and others) that require a solution from outside or that threaten public interest. Therefore, policy affecting families is most often applied as a consequence of the breakup of families: divorce, alimony and property settlements, and child-custody and child-support arrangements.

There are two ways of looking at family-law issues and women's rights. One is to focus on gender roles, comparing the rights and responsibilities of women with those of men. As with other types of policy, underlying theories of proper gender roles give meaning to the content of official rules and regulations. The second way to study family law follows the first: the effects of gender-role theories on the status of women. This might be a fairly simple task if there were a consensus on values relating to family life in the United States. But there is little agreement and growing unrest. To enact statutes, legislators try to come to some agreement on an official view of family roles. They are unable, however, to control the private views of judges, lawyers, and family members. And it is doubtful that there has ever been complete agreement between the official views and private practices related to the proper roles of women and men in the family. Today, these theories are affected by the diversity of the state cultures, as well as by changing patterns of family relationships. Women's lives and the social attitudes about their roles are in turmoil. Men's place is no more certain, as far as their family lives are concerned.

Feminists have not been central to the debates over family law in legislatures and courts. For one thing, they have not often agreed on what theories and laws would do the most for women's rights. For another, family-law debates have usually been dominated by lawyers who take a special proprietary interest in policy areas that require extensive court litigation. Women's rights activists were most visible in the nineteenth century when campaigns for the reform of family law were central to the movement for women's rights. Before they could claim the vote, married women had to gain some legal independence.

BOX 6.1

Family and the Role of Women

Theorists have notions of women's place in the family, and relate these ideas to general views of society. Here are three different views:

"The rise of capitalism isolated the family from socialized production as it created a historically new sphere of personal life among the masses of people. The family now became the major space in society in which the individual self could be valued 'for itself.' This process, the 'private' accompaniment of industrial development, cut women off from men in a drastic way and gave a new meaning to male supremacy. While housewives and mothers continued their traditional tasks of production—housework, child-rearing, etc.—their labour was devalued through its isolation from the socialized production of surplus value."

Eli Zaretsky, *Capitalism, the Family, and Personal Life* (1976, pp. 31–32).

"It is the isolation and debasement of women under terms of male-dominated ideology and social structures that must be fought, not the activity, the humanizing imperative, of mothering, or of being a parent, itself. Too frequently mothering has been over assimilated to what feminists call 'the shitwork.' Mothers were demeaned under the guise of 'liberating' them. In many early feminist accounts mothering was portrayed as a condition of terminal psychological and social decay, total self-abnegation, physical deterioration and absence of self-respect. Women, already victims of an image that denigrated their social identity under the terms of the male American success ethos, now found themselves assaulted by the very group that would liberate them."

Jean Bethke Elshtain, *Public Man, Private Woman* (1981, pp. 333–334).

"If we are to aim at making the family, our most fundamental social grouping, more just, we must work toward eradicating the socially created vulnerabilities of women that stem from the division of labor and the resultant division of power within it. . . . In order to do anything effective about the cycle of women's socially created vulnerability we must take into account the current lack of clarity in law, public policy, and public opinion about *what marriage is*. Since evidently we

BOX 6.1 *(continued)*

do not all agree about what it is or should be, we must think in terms of building family and work institutions that enable people to structure their personal lives in different ways. If they are to avoid injustice to women and children, these institutions must encourage the avoidance of socially created vulnerabilities by facilitating and reinforcing the equal sharing of paid and unpaid work between men and women, and consequently the equalizing of their opportunities and obligations in general."

Susan Moller Okin, *Justice, Gender, and the Family* (1989, pp. 168–169).

The contemporary women's movement has been especially affected by ambivalence about the family in the context of the changes in women's economic and family roles since 1950. Feminist theory attacks family relationships as the foundation of patriarchal domination of women. To many feminists, power, equality, and liberation for women require a transformation of the intimate relations between men, women, and children. As families adapt to social and economic changes, especially the increased frequency of divorce and single parenthood, advocates for women's rights have struggled to reconcile women's activities in child rearing with their ideals of equity and justice. Some women search for ways to have it all: a career, a husband, children, and a happy home life. Others turn toward other women to create permanent families. But most women live in untransformed families. Research into the contemporary division of labor in families reveals that in most families, women have an unequal burden with both work and family responsibilities. Other women are economically dependent homemakers who may need special protection. Finding a gender-role theory of family rights and responsibilities that improves the status of all women is a problem.

This chapter focuses on major trends in the debate over gender roles in the family as they pertain to laws on marriage, divorce, and parental rights and responsibilities. In each area, the rights and responsibilities of women and men are compared. The effects of these laws on the status of women and the feminist response concludes each section. A final discussion focuses on the laws that affect households and families outside of marriage, with special emphasis on property rights and the custody and support of children.

Marriage

> Other contracts can be modified, restricted, or enlarged, or entirely released upon consent of the parties. Not so with marriage. The relation, once formed, the law steps in and holds the parties to various obligations and liabilities. It is an institution, in the maintenance of which in its purity the public is deeply interested, for it is the foundation of the family and of society, without which there would be neither civilization nor progress. (*Maynard v. Hill*, 1887, p. 211)

Marriage is a special kind of contract: the duties and rewards are specified by the government, not the parties. Although there has been no law against private contracts, courts have tended to take the position that they contradicted public policy defining the duties and privileges of husband and wife. This meant little to couples unless they called upon the courts to enforce private nuptial contracts. Since the courts discouraged suits between spouses in intact marriages, such contractual issues were likely to arise only in cases of separation, divorce, or death. In the 1980s, states began to drop their opposition to prenuptial contracts. Since 1983, half the states have adopted the Uniform Premarital Agreement Act, which sets forth specific categories of marital rights and obligations, particularly in the areas of property and support that can be established through private contract. In determining the obligations of husband and wife, authorities are guided both by prevailing ideologies of gender roles, that is, how men and women should relate in marriage, and by observation of how they do relate.

Gender-Role Relationships Within Marriage

As family law has developed since the founding of the United States, it has been affected by three successive theories of gender-role relationships in marriage—(a) a unity of husband and wife, (b) a separate-but-equal legal status, and (c) a shared equal partnership. Although one or another of these theories has predominated at different times in U.S. history, present family law contains elements of all three.

Coverture: Unity of Husband and Wife

The colonists brought common-law concepts of marriage to America, and the doctrine of coverture became the foundation of marriage law in nearly all the states. *Coverture* (a term describing the status of *femme couverte*, or a covered woman) was based on the concept of marriage as a *unity* of husband and wife. At marriage, a woman's separate status (*femme sole*) disappeared as she came under the legal responsibility and protection of her husband: "By marriage, the husband and wife are one person in law: that is, the very being or existence of the woman is suspended during marriage, or at least is incorporated and consolidated into that of the husband" (Blackstone, 1803, p. 442). All the legal rights and responsibilities a woman had when single transferred to her husband upon marriage. All her property, including wages, came under his control. She had no right to enter into contracts or to sue or be sued. If she committed a tort, the plaintiff had to sue her husband. Since her husband was responsible for her acts, he could restrain her and correct her behavior. The husband's obligations included paying her debts before marriage and providing support afterwards. Common-law coverture made a woman completely financially dependent on her husband for all legal acts: these provisions were called *a married woman's legal disabilities*.

While common law reinforced patriarchal family structures, many of the limitations on women were intended, at least symbolically, for the protection of the wife and mother. But the lawmakers did not intend such protections to extend to African American slaves or Native American women. Then, and since, ethnic minorities have been valued as workers and, in the case of the slaves, as breeders. For many women of color, to be protected by coverture might have seemed an improvement in comparison with their vulnerability to various forms of economic and sexual exploitation. In any case, the questions pertaining to coverture primarily involved wealthy middle-class white women.

The first challenges to coverture came not from emancipated women but from the fathers of wealthy women who sought to keep their family property away from shiftless, irresponsible, or fortune-hunting sons-in-law. One way was to separate such property in an antenuptial marriage settlement. These were made not to give married women property but to protect the property from the husband's creditors and to safeguard it for future generations. The first Married Women's Property Acts (MWPAs) in the United States were enacted in Mississippi in 1839 and Maryland in 1843, and they simply removed a wife's property from liability for her husband's debts.

BOX 6.2

The Debate on Coverture—New York, February 20, 1854

"Look at the position of woman as wife. Your laws relating to marriage—founded as they are on the old common law of England, a compound of barbarous usages, but partially modified by progressive civilization—are in open violation of our enlightened ideas of justice and of the holiest feelings of our nature. . . . Do not by your special legislation for this one kind of contract, involve yourselves in the grossest absurdities and contradictions."

Elizabeth Cady Stanton, woman's rights leader

" . . . the object of these unsexed women is to overthrow the most sacred of our institutions, to set at defiance the Divine law which declares man and wife to be one, and establish on its ruins what will be in fact and in principle but a species of legalized adultery. . . . Are we to put the stamp of truth upon the libel here set forth, that men and women, in the matrimonial relation, are to be equal?"

Mr. Burnett, chair of the New York Judiciary Committee

Source: Elizabeth Cady Stanton, Susan B. Anthony, and Matilda Joslyn Gage. *History of Woman Suffrage,* Vol 1. 1848–1861, Rochester, N.Y.: Charles Mann, 1889, pp. 598, 613.

Although not inspired by concerns for the rights of a married woman to her property or by a desire to change concepts of gender roles in marriage, these statutes were the beginning of a process of statutory reform that gradually chipped away at common-law coverture. During the nineteenth century, MWPAs were adopted in every state. They were amended many times and the subject of much interpretation by the courts.

Women's rights advocates were active in lobbying for many MWPAs, especially in New York (Flexner, 1975; Speth, 1982). Their campaign had more effect on the women's movement itself than it did on the laws that were passed. Some legislators began to claim that the women's rights advocates were "unsexed women" who threatened the stability of society. Many others found pleas for equal rights for wives more amusing than convincing. Most legislators were moved more by the pleas of creditors and lawyers for codification of property rights than they were by the arguments of leaders of the woman movement. But the campaign experience taught the feminists how much they were handicapped by not having the vote. After the Civil War, they settled down to work on the suffrage nearly full time.

The pattern of reform through the MWPAs was piecemeal and gradual. First, real property was protected from creditors. Later, married women received the right to control their earnings. Additional statutes eventually restored women's contract and liability status. However, none of these statutes directly overturned common-law unity concepts. Still, the result was the gradual evening of the legal status of the husband and wife, even though they retained their separate spheres: husband as breadwinner and wife as homemaker. The reforms of the MWPAs helped bring a new theory of sex roles in marriage to the forefront of family law: marriage was a union of two individuals, a man and a woman *in separate spheres but with equal legal status* (Rothman, 1978).

Equal Citizens, Separate Domestic Roles

By the early 1900s, this theory of marriage as a contract of equal citizens with separate domestic roles became dominant, and it remained so until the 1960s. As late as 1963, the President's Commission on the Status of Women continued to advocate this view: "Marriage as a partnership in which each spouse makes a different but equally important contribution is increasingly recognized as a reality in this country" (Mead and Kaplan, 1965, p. 69). Apparently, however, equality in marriage had still not been achieved in every state. The commission called for laws equalizing the civil capacity of married men and women. As late as 1968, married women in some jurisdictions still retained common-law legal disabilities.

Shared Equal Partnership

Also in the late 1960s, a third theory of gender roles in marriage was beginning to attract attention: marriage as a *shared equal partnership*. This coincided with the increase in the number of married women in the work force. Unlike the separate-but-equal theory, the shared-partnership theory depended on an overlapping of marital duties rather than duties assigned according to sex. Spouses would share in providing support for the family as well as in homemaking and child care. To have public policy consistent with this theory of marriage as a shared partnership did not necessitate a massive overhaul of the reformed common law that was the substance of family law in nearly every state. The pattern of piecemeal change that had characterized decision making in family laws since the nineteenth century could continue to accommodate—in fact, integrate—the new concepts. Legislators and judges could incorporate the idea of marriage as a shared partnership by inserting gender-neutral terms for male and female terms in existing laws: *spouse* for *husband* and *wife*; *parent* for *mother* and *father*; *primary care-giver* for *mother*; *primary earner* for *male breadwinner*.

Like the MWPAs, shared-partnership reforms have varied from state to state. The Supreme Court has declined to establish a national standard. In the 1960s, for example, the Court had an opportunity to establish a federal definition of marriage rights that would have obliterated common-law unity and separate spheres throughout the country. Although the Court agreed "the institution of coverture is peculiar and obsolete," it bowed to states' rights: "Both theory and precedents of this court teach us solicitude for state interests, particularly in the field of family and family property relations" (*U.S. v. Yazell*, 1966, pp. 351–352). Nevertheless, from time to time in their *obiter dicta* the justices do set forth their views of gender roles in marriage.

There were efforts to encourage state governments to wipe out the hodgepodge of reforms and adopt new coherent and complete family-law statutes. In the 1970s, lawyers were the prime movers in the reform of family laws. Many hoped to eliminate some of the variety in state laws. The National Conference of Commissioners on Uniform State Laws (NCCUSL) offered the the Uniform Marriage and Divorce Act (UMDA) as a model for states to follow in enacting shared-partnership, gender-neutral laws.[3] In addition, state and national bar associations urged courts to adopt new concepts of marriage when ruling on divorce cases.

Feminist groups also sought the massive reform of family law that would incorporate shared-partnership concepts. In 1970, the Marriage, Divorce, and Family Relations Task Force of the National Organization for Women (NOW) resolved that "marriage should be an equal partnership with shared economic and household responsibility and shared care of the children." The debates over the national Equal Rights Amendment (ERA) and the passage of state ERAs moved some state lawmakers. Ratification debates prompted legislators to comb their law codes for remnants of common-law disabilities and traditional gender roles. State ERAs required states such as Pennsylvania and Montana to rewrite their family-law codes. The Supreme Court boosted these efforts by declaring, "No longer is the female destined solely for the home and rearing of the family, and only the male for the marketplace and the world of ideas" (*Stanton v. Stanton*, 1975, pp. 14–15).

In 1977, the International Women's Year Conference resolved: "The Federal Government and state legislatures should base their laws relating to marital property, inheritance and domestic relations on the principle that marriage is a partnership in which the contribution of each spouse is of equal importance and value "(Bird, 1979, p. 129). Note that this statement still allows for families where one spouse is primarily involved in homemaking duties. It is scrupulously gender neutral but is more sensitive to the concerns of women who are full-time homemakers than was the 1970 NOW resolution.[4]

Over the years since 1789, U.S. policy makers have been informed by these three theories about the proper and expected roles of husband and wife in marriage: (1) *unity*, in which the husband is dominant and the wife has few rights or responsibilities; (2) *separate but equal*, in which the wife-mother and the husband-breadwinner have similar legal rights but different responsibilities; and (3) *shared partnership*, in which the husband and the wife have equal rights and overlapping responsibilities. Each theory gained dominance in the policy debate in a particular historical context. Yet, the development of a new theory did not abolish all trace of previous theories. Despite efforts by feminists and lawyers to secure national standards of equity and shared partnership between marriage partners, contemporary laws retain elements of all three concepts of marriage. Each state has its own pattern of family law reflecting its own combination of concepts and theories. Because of the complexity and diversity among the states and their case law in family matters, we can only review general trends here. An interesting project would be to trace the pattern of law reform in your state and the relative importance of theories of unity, separate but equal, and shared partnership in statutes and court interpretations.

Marriage Regulations

Acceptable Partners

The first topic in each state's marriage laws usually outlines who is permitted to marry whom and the necessary fees and licenses involved. Historically there have been racial as well as sex restrictions. Anti-miscegenation laws were declared unconstitutional in 1967 (*Loving v. Virginia*). Thus far, sex restrictions remain; one can marry only someone of the opposite sex. Campaigns to permit same-sex marriages provoke intense opposition from moral conservatives (see Chapter 9).[5]

Minimum Age for Marriage

There are two age limits: one for marrying with parental consent and another for marrying without parental consent. (There is no age limit if the bride is pregnant.) Originally the ages were different for males and females. According to common law, the minimum age with parental consent was twelve for girls and fourteen for boys. For marrying without parental consent, most states adopted eighteen for girls and twenty-one for boys. These different ages were consistent with theories of unity: boys needed the extra time to prepare themselves to earn a living, but girls were considered ready to assume marital homemaking duties at a younger age. These different ages survived the shift to the theory of separate-but-equal roles.

Now, however, the minimum ages at marriage are the same for men and women. All states have set eighteen as the age for marrying without consent; with consent, ages range from fourteen to eighteen. A few require a court order to marry under the age of consent. Several factors motivated legislatures to equalize the minimum ages. Most important was the change in age of majority and the minimum voting age to eighteen under the Twenty-Sixth Amendment, which was ratified in 1971. The legislators also wanted to satisfy the demands for constitutional equality by removing this obvious sex-based classification. It was a state age-at-majority law that moved the Supreme Court to drop its own separate-spheres ideology in 1975 (*Stanton v. Stanton*, 1975). By then, most states had already equalized marriage ages.

Surname After Marriage

In contrast with age at marriage, for which there are specific statutes and uniformity, there is variety and little legislative action on the subject of name. Common law was never very rigid about the regulation of names. A person could use any name she or he wished as long as there was no intent to defraud creditors. It was a common-law practice that children be registered on the birth certificate in the father's name, but the married woman was not required to take her husband's name. That most women still do so is because of custom rather than regulation. The custom reflects unity concepts of marriage, with the husband as lord and master of the home and the wife and children taking their identity from him. Although women are more likely than men to change their names in marriage and divorce, some women prefer to keep their birth names throughout. There are special costs involved, regardless of which choice a woman makes.

Although a woman can use her birth name for most purposes, some states require that a wife use her husband's name on state documents and records, such as her driver's license or tax forms. And the courts have upheld states' constitutional power to require this only of married women (*Forbush v. Wallace*, 1971). This probably constitutes a de facto policy that a wife take her husband's name, since it is difficult to use one name on state records and another for business and social purposes.

Other states have enacted statutes guaranteeing that each spouse may choose a surname during the marriage: birth name, spouse's name, or a combination. No matter what policy the state has, married couples with different names sometimes find it necessary to explain their status when they deal with bankers, welfare agencies, health insurance companies, real-estate brokers, hotel clerks, and in other circumstances in which marital status is important. Credit records are likely to be more complete if the same name is used on all transactions and financial accounts. And Social Security administrators recommend that a person use the same name on employment, tax, and Social Security records to facilitate the collection of benefits.

Changing one's name with marriage has disadvantages. A woman who marries and then divorces and remarries may have to change her name on all sorts of public and credit records several times. A man with the same uneven family status sails through life with his public identity intact. Some women have found it easier in the long run to get a court order giving them permission to use their birth name on all official documents. In the area of name, the law in practice and custom remains inspired by common-law unity and coverture.

Domicile Laws

Domicile laws retain important aspects of coverture as well. A person's domicile, or permanent residence, establishes that person's rights in many areas of public policy—from purchasing licenses to suing in court. The common law assumption that the domicile of a family is that of the husband still prevails in many states. The courts in other states have interpreted the MWPA to nullify this preference, along with the elimination of unity. In still others, courts say that the unity of the home continues, supporting the idea that there should be only one domicile for husband and wife. Why it should be determined by the husband was explained in the oft-cited case of *Carlson v. Carlson* (1953):

> The general rule by the great weight of authority is that the wife must adopt the residence of the husband and that she cannot, without just cause, maintain a separate domicile. There are sound reasons for this rule. The law imposes on the husband the burden and obligation of the support, maintenance and care of the family and almost of necessity he must have the right of choice of the situs of the home. There can be no decision by majority rule as to where the family home shall be maintained, and a reasonable accompaniment of the imposition of the obligation is the right of selection. (p. 250)

The judge went on to say that this reasoning did not mean the merger of husband and wife, but rather the maintenance of one family unit.

Why have these domicile laws so reminiscent of common-law unity theories remained in force for so long? For one thing, most intact families live in the same residence and have little occasion to feel the effects of these laws. Second, those few who live in separate residences have successfully sought exceptions to the domicile rules. At first, married women won the right to establish separate domicile only on an exceptional basis, for purposes such as voting, university tuition, holding public office, jury service, taxation, or probate. The increased incidence of two-career marriages has rendered many traditional domicile laws ineffective. In practice, each spouse has a right to establish separate residence or domicile for whatever reason (see *Corpus Juris Secundum*, vol. 41, under Husband and Wife). Still, only a few states have blanket laws giving husband and wife the statutory equal right to choose the domicile.

Interspousal Immunity

Unity theory made the husband and the wife one legal entity; they could not make contracts or sue each other in court. This is called *interspousal immunity*. Although MWPAs gave married women separate standing in court, most MWPAs were silent on the question of interspousal immunity. When wives tried to bring suit against their husbands, often for assault, state courts' rulings varied. Some state courts concluded that the MWPAs had eliminated the concept of unity entirely. These courts permitted the suits. Other state courts saw the MWPAs as specific remedies that otherwise left unity intact. These courts refused to allow civil suits between spouses in the absence of legislative action. The Supreme Court made such a ruling in 1910 in interpreting the MWPA for the District of Columbia: "We cannot but regard this case as another of many attempts which have failed to obtain by construction radical and far reaching changes in policy of the common law, not declared in terms of the legislation under consideration" (*Thompson v. Thompson*, 1910, p. 619).

The retention of interspousal immunity worked against women because it prevented them from gaining civil remedies in cases of abuse by their husbands. It also meant that they could not make any claims against their husband's insurance in case of auto accidents. Some lawyers and judges opposed allowing couples to bring suits against each other. Part of this was based on the traditional reluctance to bring private family matters into public courts. Framing a marital "spat" to conform to the formal adversarial systems used in the courts would undermine the chance for a harmonious resolution, these lawyers and judges reasoned. They also feared that the courts might be overwhelmed with domestic claims and that couples might be tempted to use these suits to conspire against insurance companies. For example, in the case of an auto accident in which one spouse was injured, that person might claim negligence by the other spouse who was driving the car. "In the family context, the danger of collusion is the greatest of all. Not only are the parties in a close personal relationship, but any recovery will inure to the benefit of the entire family and failure to recover will affect the entire family adversely" (*Immer v. Risko*, 56, N.J. 482, 1970, cited in Kanowitz, 1973, p. 237).

Today's renewed interest in the problem of violence in the home has pushed some legislatures to act to allow civil suits between spouses as part of a series of reforms to help battered women (see Chapter 10). As a result, most states have abolished interspousal immunity either in full or for specific cases of assault. There are an increasing number of lawsuits between spouses charging damages for infections from AIDS. But removing interspousal immunity is not an acceptance of marriage as a shared partnership or even as an alliance of equals. Rather, it is the product of a different policy debate related to sexual conflict and family violence.

The Marital-Support/Marital-Services Contract

The heart of the traditional marriage contract is the duty of the husband to support the wife, while it is the duty of the wife to provide services to the husband and home.

Marital-Support Laws

Under common-law unity, "The husband is bound to provide his wife necessaries by law, as much as himself; and, if she contracts debts for them, he is obliged to pay for them; but for any thing besides necessaries he is not chargeable" (Blackstone, 1803, p. 442). Blackstone presented this responsibility as less a concern about the welfare of the wife and the family and more as a matter of credit. The husband was to be considered liable for the debts of the family only in the area of "necessaries." When many states' marital-support laws were reformed in the 1930s to become *family-expense statutes*, they merely extended the liability for family debts to include the wife. Because of this definition, these laws have never been used effectively by wives to force husbands to support them; these laws do not require a husband to give his wife any money. His obligation is to pay the bills for "necessaries." Still, according to Blackstone, a wife might get her husband to do his duty by "pledging his credit." But this worked only as long as the husband agreed.

The first creditor to take an unwilling husband to court to pay a wife's bills no doubt ran up against one of two possible defenses: (1) the husband might claim that what the wife bought (perhaps a new formal coat) was not a "necessary"; or (2) the husband might show that he had already provided that "necessary" (perhaps the wife already had a coat). In this example, the hapless creditor probably would not accept the wife's charge a second time without the husband's permission. Creditors are not interested in the subtleties of gender-role definitions in marriage; they want their money.

The difficulties of enforcing marital-support laws became an issue during the debate on the ratification of the Equal Rights Amendment. The STOP-ERA forces argued that the ERA would abolish the state laws requiring a husband to support his dependent wife-homemaker. This argument assumed that the husband paid the bills only because the law required it and that such support laws were enforced. Feminists tried to point out that if the husband did not pay, the wife would be liable for family bills anyway, and that as long as a marriage is intact, support laws are rarely enforced. These women's rights advocates were fond of quoting *McGuire v. McGuire*, a Nebraska case in which a wife tried to get a court to require her husband to increase the standard of living he provided, in accord with his assets. The court declined, saying:

> The living standards of a family are a matter of concern to the household, and not for the courts to determine, even though the husband's

BOX 6.3

Does Marital Support Include Indoor Plumbing?

Could Mr. McGuire afford to pay for indoor plumbing for Mrs. McGuire? (Remember, these are 1953 dollars.)

In 1953, Mrs. McGuire sued Mr. McGuire, asking the court to order him to improve her standard of living. She wanted indoor plumbing, a kitchen sink, and a new furnace.

Here the judge describes Mr. McGuire's assets. Keeping in mind that these are 1953 dollars, could he afford to provide for her needs?

> It appears that the defendant owns 298 acres of land with 2 acres deeded to a church, the land being of the value of $83,960; that he has bank deposits in the sum of $12,786.81 and government bonds in the amount of $104,500; and that his income, including interest on the bonds and rental for his real estate, is $8,000 or $9,000 a year. There are apparently some Series E United States Savings Bonds listed and registered in the names of Charles W. McGuire or Lydia M. McGuire purchased in 1943, 1944, and 1945, in the amount of $2,500. Other bonds seem to be in the name of Charles W. McGuire, without a beneficiary or co-owner designated. The plaintiff has a bank account of $5,960.22. (*McGuire v. McGuire* 157 Neb. 226, 59 N.W. 2d 336 1953. Cited in Lindgren and Taub, *The Law of Sex Discrimination*, 1993, pp. 328–329)

attitude toward his wife, according to his circumstances leave little to be said on his behalf. As long as the home is maintained and the parties are living as husband and wife it may be said that the husband is legally supporting his wife and the purpose of the marriage relation is being carried out. (157 Neb. 226, 1953; cited in Kanowitz, 1973, p. 228)

Today, most states place an obligation on each spouse to support the other. All have laws with criminal penalities for abandonment, desertion, and nonsupport. Some of these penalize the husband only and state courts have upheld them as constitutional, based on social and economic differences between men and women. In other states, however, such laws have been declared unconstitutional violations of equal protection guarantees of the Fourteenth Amendment. Because the abandoned spouse must be destitute or in danger of being a public burden before the state would bring charges, it is evident that the goal of these laws is to reduce state welfare responsibilities.

The doctrine of necessaries is invoked these days primarily by creditors. Precedents generally provide that either spouse may be liable for debts of the other spouse for necessaries, defined to include food, clothing, lodging, medical assistance, and burial expenses.

Marital Services

With respect to the services part of the traditional marriage contract, the wife's duty is to provide services for her husband: "to be his helpmate, to love and care for him in such a role, to afford him her society and her person, to protect and care for him in sickness, and to labor faithfully to advance his interests" (*Rucci v. Rucci* 23 Conn. Supp. 221, 1962, p. 224; quoted in Weitzman, 1981, p. 60). Some ambitious or perhaps desperate housewives have assumed that the money their husband gives them for household expenses is a form of salary, an exchange for their services, and through judicious management of this money have put aside some savings—no longer in the proverbial sugar bowl but rather in a savings account in their own name. The courts have had occasion to shatter these illusions when they acknowledged the husband's right to lay claim to those savings. Such rulings made it clear that the services of the wife belong to the husband, are owed to him by the wife, and are not part of a labor contract. In fact, the services have no monetary or economic value that the wife can claim.

Legislators have reviewed the marital-support/marital-services contract in only a few states, primarily when the ERA debates prompted a full-scale attempt to overhaul marriage and divorce statutes. In other states, the marital-support/marital-services contract survived the shift from common-law unity to separate-but-equal marriage roles. And, the addition of contemporary notions of marriage as a shared partnership has greatly affected the pattern of case law nationwide. For example, the idea that both spouses, not just the wife, might provide services has developed through litigation. Under common law, a husband could bring a civil case for damages against anyone who injured his wife so that she was unable to provide services. He could sue for loss of her *consortium:* "The concept of consortium includes not only loss of support or services, it also embraces such elements as love, companionship, affection, society, sexual relations, solace and more" (*Millington v. Southeastern Elevator Co.,* 22 N.Y. 2d. 498, 1968; reprinted in Kanowitz, 1973, p. 242). With the adoption of the MWPAs, wives brought suits arguing that they, like their husbands, had equal rights to their spouses' consortium. Most states

BOX 6.4

Criminal Conversation: A Husband's Right to Sue for Damages to His Sexual Property

The principle of patriarchal ownership of a wife's services and progeny under common law extended to a husband's special rights to bring suit against anyone who had threatened or damaged his sexual property. Along with suits for loss of consortium (services) were suits for *criminal conversation,* a violation of a husband's exclusive right to sexual intercourse with his wife. In such cases, a husband would sue his wife's alleged lover for damages to his property, and the two men would battle it out in civil court, contending over whether the adultery had occurred. The wife was neither a party to the suit, nor was she allowed to testify. Her reputation, her access to her children, and her marriage itself could be taken away from her as a consequence of such a proceeding, but she had no right to speak for herself.

(thirty-eight) have extended suits for the loss of consortium to wives. Of the rest, six have remained with common law, and six have abolished such suits altogether. Although there have been a few legislative provisions, this right was usually extended by the courts.

Marital Property Systems

Separate Property

Under common-law unity, the husband had a monopoly on the property of the family and on the management of this property. He could sell it or save it, and the wife had no say. Government stepped in only if the family became so destitute that the poor laws applied. As the MWPAs gradually removed married women's disabilities and gave married women ownership and control over their earnings, real property, inheritance, and gifts, a system of marital property called *separate property* was eventually created in forty-two states. But it took over a century for the property rights of married men and those of married women to become equal. As late as 1968, a few states were still enforcing "free dealer" statutes, under which a woman could not buy or sell her own real property unless she either had her husband's permission to do so or had been declared by the court to be a free dealer, competent to make her own decisions.[6]

In separate-property states, the husband and the wife are treated as two separate individuals. They can join their resources in savings and property or can act entirely independently of each other. The usual exceptions are in matters affecting the family home or homestead and in matters of inheritance. For example, some states give a spouse automatic interest in the other's estate.

Community Property

Eight states—Arizona, California, Idaho, Louisiana, Nevada, New Mexico, Texas, and Washington—opted long ago for a different type of marital-property system called *community property*.[7] In these states, the formation of a marriage creates a new category of property, called community property. In the traditional community-property regime, all earnings and property acquired by either spouse after the marriage became part of the community, jointly owned by the couple. (Property acquired before the marriage or by gift or inheritance was not usually part of the community.) Although the community property was jointly held, the law gave the husband control over its management. Thus, on a day-to-day basis, a married woman's control over property and earnings was similar under both common-law coverture and under traditional community-property law. The difference was that within the community-property system a wife had claim to half the community property at her husband's death or the couple's divorce—that is, if there was any property left.

Trends toward equality in marriage had an impact on all community-property states, and there the husband's monopoly came under attack. Reforms in all eight states have now given the wife and husband equal rights to manage their community property jointly. In most states, earnings are now removed from the community, so the wife retains control of her wages.

In 1986 Wisconsin left the ranks of separate property states and adopted the Wisconsin Marital Property Act.[8] The term *marital property* is officially defined to mean a community property type of system, making Wisconsin the ninth community property state. Legislators adopted this form of property regime to bring family law in line with principles of marriage as an equal partnership between husband and wife (Erlanger and Weisberger, 1990).

Reforms of the laws related to community property and common-law property produced a convergence, although not an identity, of spouses' rights. Of course, property is rarely the subject of litigation in an ongoing marriage. It is only when death or divorce necessitates that property must be divided that the spouses learn just what property rights the law gives.

Status of Women and the Feminist Response

The idea that marriage is an equal partnership where legal responsibilities are interchangeable between the spouses continues to gain ground. At the same time, coverture and the theory of separate but equal roles persists in statutes, case law, and marriage customs. The law cooperates with marriages where the husband is the de facto head of the family and confers his name and status on his wife and children. The status of women has been affected by the expectation in so many states that the husband will have primary financial responsibility while the wife must be concerned with the care of the home. This separate-but-equal theory continues to sustain unequal domicile and interspousal-immunity laws and in some states officially deprives a homemaker's work of any economic value. This makes her dependent on her husband's decisions about the appropriate level of marital support, as well as for retirement and health insurance. According to the separate-but-equal theory, any salary a wife earns (and, remember that a majority of married women are employed) is, by definition, secondary family income, incidental to the primary work and income of the husband.[9]

Feminist organizations came out of the 1960s in favor of the new concept of marriage as a shared-and-equal partnership in which both husband and wife would earn money and care for their household and each other. Because of the diversity of attitudes and practices in U.S. marriages, however, it has been difficult to advocate only one view of gender roles. In fact, threats from STOP-ERA of imminent doom to dutiful wives forced feminist leaders to consider the demands of homemakers who feared equality would threaten their economic support. Also, gender-neutral family statutes that assume equal earning power of spouses have perpetuated women's lower status and removed some of the protections offered by the traditional laws. This was especially evident to feminists when divorce laws were reformed in the 1960s and 1970s. The 1979 NOW Bill of Rights for Homemakers showed that organization's acceptance of the continuing salience of the separate-but-equal theory.

The concept of shared partnership also disturbs many women who are making strides in careers and salaries. They don't relish committing their newly earned worldly goods to their husbands. They prefer a fourth model of the marriage relations: marriage as an *alliance* of equals who go about their separate lives, at least financially. It is evident that, with the diversity in marriage relationships, no one theory of marital gender roles will dominate policy for long.

The various theories of gender-role relationships in marriage have all developed without disturbing the fundamental idea that a family begins with a man and a woman, the "heterosexual couple—a reproductive biological pairing that is designated as divinely ordained in religion, crucial in social policy and a normative imperative in ideology" (Fineman, 1995, p. 145). Within this fundamental definition, the laws adapt to changing gender-role patterns and beliefs. Whether a woman and her husband live their lives according to unity, separate-but-equal, shared-partnership, or alliance theories, the marriage law will have little practical effect on her status and livelihood within an intact marriage. The effect of these dominant ideologies and public policy is most evident when efforts to form or maintain this heterosexual coupling fail: divorce.

Divorce

Although marriage and divorce have always been central to women's lives and status, feminists have usually been on the periphery of legislative debates over divorce reform. Part of the problem is determining what kind of divorce laws would promote women's rights. A wife's status in a divorce depends on her status in the marriage; without an overhaul of the meaning of marriage, divorce law can do little to change women's rights and responsibilities. The best that can be hoped for is that divorce laws will not increase the burdens on women.

Legal Divorce

English common law provided for no civil divorce, and the Church of England only allowed separation without remarriage. Feminists first interpreted legal divorce as a means of escape, a way of overturning autocratic policies that forced women to remain trapped in marriages to cruel husbands regardless of the suffering this entailed. Ever since, liberalization of divorce laws and procedures has been regarded as giving women choices in situations of domestic difficulty. But this support has also been tempered by the realization that divorce may hurt women. Before women had access to education and jobs, keeping a marriage intact meant economic survival. Despite improvements in employment opportunity, women continue to suffer a loss of economic and social status in divorce.

Fault-Based Divorce

When divorce first became legal, it was in the midst of widespread agreement that marriage should be for life and that divorce was immoral. The debate was grounded in a religious context, and lawmakers found justification in the Bible for their growing realization that there were some evils, such as adultery, even worse than divorce. Feminists were ready to submit that physical abuse was another such evil. Thus, early divorce laws were based on the concept of *fault;* a divorce, undesirable though it was, could be granted if one spouse could prove that the other had committed a transgression so serious that the very purpose of the marriage had been destroyed. In the United States, every state except South Carolina adopted fault-based divorce laws, and all these laws included adultery as a grounds. Most states also added cruelty and desertion; it was assumed that husbands would be more likely to sue for adultery, and wives for physical cruelty and desertion.

The demand for divorce has usually been greater than the capacity of the legal system to handle it. When divorce demands started to increase after the Civil War, debate over divorce laws spread (Hindus and Withey, 1982; Jacob, 1988; O'Neill, 1967). Liberals who saw divorce rates as symptomatic of a social problem collided with conservatives who were appalled at divorce mills in the western states and demanded a crackdown on couples trying to evade their moral responsibilities. There are usually some people in all debates on divorce law who believe that divorce rates could be reduced if laws simply made it difficult to end marriages. Well into the twentieth century, legislatures generally declined to act, leaving the courts to deal with the mounting pressure for divorce. Fault-based divorce laws were bent as couples concocted evidence, lied, and conspired to gain their freedom.

No-Fault Divorce

When liberalization of divorce laws finally began in the 1960s, it was not the product of an organized campaign for easy divorce. Instead, many lawyers quietly reported that the outmoded laws had made a shambles of courts' and judges' pretensions to being fair, impartial, and objective. They recognized that the concept of marriage as a partnership of equals was becoming more accepted in society. They reasoned that marriages

BOX 6.5

The South Carolina Paradox

In *Women and the Law of Property in Early America,* Marylynn Salmon points out a paradox that can be observed in South Carolina's policy on divorce and alimony in the postrevolutionary period.

> On the surface [that policy was] the most contradictory of any state's. Matrons there enjoyed rules allowing them significant property rights after marriage. Marriage settlements creating separate estates for women were fully recognized, as were post-nuptial separation agreements for the purpose of dividing property. South Carolina had a strong commitment to feme sole trader rights. Yet despite such general acceptance of women's financial autonomy after marriage, South Carolina refused to provide for absolute divorce. Why the contradiction? (p. 79)

Salmon suggests an explanation that ties divorce and marital property law to the traditional ideologies of race, sexuality, and masculine ideals. Her explanation proposes an exchange: The primary ground for divorce in those days was adultery, and South Carolina lawmakers—seeing the male sexual privilege to use and abuse slave women as an unequivocal right—refused to allow women to charge husbands with adultery. "To allow white women the freedom to divorce for male adultery would have meant placing a severe restriction on men's sexual behavior. . . . In exchange for the law's acceptance of male sexual privilege, South Carolina jurists gave women the right to financial autonomy within marriage" (Salmon, 1986, pp. 65, 79).

South Carolina did not permit divorced couples to remarry until the 1950s.

didn't end because one spouse was guilty of fault and the other was innocent. Marriages failed for complex reasons, and both spouses were responsible. According to these lawyers, divorce was not the result of immoral behavior, but rather the remedy for a failed marriage. They suggested that the responsibility of the courts should be to determine that marriages had in fact broken down and then to end them.

These ideas constituted a new theory of divorce based on *marital breakdown.* In 1969, California became the first state to abolish its old fault-based statute and allow divorce only for breakdown. The Uniform Marriage and Divorce Act, developed by the National Conference of

Commissioners on Uniform State Laws, offered a model statute that stimulated legislators to examine traditional divorce laws. Today, couples can get no-fault divorces throughout the United States (Elrod, 1995). Along with breakdown, no-fault grounds include incompatibility, irreconcilable differences, and separation. With separation, divorce is granted after the couple has lived apart for a specified period, usually one or two years (although a couple of states allow divorce after a six-month separation). In some states, incompatibility is a more traditional no-fault ground than separation. Eighteen states plus the District of Columbia made no-fault grounds, usually marital breakdown, the only grounds for divorce. All of the rest have added breakdown or some other no-fault ground to their fault-based provisions.

Alimony and Property Settlements

If a couple can reach an agreement about alimony and property on their own with their attorneys, the courts will usually accept it. When a husband and a wife cannot agree, however, a judge must decide.

Alimony

When unity and separate-but-equal theories of marriage prevailed, a first concern was to provide financial support for the dependent wife. Alimony was seen as the continuation of the husband's financial responsibility after the marriage ended. It was paid by a man to a woman either for the rest of her life or until she remarried and thus became dependent on another breadwinner.

The trend toward no-fault divorce and the concept of shared partnership have changed the definitions and applications of alimony laws. All statutes are now gender neutral and will probably remain so, because the Supreme Court has ruled that allocations of alimony responsibility by sex violate the Equal Protection Clause of the Fourteenth Amendment (*Orr v. Orr*, 1979). The courts also now try to end any financial commitments of divorced couples as soon as possible, leading to a decline in permanent alimony awards. One way to settle things is to order *lump sum* alimony in the form of a one-time financial settlement. The agreement that many women can and should become self-supporting after divorce has led to an increase in temporary alimony, sometimes called *rehabilitative* maintenance. The purpose of temporary alimony is to support the dependent spouse only as long as it takes for her to become self-supporting. Twenty-seven states have expressly forbidden courts to take fault or misconduct of spouses into account in making alimony arrangements, while twenty-three specifically allow fault.

Property Division

Patterns of property division between husbands and wives have depended on the marital-property regime. Under coverture, property remained with the husband. With separate-property reforms, divorce involved the unscrambling of titles, determining who paid for what. This left most of the property still in the hands of the husband in a typical divorce. An appreciation of the value of homemaking, as well as the idea of marriage as a shared partnership, have contributed to a new concept of *equal distribution in divorce* in separate-property states. This concept has little meaning during marriage, but at divorce, it entitles both spouses to an equal claim to the assets of the family. The Uniform Marriage and Divorce Act (UMDA), for example, calls for courts to divide marital property without regard to fault and to consider economic contributions of both spouses as well as that of a spouse as homemaker. Such provisions thus attribute some economic value to homemaking.

A few states have reached an equitable property-distribution policy by enacting new divorce statutes modeled after the UMDA or by amending their existing statutes. Other states rely on court rulings to guide their judges. Nearly all states require that property divisions be "equitable," or just. A majority of states order their judges to consider the contributions of the homemaker to property acquisition and maintenance. Half include work done by one spouse to further the education of the other. With respect to fault, a majority provide for misconduct to be a factor in distributing property.

Community-property states tend to begin with a clearer idea of equal division in divorce. But some of them use the term *equitable* and permit adjustments according to the circumstances of the marriage. Half of these states specifically remove fault, while others allow misconduct to deprive a spouse of an equal claim. The same convergence of effects between community-property and separate-property regimes noted in the marriage section applies to property settlements in divorce: equitable in principle, but allowing adjustments in favor of one spouse or the other.

Status of Women and the Feminist Response

Reforms in laws and practices relating to divorce, similar to many areas of family law, have been incremental, formed from a combination of statutes and case law throughout the states. Their overall form is beginning to take shape, and their effect on women's status is problematic for many feminists. In the United States, marriage is becoming an arrangement between individuals which can be legally formed and legally dissolved for just about any reason. The principle guiding the courts in settling arrangements between the spouses is gender-neutral equality, treating husband and wife the same, as though they were interchangeable.

In the period of reform since the 1970s, the financial status of women has been a main concern of women's rights advocates. With no-fault laws, divorce is easier, and the pressure to make financial settlements quickly is intense. Judges and lawyers have a great deal of discretion in settling the terms of these settlements. With more than half the states permitting issues of fault by one or another spouse to be a basis for decisions about alimony, property and the divorce itself, judges with traditional views of gender roles can punish women more harshly than men for perceived moral misconduct. Women who have spent part of their marriage economically dependent or as secondary earners are likely to lose in property settlements, especially if they must pay a lawyer a high fee to make a convincing claim to property. To remedy this situation and to strengthen women's claim to rehabilitative alimony and property, feminists have pushed for formal recognition of wives' contributions to homemaking and to building their spouse's career. They have secured broader definitions of marital property to include pensions and insurance. In 1983, under pressure from the Congressional Caucus on Women's Issues, Congress allowed military pensions to be divided as marital property.[10] Advanced degrees such as M.D.'s and J.D.'s have become part of property settlements. One divorcing wife secured a provision that allowed her half interest should her husband win the Nobel Prize. (He won.)[11]

Even if wives gain a fair share of the assets, they usually begin single life with lost earning power they can never recover, especially if they have spent time raising children. Rehabilitative alimony is supposed to take care of restoring this lost earning power, but it rarely does. What standard of living should rehabilitative alimony achieve? Many courts use self-support as the guide, even though it is often below the standard of living the wife enjoyed during the marriage. Then there are the lost investments, such as pensions and health insurance, that might have come from steady employment. How can a dependent wife make up years of lost contributions to secure adequate retirement benefits?

The mounting evidence linking the status of women in the family and their economic status has led feminist legal theorists to take another

BOX 6.6

Giving Women Credit: The Equal Credit Opportunity Act of 1974

In 1974, Congress passed the Equal Credit Opportunity Act. Both the act and the process of passing it are representative of feminist strategies on issues of economic status during the first ten years of the contemporary feminist movement. The issue of credit as a problem of sex discrimination arose during hearings in 1972 by the National Commission on Consumer Credit (Gelb and Palley, 1987). Testimony during those hearings documented the fact that, despite the increased number of women in paid employment and their access to the professions, banks and other lenders clung to traditional assumptions of the economic dependency of married women. Women, regardless of income, earning power, or marital status, were considered extra-risky as borrowers. Evidence mounted of absurd and unfair practices: middle-aged single women required to get their fathers to cosign loans; divorced women automatically stripped of their credit cards; married men denied mortgages because the income of the wives was totally discounted; married women with no credit history despite decades of continuous employment and contribution to family assets.

The coalition of feminist organizations that had successfully pushed the Equal Rights Amendment (ERA) and other bills through Congress in the early 1970s promoted their proposal as an equity issue, similar in spirit to Title VII, Title IX, and the ERA: prohibiting sex discrimination by removing sex as a permissible classification for credit transactions. The act passed Congress with little opposition; the feminist coalition kept up the pressure on the Federal Reserve Board, too, while it drafted the administrative regulations. These eliminated the automatic penalties in standard formulas of creditworthiness assigned to single, divorced, and married women. In general, the regulations sustained the concept of equity, paying special attention to the effects of marital status on credit. According to these regulations, credit accounts of married couples should be filed in the names of the husband and wife to give the two individuals equal credit histories; a husband and a wife can use a hyphenated name; income from part-time jobs cannot be discounted; a married woman (or man) need not indicate her (or his) marital status unless the applicant is relying on spouse's income to determine her (or his) eligibility and creditworthiness. Banks and creditors cannot automatically terminate credit contracts simply because a person's marital status changes. If a woman is turned down, she

BOX 6.6 *(continued)*

has the right to request justification and to examine the credit history used in making the decision. Of course, no applicant is guaranteed credit, and none of these practices would be illegal if they are truly related to creditworthiness—the ability to pay back the loan.

look at reforms of divorce laws. The prevailing standard of equality has not worked to help women. First, changes such as equality in alimony have focused on extending the idea of economic dependency to men, while reducing the obligations altogether. The campaign to recognize homemaking as equivalent to breadwinning has helped only a minority of women who are full-time housekeepers. The concept of marriage as a shared partnership in which spouses are presumed to participate equally in family and work overlooks the fact that in a majority of marriages, women do more: they provide needed financial support while at the same time continuing to do most of the work in the home.

The goal of ending all financial obligations between the spouses as soon as possible has led the courts to evade the responsibility for the continued well-being of women after the divorce. Thus the shift toward equality in divorce law has not resulted in equity; divorce continues to have devastating economic consequences for most women. These are compounded when the couple has children.

Parental Rights and Responsibilities

Legal concepts of a husband's and a wife's parental rights and responsibilities to the children of their marriage have closely paralleled the theories of marital gender roles.

From Common-Law Unity to Shared Partnership

Under unity, fathers had all rights to children, along with everything else. Children began work at an early age and were valued for their economic contribution to the family. Father controlled them, provided for their support according to his resources and preferences, and had title to their earnings. In the nineteenth century, the idea of separate spheres changed the wife's role from chattel to full-time mother with responsibility for her children's care and education while the father supported them. This change coincided with declines in child labor; children became an economic liability. Finally, the concept of marriage as a shared partnership envisions the father and the mother equally involved in parenting and thus equally responsible for the support of their children.

Today, laws regulating parental duties in an ongoing marriage tend to be gender neutral, placing rights and responsibilities on both parents equally. Nevertheless, by custom, children tend to take the name of the father, not of the mother. When the question of name is reviewed, most states recognize that naming a child is the choice of the parents. With respect to support, many states have gender-neutral statutes, placing primary responsibility on the primary earner or breadwinner; still, this person is likely to be the father. Parents retain equal rights to custody and control of their children, consistent with shared-partnership concepts. As with other aspects of family law, the parental-responsibility statutes have little direct effect on activities in families that are intact. Most of the law affects parental responsibilities and rights only when marriages break up.

Who Gets Custody After Divorce?

Policy and practice in determining custody in divorce closely paralleled changing societal views of gender roles in the family. Under common-law unity, divorce was rare but separation did occur. In either instance, the father had first claim to the children. With the growing attention to motherhood and the mother's education of the children, two principles about custody took hold. The first related to the welfare of children: states amended their statutes to award custody in the best interests of the child. Most of these statutes were gender neutral. But, in the courts, many judges followed a second principle, concluding that a child of *tender years* belonged with the mother: "Special, even mysterious bonds existed between mother and young child which, all other things being equal, made her the preferred parental custodian" (Sheppard, 1982, p. 230). These two principles resulted in placing nearly all children of divorce in the custody of the mothers.

The concepts of equality and shared partnership in marriage have since eroded the tender-years principle. Nearly all states have gender-neutral statutes declaring that either parent may be awarded custody, and nearly all give guidelines to courts in making their determination. Such guidelines include consideration of the fitness of parents, the history of being primary caretaker during the marriage, the greater ability to provide a stable home, the willingness to cooperate with the other parent, the children's wishes, and any evidence of domestic violence and abuse. The idea of equal sharing in marriage has also stimulated most states' lawmakers to allow and even to encourage joint custody, or shared responsibility for children in a divorce.

The search for a proper standard in determining custody goes on and remains controversial (Mason, 1994). The answer varies, depending on the way the problem is defined. Child-development experts focusing on the child's point of view will argue that stability and continuous care are best. This might lead to a preference for the parent who was the *primary caregiver* during the marriage. Primary-caregiver laws are gender-neutral versions of the tender-years principle. Other people argue that each parent has rights to a relationship with his or her child and that, as far as custody is concerned, mothers and fathers are interchangeable. Another version of this point of view is that children have a right to a relationship with both parents, despite a divorce. Fathers, especially, have fought for *joint-custody laws* to overcome the long-standing practice of maternal preference. There are two types: legal custody, when parents share authority to make decisions for the child, and physical custody, where the child lives with each parent for periods of time. An often repeated statistic is that 90 percent of children of divorce are with their mothers. Recent census reports show that 84 percent of divorced and separated parents with children in their custody are women. Although there have been few studies of the processes that lead to this outcome, it appears that fewer fathers seek physical custody of their children.[12]

Child Support—and Nonsupport

All but a couple of states have gender-neutral statutes regarding child support corresponding to their gender-neutral custody laws. Since mothers tend to have custody, however, most courts order the fathers to make support payments. The amounts tend to be low, and noncompliance is high. Statistics from the Census Bureau document the belief that about half of the mothers of children due support receive only partial payment or no payment at all (see Box 6.7). Thus enforcement of child-support orders has become an important women's rights issue. It is also a welfare issue, and the effects of nonsupport on welfare expenditures have brought state and federal welfare administrators into the picture in an active way (see Chapter 10).

BOX 6.7

Child-Support Awards to Mothers, 1978 to 1991

About half the mothers of children due child support receive only partial payment or no payment at all.

Status of child-support awards	1978	1981	1985	1991
Mothers awarded support	59.1%	59.2%	61.2%	55.8%
Mothers not awarded support	40.9	40.7	38.2	44.2

Actual receipt of payments	1978	1981	1985	1991
Full amount	48.9%	46.7%	48.2%	52.2%
Partial amount	22.8	25.1	25.8	24.0
No payment	28.3	28.2	26.0	23.8

Sources: U.S. Department of Commerce, Bureau of the Census, 1989. "Child Support and Alimony: 1985." *Current Population Reports*, Series P-23, No. 154, pp. 3–4; U.S. Department of Commerce, Bureau of the Census, 1995. "Child Support for Custodial Mothers and Fathers: 1991." *Current Population Reports*, Series P-60, No. 187, p. 14.

Legislatures have increased courts' authority to attach the wages and property of delinquent parents, and many counties now have offices to enforce support orders. Thus mothers need not go to court each time that the check fails to arrive. These agencies often collect directly from fathers, thereby eliminating the need for contact between parents over the money. The Uniform Reciprocal Enforcement of Support Act (URESA) enacted in every state has, at least in principle, cut off one avenue of escape: moving to another state. States pledge to enforce one another's support orders. State lottery winners also sometimes find their winnings reduced to make up for back child-support payments.

The federal government's role in child-support issues has increased ever since the establishment of the Office of Child Support in the 1970s. Parent Locator Services can trace absent parents through Social Security numbers. Income tax refunds can be withheld. Joining the armed forces to avoid support is no longer an avenue of escape either, because federal wages can be garnished. In 1992, Congress passed the Child Support Recovery Act. Under this act, a parent who is able to pay child support due his or her children living in another state and who avoids making that payment has committed a federal crime. Penalties include fines and jail time.[13] The act also authorizes funds to help states enforce their own criminal laws relating to support.

BOX 6.8

Child-Support Awards: Mothers and Fathers Compared, 1991

There are deadbeat moms as well as deadbeat dads—parents avoiding the obligation to pay child support. However, nine times as many mothers as fathers receive child-support awards.

Status of child-support awards	Mothers	Fathers
Parents awarded support	55.8%	40.9%
Parents not awarded support	44.2	59.1
	$N = 9,918,000$	1,584,000
Actual receipt of payments		
Full amount	52.2%	42.6%
Partial amount	24.0	20.1
No payment	23.8	37.3
	$N = 5,542,000$	648,000

Source: U.S. Department of Commerce, Bureau of the Census, 1995. "Child Support for Custodial Mothers and Fathers: 1991." Current Population Reports, Series P-60, No. 187, pp. 14–16.

These policies have arisen because Congress has paid special attention to the relationship of child support to welfare budgets. State aid to the poor has been defined as assistance to needy children, and when costs of welfare rise, public authorities see delinquent fathers as both a cause and a remedy. Thus, the federal government has required that states strengthen their enforcement activities as a condition of receiving federal welfare funds. Although directed at welfare recipients primarily, more effective mechanisms for the collection of child support can help all parents.

Status of Women and the Feminist Response

Aside from the perennial problems of unpaid child support, the increasing demands of fathers for rights to their children in divorce is the major parental-rights issue for feminists. As with divorce law, gender-neutral custody and support laws fail to take into account the real inequalities women face in the environment. More and more fathers seek either sole or joint custody of their children. Some studies show that, although more mothers than fathers still have custody, when custody is contested fathers often have the advantage over mothers (Chesler, 1986; Mason, 1994). This is true regardless of the state statutes and guidelines. Such studies are not conclusive, however, as others indicate that mothers will retain the advantage (Mnookin, 1990).

A presumption in favor of joint custody may cast a father in a parenting role he has never performed during the marriage. Without joint custody, however, judges may be swayed by traditional attitudes about motherhood. Judges sometimes apply gender stereotypes and double standards of morality in determining the "fitness" of mothers. As Deborah Rhode observed, "Some trial courts have been affronted by any extramarital liaison. Others have singled out Lesbian relationships for special disapproval on the basis of empirically unsupported premises; common assumptions have been that homosexual women are mentally unstable or will interfere with the 'normal' sexual and moral development of their children" (Rhode, 1989, p. 157). Differences in earning power may give fathers another advantage in that they usually can provide higher levels of material support and can pay for child care. And, when a father remarries, judges assume the new wife will provide care for the child. A mother's remarriage does not usually add a caregiver to her home.

Feminists are concerned about the implications of these trends. More involvement of men in parenting has been a goal of the National Organization for Women and other feminist groups because it would allow women to work and develop the nondomestic aspects of their lives. In addition, equal opportunity in the marketplace and politics depends on shared responsibilities in the home. Yet, some feminists argue that when fathers' rights are asserted in a male-dominated society, patriarchy is reinforced, not undermined. For example, men are winning custody battles because of continuing gender inequalities. And, although the tender-years principle gave women some power in marriage to make up for their lack of power outside of marriage, their maternal rights are once again being threatened at the same time that they continue to lack resources to assert their position either at home or in the society more generally. Even joint custody, which sounds feminist and egalitarian, hurts women when applied to still-patriarchal family gender-role patterns. Feminists observe that joint custody may often be ordered after marriage even though the fathers took little role in caring for the child when the parents were still married (Chesler, 1986). And while much of this criticism has focused on court-ordered custody arrangements, many conflicts are settled by parents or through mediation, not by a judge. In such negotiations, the unequal resources of parents are likely to affect the outcome. A father may threaten to challenge the mother's rights to custody unless his financial obligations are reduced.

What do feminists want now? First, many propose that joint custody be ordered only when truly shared parenting prevailed in the marriage. Joint responsibility requires parents to work together and get along, and this is more likely when both perceive a custody ruling as fair. Otherwise, some say, custody should be awarded to the parent who was the primary caregiver during the marriage. Not only would this person very likely be the mother, but such an arrangement would be best for the child's needs for nurturance and stability. Others are still concerned that gender-neutral principles like the primary-caretaker standard will ignore the special contribution of women in child bearing and child rearing. They propose a gender-specific standard, such as maternal deference to protect the essential relationships between mothers and their children that characterize the vast majority of families. Attention to the child's needs for care has tended to recede as custody policy has become more and more concerned with the rights of parents and justice for them.[14]

Child custody is an important contemporary battle in the war between men and women. As the battle rages, judges get more and more involved in regulating family life—determining who may live with whom and where and whether a parent can move or take a job. In court, each parent seeks to win by undermining the other parent's fitness, morally, intellectually, and financially. Some parents who lose in court defy the law and become fugitives.[15] They don't pay child support, they refuse to allow parental visits, they "steal" their children, or they deliver them to an underground network. Some even kill their children rather than lose them to the other parent.

Each year, the number of children in single-parent families increases. Since the bulk of that increase in the last ten years has been outside of marriage altogether, the laws of marriage and divorce have little effect on many of these families.

Families Without Marriage

As family relationships formed without legal marriage increase in frequency in the United States, new conflicts and demands are placed on the legal system. Policy responses in this area, as in other areas of family law, have emerged against the backdrop of common-law tradition. Judicial decisions, rather than statutes, have defined the rights and responsibilities of couples. The issues affecting women's rights parallel those within marriage: rights to property and financial status during and after cohabitation and father's and mother's rights and responsibilities to their children born out of wedlock.

Are Property Rights Recognized?

Common-law traditions reflected the religious conviction that fornication and cohabitation were immoral and thus illegal.[16] Those who practiced such behavior were fortunate to stay out of jail, let alone have grounds to assert marital-style property rights. The law usually had some sympathy, however, for a woman who might be "seduced and abandoned" or promised marriage by a man who stole her chastity and her possessions. It was not until the 1970s, when states had begun to repeal criminal sexuality statutes, that women appealed to contract or community-property principles to assert their rights to support or property from former live-in boyfriends.[17] Usually, the women based their claims on an oral or written contract, asserting that their homemaking duties gave them an interest in the property, the way that homemaking may give married women an interest in marital property.

Cohabitation is still against the law in several states. State courts in eight of them have prohibited suits for property based on contracts between cohabiting couples: the illicit sexual relationship bars the enforcement. But a majority of states have some legal precedent allowing for such suits, which can be brought by both heterosexual and homosexual couples. Some states make it clear, however, that an explicit or implied agreement that trades financial support and property for nonmarital sexual relations would not be valid. In other states, plaintiffs must prove that an agreement to share property existed, steering clear of the intimate details of the period of cohabitation. Many lawyers recommend that a cohabiting couple draw up a written contract since the law will not automatically protect the economically dependent partner in a nonmarital relationship.

Parental Rights and Responsibilities

Because of her biology and the social institutions that surround her, a mother is usually closely involved with the fate of her children. Yet the legal rights and responsibilities of the mother to children born out of wedlock often depend on the action of the father. Policies related to parental rights and responsibilities vary, depending on two categories of fathers: those who are reluctant to take an interest in their children and those who wish to be involved as parents. There is also a third category, men who are unaware they are fathers and whose rights and responsibilities are affected by adoption and welfare policy.

Legal precedents about the nonmarital child are ancient, and both legislatures and the courts have given more attention to this issue than to other aspects of nonmarital family relationships. The theoretical foundation of changes in laws parallels changes in the theories of marriage. Added to the gender-role consideration, however, is the concept of illegitimacy, that is, the legal status of the child according to circumstances of the birth. According to common law, the status of the child depended on the father, and the responsibility was the mother's. The out-of-wedlock child was the child of nobody, and unless the father recognized the child, he had no responsibility for his progeny. Concerns over child welfare in the late nineteenth century led states to require fathers to support all their children and allowed mothers and others to sue in court to establish the paternity of reluctant fathers. Successful paternity suits did not usually make the child legitimate, however. Since then, the courts have tended to undermine the distinction between legitimate and illegitimate children (Krause, 1983, pp. 818–836). In 1968, the Supreme Court, for example, used the Equal Protection Clause of the Fourteenth Amendment to strike down laws prohibiting illegitimate children from suing for the wrongful death of their mother (*Levy v. Louisiana*, 1968).

In most states, legitimacy and illegitimacy remain legal categories. Although a few states have reformed their statutes to declare all children legitimate, most still require specific actions to legitimize out-of-wedlock children, either by marriage, recognition by the father, or both. In Georgia, a father claimed an equal right to sue for a child's wrongful death, but he was denied because he had not acted to make the child legitimate (*Parnham v. Hughes*, 1979). In the common-law tradition, about half the states still give men, not women, the power to confer legitimacy on children.

Along with its growing role in enforcement of child-support obligations, Congress has taken an interest in identifying reluctant fathers of children on welfare. The Family Support Act of 1988 required states to strengthen their role in identifying fathers. With genetic matching tests that prove within a 99 percent probability the identity of a biological father, full trials are usually avoided. Today, administrative procedures in hospitals can take care of establishing paternity out of wedlock. Regulations may coerce poor mothers to name the fathers of their children in order to receive public assistance and job training. By such means, the balance between a mother's and a father's rights and responsibilities to out-of-wedlock children shifts toward the father.

The most recent issue about out-of-wedlock children is not the responsibilities of the reluctant father, but the rights of the willing father. Under old laws, the mother had sole rights to custody of the child and, if she chose not to sue for support, she could raise the child or could give the child up for adoption—either one without telling the father. Men who became fathers as a result of long-term cohabiting relationships, as well as quick sexual encounters, have used the courts to assert their interest in their children. The Supreme Court has invalidated state laws that entirely deprived fathers of their rights. These cases have not made fathers' rights completely equal with those of mothers, but they have brought them into balance. For example, *Stanley v. Illinois* (1971) tested the Illinois law that presumed the unwed father to be unfit. The Supreme Court ruled that Stanley, who had lived with the mother of his children in a long-term family relationship, had a right to a hearing for fitness. To deny him such a hearing was a violation of the Due Process and Equal Protection Clauses of the Fourteenth Amendment.

The Court has not ignored differences between the relationship of the mother and the father to the birth of their child. A father cannot, for example, ignore the mother and child for years and then come in and assert rights to visitation and custody. But "where the father has established a substantial relationship with the child and has admitted his paternity," the state may not ignore his rights to his child (*Caban v. Mohammad*, 1979, p. 389). In a subsequent case, *Lehr v. Robertson*, the Court interpreted the same New York adoption law to deny the claims of a father who had not demonstrated a commitment to his child, stating "the mere existence of a biological link does not merit equivalent constitutional protection" (1983, p. 248).

In all jurisdictions, a mother is presumed to have legal rights, whereas a father's rights are secondary. Still, actions of willing fathers seeking custody and rights to their nonmarital children have prompted new court activity and legislative reform. Their successful claims in several well-publicized cases have nullified adoptions and removed children after several months or even years from custody of adoptive parents.

Under common law, if a man had a child with a woman who was married to someone else, the presumption was that the woman's husband was the father. Now some fathers are challenging this presumption, seeking the right to establish their own paternity and rights. If successful, of course, the biological father assumes financial responsibility for the child. The Supreme Court tipped the scales in favor of marriage when it held that the biological father does not have a superior claim to that of the husband (*Michael H. v. Gerald D.*, 1989). A reform proposed in 1988, the Uniform Putative and Unknown Fathers Act, would provide ways for the biological father to rebut the presumption that goes with marriage. The goal of this reform is to define so-called putative father's rights and provide constitutionally valid norms and procedures for informing them, establishing their parental rights, and terminating those rights in case of adoption. The proposal has yet to pass in any state.

Status of Women and the Feminist Response

Feminists' concerns about the effects these policy debates and changes are having on the status of women in nonmarital family relationships parallels feminists' general concerns about women in marriage. Of greatest concern are the economic consequences of homemaking and the rights of mothers. However, in cohabitation situations, these problems are slightly worse because in many states the economically dependent woman in a living-together relationship has even less protection than that given to a married woman. For example, because of the special relationship of women to pregnancy and childbirth, the assertion of a father's rights to his children, without the legal responsibilities that flow from marriage, can increase the burdens on women. A woman with an unwanted pregnancy could become vulnerable to a man's control over her body and over her choices when the pregnancy occurs outside of marriage. Applicants for welfare can be forced to identify the fathers of their children and then be required to accept some role for the father in their family life. This may be required regardless of the possible impact of a forced relationship between two adults who may have in common only one night of casual sex. The custody and support conflicts that characterize divorce can be magnified between biological parents who have had no marriage to bring them together. Yet, at the same time, feminists are also pleased to see men take an interest in child rearing and hope men's newfound responsibilities will not work to further restrict women's choices and opportunities.

Conclusion

In other areas of policy, the potential conflicts between men and women brought about by women's struggles for equal rights are frequently muted by such calm terms as *gender neutrality, equality of opportunity, individual rights*, and even *equal pay for equal work*. Such pacific concepts have appeared in family law too: *shared partnership, joint custody, primary caregiver*, and *best interest of the child*. While such terms may ease the lives of legislators, they have not put out the fire of conflict over family relationships. Public-policy debates on family law have yielded new ideas and concepts, but they have neither found a way to protect the rights of men and women nor achieved peace in the battles between men and women. Despite the development of new uniform statutes to help states respond to changing patterns of family formation, most policy continues to take the form of court decisions on individual cases. Each wife or each mother in court has to exert her own rights. Despite the intent of divorce reformers to reduce acrimony in family disputes, the effects of new laws have been permissive, opening up the field of combat.

Statutory reforms have not in any official sense fully erased the traditional concepts of unity or separate spheres from family law. Nevertheless, gender-neutral approaches and the rhetoric of shared equal partnerships are becoming dominant. This rhetoric has not changed the fact that a woman's independent economic status is reduced by marriage and a man's is enhanced. Some feminists argue that gender-neutral family law has exacerbated existing social and economic inequalities. This outcome is clear in the facts about the economic status of single parent families headed by women. But there are consequences during marriage as well. Homemaking has little economic value; the earnings of married women continue to be regarded, even by married women themselves, as temporary or secondary income. Even in those marriages viewed by couples as alliances of two equal breadwinners, married women have much more difficulty than married men in asserting a separate identity as defined by name, domicile, credit, and claim to property.

Liberal feminists who campaigned in the 1970s for official definitions of gender roles in marriage that would emphasize equality and sharing apparently have been successful. The consequences of family law reforms have not achieved the outcomes they envisioned. The dilemma of equality and difference that plagues so many areas of policy is especially evident for those seeking a feminist system of family laws. Gender-neutral language does little to overcome the gender hierarchy and inequality outside of the family. Some feminist analysts are beginning to challenge the fundamental conception of the family in its basic form, calling for laws that embrace a variety of family forms and relationships. Agendas for such changes are still in the beginning stages, but they are likely to form the basis for the next phase of family law reform.

Notes

1. Article IV, Section I, states: "Full faith and credit shall be given in each State to the public acts, records, and judicial proceedings of every other State. And the Congress may by general laws prescribe the manner in which such acts, records, and proceedings shall be proved, and the effect thereof." The Full Faith and Credit Clause requires states to respect the laws of other states. The Supreme Court tends to interpret the requirements of this clause on a case-by-case basis. Thus, unless there are special provisions, states are not necessarily required to enforce family laws from other states. Some constitutional scholars suggest that the second sentence of the section empowers Congress to establish national uniform guidelines for family law. Thus far, it has not.

2. The *Family Law Quarterly* publishes an annual review of developments in courts and legislatures in the various states (e.g., Elrod, 1995). Legal encyclopedias, such as *Corpus Juris Secundum* (C.J.S.) and *American Jurisprudence*, 3d. ed., summarize trends nationally. There are similar encyclopedias for each state. The National Organization for Women has published a useful state-by-state guide (NOW-LDEF, 1987).

3. All in all, not a very successful effort. Only a handful of states (Arizona, Colorado, Georgia, Illinois, Kentucky, Nevada, and Washington) have enacted the UMDA in full or substantially full versions (McCabe, 1990).

4. In 1979, the National Organization for Women published the Bill of Rights for Homemakers, focusing on the economic status within and after marriage (McGlen and O'Conner, 1983, pp. 395–397).

5. Justice Warren asserted in *Loving v. Virginia* that the freedom to marry is a civil right and cannot be denied by race or class: "The freedom to marry has long been recognized as one of the vital personal rights essential to the orderly pursuit of happiness by free men" (p. 12). Those seeking legitimation of same-sex marriages might use these statements as the basis for arguing that restricting marriage to members of the opposite sex would also be unconstitutional under the Equal Protection Clause.

6. To be declared a free dealer, the woman would have to prove to the judge that she was competent to make decisions regarding her property. The declared intent of these statutes was to protect married women, who were assumed to be ignorant or especially gullible to those intent on fraud.

7. Louisiana ended up with community-property law because it was the only state to adopt France's code law, rather than England's common law, as its basic legal system. The other states with community-property laws made conscious decisions to create a community-property statute, in many cases because such a statute seemed to them more egalitarian than the separate-property system.

8. Wisconsin's law is based on the Uniform Marital Property Act, offered by the Commission on Uniform State Laws; to date, Wisconsin is the only state to enact it.

9. Census data continue to show that, despite increases in the earnings of wives, their earnings still lag far behind those of their husbands on the average. The earnings gap for spouses working full time is 43 percent.

10. The Supreme Court later interpreted this law to permit recipients of pensions to convert their pensions to disability pay, which can be excluded from property settlements (*Mansell v. Mansell*, 1989).

11. The woman was Rita C. Lucas; her former husband won the 1995 Nobel Prize in economics.

12. Mason's study (1992) of appellate court decisions shows an increase in awards to fathers between 1960 and 1990.

13. Questions have been raised about the constitutionality of this act. Congress based the law on its powers to regulate interstate commerce, but many see the issue of enforcing child support as a family matter, outside federal jurisdiction.

14. The battle between parents for their children has often been framed in terms of the children's right to have contact with both parents. This is a way to assert the place of fathers in the custody debate and to reinforce the nuclear family— mother, father, and children—in the law. It is a conservative position.

15. All states have now passed another uniform law, the Uniform Child Custody Jurisdiction Act, in which they pledge to enforce child custody orders made in other states. Thus, child-snatching parents cannot gain legal custody by moving to another state.

16. Legal marriage could be achieved for respectable couples who were unable to find a minister to perform the necessary ceremonies. If a couple declared they were married and acted as a married couple, they could achieve a legal marriage, called a *common-law marriage.* Today most states have abolished common-law marriage procedures.

17. The first famous "palimony" case involved Michele Marvin and Lee Marvin in California (18 Cal. 3d 660, 557 P. 2d 106. 1976).

References

American Jurisprudence, 2d ed. Rochester, N.Y.: Lawyers Cooperative Publishing Company, 1962– .

Bird, Caroline, ed. *What Women Want.* New York: Simon & Schuster, 1979.

Blackstone, William. *Commentaries on the Laws of England,* Book 1, 14th ed. London: Stahan, 1803.

Brown, Barbara, Freedman, Ann, Katz, Harriet, and Price, Alice. *Women's Rights and the Law: The Impact of ERA on State Laws.* New York: Praeger, 1977.

Caban v. Mohammad. 441 U.S. 380. 1979.

Carlson v. Carlson. 256 P. 2d 249, 1953.

Chesler, Phyllis. *Mothers on Trial: The Battle for Children and Custody.* New York: McGraw-Hill, 1986.

Corpus Juris Secundum (CJS). St. Paul: West Publishing, 1936–.

Eisler, Riane Tennenhaus. *Dissolution: No Fault Divorce, Marriage and Future of Women.* New York: McGraw-Hill, 1977.

Elrod, Linda. "Family Law in the Fifty States, 1993–94." *Family Law Quarterly* 28 (Winter 1995): 573–706.

Elshtain, Jean Bethke. *Public Man, Private Woman.* Princeton: Princeton University Press, 1981.

Erlanger, Howard S., and Weisberger, June M. "From Common Law Property to Community Property: Wisconsin's Marital Property Act Four Years Later." *Wisconsin Law Review* 90 (1990): 769–806.

Fineman, Martha. "Dominant Discourse, Professional Language and Legal Change in Child Custody Decisionmaking." *Harvard Law Review* 101 (February 1988): 727–774.

Fineman, Martha. *The Illusion of Equality: The Rhetoric and Reality of Divorce Reform.* Chicago: University of Chicago Press, 1991.

Fineman, Martha. *The Neutered Mother, the Sexual Family, and Other Twentieth-Century Tragedies.* New York: Routledge, 1995.

Flexner, Eleanor. *Century of Struggle: The Women's Rights Movement in the United States,* rev. ed. Cambridge: Belknap Press, 1975.

Forbush v. Wallace. 341 F. Supp. 241. 1971.

Freed, Doris, and Walker, Timothy. "Family Law in the Fifty States: An Overview." *Family Law Quarterly* 21 (Winter 1988): 417–451.

Gelb, Joyce, and Palley, Marion L. *Women and Public Policies.* Princeton: Princeton University Press, 1987.

Glendon, Mary Ann. *The Transformation of Family Law: State, Law and Family in the United States and Western Europe.* Chicago: University of Chicago Press, 1989.

Hindus, Michael, and Withey, Lynne E. "The Law of Husband and Wife in Nineteenth-Century America: Changing Views of Divorce." In *Women and the Law,* Vol. 2, edited by D. Kelly Weisberg, pp. 133–153. Cambridge: Schenkman, 1982.

Jacob, Herbert. *Silent Revolution: The Transformation of Divorce Law in the United States.* Chicago: University of Chicago Press, 1988.

Kanowitz, Leo. *Sex Roles in Law and Society: Cases and Materials.* Albuquerque: University of New Mexico Press, 1973.

Krause, Harry. *Family Law, Cases, Comments, and Questions,* 2nd ed. St Paul, Minn.: West Publishing, 1983.

Lehr v. Robertson. 463 U.S. 248. 1983.

Levy v. Louisiana. 391 U.S. 68. 1968.

Lindgren, J. Ralph, and Taub, Nadine, eds. *The Law of Sex Discrimination,* 2d ed. Minneapolis/St. Paul: West Publishing, 1993.

Loving v. Virginia. 388 U.S. 1. 1967.

McCabe, John M. "Uniform State Laws: 1988–1989." *The Book of the States,* 1990–1991. Lexington, Ky.: Council of State Government, 1990, pp. 405–448.

McGlen, Nancy, and O'Connor, Karen. *Women's Rights: The Struggle for Equality in the Nineteenth and Twentieth Centuries.* New York: Praeger, 1983.

Mansell v. Mansell. 109 s. ct. 2023. 1989.

Mason, Mary Ann. *From Father's Property to Children's Rights: The History of Child Custody in the United States.* New York: Columbia University Press, 1994.

Mason, Mary Ann. "Patterns of Appellate Court Decisions in Custody Disputes: 1920, 1960, 1990. Paper delivered at Law and Society, Philadelphia, May 1992 (cited in Mason, 1994).

Maynard v. Hill. 125 U.S. 190. 1887.

Mead, Margaret, and Kaplan, Frances Balgley. *American Women.* New York: Scribner's, 1965.

Michael H. v. Gerald D. 491 U.S. 110 1989.

Mnookin, Robert H., Maccoby, Eleanor E., Albiston, Catherine R., and Depner, Charlene E. "Private Ordering Revisited: What Custodial Arrangements Are Parents Negotiating?" In *Divorce Reform at the Crossroads,* edited by Stephen D. Sugarman and Herma Hill Kay. New Haven: Yale University Press, 1990.

NOW Legal Defense Education Fund, and Cherow-O'Leary, Renee. *The State by State Guide to Women's Legal Rights.* New York: McGraw-Hill, 1987.

Okin, Susan Moller. *Justice, Gender, and the Family.* New York: Basic Books, 1989.

O'Neill, William. *Divorce in the Progressive Era.* New Haven: Yale University Press, 1967.

Orr v. Orr. 440 U.S. 268. 1979.

Parnham v. Hughes. 441 U.S. 347. 1979.

Polikoff, Nancy D. "Why Mothers Are Losing." *Women's Rights Law Report* 7 (Spring 1982): 235–243.

Rhode, Deborah. *Justice and Gender: Sex Discrimination and the Law.* Cambridge: Harvard University Press, 1989.

Rothman, Sheila. *Woman's Proper Place: A History of Changing Ideals and Practices, 1870 to the Present*. New York: Basic Books, 1978.

Rubin, Eva. *The Supreme Court and the American Family: Ideology and Issues*. Westport, Conn.: Greenwood Press, 1986.

Salmon, Marylynn. *Women and the Law of Property in Early America*. Chapel Hill: University of North Carolina Press, 1986.

Sheppard, Annamary T. "Unspoken Premises in Custody Litigation." *Women's Rights Law Reporter* 7 (Spring 1982): 229–234.

Sloan, Irving J. *Living Together: Unmarrieds and the Law*. Dobbs Ferry, N.Y.: Oceana Publications, 1980.

Speth, Linda. "The Married Women's Property Act, 1839–1865: Reform, Reaction, or Revolution." In *Women and the Law*, vol. 21, edited by D. Kelly Weisberg, pp. 69–91. Cambridge: Schenkman, 1982.

Stanley v. Illinois. 405 U.S. 645. 1971.

Stanton, Elizabeth Cady, Anthony, Susan B., and Gage, Matilda Joslyn. *History of Woman Suffrage*, vol. 1: 1848–1861. Rochester, N.Y.: Charles Mann, 1881.

Stanton v. Stanton. 421 U.S. 7. 1975.

Statsky, William P. *Family Law*, 3rd ed. St. Paul: West Publishing, 1991.

Sugarman, Stephen D., and Kay, Herma Hill, eds. *Divorce Reform at the Crossroads*. New Haven: Yale University Press, 1990.

Thompson v. Thompson. 218 U.S. 611. 1910.

U.S. v. Yazell. 382 U.S. 341. 1966.

Walker, Timothy B., and Elrod, Linda D. "Family Law in the Fifty States: An Overview." *Family Law Quarterly* 26 (Winter 1993): 319–421.

Walters, Lynda Henley, and Abshire, Carla Rae. "Single Parenthood and the Law." *Marriage and Family Review* 20 (1995): 161–188.

Weitzman, Leonore. *The Marriage Contract: Spouses, Lovers, and the Law*. New York: Free Press, 1981.

Weitzman, Leonore. *The Divorce Revolution*. New York: Free Press, 1985.

Zaretsky, Eli. *Capitalism, the Family, and Personal Life*. London: Pluto, 1976.

CHAPTER 7

Work and Pay

A majority of women work; women have always worked. The statistics about women's employment in the United States show that since 1900, women have never been less than 19 percent of the paid work force. Their share has grown dramatically since 1960, to more than 45 percent.[1] Women earn less than men for the same work; they share in fewer rewards for their labor. The earnings gap between men and women is nearly 30 percent. The relationship of work to women's rights and the public problems that result stem from the meaning people assign to these statistics. Why do women work? What does work mean to women? What does women's participation in the work force mean to the economy and to society? How are women workers different from men workers? How does race discrimination affect women in the work force? At any time, there are a variety of answers to these questions in public debate. Some of the answers will become dominant and shape public policy, thus affecting work and pay for groups of women.

Beliefs about why women work are related to ideas about work in general, as well as to prevailing expectations about gender roles. In Western societies, there is a work ethic: work is valuable and contributes to society and human development. Thus women may work to develop their intellects and skills, to contribute to society, and to achieve maturity and independence. This has usually been a minority view. Much more popular is the belief that women work because of economic necessity, but not the same kind of necessity that puts men to work. Rather, women work when the traditional formula of male breadwinner and female homemaker fails—because of divorce, widowhood, single parenting, or the male breadwinner's inability to earn enough to meet the family's perceived needs. This perception is based on the assumption that paid work has a different place in women's lives and is in conflict with their primary roles as mothers: somehow, if things were the way they were *supposed* to be, women—especially mothers—would not have to work. If women do work, out of social need or economic necessity, they are different from men, less permanent workers, with different interests and skills—less "real" workers. When a woman works even though her husband apparently is able to support her adequately, it is often believed that her job is unimportant—she works for "pin" money, because she is bored, for personal satisfaction, or to get out of the house.

Most of these public beliefs about women, work, and gender roles have completely ignored the plight of poor women, forced to excessive work at low wages. Since the nineteenth century many more minority women than white women have worked, often in domestic and agricultural jobs, not far removed from the economy of slavery and indentured servitude. This unseen labor force, the "mules" as Zora Neale Hurston described them, did the work that permitted white women to fill the role of full-time wife, homemaker, and mother (quoted in Collins, 1990, p. 43). Yet demands to improve the working conditions of this group rarely appeared in the public debate about women and work.

Another way to look at women workers is in terms of their place, as a group, in the economy. Again, there are different interpretations. Women may be seen as a reserve labor force, called upon to serve in times of national emergency, such as war. Or the presence of women in factory labor could be a sign of social pathology, such as the failure of employers to provide decent wages to fathers or the result of a breakdown in family life through increasing divorce rates. Still another interpretation might be that changes in the economy draw women in as a source of talent in times of growth.

These different conceptions of why women work and their place in the economy produce public problems demanding government attention. Each view holds that something is wrong with women and work. Work for opportunity leads to concerns about fair treatment and equal chances. Work as social pathology demands special protection for women. A surge in the need for skills produces incentives to lure women into the work force.

Problems arising from women's participation in the paid labor force have been the concern of government for at least one hundred years. And

BOX 7.1

Why Women Worked in the U.S. Meat-Packing Industry in 1932

In 1932, the Women's Bureau reported the reasons given by more than six hundred women then employed in the slaughtering and meat-packing industry:

> Where women are supporting themselves or are the sole support of others, the importance to the family of their employment is fairly obvious. Of 634 women reporting who were not the sole support of themselves or others, it may be said in brief that roughly a third reported working because of insufficiency of husband's earnings or the need to keep up the general family expenses, and almost another third had lost their husbands through death, desertion, or divorce, or were helping relatives other than husband and children. Another large group [was] that in which the husband was unsteadily employed, either through the vicissitudes of industry or through his own incapacity. Many women reported being at work for some very definite purpose, such as to educate children, pay for a home, or pay a series of doctor and hospital bills, buy furniture, make a visit to the old country, or get a start in life and save something while young. A few specifically mentioned the high cost of living. Less than 3 per cent gave choice rather than necessity as their reason for working. (U.S. Department of Labor, Women's Bureau, 1932, p. 126)

during all that time, despite the complexity of policy debates, one basic question has stirred controversy: to what extent should women be treated as either a separate group in the work force or a part of one common group of workers, male and female? That is, should public policy recognize gender as a basis for classifying and treating workers, or should it treat all workers the same? Although first one and then the other position has prevailed, the public debate on women's work has never been free of the tension between equality and difference.

Protective Legislation

The foundation for understanding contemporary policy debates on work, pay, and women's rights is the rationale for *protective laws* enacted nearly a century ago. The first protective laws promoted by reformers trying to moderate the mistreatment of workers in the early period of industrial- ization made no distinction based on sex—the laws applied to everyone. In the grip of laissez-faire theories, the courts regularly struck down such laws as violating the constitutional freedom of contract. Faced with defeat in the courts, progressives and feminists joined together in the 1880s to help women workers. Several forces converged to produce this reform coalition. Infant-mortality rates were on the rise, and the new science of empiricism produced documentation linking infant death to demands on poor working mothers. Reformers were alarmed by the way women were used by employers—working long hours and doing heavy, exhausting work for little pay. Men were "worked" like that, too, but they were stron- ger and did not have to face pregnancy and childbirth. Feminists were moving away from the "inalienable rights" view of equality espoused by Elizabeth Cady Stanton and Susan B. Anthony and moving into a new phase extolling motherhood as a woman's primary role, of equal dignity with man's role as breadwinner. A woman had to be healthy, educated, and secure in her moral leadership in the home to give birth and raise healthy, vigorous offspring. The fledgling eugenics movement joined in, focusing on the essential contribution to the *race* made by women in their proper roles.[2]

States enacted two types of protective labor laws. One prohibited women from being employed in certain occupations considered danger- ous to their health or morality or unsuitable to woman's primary role as mother. Most common were mining jobs and jobs related to alcoholic beverages, such as bartending. But laws also restricted women from such disparate occupations as attorney and wrestler. Ohio had a huge list of male-only jobs: crossing watchman, section hand, express driver, metal molder, bellhop, gas or electric meter reader, freight or baggage elevator operator, baggage or freight handler, trucker, as well as jobs in shoeshine parlors, bowling alleys, poolrooms, and in blast furnaces or smelters.

The second type of protective law regulated work conditions. The most prevalent of these laws limited the number of hours women could work. Others required overtime pay, rest periods, and lunch breaks and prohibited night work and heavy lifting. Eventually forty-one states and the District of Columbia had such laws. Excluded from such protections were those women employed at the margins of the economy—domestic and agricultural workers—and those in states, primarily in the South, without protective laws at all.

The Test of Constitutionality: *Muller v. Oregon*

Protective laws for women survived the test of constitutionality in 1908 with the landmark decision in *Muller v. Oregon*. The Supreme Court based its decision on a new legal tool, the Brandeis brief, named after the lawyer Louis Brandeis, who had been engaged by the National Consumers' League (NCL) to defend the Oregon law. That law established ten hours as the maximum that an employer could require a woman to work each day. The brief, which was prepared in large part by Brandeis's activist sister-in-law, Josephine Goldmark, used medical and sociological data to document the adverse effects of long working hours on the health of women, especially pregnant women. The Court accepted the NCL's definition of the problem—that women and men are so different that legislation to protect women, rather than men, is fully justified to achieve equality:

> That woman's physical structure and the performance of maternal functions place her at a disadvantage in the struggle for subsistence is obvious. This is especially true when the burdens of motherhood are upon her. Even when they are not, by abundant testimony of the medical fraternity continuance for a long time on her feet at work, repeating this from day to day, tends to injurious effects upon the body, and, as healthy mothers are essential to vigorous offspring, the physical well-being of woman becomes an object of public interest and care in order to preserve the strength and vigor of the race . . . Though limitations upon personal and contractual rights may be removed by legislation, there is that in her disposition and habits of life which will operate against a full assertion of those rights. She will still be where some legislation to protect her seems necessary to secure a real equality of right. (1908, p. 421)

After official approval of protective laws for women, both the number of laws and the support for them grew. Then a third type of law, guaranteeing a minimum wage to women, was added.

Restricted Hours, but No Minimum Wage

Following Massachusetts' lead in 1912, several states passed laws guaranteeing a minimum wage for women workers. If women should be restricted in the number of hours they worked—both for their own health and for the well-being of society—then it seemed logical and just that they should also be guaranteed a minimum wage for the time they were permitted to work. Proponents used the argument about women's special place in society and as workers that had worked so well in defending other protective laws. Women needed a minimum wage, whereas men did not, because of the different moral standards of the sexes. Without adequate income, poor women were vulnerable to prostitution to earn money. Opponents, primarily employers, charged that minimum-wage laws were different from other laws to protect health. They claimed that employers would be driven into bankruptcy if forced to pay a worker more than her work produced. Minimum-wage laws, they said, were legislative price fixing.

Adkins v. Children's Hospital came to the Supreme Court in 1923 in the wake of the suffrage victory. Employers were thus able to make use of suffragists' claims to equal rights by pointing out that the minimum wage for women violated equal-protection guarantees of the Fourteenth Amendment by favoring a particular class of worker. The Court agreed with the employers' conception that the issue was not health but price-fixing.[3] The Court also questioned the greater moral needs of women:

> This is simply and exclusively a price-fixing law, confined to adult women who are legally as capable of contracting for themselves as men. . . . It is based wholly on the opinions of the members of the board . . . as to what will be necessary to provide a living for a woman, keep her in health and preserve her morals. . . . Morality rests upon other considerations than wages; and there is, certainly, no such prevalent connection between the two as to justify a broad attempt to adjust the latter with reference to the former. As a means of safeguarding morals the attempted classification, in our opinion, is without reasonable basis. No distinction can be made between women who work for others and those who do not; nor is there ground for distinction between women and men, for certainly, if women require a minimum wage to preserve their morals men require it to preserve their honesty. (pp. 554–557)

The Role of the Women's Bureau

Meanwhile, the feminists and progressives took control of the debate on women's work from inside the government. In 1920, they succeeded in persuading Congress to establish the Women's Bureau (WB). Modeled after the Children's Bureau of 1914, the Women's Bureau was charged "to promote the welfare of wage-earning women, improve their working condition, increase their efficiency, and advance their opportunities for profitable employment" (U.S. Statutes at Large, 41 Stat. 987, 1920, p. 987). By statute, the director was to be a woman. The staff was composed of ardent advocates of protective legislation for women. They believed the public problem was the threat that wage labor posed to the health and well-being of mothers and potential mothers. In study after study, they documented the conditions poor women faced in mills and factories and as household workers.[4]

The Women's Bureau was largely ignored by the Labor Department power structure. It was sustained by a coalition of women's organizations dominated by middle-class reformers, especially by the Women's Trade Union League (WTUL), the Young Women's Christian Association (YWCA), the National Consumers League (NCL), the League of Women Voters (LWV), and the American Association of University Women (AAUW). These groups interacting with the WB staff formed a full policy community with its own beliefs, values, and language. In the world of this network, women were a separate labor force. They were forced to work, but their work was incompatible with and threatened their primary responsibilities as mothers. Until something could be done to get more mothers home, protective laws were absolutely essential.

In the 1920s, the feminist movement split over the WB view of women, producing an irreconcilable division that stalled progress toward women's rights. After World War I, some women workers were beginning to understand that protective laws could work against them. Some laws had been relaxed in World War I to bring women into men's jobs. Then, after the war, women were fired. Some, such as the railway employees and printers, protested to the Women's Bureau, which was, after all, pledged to "advance their opportunities for profitable employment" (U.S. Statutes at Large, 41 Stat. 987, 1920, p. 987). The WB was unmoved, clinging to a belief that protection helped the vast majority of women workers; the WB had little sympathy for the plight of women in men's jobs.

The National Woman's Party (NWP) listened, of course; this party's commitment to an Equal Rights Amendment (ERA) meant that it supported no special treatment for women. The NWP applauded the Supreme Court's rejection of the minimum wage for women in the *Adkins* case, agreeing that women were as capable as men in contracting for their jobs. These feminists wanted women to be treated as adults: open all occupations, and let women compete. Only through fair competition with men for the good jobs could women's economic position be improved.

The disagreement developed into a bitter conflict between the Women's Bureau and its allies, called *social feminists*, and the much smaller NWP coalition, called *egalitarian feminists*. The social feminists' vision of the work-and-women issue prevailed, and they remained in control of the debate for the next thirty years. The effect carries over into women's rights today. In law and public debate, protective legislation reinforced the separation of women into a special labor force. Job segregation and unequal pay were institutionalized along with legitimation of women's separate and primary roles as wife, homemaker, and mother. Work was not considered essential for women, and women did not have a right to work. If economics necessitated, women could work at jobs suitable to their sex. In industry, they had to be treated separately. At the same time, protective laws did not affect the two jobs where most women in the 1920s worked: domestic service and agriculture. These were predominantly occupied by African American women, and the ideology of protection never applied to them. Thus, these women workers were doubly marginal, with long hours of hard work at low pay and no protection under the new legislation. It is understandable that this conflict over equality and protection would have little meaning for these black American women.

With protectionism ascendant, egalitarians did not fade away; their vision of individual rights and integration of women into the male work force gradually attracted support. They were thus ready for the major shift in women's work from institutionalized protection, segregation, and marginality to a policy community formed around goals of equal opportunity, integration, and equal pay. Although NWP egalitarians made a contribution to this transformation, the civil rights movement prepared the way. Given African American women's double marginality, it is ironic that the grip of the regime of protection was broken by piggybacking women's rights on the policy momentum for the movement for racial equality.

Equality for Working Women

Policy affecting women workers was transformed from protection to equality in the environment of social, cultural, and economic change that followed World War II. The participation of women in the work force dipped slightly at the end of the war but soon started the climb that continues to this day. Statistics showed that working for wages was becoming the norm, not the exception. Were women joining the work force because things were getting worse? No, economic development drew them in, and government helped. Public policy in the 1950s encouraged investment in defense industries and the growth of service jobs. The Department of Labor took the lead in developing the needed human resources to fuel the economic growth. The demand for educated workers became a crisis when the Soviet Union's Sputnik challenged American power. With the competition of the Cold War, resources were directed toward defense-related industries requiring skilled workers. The National Manpower Council joined with the Department of Labor and the Women's Bureau to explore ways of developing womanpower. The council recommended, among other things, that, since women were an essential part of the labor force, they should be treated according to the principles of equality of opportunity and equal pay for equal work (National Manpower Council, 1957).

Despite economic needs drawing women into the work force, public opinion about women, especially as mothers, was ambivalent. On the one hand, women's enormous participation in the war effort dispelled notions about women's fitness for many jobs. Even stronger, however, was the widespread agreement that jobs for male breadwinners, especially returning soldiers, must not be threatened. Complementing this view was a spirit of romanticism about the family and a social glorification of the central role of motherhood in child development. Despite all the sentiment about the wonders of homemaking in the suburbs, letters from women workers complaining about job discrimination and demanding equal opportunity flowed into the Women's Bureau.

Women's advocacy groups continued to disagree about basic issues of women and work and the government's role. The conflict over protective legislation and equality was still raging, led by the same coalitions and again pitting the Women's Bureau against the NWP. This split made it impossible to present a clear set of proposals to answer the demands of the growing numbers of women workers. Women workers themselves had no effective organizational voice. The old middle-class–led Women's Trade Union League (WTUL) had disbanded, and few women workers belonged to unions. Those women in the American Federation of Labor (AFL) and Congress of Industrial Organizations (CLO) maintained staunch support for protective laws.

BOX 7.2

Women Who Work; Women in the Work Force

The Women's Bureau predicts that the steady increase in participation of women in the work force will lead to parity with men in a few years.

Women as a percentage of the total U.S. work force

Year	All	White	Black	Hispanic
1975	39%	39%	45%	NA
1990	45	44	50	39
2005 (est.)	47	46	51	41

Women in the work force as a percentage of U.S. women

1980	51.5%	51.2%	53.1%	47.4%
1985	54.5	54.1	56.5	49.4
1990	57.5	57.5	57.8	53.0
2005 (est.)	63.0	n.a.	n.a.	n.a.

Source: U.S. Department of Labor, Women's Bureau. *1993 Handbook on Women Workers: Trends and Issues.* Washington, D.C.: Government Printing Office, 1994, p. 4.

This period of conflict led to the three major pieces of legislation—the Equal Pay Act of 1963; Title VII of the Civil Rights Act of 1964; and Executive Orders 11246 and 11375—that today promote the equal rights of women as workers. Equal-opportunity laws were not the result of the contemporary feminist movement of the 1960s and 1970s; they preceded it. In fact, the existence of the laws themselves stimulated the action that led to a rebirth of the women's rights movement. Finally, the way these laws operate today has been shaped by the movement they spawned. In the area of employment policy, women's rights has meant the establishment of a new policy community grounded in the interrelation among feminists within the government and those outside.

Equal Pay Act of 1963: Equal Pay for Equal Work

"Equal pay for equal work" is arguably the least controversial tenet of feminism today. Everybody now sees the inherent sense of the idea that if a woman does the same job a man does, she should get the same wage.

But it was not always such a consensus issue. The proposal for equal pay is nearly as old as waged labor itself, responding to the widespread practice in early factory work of paying women half the rate of men (Kessler-Harris, 1990). Motives behind equal-pay demands were not usually based on a sense of fairness and equality. Most male workers saw equal pay as a way to compete with lower-priced female labor. They assumed that if employers had to pay women workers the same wage men received, they would hire men. In keeping with traditional gender roles, the main salary demand of the male workers and their unions was the *family wage*.

The government flirted with equal-pay policies for special needs before the 1960s. The first equal-pay policy was in effect in World War I as a temporary war measure. Two million women entered the work force and took many traditionally male jobs. To counteract the fear that women would undercut males' wage rates, the law prevented employers from paying women's rates for male jobs. The New Deal brought another equal-pay gesture stemming from the federal government's new role in regulating employment. The Fair Labor Standards Act of 1938 established the concept of fair treatment for workers and minimum wages in certain employment categories. It stated that "no classification shall be made under this [wage order] section on the basis of age or sex" (52 Stat. 1060, p. 1064). World War II prompted orders for equal pay in war work, motivated—as in World War I—to keep wage rates up in traditionally male industrial jobs.

Until 1945, the equal-pay provisions had been designed largely to protect wage rates for men. In that year, however, social feminists introduced a bill to protect women's pay. Their position was that women were underpaid, and women's wages needed to be improved. From the perspective of special protection for women workers, it made sense to pass legislation to give women equal pay for work comparable to that done by men. The law would apply only to women and would be enforced by the Women's Bureau. Employers vigorously opposed this proposed federal intrusion into their business, and the egalitarian feminists opposed the gender bias. As it turned out, the bill did not become law. Despite an afterglow of gratitude for women's contributions to the war effort, even less crude equal-pay proposals would have had little chance in the 1940s. Political leaders were adamant in their determination to protect jobs for men. Although some people argued that women usually work because they have to, women were still seen as potential competition, taking jobs away from male breadwinners when women didn't even have to work! Many political leaders thought that improving wages for women would tempt women into the work force and right back into the men's jobs they had held during the war. Perhaps there was also the fear that more income for women would threaten family stability by giving women autonomy in marriage, divorce, childbirth, and child rearing.

The demand for equal pay remained and gathered token support during the 1950s. Several states started to enact equal-pay laws and, by 1963, twenty-three such laws were on the books. Also, the Labor Department was considering ways to attract educated women into the work force. It was not until President Kennedy's administration, however, that any bills were proposed in Congress. Under the leadership of Esther Peterson at the revitalized Women's Bureau, equal-pay law became a reality. The bureau argued that equal pay was an issue of fairness. The President's Commission on the Status of Women (PCSW) (Mead and Kaplan, 1965) strongly endorsed the concept, and Chair Eleanor Roosevelt pointed out that it was really not a difficult issue. But conflicts did erupt; they centered on the definition of equal pay for women. Until 1962, most proposals, even war measures, called for equal pay for *comparable work*. Proponents recognized that a law based on equal work might be ineffective. Employers might use standards of equal work so narrowly as to avoid the law. However, employers opposed the comparable-work language, anyway, arguing that so fuzzy a concept would mean arbitrary government interference in private business decisions. Coverage and enforcement were also issues. At stake in this debate was whether an equal pay law would be largely symbolic or would close the wage gap between men and women workers.

To get any act at all, however, the Women's Bureau and its supporters in Congress were forced to compromise and they changed *comparable work* to *equal work*. Even so, employers were working hard to limit coverage of the Equal Pay Act. And members of Congress (who were all for fairness, mind you) were still concerned that equal pay might take jobs away from men.[5] Finally, opponents gave in when convinced that the act would be more symbolic than effective because *women and men did not do equal work*. Data from the Department of Labor showed that women joining the work force in the 1950s took clerical jobs in the service sector; given such job segregation, equal-pay laws would pose little threat to men's jobs. The Equal Pay Act became an amendment to the Fair Labor Standards Act (FLSA). As such, it covered only wage and hour employees and exempted employers with fewer than twenty-five employees. The act was to be enforced by the Labor Department's Wage and Hour Division, which had the power to investigate claims of unequal pay and to order that back wages be paid.

The Equal Pay Act of 1963 provides that employers may not pay employees of one sex at rates lower than those paid to employees of the opposite sex employed in the same establishment, for equal work—that is, on jobs that require substantially equal skill, effort, and responsibility and that are performed under similar working conditions. Exceptions are allowed when sex differences in pay are due to seniority, merit, quantity or quality of production, or any factor other than sex. In 1972, the provisions of the Equal Pay Act were extended to management and professional employees, as well as to state and local government employees. Every state except Alabama and Mississippi now prohibits discrimination in pay either with an equal-pay act, usually modeled after the federal statute, or with a fair-labor-standards statute prohibiting sex discrimination in all aspects of employment, or with both (NOW-LDEF, 1987).

Civil Rights Act of 1964, Title VII: Equal Employment Opportunity

The legislative and administrative history of Title VII of the Civil Rights Act of 1964 tells of a dramatic final transformation of the public-policy definition of women and work from an ideology of protection and differentiation to one of individual rights and equality of opportunity. Before this transformation, laws were based on the assumption that women were an extraordinary category of workers. Afterwards, women officially became part of the regular work force. This switch was accomplished by the cause for women's rights hitching a piggyback ride on the civil rights movement and redesigning itself as a legitimate part of the overall demand for equality.

The story of Title VII and women's rights started in 1964, almost at the end of the long push for a federal civil rights act. Since World War II, the federal government had responded to the growing movement for racial justice with commissions, court decisions (*Brown v. Board of Education*, 347 U.S. 483, 1953), and executive orders against discrimination in government contracts. The comprehensive civil rights bill proposed by President Kennedy was to be the capstone of the long struggle. After Kennedy's assassination, the Johnson administration made the bill its top priority despite strong conservative opposition in Congress. As the bill worked its way through Congress, the National Woman's Party leaders dutifully proposed, as they had since the 1930s, that all actions to ban race discrimination include bans on sex discrimination as well. Finally, when the bill was about to be debated in the House of Representatives, the NWP convinced Howard Smith (D.-Va.) to amend Title VII, the employment section, to prohibit sex discrimination along with that based on race, national origin, and religion.

Smith's amendment divided feminists and both political parties. Many proponents saw the issue as one of white American women's rights. Most southern conservatives, however, as well as the NWP, opposed the whole idea of a federal civil rights law as an excessive interference in private affairs. But they reasoned that if the act passed and employers could not refuse to hire African Americans, or foreigners, or Jews because of Title VII, the only people they could refuse were white American, Christian women. An unusual coalition developed. Along with the conservatives, most of the women in Congress supported the amendment, aware that sex discrimination in employment was very real.

Opponents to including *sex* in Title VII included the Johnson administration, the Women's Bureau, and civil rights leaders. Some feminists still wanted to retain the principle that women's family duties sometimes warranted the different treatment of protective laws. Civil rights leaders and the Women's Bureau agreed that the problems of women were not the same or as severe as the problems of minorities, that race discrimination was far worse than anything women faced. Since women's rights was so controversial, they feared, the sex amendment might endanger the bill's passage. The association between demands for women's rights and demands for rights for African Americans has occasionally been rocky. African American advocates sometimes see women's rights leaders as representative of white American middle-class interests. Others fear the addition of women's issues will increase conflict over civil rights. Black women, subject to the intersection of both race and gender discrimination, are often forced to choose sides when such conflicts flare up.

After the amendment passed the House of Representatives, it remained in the bill, primarily because the Johnson administration did not want to send the delicate measure to a conference committee. Once the prohibition of sex discrimination in employment was in the act, the shift toward equality for women was under way. The Women's Bureau began to lobby in favor of it. At state and federal levels, the Commissions on the Status of Women (CSWs) became watchdog groups for the implementation of Title VII for women. Along the way, the contemporary women's movement was born.

Title VII states that

> it shall be an unlawful employment practice for an employer (1) to
> fail or refuse to hire or to discharge any individual, or otherwise dis-
> criminate against any individual with respect to his compensation,
> terms, conditions, or privileges of employment, because of such
> individual's race, color, religion, sex, or national origin; or (2) to limit,
> segregate, or classify his employees or applicants for employment in
> any way which would deprive or tend to deprive any individual of
> employment opportunities or otherwise adversely affect his status as
> an employee, because of such individual's race, color, religion, sex, or
> national origin. (Sec. 703(a)78 Stat. 255, 1964)

Title VII applied to employers and unions in interstate commerce
with twenty-five or more employees (in 1972 reduced to fifteen employees) and created a special Equal Employment Opportunity Commission
(EEOC) to enforce its provisions. The EEOC's first task was to issue appropriate regulations outlining which employment practices would be
permitted or prohibited. The first commissioners did not take the ban on
sex discrimination seriously. The myth had already begun to develop that
Howard Smith had added the amendment as a joke or as a ploy by anti-
civil rights southerners to defeat the act. Other than stating that sex could
be a bona fide occupational qualification (BFOQ) under certain circumstances, Congress had given little indication of what it intended by prohibiting sex discrimination in employment. Despite the four-thousand
sex-discrimination complaints filed in the first year, the EEOC's first
guidelines did little to disturb employer practices beyond the BFOQ exception. (We return to that topic later in this chapter.) The EEOC left
protective labor laws intact and refused to ban sex-segregated job advertisements.

Members of state CSWs, frustrated with inaction by the EEOC,
formed the National Organization for Women (NOW) in 1966. The bureaucrats were unlikely to act to enforce equality for women in the absence of some demonstration of organizational support like that of the
civil rights movement. Thus, NOW was organized as a civil rights organization for women's rights. The leaders, many of whom had already had
experience in the civil rights campaign, adopted an ideology of feminism
using the language of individualism and equality that had been so effective in the struggle for racial integration. This organization joined with
others to bring suits to force the EEOC to enforce Title VII. Together, they
began to argue that protective laws, so long defended by unions and
women's advocates, kept women from many jobs with good pay and had
outlived their usefulness. The courts ruled that Title VII preempted pro-

tective laws, thus invalidating their use. And, in 1969, the EEOC revised its guidelines to reflect this change. Thus, NOW's position that protection for women meant marginalization and inferiority became a principle of public policy.

The new feminist definition of equality of opportunity for women in work and pay triumphed during the 1971–1972 congressional session. The 92nd Congress, which passed the Equal Rights Amendment, Title IX, and other important legislation for women's rights, also expanded Title VII. Hearings on amendments to Title VII of the Civil Rights Act at last documented the reality and effects of sex discrimination in employment. The testimony also demonstrated that there was strong organizational support for federal laws to eliminate employment discrimination, just as civil rights advocates had shown a decade earlier. Title VII was extended to cover private employers with fifteen or more employees, as well as state and local government employment. It also prohibited discrimination against managerial and professional employees. Another debate over enforcement ended in compromise. Feminists and civil rights advocates argued for injunction powers for the EEOC.[6] They lost; the EEOC's powers were increased only to include the power to bring suit against employers.

The process of enforcing Title VII has remained largely unchanged since 1972. The EEOC does not monitor employers or investigate to find those who are breaking the law by discriminating. In fact, employers can and do violate Title VII laws undisturbed, as long as no complaints are filed. It is the *employment-discrimination complaint*, which may be filed by an employee, a group of employees, or an organization on behalf of employees, that triggers an EEOC action. The EEOC has regional and district offices throughout the country. The complaint lands on the desk of a probably overburdened investigative officer in a district office. The investigator informs the employer of a complaint against him or her and sends it, if possible, to a state or local agency for review and settlement. If the complaint is not settled, the EEOC will investigate. Its first goal is to conciliate and help the parties reach a compromise. If this effort fails, and if the EEOC has the interest, time, and staff, it can bring a suit against the employer. The vigor with which the commission attacks sex discrimination depends a great deal on the priorities of the president.[7] If the EEOC decides not to sue, the complainant can sue in a federal court. Whatever happens, a complaining employee may request a "right to sue" letter from the EEOC six months after making the complaint. This letter entitles the employee to sue in court independently of the EEOC. However, the employee can win such a suit only if she or he has the time, the resources, and an effective lawyer.

Until recently, awards for successful cases were limited to back pay and attorney's fees. The Civil Rights Act of 1991 (discussed in more detail later in this chapter) provides for assignment of punitive and compensatory damages up to $300,000 for a large firm if a worker can show that the employer engaged in intentional discrimination "with malice or with reckless indifference to federally protected rights." By and large, however, Title VII is not of much direct help to the ordinary worker; nevertheless, successful lawsuits have been part of an organized feminist-inspired campaign to gain enforcement of Title VII. The law would have little impact without the occasional chastening effect of the threat of a lawsuit, which is often enough to keep employers' policies and practices just inside the letter of the law and out of court.

Executive Orders 11246 and 11375: Affirmative Action

The third pillar of federal employment policy, affirmative action, is directed toward achieving integration of the work force. *Affirmative action* means to take positive steps to achieve a particular result. It is based on the recognition that, because of the lingering effects of previous discrimination, merely ceasing a discriminatory practice will not achieve equality since there will not be equal outcomes. For example, just removing the race restrictions from the law will not be enough to overcome racist attitudes and the effects of centuries of cultural oppression of African Americans. Similarly, removing "female only" or "male only" job categories will not overcome sexist attitudes and centuries of gender-role differentiation and inequality. And removing both race- and gender-related employment policies will not ease the double burden faced by women of color. If some discrimination has been based on membership in a group or class (all African Americans or all women), the remedy must also apply to all members of the group or class. The leaders of firms, educational institutions, and government agencies must then do more to bring members of the previously disadvantaged groups and classes into jobs and schools where there have been few such people. Affirmative action has often been criticized for contradicting the idea of individual rights that is enshrined in the 1964 Civil Rights Act. However, civil rights leaders are convinced that affirmative action is the only way to overcome the legacy of slavery and years of cultural oppression. In fact, the Civil Rights Act itself gives the courts the power to order employers found guilty of discrimination to implement affirmative action plans.

In 1965, President Johnson signed Executive Order 11246 to require firms having contracts with the federal government to "take affirmative action to ensure that applicants are employed, and that employees are treated during employment, without regard to their race, color, religion, or national origin" (30 F.R. 12319, 1968). The order also established, for the first time, a strong enforcement agency, the Office of Federal Contract Compliance (OFCC) in the Department of Labor, to monitor the order. The NWP made its usual demand to "include sex," but, in 1966, it was no longer alone in making this demand. The growing belief among feminists that sex and race discrimination were similar public problems brought in NOW, Business and Professional Women's Clubs, the Citizens' Advisory Council on the Status of Women (CACSW), and the Women's Bureau. Letters were written and memos sent, and in 1968, President Johnson's Executive Order 11375 to *include sex* went into effect.

On paper, this meant those firms that had fifty or more employees and that held contracts of at least $10,000 with the federal government could lose this lucrative business—which for many firms would bring bankruptcy—if they failed to comply with regulations of the OFCC. It wasn't until 1971 that these regulations relating to women were issued (43 F.R. 49249, 1978). Responsibility for enforcing the order and for monitoring contracts fell to the agency issuing the contract. All of these agencies were slow in implementing the orders. NOW and the Women's Equity Action League (WEAL), through suits charging noncompliance against hundreds of firms and educational institutions, led a nationwide campaign for enforcement.

Executive Orders 11246 and 11375 were important additions to equal opportunity policy because they require that most large employers do more than simply remove sex and race categories in employment policies. If it is working, Executive Order 11375 requires contractors to follow a specific affirmative-action program:

1. Prepare a study of overall employment to determine where minorities and women are underrepresented.

2. Develop a plan to increase representation in jobs where percentages of women and minorities are less than available in job pools, including goals for hiring and timetables for reaching the goals.

3. Develop recruitment strategies to increase the number of women and minorities in the applicant pool to improve the likelihood that there will be enough qualified applicants.

4. File periodic reports with the contracting agency to make sure that the employer is making progress toward the goals.

If an employer is out of compliance, the contracting agency can suspend the contract.

Other affirmative action policies range from permissive to imposed. Through collective bargaining, unions and managers may voluntarily adopt plans to increase the representation of women and minorities. At the other extreme, federal, state, and local government have approved mandatory "set-asides." These apply to distributive policies where a portion of the goods offered—contracts, licenses, radio frequencies—are reserved for minorities and women.

Implementation of Equal Employment Opportunity Laws

The principle underlying equal employment opportunity (EEO) laws is that employers must treat employees as individuals, to be evaluated on their own talents and abilities rather than on assumptions related to their race or sex. Although this principle is the basis for the Equal Pay Act, Title VII, and the Executive Orders 11246 and 11375 (all enacted over twenty-five years ago), what these laws mean for women workers depends on the way they are implemented. The enforcement of federal law is a process involving interaction among administrative agencies, federal courts, interest groups, and a wide variety of employers—from large corporations to state and local governments and educational institutions. When state governments are involved, statutes occasionally run into constitutional issues, especially those arising under the Equal Protection Clause of the Fourteenth Amendment. It is difficult to say clearly and unequivocally "It's the law!" The process of implementing equal-employment policy has yielded some accepted definitions of permitted and prohibited employer practices, as well as interpretations of the general language and intent of Congress and the president.

Sex As a BFOQ

Congress had made it clear that under Title VII sex could be a BFOQ or bona fide occupational qualification:

> [I]t shall not be an unlawful employment practice for an employer to hire and employ employees, for an employment agency to classify, or refer for employment any individual, for a labor organization to classify its membership or to classify or refer for employment any individual, or for an employer, labor organization, or joint labor-management committee controlling apprenticeship or other training or retraining programs to admit or employ any individual in any such program, on the basis of his religion, *sex*, or national origin in those certain instances where religion, *sex*, or national origin is a bona fide occupational qualification reasonably necessary to the normal operation of that particular business or enterprise. (Sec. 703[a] 78 Stat. 256, 1964)

The EEOC regulations narrowly define the circumstances in which sex can be used as a BFOQ, and they exclude most of the justifications typically used by employers to avoid receiving applications from women. Unacceptable reasons are "assumptions of the comparative employment characteristics of women in general . . . or stereotyped characterizations of the sexes . . . or because of his own personal preferences or those of his employees, customers, or clients" (Sec. 1604.2).

As implemented, Title VII rules out traditional justifications for refusing to hire women in certain jobs. Stereotypes about the ability of women or men—such as the belief that women would not be good police officers because they would not be able to break up brawls or would be afraid of guns—are not permitted as defenses of sex as a BFOQ. Even documentation that shows that most women are not strong enough to meet the physical requirements for a job such as firefighter or security guard cannot exclude a particular woman from applying for the job and trying. Assumptions about the job preferences of women also are not acceptable for overlooking women. It may be that women do not like to work weekends or that some quit to have a baby (fewer and fewer leave the work force to raise children), but employers may not refuse to interview or hire qualified women according to their assumptions about "the way women workers are."

Shifting blame to co-workers and clients won't work, either. The courts enforce EEOC regulations in this area. A prominent decision on the BFOQ issue rejected an airline's argument that its reason for not hir-

BOX 7.3

The Supreme Court Defines a BFOQ

In *Dothard v. Rawlinson* (1977), the Supreme Court considered a suit by a woman who was denied a job as a prison guard in Alabama. Rejecting her claim that the state's male-only policy was a denial of equal protection and equal employment opportunity, Justice Potter Stewart defined another instance where being female disqualifies a person for a job:

> The essence of a correctional counselor's job is to maintain prison security. A woman's relative ability to maintain order in a male, maximum-security, unclassified penitentiary of the type Alabama now runs could be directly reduced by her womanhood. There is a basis in fact for expecting that sex offenders who have criminally assaulted women in the past would be moved to do so again if access to women were established within the prison. There would also be a real risk that other inmates deprived of a normal heterosexual environment would assault women guards because they were women. (p. 335)

ing men as flight attendants was that its passengers preferred their coffee and comfort ministered by women (*Diaz v. Pan American*, 1971). Here the court referred to the statute itself—that sex as a BFOQ was acceptable only when it was a "business necessity." Similarly rejected by EEOC and the courts were arguments that policemen and their wives objected to female partners.

Conditions under which sex may be a BFOQ are limited: for authenticity and genuineness (actor, actress; model of women's clothing), for privacy (attendant in a restroom; salesperson for clothing), or if directly related to a business necessity. According to federal law, the vast majority of jobs have no sex qualifications. This has meant the renaming of jobs, for example, from *policeman* and *mailman* to *police officer* and *letter carrier*. There are jobs that, by custom, still carry a gendered connotation: nurse; lineman; kindergarten teacher; pilot; CEO of General Motors. According to law, however, no one can be barred, on the basis of sex, from applying for these jobs.

To get around the federal law, some employers tried to restrict hiring to a subcategory of a sex, such as married women, women with small children, or unwed mothers. Since they considered applicants of both sexes, they claimed that excluding applicants on the basis of *sex plus* marital status or age was not illegal. However, Title VII prohibits any hiring policy that involves classification by sex, even if it is sex plus some other category such as marital status.[8]

Criteria for Proving Sex Discrimination

Congress was more explicit in defining when sex discrimination was permitted (as a BFOQ) than in setting criteria for determining when it was prohibited. Since 1964, the standard of evidence required to prove that an employer has violated Title VII has been evolving. The main actors are EEOC, federal courts, interest groups, and, when there is an impasse among these three groups, Congress. Through a series of cases, the federal courts have established two major categories of discrimination: disparate treatment against an individual or a group, and disparate impact.

Disparate Treatment

Disparate treatment refers to the situation where the employer deliberately acts in a less favorable way toward an employee or group of employees because of their sex. This form of direct discrimination is most easily proved if there is a "smoking gun"—a letter, memo, or statement by an employer that a person is not being hired or promoted because as a woman (or a man) she (or he) would not be the right person for the position. These days such evidence is rare. Plaintiffs trying to prove direct discrimination usually must eliminate all non–gender-related reasons for the employment decision and, if possible, show motive. If the alleged discrimination is against a group, statistical evidence could show the gap in women's representation between the employer's work force and that of society generally. Even so, an employer may still come forward with a nondiscriminatory reason for the employment decisions, and the burden of proof rests with the plaintiff, who must show that the employer's reason is a pretext. (See *Texas Dept. of Community Affairs v. Burdine*, 1981, for instructions to plaintiffs.)

Disparate Impact

Disparate impact refers to employers' practices that are *facially neutral*—that is, they do not mention the gender roles or the sex of employees but they have the effect of treating men and women differently. Such neutral hiring policies discriminate because, due to social roles and behavior, women and minorities are not equally able to meet the qualifications. Examples of facially-neutral job requirements that exclude women are minimum height and weight, the ability to lift heavy loads, and weekend traveling. Do employers have to hire women even though they can't meet these qualifications?

On this question, Title VII's effects on race and sex questions is the same. Any job qualification that has a disparate impact will be acceptable only if it is shown to be necessary for the job—a business necessity. Artificial height and weight requirements that exclude women, for example, are not acceptable. This law tends to smoke out those employers who add unnecessary and discriminatory qualifications just to reduce the number of women applicants they have to consider.

An example of a legal gender-neutral hiring practice that has a disparate impact is giving preference to veterans. Because of conscious discriminatory quotas on female recruitment in the armed forces, individuals who benefit from veterans' preference are overwhelmingly male. When states have given such preference to hiring veterans, the courts have ruled that such policies do not violate the Equal Protection Clause of the Fourteenth Amendment because their purpose is to reward military service, not to discriminate against women (*Personnel Administrator v. Feeney*, 1979). To be unconstitutional, veterans' preference policies would have to be developed as a pretext for keeping women out of government jobs.

While disparate impact policy is fairly easy to define, the question of proof in court has been especially contentious. In 1971, the Supreme Court took Title VII on a course that was different from the equal protection idea developed in *Feeney*. In *Griggs v. Duke Power Co.*, the justices gave notice that, while facially neutral policies that had a disparate impact on women and minorities would be acceptable if related to business necessity, the *burden of proof* as to whether such practices were such a necessity rested with the employer, not with the plaintiff who alleged illegal discrimination. Under *Griggs*, plaintiffs could demonstrate that a company's hiring policies had a disparate impact on women by using statistical data to show that the percentage of women in certain jobs at that company differed from the percentage of qualified women available in recruitment pools. Plaintiffs did not have to show that the employer intended to discriminate (a requirement the court used in dealing with the constitutionality of veterans' preference laws). Rather, the employer had to prove that he or she was not discriminating and show evidence that job qualifications and hiring procedures were closely related to a business necessity.

Many employers objected to the *Griggs* test and continued to challenge its usage as a means of determining the legality of various employment practices. The changing membership of the Court in the 1980s to include more judicial and ideological conservatives finally resulted in a win for the employers in *Wards Cove Packing v. Atonio* (1989). In that case, the Court shifted to the plaintiffs the burden of proof in disparate impact cases. As a result, the plaintiff had to give evidence to show how the employer's practices failed to meet the business necessity test. For women's rights and civil rights activists, the *Wards Cove* case seriously weakened the effectiveness of all civil rights laws that used the disparate impact definitions of discrimination. These groups launched an effective two-year lobbying effort in Congress to reverse the trend away from workers' rights. The Civil Rights Act of 1991 codified the ruling in *Griggs*. Thus, the Courts are now bound by Congress to place on the employers charged with a disparate impact form of employment discrimination the burden of proof for showing that their policies and practices are related to business necessity.

The Continuing Debate over Affirmative Action

While individualism as a means to achieve legal equality of the sexes in employment is well established in U.S. labor law, less secure is the more activist policy of affirmative action. It is difficult to reconcile a class approach to substantive equality with the individualist credo that race and sex should be irrelevant to employment decisions. Effective affirmative action plans in training, hiring, or promotion require some sort of preferential treatment for a racial or gender group. White American males have charged that they are denied the right to be treated on their individual merits and that the result is *reverse discrimination*.

Although Executive Order 11375 was written about three decades ago, the debate over affirmative action continues because of the difficulty of reconciling preference with equality. The Supreme Court has accepted the principle of preference as a way of overcoming past discrimination, even when the individuals who benefit have not personally been victims, and it considers each plan on a case-by-case basis.[9] Most of the plans and most of the cases involve affirmative action for racial minorities. However, in *Johnson v. Transportation Agency of Santa Clara County* (1987), the Supreme Court for the first time examined an affirmative action plan for women. Johnson claimed that, since the county agency had hired

BOX 7.4

Qualifications of Teresa Joyce and Paul Johnson for Promotion to Road Dispatcher

In *Johnson v. Transportation Agency of Santa Clara County* (1987), the Supreme Court first examined an affirmative action plan for women. The Court found the plan consistent with Title VII guidelines. The applicants' qualifications were as follows:

"Nine of the applicants, including Joyce and Johnson, were deemed qualified for the job, and were interviewed by a two-person board. Seven of the applicants scored above 70 on this interview, which meant that they were certified as eligible for selection by the appointing authority. Johnson was tied for second with a score of 75, while Joyce ranked next with a score of 73. . . .

"The certification form naming Joyce as the person promoted to the dispatcher position stated that both she and Johnson were rated as well-qualified for the job. The evaluation of Joyce read: 'Well-qualified by virtue of 18 years of past clerical experience including 3 1/2 years at West Yard plus almost 5 years as a [road maintenance worker].' The evaluation of Johnson was as follows: 'Well-qualified applicant; two years of [road maintenance worker] experience plus 11 years of Road Yard Clerk. He had previous outside Dispatch experience but that was 13 years ago." (*Johnson v. Transportation Agency of Santa Clara County* [1987], pp. 623–625)

Teresa Joyce—instead of him—to a supervisor position because of her sex, he was the victim of illegal reverse discrimination. The Court made it clear, as they had in previous affirmative action cases, that making employment decisions only on the basis of race or sex is not acceptable but that under certain circumstances employers may take race or sex into account. The Court found the Santa Clara County agency's plan acceptable; Justice Brennan described the plan as

an affirmative action plan that represents a moderate, flexible case-by-case approach to effecting a gradual improvement in the representation of minorities and women in the Agency's work force. Such a plan is fully consistent with Title VII, for it embodies the contribution that voluntary employer action can make in eliminating the vestiges of discrimination in the workplace. (p. 642)

In the *Johnson* case, the Court applied guidelines, set forth in *United Steelworkers v. Weber* (1979), for determining whether voluntary affirmative action policies violated Title VII's antidiscrimination goals. In *Weber*, the Court examined a voluntary labor contract that gave preference to black employees in job training. It ruled that Title VII permitted such plans as long as they were temporary, did not "unnecessarily trammel the interests of the white employees," and were intended to "eliminate a manifest racial imbalance" (208).

Affirmative action plans may be permitted under Title VII, but is it constitutional for the government to give preference to women and minorities in its own policies? In 1995, the Supreme Court gave notice that there are severe constitutional limits on such efforts. In *Adarand Constructors v. Pena* (1995), the Court did not find that federal affirmative action programs, such as set-asides for contractors, are unconstitutional, but the majority ruled that such plans would be subjected to strict scrutiny. (State and local plans had been reviewed under the strict standard since 1989.) To survive the tougher test, the government has to show that there is compelling state interest for giving racial or sex preferences and the plans must be "narrowly tailored" to achieve these goals.[10]

Some dissenting justices wanted to abolish government affirmative action plans altogether. Instead, the Court affirmed that individual rights are superior to group rights. The decision stimulated opponents of affirmative action in Congress and in many states to try once again to eliminate all affirmative action plans, including the Executive Order, government hiring plans, and efforts to maintain racial and ethnic diversity in state universities. Whether they will be successful remains to be seen, but affirmative action is back on the public agenda.

Equal Pay and Nondiscrimination in Compensation

The Equal Pay Act, calling for equal pay for equal work, was followed one year later by Title VII, intended to prevent sex discrimination in compensation. In the last days of the debate on Title VII, Senator Wallace Bennett (R.-Utah) succeeded in adding an amendment that permitted employers to pay different wages as long as it was permitted under the Equal Pay Act. Guided by the Bennett Amendment, the EEOC and the Courts at first interpreted Title VII's language about wages in the same way they interpreted the Equal Pay Act.[11]

The implementation of the Equal Pay Act has been more flexible than the narrow concept of "equal pay for equal work" implied at the time of the act's passage. Men and women do not need to be doing identical work to qualify for equal pay. Court interpretations of what is meant by jobs with similar skills, effort, responsibility, and conditions of employment allow for consideration of differences in the way jobs are performed. The courts have examined the actual performance of jobs held by men and women that employers alleged were different jobs—such as orderly and nurse's aide in medical care institutions, or checker and stock boy in supermarkets. The courts have evaluated the mental and physical exertion required on these pairs of jobs—criteria often used to segregate and value men's jobs over women's—and have determined that the jobs are equivalent.

The Equal Pay Act was enforced within the limits of its definitions and exceptions, and many pay settlements and back-pay cases were awarded.[12] This act eliminated the blatant sex differentials, as well as the fake job-classification schemes that masked them in many large corporations. Nonetheless, the act applied to relatively few women workers and the wage gap has persisted.

Overcoming the Wage Gap

After thirty years of equal employment opportunity (EEO) policy, the disparity in employment status between men and women remains most visible in the statistics comparing median year-round earnings of men and women—the wage gap (see Box 7.5). In 1961, the gap stood at 40 percent: women's wages were 60 percent of men's. Since 1990, the gap has hovered around 30 percent. Can we attribute the reduction of the gap to EEO policies? These general figures cover a very complex array of employment situations of millions of workers; no one factor can explain changes in them. However, there is widespread agreement about the reason for persistence of the wage gap: gender-based job segregation.

As Congress realized in 1963, men and women do not usually work in similar jobs for the same employers. Women are segregated into a few job categories that pay less than the job categories held primarily by men.[13] The Equal Pay Act has done little to overcome the wage gap caused by continuing patterns of job segregation in the work force. Many equal employment policy debates arise from different theories about the reasons for the persistence of job segregation and possible ways to remedy it and its effects. One side argues that gender-based job segregation persists

BOX 7.5

The Wage Gap Between Men and Women

The following figures show the median annual earnings in current dollars (not adjusted for inflation) for year-round full-time workers, by sex:

Year	Women	Men	Women's Earnings As a Percentage of Mens's
1951	$ 2,305	$ 3,605	63.9%
1961	3,351	5,644	59.3
1971	5,563	9,399	59.1
1981	12,001	20,260	59.2
1991	20,553	29,421	69.8

Source: U.S. Department of Labor, Women's Bureau. *1993 Handbook on Women Workers: Trends and Issues.* Washington, D.C.: Government Printing Office, 1994, p. 32.

because of continuing discrimination that has thus far eluded the remedies available in the law. According to this view, it can be overcome by more energetic policies to bring more women into higher-paying jobs. The other side notes that despite increased opportunity, women continue to flock (or "herd") together in certain occupations because they better accommodate demands of work and family, still a heavier burden for women than for men. Advocates for improving women's status and pay in the work force have supported policy proposals based on both explanations of job segregation. This section reviews some of these policy initiatives and the debates they have provoked.

Moving Women into Better-Paying Jobs

Antidiscrimination laws have resulted in many women obtaining professional degrees in law, medicine, and business and in obtaining entry-level positions in government, business, and industry. In such top positions as corporate boards of directors, law partners, and tenured full professors, however, women occupy mainly token roles. Barriers remain, and many observers argue that among them are subtle patterns of discrimination: stereotypes, tendencies to want to associate with similar people, personal connections, and unequal performance standards that are gender biased. All of these barriers are components of the *glass ceiling*.

Efforts to bring women into better-paying jobs focus on the more aggressive use of available policy tools. Critics have charged that neither EEOC nor the courts have been active enough in enforcing Title VII to remove discriminatory practices in the top-level jobs (Baron, 1994). The court-imposed requirements to prove unlawful *disparate treatment* make it extremely difficult to root out the subtle cultural and personal practices that sustain the glass ceiling (*Price Waterhouse v. Hopkins,* 1989). Such arguments reinforce the continuing need for affirmative action policies.

Congress has recognized the problem but has thus far resorted only to a symbolic remedy: the investigative commission. The 1991 Civil Rights Act included a provision establishing the Glass Ceiling Commission to conduct studies of the opportunities for and barriers to advancement of women and minorities to management positions in "corporate America." Their reports, issued in 1995, documented gender-based job segregation at management levels and included among the barriers to advancement the "lack of vigorous consistent monitoring and law enforcement." (Executive Summary, p. 8)

Federal authorities have paid some limited attention to the segregation produced in the United States by the vocational education and job training practices described in Chapter 5. The federal government itself does not conduct job-training programs, but it uses its funds to encourage states to promote certain goals and may designate women as a special target population. Such was the amendment to the Job Training Partnership Act (JTPA) in 1991, which required state employment and training agencies receiving federal funds to set goals for placing women in programs for nontraditional jobs. Efforts by opponents of affirmative action to eliminate set-asides would threaten even these limited efforts to overcome job segregation.

Raising the Pay for Women's Jobs

An alternate route to overcoming the wage gap is to accept gender-based job segregation but seek a way to raise the pay of jobs held primarily by women. Some of those jobs—such as nurse, child care worker, or bookkeeper—make important contributions, but salaries remain low. When compared with the importance of some jobs held by men that pay more—truck driver, tree trimmer—there seems no justification for this wage gap. Wage patterns retain the vestiges of past levels of discrimination, and women's work has traditionally been paid less because it was done by women. To attain true equal pay, jobs must be compared according to their worth, not just their description.

The idea of *comparable worth* is to assess the value of jobs and to compare salaries across job categories by using job-evaluation plans. Job evaluation, long a way of determining salaries, assigns points to jobs according to standard measures of skill, effort, responsibility, and working conditions. When such plans are applied to evaluate women's pay, they usually reveal that, although jobs held by women in a company or agency receive points similar to those assigned to men's jobs, the salaries attached to women's jobs are substantially lower, both because of the traditional gender-role division of labor and because of sex discrimination.

A comparable-worth policy consists of two parts. The first is a statement that defines unequal pay for jobs of comparable worth as sex discrimination, which is prohibited. The second part is a job-evaluation plan to implement a comparable-worth policy by adjusting pay levels so the pay level matches the value of each job category.

With the support of public employees' unions, feminists revived the demand for equal pay for comparable worth in the 1970s. At first, demands for comparable worth were defined by state legislators as primarily a distributive matter—a question of dispensing some assistance to certain interest groups. Job evaluation alone involves a modest one-time appropriation of funds to a consulting firm. Politicians found it fairly easy to satisfy demands by union and feminist lobbyists for "innocuous" studies of pay patterns of state employees. However, when the studies found that women's jobs pay less than men's (as they invariably do), the stakes changed. Then, advocates charged the state with sex discrimination and demanded that salaries be raised. In the state of Washington, such an innocuous study resulted in a federal court ruling that failure to raise salaries in accord with the study was sex discrimination, as well as an order for millions of dollars in back pay.[14] Legislators began to see the issue as a regulative matter, with the court determining salary raises. Even more seriously, the effect of proposed remedies would be redistributive, since large amounts of funds from taxes would be reassigned to compensate women employees. The debate heated up.

The lines of the debate became clearer as feminists and union leaders continued to press their demands. Proponents and opponents can agree that women's low wages are linked to job segregation. (There is no argument from opponents here; the evidence is too clear.) The two sides differ, however, on the reasons for the low pay. Proponents of comparable worth argue that these problems result from sex discrimination in society: Undervaluing of women's work, historical pay patterns that paid men a "family wage," and assumptions that women are "secondary earners." Opponents argue that the worth of different jobs cannot be measured and that wages should be set by the market. Comparable-worth programs would interfere with these market mechanisms. In fact, they maintain, if employers are forced to pay more than market rates, costs will increase and jobs will decrease. Women will lose because there will be fewer jobs available. And, they point out, women seek these jobs in the first place and accept lower wages for the flexibility they offer.

Employers also bring up the standard arguments used against government interfering with wages: the cost is too high; paying more than market wages drives up prices; employers will go bankrupt; government regulation is just plain bad for business. Phyllis Schlafly added a challenge to individual rights. As she pointed out in a debate on women's rights at Florida Atlantic University: "Do you want some government bureaucrat [she shuddered at the mention of bureaucrat] telling you what you are worth?"

Proponents counter that the market is not neutral. In fact, they argue, there is a dual labor market, closely allied with sex segregation. The women's job market and the men's market are different and aren't governed by the same laws of supply and demand. According to market mechanisms, wages are supposed to increase when the supply of workers is low. But this rarely works for women's jobs such as nurse, secretary, and child-care worker, which are undervalued everywhere even though the demand for these workers is high. The job-segregated earnings gap is institutionalized in the labor market, say proponents of a comparable-worth policy. Only breaking the pattern and raising the salaries of women in public employment will prod private employers to compete for workers by raising their salaries.

So far, most of the policy activity on comparable worth has been in state legislatures. About one-quarter of the states have passed a statute with language prohibiting discrimination in work done primarily by women in public employment and have followed it up with a job-evaluation study of state employees to implement the statute. Another quarter of the states have either enacted a statute or have commissioned a study. Only seven states—Minnesota, Iowa, Oregon, Washington, New York, Wisconsin, and Connecticut—have comprehensive reforms (McCann, 1994; Sorenson, 1994). Proposals for a pay-equity statute and job-evaluation scheme for federal employees have been unsuccessful.

Title VII has the potential to be an avenue for developing a comparable-worth policy. The Bennett Amendment incorporated the provisions of the Equal Pay Act, but the parameters of just what was to be transferred to Title VII were not made clear. Was it the entire EPA, requiring the work of men and women to be substantially equal, thus eliminating comparable worth cases? Or was it just the four affirmative defenses (seniority, merit, quality and quantity of production, and factors other than sex)? In *County of Washington v. Gunther* (1981), the Supreme Court opened the door to comparable-worth suits under Title VII. But the court-stipulated requirement—that plaintiffs must prove employers used pay policy intentionally to discriminate—has meant that few such claims are likely to be satisfied. The more successful cases have been those in which job-evaluation plans have been completed and employers have refused to implement them. But many courts have accepted the employers' arguments that setting salaries according to the labor market is gender neutral, a business necessity, and a "factor other than sex," and not sex discrimination. A vigorous policy directed at erasing the earnings gap resulting from job segregation will ultimately require congressional action, that is, the amending of Title VII. However, the issue is too controversial for Congress to act on any time soon.

Conclusion

The transformation of the debate about women and work from a framework of protection and difference to one of equal opportunity and individual rights has been a complex policy process that has affected not only women's rights but also the politics of the women's rights movement. It has removed barriers to jobs and promotion for millions of women and has eased their movement into the American work force. The interaction between feminists in the government, women's organizations, and policymakers in legislatures, bureaucracies, and the courts has reinforced a policy community for women's rights in the area of employment.

There remain, however, limits in the equal-opportunity policies because of inadequacies both in the policy itself and in the definition of women's employment. The coverage of equal-opportunity laws is incomplete. For example, women tend to be overrepresented among employees in small businesses not covered by Title VII and Executive Order 11375.

BOX 7.6

Job Opportunities for Women in the U.S. Military: A Chronology

Congress, the Secretary of Defense, the generals, and the admirals are responsible for the state of sex discrimination in the military. Since World War II, removal of legal barriers has been gradual:

1948 Women's Armed Services Integration Act sets a quota for women in the military at 2 percent, permits involuntary discharge for pregnancy, and limits promotion of female officers.

1956 Congress passes statute prohibiting women from combat in Navy and Air Force.

1967 Public Law 90–130 removes the 2 percent quota and formal restrictions on female officers' careers.

1977 Army Combat Exclusion policy prevents women from serving in certain designated combat positions.

1991 Congress repeals 1956 prohibition on women as combat pilots; creates commission to study role of women in combat generally.

1992 Commission issues report; recommends that women be permitted to serve on Navy combat ships.

1993 Congress repeals prohibition on women on combat ships.

1994 Secretary of Defense orders that women be allowed to apply for combat support positions in the Army and Marine Corps. Henceforth women could be excluded only from direct combat: "engaging an enemy on the ground with . . . weapons, while being exposed to hostile fire and to a high probability of direct physical contact with" enemy troops. New policy opens 18,000 positions to women.

Since the draft ended in 1973 the percentage of women in the military has increased from 2 to 11 percent. There are no hard and fast quotas, but enlistments are guided by accession plans that prescribe the number of women to be inducted. Many women in the military believe that opportunity for women officers will improve as a result of the repeal of combat-exclusion policies. At the same time, integration has coincided with attention to sexual harassment (see Chapter 9).

Until recently, important parts of public employment have been exempt from the policy, notably, the military and patronage appointments in legislative staffs. Changing attitudes, especially among women seeking equal opportunities, have broken down barriers even in these sacred institutions.

The enforcement of equal-opportunity legislation is another barrier to the effectiveness of policy in improving the status of women workers.

Much of the burden of enforcement is placed on the individual woman who believes she may be the victim of unlawful discrimination. She may receive only limited assistance with her complaints from the EEOC because of that agency's inadequate staffing and uninterested administrators. In addition, the courts' stringent requirements for proof mean that producing credible evidence is often difficult. Coordinated campaigns of litigation with resources from a coalition of organizations continue to be the only effective way to enforce equal-employment policy.

It may be that the individual equal rights approach has run its course. Efforts are increasing to change the debate to look at substantive equality—the share of economic resources women enjoy from their share of the work. The chronic inequities in pay that result from job segregation resist antidiscrimination laws. The policies designed thus far to overcome job segregation are inadequate. Affirmative action has broken down some of the resistance to token representation of women in all-male fields. The glass ceiling persists, as does job segregation. Affirmative action has done nothing to increase representation of men in all-female jobs. Comparable-worth remedies are costly and are considered redistributive. State legislatures resist them, and the existing policies under Title VII are weak.

The analogy between race discrimination and sex discrimination that has been the foundation of employment policy for women has its own limits. In their most direct form, sex-discrimination and race-discrimination practices in employment—for example, strict quotas or outright refusal to employ women or racial minorities in certain jobs—are similar. But once these crude barriers had been removed by antidiscrimination laws, the differences between the problems of women workers and those of racial minorities became evident. Racial minorities combat the legacy of slavery. Women struggle to reconcile their desire for jobs that offer status and fair pay with the demands of work and family.

The complex issues raised by the interplay between race and gender discrimination direct our attention to the workers whose status reflects them both: African American women. Evidence suggests that these women—historically considered the "mules," as Hurston called them—have benefited most from equal opportunity policy. Of course, they also started from the lowest status. "A combination of new jobs, equal opportunity laws, and educational gains helped black women move from domestic employment to mainstream work" (Woody, 1992, p. 2)

Occupational segregation has declined more between black women and white women than between the sexes (Jacobsen, 1994). Structural

BOX 7.7

The Pay Gap Is Closing ... White Men Retain the Advantage

Since the 1970s, the earnings of both black women and white women have increased in relation to the earnings of white men. The gap has narrowed in part because of the decline in the growth of earnings of white men. Still, race and gender structures persist, with white and minority women and minority men on the bottom rungs of the income ladder.

Wage Earner	Earnings As a Percentage of White Men's Earnings		
	*1979**	*1986**	*1996**
White men	100%	100%	100%
Black men	73.4	68.6	71.2
White women	58.7	62.6	74.5
Black women	54.3	56.0	61.0
Hispanic men	n.a.	n.a.	60.5
Hispanic women	n.a.	n.a.	53.6

*Figures for 1979 and 1986 are based on median annual earnings; figures for 1996 are based on monthly earnings for June 1996.

Sources: Cynthia Taeuber, ed. *Statistical Handbook on Women in America.* Phoenix, Ariz.: Oryx Press, 1991, p. 92; U.S. Department of Labor, Bureau of Labor Statistics. *Usual Weekly Earnings of Wage and Salary Workers: Second Quarter 1996.* No. 96–291. Washington, D.C.: Government Printing Office, 1996.

and situational factors that reinforce gender-based job segregation seem more resistant to antidiscrimination efforts than those based on race. Still, African American and Hispanic/Latina women lag behind both white women and men in the access to professions and in salaries.

Some equality policy—for example, that pertaining to reproductive hazards in the workplace—affects gender and not race. In the late 1970s, employers began to establish fetal-protection policies that revived protective regulations and thinking about women workers. Blanket policies restricted women from certain jobs that were deemed to have potential hazards to pregnant women and fetuses. These policies excluded women from job opportunities based on assumptions about their reproductive health and capacities. The EEOC permitted fetal-protection policies as long as employers could offer scientific proof that the hazards leading to

such a policy did not also pose a risk to male employees and their offspring.

In *U.A.W. v. Johnson Controls* (1991) the Supreme Court ruled that
fetal-protection policies violated Title VII because they classified employees on the basis of gender and child-bearing capacity, rather than on their
individual circumstances. The employer tried to argue that its policy was
a legitimate application of BFOQ, protecting the health of offspring. Justice Blackmun disagreed: "Decisions about the welfare of future children
must be left to the parents who conceive, bear, support, and raise rather
than the employers who hire those parents" (p. 207). Prior to the *Johnson
Controls* case, employers who treated all women employees as if they were
potentially pregnant could evade Title VII's antidiscrimination net. By
using individual-rights theory to undermine these policies, the courts
have not stilled the debate over the conflict between work and family responsibilities that women face.

Protective laws in the past were based on making reproduction the
most important thing about women workers. Now, equal-employment
policies tend to ignore family and reproduction altogether. Sometimes,
women suffer because of their inability to compete equally with men. Yet
feminists, fully aware of the negative effects of protections only for
women, search for gender-neutral solutions to cover areas where reproductive differences affect job status. Thus far, the policy story of women
and work is only half-finished: the rest of the story, which involves government efforts to accommodate the conflicts between work and family,
is discussed in Chapter 8.

Notes

1. For statistics on women's participation and wages in the present work force, see
   the *Earnings and Employment Survey,* published monthly by the U.S.
   Department of Labor. For trends, see the U.S. Department of Labor, *Handbook
   on Women Workers*, 1975, 1983, and 1993; U.S. Department of Commerce,
   Bureau of the Census, *Historical Statistics of the U.S., Colonial Times to 1970*,
   1976.
2. The concept of race had double meaning. It referred to the human race but was
   also used in a special way by many groups concerned about "race suicide" of
   Northern European whites because of the increase in the numbers of
   immigrants from southern and eastern Europe.
3. The *Adkins* case is, technically, the first case to strike down a sex-discriminatory
   law as unconstitutional under the Fourteenth Amendment. But it did not reach
   the status of precedent; feminists would wait fifty years for the Supreme Court
   to make it clear in *Reed v. Reed* (1971) that sex classifications must bear a
   reasonable relationship to a legitimate state objective. See Chapter 2.

4. Reports of the Women's Bureau in the 1920s and 1930s now make up a valuable source of data about the experiences of women in the work force between the two world wars. These reports are available in government document collections. A list can be found in Sealander (1983), an excellent study of the Women's Bureau. See Stetson (1995) for a study of recent activities of the bureau.

5. This is a switch on the earlier argument that unequal pay took jobs away from men and that equal pay would undercut competition from women in the labor force.

6. Powers of injunction would allow the EEOC to issue binding orders to employers to change their practices, orders that carry the enforcement powers of court orders.

7. Two contrasting styles at the EEOC were those of Eleanor Holmes Norton, who in the 1970s took an activist stance to improve the status of women workers by endorsing affirmative action and comparable-worth proposals and those of Clarence Thomas, who in the 1980s opposed affirmative action and comparable worth.

8. As Chapter 8 will discuss, the Supreme Court did not rule out some discrimination against or in favor of pregnant women. The Court got around this problem by calling them "pregnant persons."

9. The Supreme Court may reject some plans or change the standards of proof necessary to establish patterns of discrimination that warrant affirmative action.

10. This is the same idea as the strict scrutiny tests applied to race classification described in Chapter 2. Before *Adarand*, the Court had used the middle-level scrutiny test for federal affirmative action policies.

11. In considering whether Title VII permitted a consideration of comparable worth in 1981, the Supreme Court drove a wedge between the Equal Pay Act and Title VII that has still not been reconciled. Cases charging discrimination in pay have been interpreted differently in various federal courts ever since (see Greenlaw andd Kohl, 1994).

12. Most casebooks on sex-discrimination law, such as Kay (1981), include the major court interpretations of the Equal Pay Act: *Schultz v. Wheaton Glass Co.* 421 F. 2d 259, cert. denied 398 U.S. 905 (1970); *Corning Glass Works v. Brennan*, 417 U.S. 188 (1974); and *Hodgson v. Robert Hall Clothes, Inc.*, 473 F. 2d 589, cert. denied 414 U.S. 866 (1973).

13. Of the twenty leading occupations for women, eleven are known as traditional "female jobs" with low wages: secretary, cashier, bookkeeper, nurse, nurse's aide, waitress, child-care worker, elementary school teacher, hairdresser, office clerk, and sales clerk (U.S. Department of Labor, Women's Bureau, 1994).

14. The ruling was eventually overturned by the federal circuit court.

References

Abrams, Kathryn. "Gender in the Military: Androcentrism and Institutional Reform. *Law and Contemporary Problems* 56 (1993): 217–241.

Acker, Joan. *Doing Comparable Worth: Gender, Class, and Pay Equity*. Philadelphia: Temple University Press, 1989.

Adarand Constructors v. Pena. 115 S.Ct. 2097. 1995

Adkins v. Children's Hospital. 261 U.S. 525. 1923.

Baron, Tracy Anbinder. "Keeping Women Out of the Executive Suite: The Courts' Failure to Apply Title VII Scrutiny to Upper-Level Jobs." *University of Pennsylvania Law Review* 43 (November 1994): 267–320.

Brauer, Carl. "Women Activists, Southern Conservatives, and the Prohibition of Sex Discrimination in Title VII of the 1964 Civil Rights Act." *Journal of Southern History* 49 (February 1983): 37–56.

Chavkin, Wendy. *Women's Health: Hazards on the Job and at Home.* New York: Monthly Review Press, 1984.

Collins, Patricia Hill. *Black Feminist Thought: Knowledge, Consciousness, and the Politics of Empowerment.* Boston: Unwin Hyman, 1990.

"Compliance Responsibility for Equal Opportunity." Revised Order No. 4. 43 F.R. 49249, 1978.

County of Washington v. Gunther. 452 U.S. 161. 1981.

Diaz v. Pan American. 422 F 2d 385. 1971.

Dothard v. Rawlinson. 433 U.S. 321. 1977.

Evans, Sara M., and Nelson, Barbara J. *Wage Justice: Comparable Worth and the Paradox of Technocratic Reform.* Chicago: University of Chicago Press, 1989.

Executive Summary. Glass Ceiling Commission, 1995.

Feldberg, Rosalyn. "Comparable Worth: Toward Theory and Practice in the United States." *Signs* 10 (1984): 311–328.

Freeman, Jo. *The Politics of Women's Liberation.* New York: Longman, 1975.

Griggs v. Duke Power Co. 401 U.S. 424. 1971.

Greenlaw, Paul S., and Kohl, John P. "Thirty Years of Civil Rights: The EPA/Title VII Sex-Based Wage Discrimination Controversy." *Labor Law Journal* 45 (April 1994): 240–247.

Harris, Cynthia. *On Account of Sex: The Politics of Women's Issues, 1945–68.* Berkeley: University of California Press, 1988.

Holm, Jeannie. *Women and the Military.* Novato, Calif.: Presidio Press, 1982.

Jacobsen, Joyce. "Trends in Work Force Sex Segregation, 1960–1990." *Social Science Quarterly* 75 (March 1994): 204–211.

Johansen, Elaine. *Comparable Worth: The Myth and the Movement.* Boulder: Westview Press, 1984.

Johnson v. Transportation Agency of Santa Clara County. 480 U.S. 616. 1987.

Kamerman, Sheila B., and Kahn, Alfred J. *The Responsive Workplace: Employers and a Changing Labor Force.* New York: Columbia University Press, 1987.

Kay, Herma H. *Sex Discrimination,* 2nd ed. St. Paul: West Publishing, 1981.

Kessler-Harris, Alice. *Out of Work.* New York: Oxford University Press, 1982.

Kessler-Harris, Alice. *A Woman's Wage: Historical Meanings and Social Consequences.* Lexington: University Press of Kentucky, 1990.

Lehrer, Susan. *The Origins of Protective Labor Legislation for Women, 1905–1925.* New York: State University of New York Press, 1987.

McCaffery, Edward J. "Slouching Towards Equality: Gender Discrimination, Market Efficiency, and Social Change." *Yale Law Journal* 103, no. 3 (December 1993): 595–675.

McCann, Michael W. *Rights at Work: Pay Equity Reform and the Politics of Legal Mobilization.* Chicago: University of Chicago Press, 1994.

Mead, Margaret, and Kaplan, Frances Balgley, eds. *American Women: The Report of the President's Commission on the Status of Women and Other Publications of the Commission.* New York: Scribner's, 1965.

Muller v. Oregon. 208 U.S. 412. 1908.

National Manpower Council. *Womanpower.* New York: Columbia University Press, 1957.

NOW-LDEF, and Cherow-O'Leary, Renee. *The State by State Guide to Women's Legal Rights.* New York: McGraw-Hill, 1987.

Personnel Administrator v. Feeney. 442 U.S. 256. 1979.

Price Waterhouse v. Hopkins. 490 U.S. 228. 1989.

Reed v. Reed. 404 U.S. 71. 1971.

Rothman, Sheila. *A Woman's Proper Place.* New York: Basic Books, 1978.

Samuels, Suzanne Uttaro. *Fetal Rights, Women's Rights: Gender Equality in the Workplace.* Madison: University of Wisconsin Press, 1995.

Sealander, Judith. *As Minority Becomes Majority: Federal Reaction to the Phenomenon of Women in the Work Force, 1920–1963.* Westport, Conn.: Greenwood Press, 1983.

Sorensen, Elaine. *Comparable Worth: Is It a Worthy Policy?* Princeton: Princeton University Press, 1994.

Stetson, Dorothy McBride. "The Oldest Women's Policy Agency: The Women's Bureau in the United States." In *Comparative State Feminism*, edited by Dorothy McBride Stetson and Amy G. Mazur. Thousand Oaks, Calif.: Sage Publications, 1995, pp. 254–271.

Stiehm, Judith. *Arms and the Enlisted Woman*. Philadelphia: Temple University Press, 1989.

Texas Department of Community Affairs v. Burdine. 450 U.S. 248. 1981.

U.A.W. v. Johnson Controls. 499 U.S. 187. 1991.

United Steelworkers v. Weber. 443 U.S. 193. 1979.

U.S. Federal Glass Ceiling Commission. *A Solid Investment: Making Full Use of the Nation's Human Capital: Recommendations of the Glass Ceiling Commission*. Washington, D.C.: Government Printing Office, 1995.

U.S. Department of Labor, Women's Bureau. "The Employment of Women in Slaughtering and Meat Packing." *Bulletin of the Women's Bureau*, No. 88, 1932.

U.S. Department of Labor, Women's Bureau. *1993 Handbook on Women Workers: Trends and Issues*. Washington, D.C.: Government Printing Office, 1994.

Wards Cove Packing v. Atonio. 490 U.S. 642. 1989.

Woody, Bette. *Black Women in the Workplace*. Westport, Conn.: Greenwood Press, 1992.

CHAPTER **8**

Work and Family

The feature that distinguishes most women workers from other workers is the difficulty of resolving conflicts between the needs of their families and the demands of their work. Before industrialization brought workers off the farms and out of the home, there was little difference between men and women in reconciling the demands of work and family. Children could be easily integrated into the routine of the farm, and extended family members were there to help out when a mother got sick or pregnant. In the nineteenth century, work moved out of the home, and the ideology of separate spheres became dominant. These developments separated men and women into two categories of workers. For most men, family responsibilities complemented their roles as workers. For many women, the roles were in deadly contradiction. Protective laws encouraged women to resolve this contradiction in favor of the family. At the same time, women in poor communities had little choice because, to survive, everyone, even children, had to bring in money. Now that work has become a means of economic independence and fulfillment for both men and women, the conflict between work and family acts as a handicap for women and prevents them from achieving their rights as workers.

The persistent economic inequality and dependency of women can be directly attributed to gender differences in family responsibilities. Family responsibilities include family formation and the care and support of family members. The needs of families change with the life stages of family members—through pregnancy, childbirth, infant care, preschool care, afterschool supervision, care of a sick child, and care of an elderly family member. Family responsibilities include, in principle, both financial and emotional support. Financial support is fully consistent with demands of work. Emotional support and care giving are usually incompatible with work responsibilities.

Two theories link care giving to women's lower work status and earning capacity. The first explains work status in terms of dominant gender roles, still strikingly close to the separate-spheres ideology. Women's roles as mothers and primary care givers diminish the time and energy they can devote to the demands of highly skilled, high-paying jobs. The other theory blames the discrimination against women in the labor market for driving women into mothering. Their pay and job status, usually lower than that of their husband, makes their assignment to care giving a rational one—at least to economists. In Chapter 7 we examined the limits of antidiscrimination policies. In this chapter we assess government's reluctant role in aiding women to overcome the conflict between responsibilities at home and equal status in the work force.

Most other industrial countries have national government policies that aid women workers in managing their family responsibilities without losing their job status and income. Such policies include health care, paid maternity and parental leaves, child-care centers, and family allowances. The United States has had few of these policies on a national level. Until the 1980s, the public debate on women and work did not include demands for these policies. The issue of work and family was not on the public agenda. This does not mean that there was no discussion of child care or maternal health. The subjects of women, childbirth, children, and work have from time to time been debated, and policies have resulted. But these subjects have not been discussed in such a way as to link family duties with rights to equality and employment. Instead, these issues have been part of other policy debates, and their discussion has served different agendas. The result is a patchwork of government-funded and privately funded programs that affect the children of workers. National policies to help relieve the conflicts between work and family for women workers have, however, been few.

For such national policies to develop, the United States must overcome its long history of acceptance of a dichotomy between the public worlds of work and government and the private worlds of family and children. Despite a lot of rhetoric about the crucial importance of families to social and political health, officials in Congress, the courts, and the executive branch define the family as private, that is, not the responsibility of the government. Occasionally, some abstract notion of "saving chil-

dren" sparks the politicians' interests, but what citizens decide with respect to their families has not traditionally been of interest to the government, especially not to the federal government. Some believe, in fact, that
government programs are an unconstitutional intrusion into people's
lives. Only when family demands might impinge on solving a perceived
national problem, such as recruiting workers for emergency work during
a war or relieving the economic burdens of poverty and welfare, has government been concerned. A nationalist policy of pronatalism, like those
found in France and Sweden, has rarely motivated American political
leaders in their consideration of families.

Work and family have been officially separate areas of concern. Add
woman to the scheme, and she was assigned to the family—the private
world. Although women have been in the work sphere for generations,
the official conception has persisted that they did not belong there—that
some sort of social or economic pathology must have put them there.
They had to work and would have chosen not to work if they had someone to support them and their children adequately. The assumption still
underlying much public discussion is that once such pathologies are
cured, women, mothers anyway, will not work. The few who are career-
oriented could buy the services necessary to accommodate family responsibilities, just as the wealthy have always managed to engage nursemaids
and nannies.

Forty years ago, European governments started accepting the idea
that women had a proper and expected role in the work force, as well as
in the nursery. Alva Myrdal and Viola Klein in their book, *Women's Two
Roles* (1956), outlined policies necessary to help women take care of their
two responsibilities. Starting in the 1950s, most European governments
established comprehensive child care, paid maternity and parental leave,
and equal rights and benefits for part-time workers.

The idea of women's two roles has been slow to catch on in the
United States. Not only has government been slow in recognizing the issues, but feminists have rarely presented demands in these terms. Tensions between concern for the obvious needs of women and fear of the
effects of special treatment have cast feminists on both sides of proposals
for maternity leave and child-care tax credits. Complex theoretical questions of the relation of work and family have divided women's rights advocates. They disagree about the proper role of women in the family and
have not made a clear commitment that paid work is a component in
women's liberation. They cannot agree which policies will promote the
status of women and increase women's power. There are contradictions

BOX 8.1

Mothers in the Work Force: Then and Now

The percentage of mothers with children under 18 who are in the work force has grown dramatically since 1960. In the 1990s, even among mothers with small children, most work outside the home.

Age of children	1960	1975	1980	1993
Under 18	35%	42%	52%	67%
Under 3	n.a.	31	42	54
Under 6	19	49	49	58
Between 6 and 18	39	61	68	75

Sources: U.S. Department of Labor, Women's Bureau. *Working Women Count!* Washington, D.C.: Government Printing Office, 1994, p. 31; Cynthia Taeuber, ed. *Statistical Handbook on Women in America.* Phoenix, Ariz.: Oryx Press, 1991, pp. 108, 159.

between radical feminist visions of a future without patriarchy and the demands of real-life women today with families, jobs, and limited gender consciousness.

Pregnancy and Childbirth

Employment difficulties caused by pregnancy and childbirth pertain exclusively to women workers, thus making maternity leave a central issue for the rights of women workers. Yet, the women's movement has not produced a clear set of demands for job-protected maternity leave, let alone a common way of thinking about the interrelationship between motherhood and work. Feminists have been ambivalent about motherhood. On the one hand, they see a basic source of oppression in the social construction of motherhood as a career and the exclusive assignment of women to that role on the basis of biology. They point out that childbirth and child rearing need not occupy a woman's entire adult life; restricting her to motherhood deprives her of any opportunity to develop her talents and to attain economic independence. They contend that for women and men ever to be equal, their relationship to reproduction must be more and more alike. At the same time, many feminists believe that biological differences give women a special world that men can never enter. For example, children develop gender identities and personalities in large part because of the relationship they have with their mothers in the first few weeks of life. Feminists suggest that it is not mothering that oppresses, but the way it has been defined and undervalued by men. They conclude that women need to gain control of what it means to give life and rear children. Of special interest is Sara Ruddick's exposition on maternal practice as a form of work that demands and yields special forms of thinking. This "maternal" thinking—preservative love, fostering growth, and special training—constitutes a largely undiscovered yet potentially powerful form of feminist transformation (Ruddick, 1995).

Maternity Protection

Disagreements among feminists about motherhood and equality have been part of all the various women's movements, but never more so than when the conflict between demands of childbirth and work first came to the attention of policy makers in the 1890s. The discussion was brought up in the context of the campaign for protective labor legislation. Labor activists in new labor unions tried to convince government to help all workers by setting minimal standards and preventing excessive exploitation. These proposals were fervently opposed by laissez-faire liberals of the time, who feared excessive interference by government in the marketplace.[1] The Supreme Court regularly struck down such labor legislation. The strongest voices for reform came from the social feminists who led the National Consumers' League (NCL). They considered work to be harmful to women, especially pregnant women. The grim conditions of the sweatshops and factories threatened women's health. These social feminists were able to convince several state governments that the public had an interest in the health of children, and that interest justified government interference with the market in order to protect women. That justification focused on women's childbearing function.

The policy solution was the protective legislation passed in many states to limit the hours of work and the access to dangerous jobs for women. In 1908, these laws were upheld in *Muller v. Oregon*:

> Even though all restrictions on political, personal, and contractual rights were taken away, and [woman] stood, so far as statutes are concerned, upon an absolutely equal plane with [man], it would still be true that she is so constituted that she will rest upon and look to him for protection: that her physical structure and proper discharge of her maternal functions—having in view not merely her own health, but the well-being of the race—justify legislation to protect her from the greed as well as the passion of man. The limitations which this

statute places upon her contractual powers, upon her right to agree with her employer as to the time she shall labor, are not imposed solely for her benefit, but also largely for the benefit of all. (p. 422)

It seems odd from our perspective that there was no proposal, such as *maternity leave*, pertaining directly to the *maternal functions* of women workers. Leave would have given them the right to stay home and rest before and after giving birth. Feminists did not mention such a thing, even though maternity-leave laws had already been enacted in several other countries.[2] Lack of such demands is evidence of the strong conviction of many social feminists that women would or should quit their jobs altogether when they had their first child. If mothers had to work because they were poor, or because they had been deserted by their husbands, it was a tragedy. Perhaps the feminists assumed that such unfortunate women would have to pick up where they left off when they returned to work. At the bottom of the work ladder, there was no status or seniority to be lost.

The social feminists went on after World War I to lobby for a maternal health bill, the Sheppard-Towner Act. In this effort, they separated maternity policy from labor policy altogether. The Sheppard-Towner Act of 1921 was the first major federal social legislation in the United States. It gave grants to states to provide health care for mothers and children, regardless of a mother's work or economic status. The act was the first lobbying success for the newly enfranchised women voters and the last for the suffrage movement. In 1920, women got the vote. In 1921, while Congressmen were still unsure of the electoral effect of the Nineteenth Amendment, a coalition of women's rights groups formed the Women's Joint Congressional Committee to push the act through Congress. After the 1922 elections, the politicians believed that women did not vote as a bloc and that their turnout was low. As a result, women's rights lobbyists could neither follow up on the 1921 victory nor protect the Sheppard-Towner Act when it was allowed to lapse in 1929.

Since the 1890s, egalitarian feminists had continued to challenge social feminists' preoccupation with protecting mothers. A minority in the women's movement, these egalitarian feminists denounced special treatment for women and wanted laws to pertain to all workers equally. They ignored motherhood altogether, while the social feminists remained uneasy with the idea of women in the work force. In 1920, the protectionist view prevailed and was institutionalized at the Women's Bureau in the Department of Labor. The Women's Bureau had two goals: protection of

BOX 8.2

Sheppard-Towner: The "Red Menace"

At first, the intent of the Sheppard-Towner Act was to improve the health of women and children. In the early 1920s, the Women's Joint Congressional Committee, a coalition of pro-suffrage interest groups, was successful in defining the issue as a help to needy families. The main opposition came from the American Medical Association, which labeled the program excessive "federal interference." The egalitarian feminists of the National Woman's Party balked as well, unhappy with the act's assumption that all women were mothers. But this conflict took a back seat to the wave of patriotic right-wing opposition that arose in the late 1920s.

Although Sheppard-Towner was intended to be a permanent program, the Congress had to act to continue funding after 1927. By then, the terms of the debate had changed dramatically. From being a health measure for mothers and infants, it became a symbol of the insidious infiltration of dreaded Bolshevism into the United States. The patriots, considering feminism and socialism as twin evils, turned a watchful eye on many women's rights organizations who had supported such "socialized" medical schemes. Thus, supporting federal health care for mothers and babies became unpatriotic. No wonder few legislators stood up to protect the Sheppard-Towner Act when it was allowed to lapse in 1929. (See Lemons, 1973, pp. 153–180; Woloch, 1984, pp. 249–250.)

potential mothers and the economic advancement of women workers. When these goals proved contradictory, protection prevailed. This perspective dominated governmental policy toward women workers and maternity throughout World War II and into the 1950s.

In 1942, the Women's Bureau joined with the Children's Bureau to recommend standards for the maternal health of employed women. Together, they recommended prenatal care, limited hours of work, rest periods, six weeks of prenatal leave, and two months of postnatal leave. Although the bureaus were mainly interested in health care, they added that childbirth leave should not jeopardize a mother's employment or seniority. However, neither the states nor the federal government adopted these recommendations as employment practice. And, although private employers' policies varied, it was "generally understood" that most women would quit working to care for a newborn child and did not need job protection.

Pregnancy As Disability

A new definition of the relation between pregnancy, childbirth, and work arose between the 1940s and the 1970s and led to a national policy on pregnancy leave. This development coincided with changes in the federal government's conception of women as workers and the relentless increases in the numbers and percentages of women in the work force. How did the federal government's view of women workers change? The evidence is found in the changes at the Women's Bureau. In its first thirty years of existence, the bureau was run by middle-class social reformers considered largely on the periphery of the real work of the Department of Labor. By the 1950s, the role and the constituency of the bureau had changed. The Department of Labor began to focus on improving *manpower* resources in the country and, using the generic sense of the term, included women as a potential source of manpower. The Women's Bureau was assigned a new role to improve this labor resource. This meant accepting women as a regular part of the work force, entitled to fair and equal treatment.

The bureau dropped its protective stance toward protective laws after 1956 and began to work for an Equal Pay Act. Sex discrimination in employment and pay was outlawed in the early 1960s. The massive shift in the official view of women workers toward equality and individual rights was well under way. Any special treatment, such as maternity leave, was off-limits. The bureau had to find a new way to look at pregnancy. Bureau Director Esther Peterson worked closely with President Kennedy's Commission on the Status of Women (1960 to 1963) and its descendant, the Citizens' Advisory Council on the Status of Women (CACSW). Together, they developed the concept of pregnancy as a disability:

> Childbirth and complications of pregnancy are, for all *job-related purposes*, temporary disabilities and should be treated as such under any health insurance, temporary disability insurance or sick leave plan of an employer, union, or fraternal society. Any policies or practices of an employer or union, written or unwritten, applied to instances of temporary disability other than pregnancy should be applied to incapacity due to pregnancy or childbirth including policies or practices relating to leave of absence, restoration or recall to duty and seniority. No additional or different benefits or restrictions should be applied to disability because of pregnancy or childbirth, and no pregnant woman employee should be in a better position in relation to job-related practices or benefits than an employee similarly situated

suffering from any other disability. (U.S. Citizens' Advisory Council on the Status of Women, 1971, p.4)

There are several important elements to this definition. It separates the functions of childbirth and child rearing: only childbirth has any relevance to work. Pregnancy and childbirth are seen in terms of their effects on women's ability to work. This definition makes pregnancy equivalent to something that happens to men, namely, a job-related disability. Therefore, employers need concern themselves with pregnancy only if they also have a concern with a job-related disability. If leave for a disability is a worker's right, then leave for pregnancy should be a worker's right as well. Not to provide it would be sex discrimination. Yet there should be no special treatment for women.

This definition is consistent with the theories of antidiscrimination and individualism and was supported by egalitarian and reform feminists. In advocating a view of pregnancy as a disability, reform feminists sought to control the terms of debate in order to promote women's role as workers and to eliminate the discrimination resulting from traditional roles in the family. Quite simply, this framework excluded from the workplace and employment policy concern with motherhood, children, family, and health, and it focused only on effect of pregnancy on the physical fitness of women as members of the labor force.

Opponents of this definition of pregnancy as a job-related disability protected by antidiscrimination law responded to several parts of the CACSW argument. They maintained that pregnancy is a natural function, not a disability; it is private and usually voluntary. They noted that since pregnancy is normal, rather than a disease or an accident, it is widespread and that no employment policies give leave for such natural functions. If they did, their implementation would prove too costly, the opponents said, especially if these employment policies included disability insurance and health insurance benefits, too. The opponents also pointed out that women tend not to return to work after pregnancy, making its effects quite different from those of "real" disabilities. To them, excluding pregnancy from disability plans might just be prudent business, not sex discrimination.

Two Supreme Court decisions enshrined these opposition arguments in constitutional and antidiscrimination law. *Geduldig v. Aiello* (1974) considered whether a state's refusal to include pregnancy as a disability under a benefit plan for state employees violated the Equal Protection Clause of the Fourteenth Amendment. *General Electric v. Gilbert* (1976) considered whether similar plans of private employers violated Title VII. These cases were part of a series dealing with pregnancy and work in the 1970s. In 1973, the Court ruled that mandatory maternity leave on a certain date, regardless of the circumstances of an individual's pregnancy, was a violation of due process (*Cleveland Board of Education v. LaFleur*). In 1976, a federal circuit court extended this ruling to apply to military personnel (*Crawford v. Cushman*). In a Title VII case, the Supreme Court ruled that the Nashville Gas Company had violated prohibitions against sex discrimination by denying employees seniority after leave for pregnancy (*Nashville Gas Co. v. Satty*, 1977). The reasoning of the Court in these cases was that employment policies were discriminatory if they treated pregnant employees harshly by placing burdens on them that other employees with other disabilities did not face. But the *Geduldig* and *General Electric* cases involved disability *benefits*—income replacement and health insurance for the disabled employees. On this subject, the Court ruled that failure to include pregnancy in a benefit plan was not sex discrimination and therefore not prohibited by the Fourteenth Amendment or Title VII.

In both cases, the Court reasoned that the employment practice of removing pregnancy from a list of disabilities was not sex discrimination because only a subclass of women, not all women, would be affected: "There is no risk from which women are protected and men are not" (*Geduldig v. Aiello*, 1974, pp. 496–497).[3] The Court seemed to consider pregnancy to be a natural function:

> Normal pregnancy is an objectively identifiable physical condition with unique characteristics. Absent a showing that distinctions involving pregnancy are mere pretexts designed to effect an invidious discrimination against the members of one sex or the other, law makers are constitutionally free to include or exclude pregnancy from the coverage of legislation such as this on any reasonable basis, just as with respect to any other physical condition." (pp. 496–497, n. 20)

Although the feminist lobby lost the battle in court, they eventually won the war. The final redress for an adverse Supreme Court decision is to go to Congress for an amendment to the statute in question, or, if a constitutional issue is involved, to try for an amendment to the Constitution. In this case, changing Title VII was all that was necessary, since it covers both private and state employers and extends to federal government employees. Feminists joined with representatives from unions and civil rights groups to form the Campaign to End Discrimination Against

Pregnant Workers. This was one of the most successful lobbying efforts by feminists in the 1970s (Gelb and Palley, 1987, pp. 162–174). After only twenty-two months, their proposal, the Pregnancy Discrimination Act (PDA), became law.

The PDA constitutes the first U.S. national policy for pregnant workers. Into Title VII it adds language that prohibits discrimination against pregnant women in all aspects of employment, including hiring, firing, job security, seniority, and fringe benefits. The PDA also spells out the requirement that employers with disability-benefit and health-insurance plans extend coverage to include pregnancy. The coalition for the PDA enjoyed support from more than three hundred groups, including representatives of pro-life antiabortion groups. While this rare common effort of feminists and pro-lifers helped reduce the conservatives' usual stalling tactics used on equal-rights legislation, there was a cost to feminists. The final language of the bill allows employers to exempt elective abortions from insurance coverage except to save the life of the mother; still, employers may provide such benefits if they wish.

The PDA was the formal recognition of the CACSW's definition of the issue of pregnancy, childbirth, and work. It marked the complete shift from the conclusions expressed in *Muller v. Oregon* (1908), based on a description of women workers almost exclusively in terms of their capacity for motherhood, to a definition of women only as workers and ignoring their capacity for motherhood. In 1920, the Women's Bureau had expected that all women workers would become mothers; in 1980, the expectation seemed to be that few women workers were likely to become pregnant. They could fit all the necessary details into the time it took to recover from appendicitis. Despite the limited perspective, defining pregnancy as a temporary disability signaled the official acceptance of women as members of the work force. For the first time, women workers who gave birth had some job security. It was a victory for feminists, whose goal was to make pregnancy an issue of sex discrimination.

But many women had neither job protection nor financial support. The PDA applied only to those workers covered by Title VII. That group was further limited by the stipulation that only employers with temporary disability insurance (TDI) plans had to give benefits for pregnancy. Only five states—California, Hawaii, New Jersey, New York, and Rhode Island—require employers to have TDI plans for their employees. Many women workers have to use a combination of sick leave, annual leave, and leave without pay when they give birth. Estimates of the percentage of women workers who have no income-protected leave for pregnancy run as high as 60 percent.

Maternity/Parental Leave

After 1978, new proposals for a more comprehensive policy to deal with pregnancy and childbirth for women workers stirred debate among feminists. The question—whether women should get special treatment for maternity—was not new. Generations of feminists have tried to reconcile biological differences with equality. While rigidly equitable and gender neutral, the PDA falls short in both coverage and the length of leave provided. Critics charge that because it conforms to a male work standard of disability, it is inadequate for the needs of maternity.

In the late 1970s, Betty Friedan became an outspoken critic of feminists who refused to take into account the special needs of women. With her book *The Second Stage* (1981), she became one of the first leaders in the U.S. women's rights movement to promote the idea of *women's two roles*. While Friedan supported all the gains made toward legal equality of the sexes, she considered them only a first step, not the final goal. Without adequate attention to the family demands on women, she noted, legal equality places women in an impossible position: two full-time jobs and no support services. According to Friedan, the second stage of the women's movement must be a full-scale campaign for services, especially for maternity leave and child care, along with more involvement by fathers in family responsibilities. Men should have two roles, too!

In the 1970s and 1980s, the increases in labor force participation came from white mothers with children at home. This upward trend gradually closed the work gap between white women and women of color. These new workers saw the problems of work and family that many minority-group women had always faced. This convergence provided common ground for a cooperative effort to gain government support. The feminists seeking solutions to the problems were able to form coalitions with unions of working class women, many of color, such as American Federation of State, County, and Municipal Employees (AFSCME) and Service Workers International.

There were disagreements over the approach to the issue. Friedan spoke for maternity leave, but reform feminists adamantly opposed any kind of special-treatment approach. They contend that all policies must be gender neutral, not singling women out for special treatment—even for pregnancy and childbirth. They cite the effects of protective legislation still felt in job segregation and wage gaps. For the reformers, any special treatment means a renewal of those processes.

The two views met in debate at the Supreme Court in 1987. Responding to demands for adequate pregnancy leave, a few states (Montana, Massachusetts, California, and Connecticut) have enacted maternity-leave statutes.[4] Montana's law actually requires *maternity leave*. The motive was to ensure "real sexual equality while encouraging stable and workable family and societal relationships." Both the Montana Supreme Court and the federal district court had upheld the statute. In doing so, the courts affirmed a definition of equality that would be consistent with special leaves for childbirth: "The MMLA (Montana Maternity Leave Act) would protect the right of husband and wife, man and woman alike, to procreate and raise a family without sacrificing the right of the wife to work and help support the family after her pregnancy. The MMLA would ensure that both men and women would choose together to raise a family without permanently relinquishing the necessary income of the working wife" (*Miller-Wohl v. Commissioner of Labor and Industry, State of Montana*, 1981, pp. 1266–1267).

California's statute used the language of disability but required extra disability leave for pregnancy. California Federal Savings and Loan (CalFed) brought suit against the state of California. The financial institution charged that the law requiring a special disability leave for pregnancy was incompatible with Title VII. CalFed argued that Title VII, which prohibits sex discrimination, would preempt the California law as far as eligible employers were concerned. The two feminist groups filed briefs. Betty Friedan and the Planned Parenthood Federation of America supported the position that extra leave for pregnancy and childbirth gave women the same right to jobs and children that men had. The National Organization for Women (NOW), the Women's Legal Defense Fund, and the League of Women Voters sided with CalFed. These women's rights groups argued that the special leave violated Title VII. They wanted adequate leave and more coverage than that provided by the PDA, but they feared the marginalizing effects of protection and unequal treatment.

The U.S. Supreme Court agreed with the state of California that Title VII did not preempt the state pregnancy-leave law. The majority opinion rested its interpretation on Congress's intent in passing the PDA amendment to Title VII in 1978. Congress meant to prohibit discrimination against pregnant workers, not to rule out special benefits for them. Along the way, Justice Thurgood Marshall made reference to the two-roles argument of Friedan: "By 'taking pregnancy into account' California's preg-

BOX 8.3

New Definitions of Equality

These maternity leave and pregnancy leave cases show the effects of efforts to combine special treatment for women's reproductive needs with equality and equal treatment. To balance these seemingly contradictory goals requires changing the context of judging equality from a framework based on legal classifications to one of substantive equity *given* the different biological and social imperatives on women and men as workers and family members. As Friedan wrote, it involves equality not only between men and women but, within their lives, equality between work and family:

> In the second stage of this struggle that is changing everyone's life, men's and women's needs converge. There are conscious choices now, for men as well as women—to set up their lives in such a way as to achieve a more equitable balance between success in work and gratification in personal life. (1981, 1986, p. 160)

nancy disability statute allows women as well as men to have families without losing their jobs" (*California Federal Savings and Loan v. Guerra*, 1987, p. 694).

Meanwhile, reform feminists sought in Congress a gender-neutral solution to the problem of inadequate leave for maternity. Their proposal involved a new definition of the issue of childbirth and work and a recognition of women's two roles at home and work. The new definition, however, extended the idea of women's two roles to men. If women and men are to share equally in the work force, they must share in home and family responsibilities.

Working with members of Congress, reform feminists fashioned a bill that shifted the definition of pregnancy from a disabling to a medical condition, while requiring employers to provide adequate leave with job security. Then, the law would require employers to provide family leave (it need not be paid leave), for any worker, male or female, to care for a newborn, an adopted infant, or a sick child, with job protection and no loss of pay level or seniority.

Although the proposal quickly gained supporters from labor unions and child-advocacy groups, they often had different definitions of the issue. Many did not support family leave as a measure to improve the status of women. Instead, they saw it as a labor issue, a way to extend job-protected leave to a new category of employees, or as a children's issue, a way to encourage strong parent-child bonding. Does it really matter how the proposal for parental leave was defined? Yes, because particular definitions lead to particular constellations of proponents and opponents.

Opponents of parental-leave policies were content to have the issue treated as another piece of labor legislation. As such, it mobilized defenders of business and states' rights interests who have opposed federal labor policies since the 1930s. They trotted out their time-worn arguments to oppose the FMLA: federal regulations lead to excessive costs, to unacceptable burdens on small business, to government interference in the private sector, to a break with the tradition of providing benefits through labor-management contracts, to a first step down the slippery slope to paid maternity and family leave, and to a serious handicap on the international competitiveness of American firms, threatening a loss of jobs. If family leave were seen as a women's or children's issue, opponents would have to oppose help for families or argue that women belong at home—both risky and volatile positions. As labor legislation, the bill had to compete with other labor bills for scarce time. At the end of the Reagan era, many labor bills were backed up and some, such as mandatory sixty-day notification of plant closings, were seen as more urgent.

The battle over national family leave turned out to be a protracted struggle, resolved only with a change in the party in the White House. First introduced by representatives Patricia Schroeder (D.-Colo.) and William Clay (D.-Mo.) in 1985, the Family and Medical Leave Act finally passed both houses of Congress in spring of 1990. In its final form, the act was still primarily defined as a labor rights issue, not a women's rights issue. Thus, for the most part proponents and opponents lined up along party lines, with Democrats, who traditionally support labor rights, in favor and Republicans, who traditionally respond to business interests, against. Some Republican legislators broke ranks with their party and sponsored the act, arguing it was a family measure that would help workers, especially women, to cope with demands of work and family. They appealed to President Bush to treat the act as an aid to families, not a burden on business.

They failed, however, to shift the White House view, and on June 29, 1990, President Bush vetoed the FMLA. In his veto message he praised the idea of employers granting leave to workers but objected to the idea that federal government should dictate practices to employers in the name of labor rights:

> America faces its stiffest economic competition in history. If our
> Nation's employers are to succeed in an increasingly complex and

competitive global marketplace, they must have the flexibility to meet both this challenge and the needs of their employees. We must ensure that Federal policies do not stifle the creation of new jobs, nor result in the elimination of existing jobs. The administration is committed to policies that create jobs throughout the economy—serving the most fundamental needs of working families. (*Congressional Quarterly Almanac,* p. 361)

He went on to assert that employees as well as employers prefer diversity, not government-mandated uniformity. Bush called family leave a matter for private negotiation, not public mandate.

The 1990 FMLA scenario was repeated in 1991–1992: Both houses of Congress passed the FMLA and President Bush again vetoed it, giving identical reasons. In fact, the debate remained unchanged (*Congressional Digest,* 1991, 1993). The advocates had made some progress: the second time the Senate overrode the president's veto (although the House of Representatives did not). The issue became part of the presidential election campaign of 1992, when Bill Clinton pledged that one of his first acts as president would be to sign the Family and Medical Leave Act. Bush, who was running for reelection, added something new to his veto message: his intention to introduce a bill that would reward employers for providing parental-leave benefits to employees. Known as the Family Leave Tax Credit Act, it would offer a refundable tax credit for businesses that establish family leave policies for employees. This proved to be little more than a symbolic gesture, however. After the Democrats won the presidency in 1992, Congress enacted the FMLA for the third time, and newly inaugurated President Clinton signed it into law in February 1993.

The Family and Medical Leave Act applies to private employers with more than fifty employees and to public agencies. It requires that they provide up to twelve weeks of leave (which need not be paid) in a twelve-month period for birth or adoption of a child; for acquiring a foster child; for purposes of caring for a child, spouse, or parent with a serious health condition; or for the worker's own serious illness preventing performance of the job. After an employee returns to work following this leave, the employer is required to restore the worker to the same or equivalent position with same pay, benefits, and conditions. Many advocates for women workers see the FMLA as a partial victory at best. The Women's Legal Defense Fund estimates that the act covers 60 percent of American workers; it probably covers a lower percentage of women workers, however, for they tend to be more concentrated in small businesses (Slaughter, 1995). In addition, the gender-neutral approach assumes a sharing of family care activities between men and women, which does not exist. Even if men and women share such activities with good will, gender inequities that permeate the workplace continue to constrain women to the double shift and lower status. Follow the arithmetic: women tend to be in jobs that pay less than men's jobs, plus family medical and parental leave is unpaid, plus families are more likely to sacrifice the income from the worker with the lower pay. Taken together, this all equals reinforcement of separate spheres.

Relief for the Sandwich Generation?

The Family and Medical Leave Act of 1993 provides leave for more than childbirth and child care; it is the first U.S. national policy to provide substantive relief for the sandwich generation. The care of elderly family members is not a new public issue, but until the FMLA debates it had not received much national attention as a family issue, let alone as a women's work issue. Government interest in older people usually focuses on providing adequate income and health care. But the concept of the sandwich generation defines care of the aged as another work-and-family issue primarily affecting women. Health care is still a major need for the elderly but, as with the child-care issue, converging demographics are helping press the problem on lawmakers in a new form.

In the old days, the care of elderly family members was the responsibility of younger family members. But excessive demands on the time and money of the younger family members caused a strain that they often sought to avoid. Dramatic stories of sending grandpa "over the hill to the poorhouse" surfaced in the nineteenth century. By the 1930s, thirty-seven states had statutes requiring the family to take responsibility for aged parents, as the family was required to do for children. In the 1960s, as the population aged and more nursing homes were built, there was a national debate on the extent to which families continued to shirk their responsibility by parking older Americans in those nursing homes, expensive contemporary counterparts of the nineteenth-century poorhouse. Despite this image, however, 90 percent of the dependent elderly needing some care are still taken care of by family members—and the vast majority of these are the responsibility of women, usually wives or daughters (U.S. Congress, House, Select Committee on Aging, 1988).

Here is where the demographics come in: (1) With a longer life expectancy, the percentage of elderly people in the U.S. population is steadily increasing, thus increasing the demand for long-term care. (2) Middle-aged women, the primary caretakers for everyone—their own parents, their in-laws, their children, and their grandchildren—have been entering and staying in the labor force in growing numbers. (3) Higher divorce rates are beginning to reduce the number of elderly people who are able to rely on spouses for care. The result is that middle-aged parents have their frail parents to look after along with their own children, and sometimes grandchildren.

Men and women share in the "squeeze" on the sandwich generation, but the threat to work status is greater for women. Traditional attitudes associate caregiving activities with the maternal role. (Think of the kinds of help needed by a frail elderly person: cooking, dressing, bathroom help, administering medications.) Women are more likely than men to reduce their work hours or give up their jobs to care for an aging parent. Recent studies show that when the elderly parent moves in with a two-earner couple, the woman withdraws from the work force. This phenomenon is growing to such an extent that it is likely to have an impact on the future labor supply (Ettner, 1995). For women's work status, the effects can be devastating. As with the demands of pregnancy and child care, women pay extra costs of care in lost wages, lost opportunity and status, and lost pension and insurance benefits.

Until the mid-1980s, the problem of care of the elderly was not considered a women's issue, but it did piggyback on some child-care legislation. The Economic Recovery Tax Act of 1981 provided tax credit that could be used for all dependent-care expenses, but its provisions, inspired by the parent-child model, were very narrow and did not apply to many elder-care situations. It also gave some tax benefits to employers who assisted with dependent care for employees. All these provisions were consistent with the Reagan administration's efforts to encourage but not require employers to provide the assistance workers needed to meet their family obligations. The Dependent Care Planning and Development Grant program of 1986 provided some assistance to resource and referral programs for access to care facilities.

During its early stages, the debate on the Family and Medical Leave Act (FMLA) entertained the idea of extending job-protected parental leave to a more general leave for care of elderly parents. There were various definitions of these elder-care provisions. Some groups, such as the American Association of Retired Persons (AARP), saw the act as assistance to senior citizens. As a labor issue, it extended job protection. A few testified before the congressional committee that it was a special help for women workers. Political effects were mixed. The proposed expansion of the coverage broadened the coalition to include AARP, with its 24 million members, but it also raised the burden on employers and sharpened the opposition, probably prolonging the struggle over the act. As a part of the bill in the House of Representatives, the expansion survived negotiation with the more conservative Senate and became part of the FMLA.

Child Care

Federal and state governments have been involved more in the care of children than in helping ease the burdens of pregnancy and childbirth for women workers. In the middle 1800s, with the expansion of free public education, governments focused on the education of children. By the 1860s, the kindergarten movement approached the idea of combining care with learning. For the most part, however, the first infant and pre-school services were philanthropic projects with no government funds. Some were projects for women active in reform work among poor and newly arrived immigrant families. Community day nurseries to supervise children of mothers who worked in the new factories date from the 1880s. By 1910, there were 450 centers nationwide, with 85 in New York City alone.

The first federal government money to be spent on nonschool child care was spent in the 1930s under the New Deal. This money was not intended to help working mothers, however, but was meant to provide jobs for unemployed teachers, nurses, and social workers. In 1941, under pressure to crank up defense production, Congress quickly saw the relation between attracting women workers and availability of child care. The Community Facilities Act, or Lanham Act, of 1941 allocated federal funds to provide day care for children of workers in defense plants. At the peak of this act, 1.5 million children were in public day-care facilities. Since the program was an emergency war measure, however, these federal funds for child care were stopped in 1946.

The worry about who was caring for the children of the poor brought government back into the business of child care in the 1960s. The Social Security Act of 1935, with its allocation of Aid to Families with (Dependent) Children, had been passed to solve the problem of needy children by giving their mothers aid to allow them to stay home. As more women joined the labor force in the 1950s and 1960s and official attitudes toward women workers changed, this welfare program became increasingly unpopular. Federal and state governments looked for ways to reduce welfare rolls by putting mothers to work. Since that time, during periodic attempts to plug holes in welfare policies that discourage work, Congress has given more attention to the lack of affordable and available child care for welfare mothers. In 1967, Congress provided funds for day care to welfare mothers enrolled in the Work Incentive (WIN) programs. In 1974, Title XX of the Social Security Act extended grants to states to fund day-care centers for low-income and moderate-income families, half in welfare-related categories. In 1981, the funds for such centers were cut by one-fourth as Title XX was folded into block grants to the states, and this has continued through subsequent welfare legislation. In 1988, the Family Support Act required states to provide child-care services for any welfare recipients who are enrolled in a job-training program. Under 1996 welfare reform, federal funds for child care are available to states to help move welfare recipients to permanent jobs (see Chapter 10).

Another stimulus for the child-care policy debate—along with welfare—is the state of research into child development. In the 1940s, child psychologists extolled the essential role played by mothers in the development of their children. Care outside the home was a signal of pathology in the family. By the 1960s, evidence showed that some children were deprived of necessary stimulation, even if they were cared for at home. The idea of deprivation in child rearing did not challenge the importance of mother-care, but showed that some mothers, themselves poor and uneducated, were not able to give their children an even chance in competing with more advantaged children. This argument led in 1964 to the Head Start Program to provide preschool education for young children of the poor. Head Start was not a day-care solution for working mothers, since many centers offered only half-day programs. But the idea that day care might be more than custodial and of benefit to children was planted into public policy with the Head Start Program.

Child Development Act of 1971

Until the 1970s, the official perception was that out-of-home day care was an exceptional solution to whatever forces might interfere with the natural role of the mother in rearing her children, day and night, at home. Child-care services might be an answer to problems caused by war, depression, temporary poverty, or cultural disadvantage, but no general social need for them was recognized. After Head Start, however, feminist and civil rights leaders joined with child-development advocates and Labor Department experts to push for a redefinition of the issue that would give the federal government a permanent role in providing child-care services to all.

This coalition wanted a federally funded network of centers throughout the country. Child-development advocates in the government, universities, and social agencies sought to provide and expand early-childhood education to as many as possible, especially to poor children. They were encouraged by President Richard Nixon's pledge in 1969: "a national commitment to providing all American children an opportunity for healthful and stimulating development during the first five years of life" (quoted in Steiner, 1976, p. 11). Activists in the civil rights movement saw community-based child-care centers as an instrument of change. Manpower specialists in the government saw day care as a way of permitting more women to work.

Leaders of the women's rights movement saw child care as necessary to the liberation of women. Free child-care centers, open twenty-four hours a day, was one of the first demands of the women's movement. Most feminist theorists considered public child care a way to free women from the trap of their traditional domestic roles. In 1964, Alice Rossi challenged the psychologists' conclusions that any alternative to full-time mothering was pathological. Such patriarchal delusions, she said, kept women from developing their intellectual potential and kept them economically dependent. She called for a network of child-care centers as an "institutional lever for achieving sex equality" (p. 628). Feminists described profit-making day-care franchise businesses (called KFC: "Kentucky Fried Children") that substituted poorly paid baby custodians for dependent mothers and warned that "any old care" was not the answer. They felt that rearing children should be a responsibility of the entire society. With community-controlled child-care programs, the next generation would be reared free from stultifying sexist stereotypes.

NOW was the most vocal feminist group active in promoting child-care legislation. "We demand that child care facilities be established by law on the same basis as parks, libraries, and public schools, adequate to the needs of children from the pre-school years through adolescence, as a community resource to be used by all children from all income levels" (quoted in Deckard, 1979, p. 419). The Child Development Act of 1971 came close to meeting these demands. It called for a substantial federal

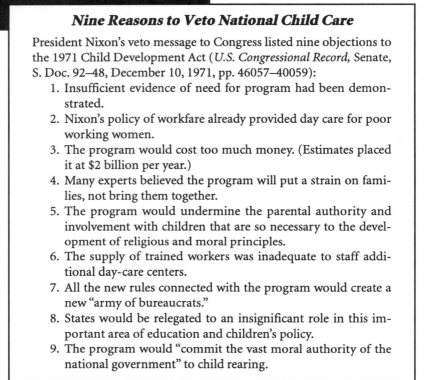

BOX 8.4

Nine Reasons to Veto National Child Care

President Nixon's veto message to Congress listed nine objections to the 1971 Child Development Act (*U.S. Congressional Record,* Senate, S. Doc. 92–48, December 10, 1971, pp. 46057–40059):

1. Insufficient evidence of need for program had been demonstrated.
2. Nixon's policy of workfare already provided day care for poor working women.
3. The program would cost too much money. (Estimates placed it at $2 billion per year.)
4. Many experts believed the program will put a strain on families, not bring them together.
5. The program would undermine the parental authority and involvement with children that are so necessary to the development of religious and moral principles.
6. The supply of trained workers was inadequate to staff additional day-care centers.
7. All the new rules connected with the program would create a new "army of bureaucrats."
8. States would be relegated to an insignificant role in this important area of education and children's policy.
9. The program would "commit the vast moral authority of the national government" to child rearing.

appropriation for a network of centers meeting high national standards and emphasizing development programs. These would be available to all children regardless of financial status because payment would be made on a sliding scale. Thus, the act broke the association of day care with welfare or deviant family situations.

In the final debates, the bill's sponsor, Senator Walter Mondale (D.-Minn.) declared that the purpose was to "strengthen the family." This statement, that out-of-home structured care for young children will strengthen the family, was a signal that the idea of a national comprehensive child-care system was under attack. In earlier discussions of the bill, issues of child development, support for working women, and national standards of care had been emphasized. Then Mondale seemed to respond to a new definition of public child care put forth by opponents: that it threatened the integrity of the traditional nuclear family. The argument proved to be very important. In 1971, the conservative right was just beginning to gear up the juggernaut that would end all the social-welfare fantasies of the 1960s.

President Nixon "saved" the country by vetoing the Child Development Act of 1971, ending the chances for such a program for the next decade. In doing so, he abruptly changed his administration's definition of the issue of public child care. Administrative departments and agencies, especially the child-development agencies, had supported the bill, and the president himself had advocated such a bill in 1969. The veto message of 1971, however, rejected public child care as excessive government interference with the family, the kind associated with communist systems: "For the Federal Government to plunge headlong financially into supporting child development would commit the vast moral authority of the National Government to the side of command approaches to child rearing over (and) against the family centered approach" (U.S. Congress, Senate, *U.S. Congressional Record*, 1971, p. 46059).

The association of child care with attacks on the family, along with economic crises and growing unemployment, kept the issue of public services off Congress's agenda for the next ten years. The problem of child care for working mothers received occasional mention. The regulations that implemented Executive Order 11375 included child care as part of the recommended action for affirmative action programs for government contractors. Tax deductions for child care, which have existed in one form or another since 1954, were extended in 1976 with a tax credit for child-care costs that relieved working parents of about 20 percent of the costs of care. State and local governments developed various services. Some of the most successful have focused on providing information about the wide variety of services available in a community. States have also been roused from their reluctance to get involved with potentially costly programs by occasional scandals over the standards and quality of private centers. In the 1980s, the scandals focused on sexual abuse, and a few well-publicized trials have led to some increased standards for child-care workers. These measures have further increased the cost of programs, but standards and services remain uneven across the country.

Child-Care Debates Continue

Although NOW worked hard for the 1971 act, the Washington women's rights lobbyists have not been on the forefront of the issue since. At first, feminists associated child care with the liberation of women from traditional roles in the family. They did not make a full transition to embrace the two-roles theory with enthusiasm. Although they supported proposals to expand services, they did not place the balancing of work and family roles at the top of the feminist agenda. Feminists went on to other campaigns, especially those for the Equal Rights Amendment (ERA) and for abortion rights.

Child care is one of those issues that keeps coming back. There were occasional committee hearings during the 1970s. The atmosphere set by the Reagan administration did not nurture the idea of federally funded child-care services. The states were the main places for policy and action. Title XX funds were turned into block grants, federal funds declined, and federal minimum standards were eliminated. The president also sought solutions in the private sector. Tax reforms enacted in 1981 gave incentives to employers to provide services for employees.[5] The decreasing number of available child-care spaces and the increasing numbers of mothers in the work force put the squeeze on Congress in the early 1980s. In 1984, the Select Committee on Children, Youth, and Families of the House of Representatives began a series of hearings to build support for a greater federal role in child care once again. George Miller (D.-Calif.) hoped to build a broad coalition: "Child care as an issue has a common border with just about every major domestic goal, from full employment to economic growth, from improving education to reducing child abuse, from providing early developmental opportunities for the handicapped and respect for the parents, to helping teenage parents stay in school" (U.S. Congress, House, 1984, p. 2). A notable exception in Miller's list of goals was women's rights to employment.

As revealed in these hearings, the 1980s version of the child-care issue focused on the need for services for children in families with two working parents and, secondarily, for single-parent families. It is the increase in the number of working mothers that has sparked demand. Why are mothers working? Out of economic necessity, answered the advocates of child care: their husbands don't earn enough to support their families, or the mothers are single. Most working mothers are in lower-paying jobs, and their need is for *affordable child-care*, said these advocates. And the *patchwork child-care system* in the United States is just inadequate to meet the need. A related theme in the discussion is the benefit to the economy and employers: decreased turnover, lower absenteeism, and improved productivity (thus reinforcing radical feminist suspicions that female labor is valuable to capitalism). Arguments from earlier debates re-

BOX 8.5

Who's Caring for Preschool Kids While Mom Works?

In the fall of 1991, the Bureau of the Census reported results of surveys to show who was caring for the 31 million children under age fifteen living with employed mothers. For the preschool youngsters, Mom reported a variety of solutions:

1. In child's home	35.8%
father	20.0
grandparent	7.2
other relatives	3.2
non-relative	5.4
2. Care in another home	31.0
grandparent	8.6
other relative	4.5
non-relative	17.9
3. Organized child-care facilities	23.1
day-/group-care center	15.8
nursery/preschool	7.3
4. Kindergarten	1.1
5. Mother cares for child at work	8.7

Source: U.S. Department of Commerce, Bureau of the Census. "Who's Minding the Kids? Child Care Arrangements: Fall 1991." *Current Population Reports,* P-70. Washington, D.C.: Government Printing Office, 1994, p. 5.

mained: the need of child development and the importance of child care to welfare mothers. In its reports, the House committee rarely linked child care to women's work status and economic independence. Economic productivity and family stability—traditional apple-pie themes—predominated, along with rhetoric about investing in our nation's "most precious resource"—children.

The 1980s hearings provoked more child-care bills each year. By 1988, when one hundred bills were filed, one had emerged for debate: the Act for Better Child Care (ABC). It was the next generation of the 1971 approach: $2.5 billion in federal grants to states, coupled with federal standards for child care. Users would pay for the service on a sliding scale

BOX 8.6

Tax Laws and Child Care

Some limited financial relief is available to working parents from the federal government. This aid takes the form of direct credits or tax-free dependent care assistance.

Child-Care and Dependent-Care Tax Credit

A tax credit of up to $2,400 for one dependent and $4,800 for two or more dependents is available to tax-paying working families with expenses for care of a child (under age thirteen) or a dependent (disabled person living at home). Up to 30 percent of the amount spent may be credited, depending on income, and the credit cannot exceed the total earnings of the spouse with the lower income. Payments to a grandparent may qualify, if the grandparent is not a dependent of the taxpayer.

Dependent-Care Assistance Program

The Internal Revenue Code provides for companies to offer employees a tax-free dependent-care assistance program for the care of children and disabled dependents. The program allows employees to use up to $5,000 (or $2,500 each for a married couple filing separate returns) in pretax income to pay for care expenses, thus reducing the gross income by a corresponding amount.

No Double Dipping

Employees eligible for both tax credits and the tax-free assistance program may not receive financial relief totaling more than a limit of $2,400 for one child and $4,800 for all children.

Source: U.S. Department of Labor. Women's Bureau. *1993 Handbook on Women Workers: Trends and Issues.* Washington, D.C.: Government Printing Office, 1994a, pp. 223–224.

according to their income. Child care became an issue in the 1988 presidential campaign, with Michael Dukakis supporting the ABC federal-funding proposal and George Bush emphasizing direct assistance to parents through tax credits. ABC never became law. Instead Congress passed the Child Care and Development Block Grant of 1990, providing $750 million to states for child-care services targeted to low-income families.

It is evident from tracing the development of debate over the question of government's responsibility for child care that the boundaries of the issue are porous: some child-care topics arise during consideration of seemingly unrelated questions; other policy debates infiltrate ongoing child-care discussions.

One famous case in which child-care arrangements led to a debate on other issues was the nomination of Zoe Baird for attorney general in 1993. Baird's nomination was suddenly derailed by the revelations of her solution to a common child-care problem. Wages for child-care providers remain low, and finding competent workers and keeping costs affordable is difficult for both agencies and individuals. Many have recruited immigrant women, often highly skilled and willing to work for low wages because they cannot get other jobs. However, the law has stringent rules for hiring immigrant workers (mostly designed for business employers, not individual families), including satisfying immigration work regulations and paying Social Security and withholding taxes. Baird hired an immigrant illegally as a nanny and failed to pay Social Security taxes. Prior to the Baird case, people hiring individuals to work at their homes were either unaware of the regulations or ignored them, in both cases breaking the law. When it turned out that the candidate for the top law-enforcement position—a working mother charged with responsibility for providing care for her child—had been guilty of taking this illegal way out, she was forced to withdraw.[6] As is so often the case in American politics, the publicity surrounding a single case raised awareness of a more general problem—the interrelation between the inadequate services for child care, the desire of immigrant women for employment, and a growing conflict about both legal and illegal immigration.

As we have seen, the child-care issue has been intertwined with the question of welfare policy for decades. In the 1990s, this debate was complicated by even stronger proposals for forcing welfare recipients into the work force. Advocates for strong work requirements at the federal and state government levels were once again cautioned that welfare mothers could not join the work force in the absence of adequate child care. Soon this debate was altered by the ascendance of the "family values" ideology. Based on a fundamental premise that solutions to all social problems are best handled in traditional families and not by the government, this approach undercuts many efforts to fund social programs. For a time, the Republican party majority in Congress was successful in making the family values perspective dominant, and many advocates for child care shifted focus from women's needs for help with family duties to emotional treatises on children and their welfare.

This review of the ebb and flow of public debates on child care suggests that it is unlikely that the U.S. government is capable of providing a coherent solution to the problem for working mothers. Some feminists maintain that only a change in the family gender-role ideology and the legal status of business would alter things. Mothers, of course, are not able to wait for that sea change in the culture and daily must put together a solution while maintaining their jobs and income.

Conclusion

Despite the centrality of work-and-family issues to the rights of women as workers and mothers, feminists have been, for the most part, in the background during policy debates. The tensions between equality and difference especially plague feminists in trying to reach agreement on a policy definition and solution. A core of the national women's rights policy network equates different treatment with inferiority. To them, *protection* is a bad word. Yet gender-neutral solutions thus far have not made room for the special problems faced by real-life women workers. Feminists have yet to agree that they can accept consciously pro-women policies, such as maternity leave and child-care services, without sacrificing opportunities for women at work.

The issues that arise under the subject of work and family, such as work status, family leave, and child care, have been in the policy arena for decades. They attract many diverse interest groups, all with their own self-serving versions of what the problem is and how it should be solved. Consideration of parental leave and child-care bills provokes only peripheral attention to gender questions, usually refering to increases in mothers in the work force or requiring welfare mothers to work. The argument that women have a right to work for occupational status and for financial autonomy is rarely heard. Thus, always lurking near the surface of the discussion is the sentiment that if things were right, parental leave and out-of-home child care would not be necessary except for the unfortunate few.

The search for solutions to the conflicts between work and family responsibilities through government social policies or regulations may have run its course. The protectionist dilemma presented by gender-neutral solutions may stymie any coherent feminist campaign. For the time being, women-oriented leave policies in states coexist with the federal gender-neutral Family and Medical Leave Act.

Nothing prevents employers from giving help to workers with family responsibilities. Incentives in the tax law have increased employer involvement in child care through on-site centers or, more frequently, through information and referral services. Some employers also have departed from the conventional 9-to-5 workday through job sharing, flextime, and part-time work. In fact, the so-called contingent workers are a growing component of the labor force.[7] Maintaining job benefits and status for workers who take these options is a problem.

Advocates for women's employment equality flirt with the notion that laws could be used to require more employers to accommodate work and family responsibilities by an attack on "labor hostility to working mothers" (Frug, 1979). They observe that, to many employers, the ideal employees, especially in management and professional levels, are those willing to devote their lives to the business. The courts accept this ideal as well. As we saw in Chapter 7, judges are willing to accept any discriminatory policy as long as employers can prove they serve a "business necessity." Some feminists ask: What if the courts started applying the disparate-impact law to employers whose failure to accommodate family demands relegates women to lower job status, achievement, and income? A step was already made through the Pregnancy Discrimination Act— failure to accommodate pregnancy is defined as sex discrimination. Should failure to provide paid pregnancy leave also be deemed sex discrimination? If so, then to comply with Title VII and the Executive Order 11375, employers would have to institute other family-friendly policies, such as paid leave, child-care assistance, flextime, and perhaps even home-working opportunities, while at the same time guaranteeing that status, pay levels, and benefits would be maintained.

Fantasies of using disparate-impact analysis to provide child care and other supports eventually confront the real obstacle to equal employment opportunity: gender roles in the family. As long as women have the primary family responsibilities and as long as they are the ones who take advantage of employers' grudging compliance with their needs, men will have the time and energy to devote to the employers' goals and, in fairness, will be compensated for it. Tracks that reduce career opportunities inevitably develop for women with children or with other major family responsibilities.[8] In Chapter 10 we return to this topic, with a full discussion of the intersection of gender roles in the family and work and their implications for women's relative economic status in the United States.

Notes

1. Nineteenth-century liberalism was based on theories of laissez-faire economics and limited government. In the twentieth century, the term *liberalism* has come to be associated with support for social programs first launched by President Franklin Roosevelt's New Deal in the 1930s.

2. The first maternity-leave laws in other countries restricted employers from requiring women to work in the last stages of pregnancy and after childbirth, usually four to six weeks altogether. These laws did not protect the jobs or pay of working women, however. Employers could fire workers and then rehire them at lower wages after the birth.

3. In writing the opinion for the Supreme Court in the *General Electric v. Gilbert* (1976) case, Justice William Rehnquist followed the *Geduldig v. Aiello* (1974) reasoning closely: "We think therefore that our decision in *Geduldig v. Aiello* dealing with a strikingly similar disability plan is quite relevant in determining whether or not the pregnancy exclusion did discriminate on the basis of sex" (p. 133).

4. Connecticut's 1977 statute, which predated the Pregnancy Discrimination Act (PDA) included language that said it was an "unfair employment practice for employers to refuse to grant a pregnant employee a reasonable leave of absence for disability resulting from such pregnancy." Justice Thurgood Marshall used this language as proof that the PDA did not preempt state pregnancy-disability statutes (*California Federal Savings & Loan v. Guerra* (1987). Agencies in Hawaii, Illinois, New Hampshire, Ohio, and Washington administering antidiscrimination laws have added regulations for job-protected maternity leave (Finley, 1986, p. 1128).

5. The Women's Bureau of the Department of Labor has established a clearinghouse to help employers provide assistance to workers with child and elder care. It includes a data base of existing programs and policy options (U.S. Department of Labor, 1994b, p. 86).

6. The media remained alert to the so-called nannygate issue during subsequent nominations. The next nomination for attorney general, that of Kimba Wood, fizzled before confirmation hearings over the same issue. Although child care came up during consideration of Stephen Breyer for the Supreme Court, senators did not seem to consider this father's solutions to child-care questions to be very important.

7. The Women's Bureau defines the *contingent work force* as including part-time and temporary workers; workers lacking traditional labor rights, such as job security, training advancement, and benefits; and home-based workers. Estimated at 32 million in 1993, the contingent work force has grown faster than the labor force as a whole. And it is predominantly female: two-thirds of the part-time workers are women, as are three-fifths of the temporary workers (U.S. Department of Labor, 1994a).

8. Felice Schwartz (1989) made quite a stir with her recommendation that corporate management develop two tracks for young trainees: the so-called mommy track would take account of the family needs of women but would offer only limited opportunities for advancement.

References

Adams, Carlyn T., and Winston, Kathryn T. *Mothers at Work*. New York: Longman, 1980.

Becker, Mary, Bowman, Cynthia Grant, and Torrey, Morrison. *Cases and Materials on Feminist Jurisprudence: Taking Women Seriously*. St. Paul: West Publishing, 1994.

California Federal Savings and Loan v. Guerra. 107 S. Ct. 683. 1987.

Cleveland Board of Education v. LaFleur. 414 U.S. 632. 1973.

Collins, Patricia. *Black Feminist Thought: Knowledge, Consciousness, and the Politics of Empowerment*. Boston: Unwin Hyman, 1990.

Congressional Digest: Symposium on Family and Medical Leave Legislation, April 1991.

Congressional Digest: Symposium on Family and Medical Leave Legislation, January 1993.

Congressional Quarterly Almanac, 101st Cong., 2nd sess., 46 (1990), p. 361.

Crawford v. Cushman. 531 F. 2nd 114. 1976.

Deckard, Barbara Sinclair. *The Women's Movement*. New York: Harper & Row, 1979.

Diamond, Irene, ed. *Families, Politics, and Public Policy*. New York: Longman, 1983.

Erickson, Nancy. "Pregnancy Discrimination: An Analytical Approach." *Women's Rights Law Reporter* 5 (Winter/Spring 1979): 83–105.

Ettner, Susan L. "The Impact of 'Parent Care' on Female Labor Supply Decisions." *Demography* 32 (September 1995): 63–80.

Finley, Lucinda. "Transcending Equality Theory: A Way Out of the Maternity and the Workplace Debate." *Columbia Law Review* 86 (1986): 1118–1182.

Finley, Lucinda. "Legal Aspects of Child Care: The Policy Debate over the Appropriate Amount of Public Responsibility." In *Parental Leave and Child Care: Setting a Research and Policy Agenda*, edited by Janet S. Hyde and Marilyn J. Essex, pp. 125–161. Philadelphia: Temple University Press, 1991.

Friedan, Betty. *The Second Stage*, originally published in 1981; rev. ed. New York: Summit, 1986.

Frug, Mary Joe. "Securing Job Equality for Women: Labor Market Hostility to Working Mothers." *Boston University Law Review* 59 (1979): 55–103.

Geduldig v. Aiello. 417 U.S. 484. 1974.

Gelb, Joyce, and Palley, Marion Lief. *Women and Public Policies*, rev. ed. Princeton: Princeton University Press, 1987.

General Electric v. Gilbert. 429 U.S. 125. 1976.

Hutchinson, Elizabeth D. "Child Welfare As a Woman's Issue." *Families in Society: The Journal of Contemporary Human Services* 73 (February 1992): 67–77.

Hyde, Janet S., and Essex, Marilyn S., eds. *Parental Leave and Child Care: Setting a Research and Policy Agenda*. Philadelphia: Temple University Press, 1990.

Kahn, Alfred J., and Kamerman, Sheila B. *Child Care: Facing the Hard Choices*. Dover, Mass.: Auburn House Publishing, 1987.

Krieger, Linda, and Cooney, Patricia N. 1983. "The Miller-Wohl Controversy: Equal Treatment, Positive Action, and the Meaning of Women's Equality." *Golden Gate University Law Review* 13 (1983): 513–572.

Lemons, J. Stanley. *The Woman Citizen: Social Feminism in the Twenties*. Urbana: University of Illinois Press, 1973.

Mahony, Rhona. *Kidding Ourselves: Breadwinning, Babies, and Bargaining Power*. New York: Basic Books, 1995.

Miller-Wohl v. Commissioner of Labor and Industry, State of Montana. 515 F. Supp. 1264. 1981.

Muller v. Oregon. 208 U.S. 412. 1908.

Myrdal, Alva, and Klein, Viola. *Women's Two Roles*. London: Routledge & Kegan Paul, 1956.

Nashville Gas Co. v. Satty. 434 U.S. 136. 1977.

Reskin, Barbara, and Padovic, Irene. *Women and Men at Work*. Thousand Oaks, Calif.: Pine Forge Press, 1994.

Rossi, Alice. "Equality Between the Sexes: An Immodest Proposal." *Daedalus* 93 (Spring 1964): 607–652.
Ruddick, Sara. *Maternal Thinking: Toward a Politics of Peace.* Boston: Beacon Press, 1995 (orig. pub, 1989).
Schwartz, Felice. "Management, Women, and the New Facts of Life." *Harvard Business Review* 67 (January–February 1989): 65–76.
Slaughter, M. M. "The Legal Construction of 'Mother.'" In *Mothers in Law: Feminist Theory and the Legal Regulation of Motherhood,* edited by M. A. Fineman and I. Karpin, pp. 73–100. New York: Columbia University Press, 1995.
Steiner, Gilbert. *The Children's Cause.* Washington, D.C.: Brookings Institution, 1976.
Steinfels, Margaret O'Brien. *Who's Minding the Children?* New York: Simon & Schuster, 1973.
U.S. Citizens' Advisory Council on the Status of Women. *Women in 1970.* Washington, D.C.: Government Printing Office, 1971.
U.S. Congress. House Select Committee on Aging. Subcommittee on Human Services. *Exploding the Myths: Caregiving in America.* 100th Cong., 2nd sess., August 1988.
U.S. Congress. House. Select Committee on Children, Youth, and Families. *Improving Child-Care Services: What Can Be Done.* 98th Cong., 2nd sess., September 5–6, 1984.
U.S. Congress. Senate. "Veto Message." *Congressional Record.* December 10, 1971, pp. 46057–46059. S. Doc. 92–48.
U.S. Department of Commerce. Bureau of the Census. "Who's Minding the Kids? Child Care Arrangements: Fall 1991." *Current Population Reports,* P-70. Washington, D.C.: Government Printing Office, 1994.
U.S. Department of Labor. Women's Bureau. *1993 Handbook on Women Workers: Trends and Issues.* Washington, D.C.: Government Printing Office, 1994a.
U.S. Department of Labor. Women's Bureau. *Working Women Count! A Report to the Nation.* Washington, D.C.: Government Printing Office, 1994b.
Williams, Wendy. "Equality Riddle: Pregnancy and Equal Treatment/Special Treatment Debate." *Review of Law and Social Change* 13 (1984–1985): 325–380.
Woloch, Nancy. *Women and the American Experience.* New York: Knopf, 1984.
Zigler, E. F., and Frank, M. *The Parental Leave Crisis: Toward a National Policy.* New Haven: Yale University Press, 1988.

CHAPTER 9

Sexuality

A fundamental part of the social organization of human beings is the regulation of sexual behavior. All societies have rules about who may be intimate with whom, how, and under what circumstances. Punishment for violations of the rules ranges from ostracism to imprisonment and even death. The United States, with its many cultural groupings, has a variety of norms prescribing desired—and tolerated—sexual practice for women. Beliefs about proper sexual conduct are often intensely held. Conflicts about what these rules should be are quite difficult to resolve. Women have a deep interest in such conflicts because, historically, regulation of sexuality has been synonymous with regulation of women, and, their rebelling against the culture may take the form of sexual rebellion (Espin, 1986).

In the United States, as in many contemporary societies, conflicts over sexuality issues have involved the question of what governmental policy should be with respect to varieties of sexual behavior and also whether government should be involved at all. The ordinary politics of distribution and compromise do not apply. Instead, the debates are ideological, often with moral and religious foundations, and they defy democratic processes of bargaining and compromise. At the same time, sexual behavior is widespread, varied, and private. Laws made and enforced in this political environment have little chance of accomplishing their goals.

Many policy areas that affect women's rights have elements that pertain to sexuality. Just how much policies related to education, employment opportunity, political rights, and family law are affected by attempts to control female sexuality is an issue of radical feminist ideology. This chapter discusses policy issues concerned primarily with the definition and regulation of women as sexual beings.

The issues of prostitution, pornography, and rape have been in the American political arena for more than 150 years; other sexuality issues, such as sexual harassment and gay and lesbian rights, have arrived more recently. Regardless of when they have arisen, sexuality issues have been framed in U.S. public debate by an ongoing conflict between moralists and libertarians. Moralists, inspired by religious convictions and rules, want to use public policy to contain sexual expression within hetero-sexual marriage and procreation and to punish deviations from the norm. Libertarians discourage coercive moral standards and ask govern-ment to leave people alone to live their sexual lives in private. These two great ideologies of sexuality policy have persisted in public debate since colonial times through massive changes in the American society, economy, and culture. Neither side shows signs of leaving the battlefield to the other.

Whenever an issue such as prostitution or rape comes to the public arena for debate, the moralist-libertarian axis is likely to be the primary conflict. Other questions—such as issues related to health, economic sta-tus, employment, or crime—may also arise. The outcome of each debate will be affected by the particular mix of issues and interests. Thus, gov-ernment is unlikely to maintain a consistent stance on major sexuality laws. Policies will be more liberal in some areas, more conservative in others, and possibly feminist in a few, thus differing from issue to issue and from state to state.

The traditional moralist-libertarian controversy has not had a lot to do with the effect of policy options on women. For most of the history of sexuality policy, feminists have flitted about on the edges, from time to time trying to enter the debate to promote women's rights. They have rarely been in agreement on a feminist vision of the policy that would achieve that goal. Often, feminists have accepted the moralist-libertarian axis and looked for the side that would be best for women. They have sometimes allied themselves with the moralists and at other times with the libertarians. Since the 1970s, however, liberal and radical feminists have engaged in their own debate (Duggan and Hunter, 1995; Ferguson et al., 1984; MacKinnon, 1993; Stan, 1995).

The liberal feminists protest the regulation of women by sexuality laws and mores. For them, the liberation of women involves not only op-portunities for education, employment, and political power but also for liberation of sexual life as well. In line with this thinking, the principles of choice, consent, and equality should guide public policy. There should be no constraints on what can be said, written, or shown about sex. Liberal feminists point out that silence and ignorance have historically been used to control and limit women. They say that women should be free to seek their own fulfillment and enjoyment without conforming to any outsider's idea of "politically correct" behavior. Liberal feminists argue that, given the right legal and cultural norms and institutions, women can have egalitarian sexual relations with men or women. Laws do make a difference, they contend, and feminists should seek reforms that enhance women's choices.

The radical feminists label all sexuality questions as part of the basic structure of male domination. As they see it, sexual identity and practice are created, this is, constructed, by patriarchy. Through heterosexual values, norms, and practices, men dominate women by defining their sexuality—their female essence. Practices and institutions such as intercourse, dating, courtship, marriage, prostitution, pornography, rape, wife abuse, sexual harassment, and homosexuality are thus interrelated. Therefore, the radical feminists say, it is the male perspective, not the female (let alone feminist), that defines what it means to be heterosexual. For women to be free and equal, they contend, women must fight this male domination. The only way to attack the tool of that domination—the regulation through heterosexuality—is by reconstructing sexuality. Laws are just vestiges of the domination pattern. Without reconstruction of sexuality, say the radical feminists, changing laws will either be impossible or have little effect on women's rights.

On the margins of the liberal-radical feminist debate are voices representing the perspectives of women of color. Many Hispanic/Latina women must contend with sexuality norms closely entwined with the family, community, and social status. African American feminists assert that sexual exploitation of black women has been especially severe, grounded in myths of sexual promiscuity and the use of slave women by white masters. Sexual myths about the "black rapist" and the "black whore" repress both men and women (Davis, 1981). These feminists have felt uncomfortable with simple liberal feminist assumptions about equality that overlook sexual exploitation based on racism. Radical feminists are faulted, too, for a blanket vilification of male domination—a view that fails to recognize the intersection of class and race oppression that keeps African American men subservient through myths, stereotypes, and abusive police tactics.

Whereas women of color have remained in the background, both radical and liberal feminists have attempted to influence the public debate on sexuality issues. The activists risk losing control of definitions and proposals by being incorporated into the ideological conflict between moralists and libertarians, but they are aware of this risk. They are careful to heed the lessons of earlier generations of feminists who lost to the other agendas and definitions of female sexuality.

Nevertheless, both liberal feminists and radical feminists have formed at least temporary coalitions with other activists. Liberal feminists have formed coalitions with civil libertarians from time to time because these two groups share values of privacy, choice, consent, and equality in sexual matters. Radical feminists seeking government regulation of sexual behavior have occasionally found themselves allied with moralists. Radical feminists have criticized liberal feminists for ignoring the effect of patriarchy on the status of women when laws are neutral and sexual practices are private. The liberal feminists have in turn warned that moralists will use regulations on sexual behavior not to improve women's autonomy from men but to limit freedom for women.

The sequence of topics within this chapter forces the author and reader to confront the sexuality debate itself. What issues should be included in a sexuality chapter of a book on women's rights? Is sexual harassment a sexuality issue or an employment issue? Do discussions of prostitution and pornography belong together, or should prostitution be discussed as a criminal law with rape and wife battery? Is lesbianism a primary and essential question of women's rights, or is it a part of the gay rights movement? Answers to such questions are not always obvious. The topics that follow in this chapter are included according to the definitions of feminist writers who have described the sexuality debates. Their order is according to their histories as issues of public concern, beginning with the oldest public issues, prostitution and pornography, and ending with the most recent, the status of lesbians.

Prostitution

Prostitution is popularly known as the "world's oldest profession." This rubric implies that selling sex, no matter its causes or effects, is inevitable: where you find human beings, you find prostitution. But prostitution has many meanings and definitions in different societies, as well as within the American society. For example, the exchange of sex for material goods may not be noticed or named in some societies. In others, it may be fully accepted and respected or reviled and punished. In ancient civilizations, women may have practiced prostitution as a religious ritual (Frazer, 1922, pp. 330–331).

The various meanings of prostitution make it a difficult policy issue. For example, seeing prostitution as a work contract; a commercial transaction; a coercive relationship; a problem of public decency, morality, and health; or a symptom of poverty can lead to an active role for government. Any of these definitions relates the transaction to a legitimate governmental role in protecting citizens' health and welfare or in regulating commerce. Other conceptions of prostitution are consistent with limited governmental action, for example, seeing it as a private sexual relationship or a service for which people can earn money, just as many other personal services are offered for money. Because of the variety of its meanings, whenever prostitution has been on the public agenda since colonial times, it has stimulated an intense and conflictual debate. Prostitution is now illegal in every state except Nevada, where it is regulated. The state laws and the way they are enforced bear the imprint of these past battles, and the impact that prostitution policies have on women's rights remains a matter of debate.

Prostitution became a public problem early in the nineteenth century, and its rise in the nation's social consciousness coincided with urbanization. With people living closer together in cities, they became aware of brothels and their clientele. Early reactions came from church reformers, who considered prostitution to be evidence of social evil, individual sin, and the moral weakness of women. To these reformers, the sin was in the character of the prostitute. At first, they didn't demand new laws but instead urged the police to use vagrancy laws to keep the prostitutes away from the "decent people." Police officials in big cities, however, were also aware of European theories and practices that treated prostitution as an inevitable, even necessary, evil. The way to control its ill effects, urban police decided, was to regulate prostitutes, to limit their activities, and to subject them to strict health inspections in order to limit venereal disease.

Efforts by some police officers and medical doctors to pass regulations to control prostitutes were thwarted successfully by women's rights activists who opposed any policy that might perpetuate or support prostitution. These feminists saw prostitution as an evil perpetrated by men on women. Inspired by extant theories of separate spheres and motherhood, many of these feminists believed that women were by nature more

BOX 9.1

Contagious Diseases Acts in England: 1864

Government can be especially vigilant about prostitution when military policy is involved. The British parliament passed the Contagious Diseases Acts to control venereal disease: "That the peculiar conditions of the naval and military services, and the temptation to which men are exposed, justifies special precautions for the protection of their health and their maintenance in a state of physical efficiency" (Petrie, 1971, p. 11).

The acts empowered police in ports and garrison towns to force any woman suspected of being a prostitute to undergo tests and treatment for venereal disease. Josephine Butler devoted her energies and social status to a twenty-year campaign to repeal these acts. She argued that the laws burdened women with full responsibility for prostitution and left the poor and uneducated vulnerable to abuse. Not only was any woman liable to being labeled a prostitute, but the state was in the business of certifying healthy women for purchase by men. Josephine Butler's crusade inspired feminists throughout the United States and Europe.

moral then men. If women became prostitutes, it was because men forced them into "the life" through seduction, rape, poverty, and even bondage. In this way, prostitutes were the victims of unregulated sexual aggression by men. According to these feminists, there were other female victims of male aggression in marriage—women forced by male sexual appetites to ruin their health bearing too many children. Women suffered from the double standard; an equally high standard for men would bring relief, these feminists believed. For nineteenth-century feminists, the prostitute was not immoral or evil, but a victim, in the words of the old song, "more to be pitied than censured."

Feminists sought to reclaim the victims and to protect other women, especially young working girls, who were especially vulnerable to male seduction. After the Civil War, feminists joined with moral reformers in the social-purity movement. Their shared goal was to regulate and control male sexual aggression with laws and social services. States began to enact laws to punish men who seduced women. Most states raised the age of sexual consent from age ten to age sixteen or even as high as age eighteen. Any person having sexual relations with a girl under the age of consent could be charged with rape, that is, *statutory rape*. By 1900, the social-purity allies had launched a national campaign to suppress prostitution

(Hobson, 1987; Pivar, 1973). They had gained control of the debate and the definition of the issue from those who supported regulation. Over the next three decades, prostitution itself would become criminalized.

Criminalization of Prostitution

After 1900, the social-purity movement developed into an even broader, more successful coalition that gained control of the issue of prostitution and won new laws at the federal level and in every state in the union. These laws made most aspects of prostitution subject to police action and criminal prosecution. The alliance of feminists, doctors, prohibitionists, social workers, and progressives made war on red-light districts, pimps and procurers, organized vice rings, and prostitutes themselves.

Today, state laws continue to bear the mark of this successful national campaign against prostitution. Along the way, however, the feminists' view of male power disappeared, and prostitutes themselves became the object of government control. Feminists lost control of the issue when policy makers accepted the term *vice* to refer to problems of prostitution. This concept expands the definition of the problem because it not only implies immorality but also adds the concepts of crime, disease, and threat to the public welfare. No longer seen as a necessary and inevitable evil that government should contain, prostitution became a serious criminal problem that warranted police control.

Between 1900 and 1930, states enacted laws making prostitution transactions criminal—both the act of trading sex for money and the act of *soliciting*, asking for or offering someone money for sex. State laws expanded to capture pimps and brothel or hotel owners. It became a criminal act to live off the earnings of prostitution, to live in a house of prostitution, or to own property where these practices occurred. In large cities, funds were channeled into special police units to close down red-light districts and to break up commercial prostitution rings as well as to arrest individual women for soliciting. To lawmakers and the police, prostitution was a women's crime, but prostitution was sustained and expanded by commercial networks of men, who were also criminally responsible.

The idea of prostitution as "traffic in women" inspired federal policy as well. In 1910, Congress passed the White Slave Traffic Act (Chap. 395, 36 Stat. 825–827, 1910; codified at 18 U.S.C. S.S. 2421–2424), also known as the Mann Act. Patterned after an 1875 act that forbade the importation of women from foreign countries for the purposes of prostitution, the

Mann Act was aimed at pimps and procurers who brought women across state lines as prostitutes and was meant to protect women. Such laws were inspired by lurid stories of young white girls being kidnapped and held in bondage as sexual slaves traded from one pimp to another. The analogy to slavery led to laws similar to the laws prohibiting slavery. The Mann Act, however, went beyond prohibiting prostitution and made it a federal crime to transport in interstate commerce "any woman or girl for the purpose of prostitution or debauchery or for any other immoral purpose." This broadened language permitted the Federal Bureau of Investigation (FBI) to prosecute both men and women for sexual behavior other than prostitution, such as extramarital or premarital sex.

The Mann Act remains on the federal statute book. Between 1970 and 1982, one study showed, 439 defendants—including 35 women—were in prison for violating the Mann Act (Beckman, 1984). Congress amended the act in 1986 to make it gender neutral and to remove the federal role in policing activities deemed immoral. It is now a federal crime to transport a person, male or female, across state lines for any sexual activity deemed to be a criminal offense in the destination state. Today the Mann Act has been used to prosecute men who lure women from one state to another and then rape them, as well as for interstate traffic for prostitution (Langum, 1994).

By 1910, the feminist idea of the prostitute as the unfortunate victim of male sexual aggression had already receded from the debate, overwhelmed by the concept of criminal vice. During World War I, federal policy turned its full force against prostitutes, and prostitution became a female crime. The mobilization of soldiers led to increases in venereal disease (VD), which, in turn, made War Department officials fear for the nation's defense. The campaign to keep soldiers healthy—"fit to fight"—turned into an assault on women's rights that has received little attention from historians. While we know all about the internment of Japanese Americans during World War II, we know little about the internment of women on suspicion of prostitution during World War I. Like the Japanese Americans, the women were detained by military and local police because of their biological characteristics, not for their behavior. Local health officials had the power to require "suspicious" women to have health exams. If the women tested positive for a venereal disease, they were quarantined. The entire burden for preventing the spread of venereal disease fell to women, not to the soldiers. Feminists were unable to prevent this discrimination, and the events reinforced the conclusion that the state regulation of prostitution means the state regulation of women, not men. By the 1920s, laws and official conceptions of prostitution that defined it as a woman-centered crime were firmly in place. Feminists had lost their demand that ways be found to force men to limit their sexual aggression.

Reform Efforts and Effects

Beginning in the 1970s, plans to reform criminal prostitution laws enacted in the early 1900s appeared on the public agenda. The civil libertarians, the first to raise criticisms of prostitution laws, focused on the content of prostitution laws and the way the laws were enforced. They attacked the policies represented by these laws as unconstitutional on several fronts. In making a sexual act a crime, the policies violated the privacy of consenting adults. The laws also violated due-process guarantees: they were vague and often made a person's status (that is, being a prostitute) rather than a person's act (that is, selling sexual favors) a crime. The laws were vulnerable to review under the Equal Protection Clause of the Fourteenth Amendment because they discriminated against women; some even defined a prostitute as "a woman who . . . " and clearly excluded men from prosecution for selling sex. Even more discriminatory, civil libertarians believed, male patrons of prostitutes were exempt from prosecution by law or by practice, even though the illegal transaction could not occur without their participation. Beyond their questionable constitutionality, the policies they reflected were clearly ineffective in eliminating or suppressing prostitution, their original intent. Thus, the laws became vehicles for police to harass prostitutes, especially those who were poor. In addition, they increased the power of pimps.

The American Civil Liberties Union (ACLU) and the American Law Institute took the lead in challenging the unconstitutional features of state prostitution laws. Litigation changed some state laws in the 1970s (Parnas, 1981). Eventually efforts at legislative reform were more successful. In the 1960s and 1970s, more than one half of the state legislatures amended their laws to incorporate up to three changes: (1) substituting gender-neutral language, (2) including homosexual acts, and (3) providing penalties for patrons similar to those for prostitutes. Despite these reforms, women, especially African American women, are still the most likely to suffer arrest and prosecution for trading sex for money.[1]

Police and some legislators have proposed schemes to save law enforcement resources and increase taxes by legalizing prostitution and licensing it as a business. Only one state has adopted this regulation policy. In 1971, Nevada enacted a statute allowing counties with fewer than 250,000 residents (increased to 400,000 in 1991) to license, tax, regulate, or prohibit brothels; this number by definition excludes Las Vegas and Reno. Prostitutes are allowed in all but three of Nevada's eligible counties but are subject to a variety of regulations. In general, prostitution is restricted to licensed brothels, and only women may be employed. Every aspect of the business and of the life of the employees (the "girls," as they are called) may be strictly regulated, including where they can go in the community and the people with whom they can associate. A "girl" may not be allowed to rent a hotel room in town, for example, or go to a bar, or go anywhere with a male escort, or visit friends in town. Of course, each "girl" is required to submit to regular health inspections to retain her license. Outside this regulatory scheme, prostitution remains illegal and criminalized.

Feminists are united in their opposition to systems of state-regulated prostitution such as that in Nevada. Such systems bring the state into the business of supplying disease-free women for the use and pleasure of men. Although no one is arrested within the licensed system, women's lives are controlled and through their fingerprints they are marked for life as prostitutes. Any woman who accepts money for sex outside the regulated system is liable to arrest and prosecution. And, in their zeal to eliminate illegal prostitution, police may harass any woman on the street or in a bar as a possible prostitute.

Despite feminists' agreement on the question of regulated prostitution, divisions about the meaning of prostitution hamper their efforts at further changes in the law. Liberal feminist attention to the issue of regulated prostitution is based on the assumption that selling sexual services is a form of *work* that women may freely choose; it follows that it should be treated as a work issue. Women have the right to be sex workers, liberal feminists argue. Prostitution should therefore be renamed as sex work, and states should repeal codes that make voluntary sex work a crime. States could use existing business and commercial codes to manage the work. According to this view, decriminalization would make sex work much less dangerous and allow prosecution of those who abuse prostitutes.

Another group of feminists interested in the issue take what has been called the "abolitionist" position: they wish to eliminate the practice of prostitution altogether because it inherently involves the sexual use and abuse of women by dominant male culture. Abolitionists focus their arguments on the assumption that women do not choose prostitution voluntarily. Rather, systems of exploitation trap women into prostitution through drug addiction, economic deprivation, and coercion. Abolitionists disagree with the feminists who label prostitution as a form of work. It is not a service or work, they say, it is the selling of the body, in fact, of the self. At its base, prostitution is "men's perceived need, and self-proclaimed right, to buy and sell women's bodies for sexual use" (Wynter, 1987, p. 266).

Other analysts insist that race and class factors must be part of the assessment of prostitution and thus of its remedies. The number of people engaged in prostitution is probably unknowable. However, there is little doubt about who is arrested: "Black women are 7 times more likely to be arrested for prostitution than non-black women, with the highest proportion of arrests occurring in inner cities where living standards are low, the level of desperation high, and policy prejudice endemic" (Flowers, 1994, p. 173). Any proposed solution to the problem of prostitution must recognize the special vulnerability of women of color to exploitation both by men and by the police.

Beginning in 1973 with the organization of COYOTE (Call Off Your Old Tired Ethics), advocates for decriminalization of prostitution staged a campaign. The leader of COYOTE was Margo St. James who had worked briefly as a prostitute. The organization presented itself as a union of prostitutes, although in fact prostitutes made up only a tiny minority of the membership. COYOTE sought links with the National Organization for Women (NOW) and the ACLU, and in the late 1970s it began a national effort to gain repeal of prostitution laws, claiming that prostitution was a civil rights issue. Despite some interest in the national press from time to time, COYOTE's campaign was a failure. A few states flirted with the idea of decriminalization as a way to reduce costs of law enforcement, but no state has decriminalized prostitution. Efforts to change the terms of the prostitution debate from a question of morality and crime to one of work and civil rights had limited impact; the press continued to use traditional terminology.

In the mid-1980s, COYOTE's campaign met feminist opposition from a new organization, WHISPER (Women Hurt in Systems of Prostitution Engaged in Revolt). This organization was closely related to international efforts to abolish prostitution (Barry, 1995). WHISPER opposed decriminalization, arguing it would have the effect of freeing the pimps and procurers to exploit women for sex with no interference. Instead, they advocated social programs to aid runaway girls and to help prostitutes find alternatives to selling sex.[2]

Neither COYOTE nor WHISPER has enjoyed success in getting policy makers to consider reforms that would improve the status and rights of women engaged in prostitution. Neither organization has been able to mobilize much support, even from its main constituency, prostitutes themselves (Weitzer, 1991). COYOTE found it difficult to form coalitions with more mainstream feminist and civil liberties groups.[3] WHISPER's allies were in the international feminist community. Thus, on occasions when the prostitution issue has risen to the public agenda in recent years it has tended to coincide with efforts to crack down on street walkers and to prosecute prostitutes who have acquired immunodeficiency syndrome (AIDS). Policy makers are reluctant to take up reform proposals. While opinion data are sketchy, evidence shows that regulation, not decriminalization or treatment programs, gains the most support from the public. Regulation is an alternative opposed by both COYOTE and WHISPER.

Thus, prostitution remains a criminal activity, with enforcement aimed at limiting its public aspects, especially soliciting and the operation of brothels, massage parlors, tanning salons, and the like. Occasionally some attention is paid to the victimization of women and girls by pimps and to the victims' vulnerability to drugs and violence. Descriptions reminiscent of nineteenth-century views warn the public of the dangers represented by prostitutes as carriers of sexually transmitted diseases (STDs), especially AIDS. Prostitution may not be the oldest profession, but the debates about it seem timeless.

Pornography

Pornography is at least as old as prostitution, or at least as old as literate prostitutes (the word *pornography* has its origins in the Greek language, in which it means the "writing of harlots"). What makes something pornographic depends on its intent to stimulate sexual excitement. Whether a particular book, film, or poster does so stimulate and whether that item poses a public problem is the political question. In the United States, government has always had authority to regulate pornography. Debate has focused primarily on the extent of that authority and on whether all sexually explicit representational materials are intrinsically stimulating and thus pornographic.

Pornography As Obscenity

From early in the nineteenth century, the issue of pornography was defined as a question of *obscenity* and protecting public morals. At the time, moralists considered obscenity, which they defined as the unnatural abuse of sexual or excretory functions, to be identical with the representation of sexual acts. They successfully pushed for local and national laws to suppress such materials and keep them out of the marketplace. This campaign peaked in 1873 when Congress passed the Comstock Act (the Act for Suppression of Trade in and Circulation of Obscene Literature and Articles of Immoral Use), which banned the importation and mailing of obscene materials, including sexually explicit books and pictures as well as contraceptive devices and information (see Chapter 4).

The moralist argument dominated the issue for decades and still remains a major aspect of the debate. The libertarian challenge to the moralists began in the early 1900s, when books deemed important literary contributions, such as James Joyce's *Ulysses*, were either declared illegal imports or "banned in Boston" and other communities. The libertarians argued that obscenity laws violated the First Amendment's guarantee of freedom of speech. They initiated cases to provoke a wide judicial interpretation of this amendment's free-speech guarantees. Traditionally, the amendment had been interpreted as protecting civic or political speech. Libertarians simply contended that sexually related speech and writing should also be protected. They said that any curtailing of free expression could ultimately have a debilitating effect on citizens' rights.

Case law mounted up as courts moved away from considering the merits of importing individual films and books and toward establishing guidelines that balanced the rights of free speech and free press with the community interest in public safety and morals. So far, however, the Supreme Court has rejected the idea that obscene materials are protected by the First Amendment (*Roth v. United States*, 1957). Instead, the Court has developed a test for determining if materials are obscene and subject to regulation or prohibition by state and local governments. The test criteria are

> (a) Whether the average person, applying contemporary community standards would find that the work, taken as a whole, appeals to the

BOX 9.2

Two Commissions, Two Conclusions

In 1970, President Johnson assembled a commission on obscenity and pornography to study various aspects of these issues. That commission found no evidence of a relation between sexually explicit materials and crime:

> In sum, empirical research designed to clarify the question has found no evidence to date that exposure to explicit sexual materials plays a significant role in the causation of delinquent or criminal behavior among youth or adults. The commission cannot conclude that exposure to erotic materials is a factor in the causation of sex crime or sex delinquency. (U.S. Commission on Obscenity and Pornography, 1970, p. 27)

In 1986, President Reagan assembled a similar commission, which came to be known as the Meese Commission. Citing changes in both media and pornography, the Meese Commission reached a conclusion opposite that of the 1970 commission:

> Since the clinical and experimental evidence supports the conclusion that there is a causal relationship between exposure to sexually violent materials and an increase in aggressive behavior directed towards women, and since we believe that an increase in aggressive behavior towards women will in a population increase the incidence of sexual violence in that population, we have reached the conclusion, unanimously and confidently, that the available evidence strongly supports the hypothesis that substantial exposure to sexually violent materials as described here bears a causal relationship to anti-social acts of sexual violence and, for the same sick groups, possibly to unlawful acts of sexual violence. (U.S. Department of Justice, 1986, pp. 325–26)

prurient interest . . . ; (b) whether the work depicts or describes, in a patently offensive way, sexual conduct specifically defined by the applicable state law; and (c) whether the work, taken as a whole, lacks serious literary, artistic, political, or scientific value. (*Miller v. California*, 1973, p. 24)

The Court's test elaborated in the *Miller* and *Paris Adult Theatre* (1973) cases is essentially a compromise between the libertarian and moralist positions. When the test criteria were outlined in 1973, the public debate was changing. The antipornography group relied less and less on moralistic arguments of religion and purity (except when dealing with child pornography) and began to assert that pornography was a danger because it provoked violent crime. They noted government's constitutional power to protect the public from expression that would incite violence. (The often-cited analogy is that of shouting "Fire!" in a crowded theater.) To consider the evidence on both sides of the public debate over pornography, President Johnson assembled a commission to study obscenity and pornography. The commission concluded that pornography was not dangerous (U.S. Commission on Obscenity and Pornography, 1970). Fifteen years later, President Reagan assembled another commission. It came to the opposite conclusion (U.S. Department of Justice, 1986). Both commissions relied on published scholarly research in reaching their conclusions, and both have been criticized by skeptics and opponents for bias in their selection of research to study and for inadequacies in their research methodologies. It is very difficult to prove, beyond doubt, a causal link between one type of reading material and one type of subsequent action. There are too many other variables to be eliminated. Thus, such studies usually have little impact on those who are not predisposed to agree with their conclusions.

The Feminist Debate

Feminists became active on the pornography issue in the 1970s in response to increased public exposure to films, billboards, and shop displays that graphically linked extreme violence against women with sexual stimulation. Many feminists formed activist organizations such as Women Against Violence Against Women (WAVAW), Women Against Violence in Pornography and Media (WAVPM), and Women Against Pornography (WAP). They organized direct-action protests against movies and advertisements, holding demonstrations, circulating petitions, and publishing newsletters to raise public consciousness. WAP conducted tours of pornography shops on Times Square in New York City to call attention to the portrayal of women as sex objects: that is, as sexually aroused by violence and as enjoying violence and degradation at the hands of men. This group staged "Take Back the Night" rallies, denouncing pornography as part of an effort to intimidate and control women.

Based on the experience of direct action, antipornography feminists developed a theory linking pornography to criminal violence against women and the patriarchal culture of male domination and oppression. "Pornography is the theory, rape the practice," wrote Robin Morgan

(1977, p. 169). Susan Brownmiller made the following point in her classic study of rape:

> Pornography, like rape, is a male invention, designed to dehumanize women, to reduce the female to an object of sexual access, not to free sensuality from moralistic or parental inhibition. The staple of pornography will always be the naked female body, breasts and genitals exposed, because as man devised it, her naked body is the female's "shame," her private parts the private property of man, while his are the ancient, holy universal, patriarchal instrument of his power, his rule by force over her. (Brownmiller, 1975, p. 394)

Antipornography feminists make a distinction between *erotica*—sexually explicit materials designed to stimulate arousal through love, pleasure, and sensuality—and *pornography* or *gyno-thanatica*—sexually explicit materials designed to emphasize pain, dominance, and violence (Steinem, 1978, p. 53; Tong, 1984, pp. 9–32). Feminist legal theorists refined the argument into a detailed analysis of sexual repression and politics (MacKinnon, 1982, 1983).

Civil libertarians were astonished at the antipornography stance these feminists had developed. From the first antipornography demonstration by feminists, the libertarians labeled them as "prudes," throwbacks to their uptight ancestors in the nineteenth-century social-purity crusades. The so-called sexual revolution had freed women to be sexual creatures; the libertarians discounted women against pornography either as women who were frightened of sex or as deviant anti-male lesbians.

Antipornography feminists persevered and formulated a definition of *pornography* as cultural discrimination against women. Andrea Dworkin (1981) and Catharine MacKinnon (1987) offered a legal solution to the problem: persuade local governments to declare pornography a form of sex discrimination and empower women to sue pornographers (producers and sellers) for civil damages based on personal harm. These two women successfully lobbied city councils in Minneapolis in 1983 and in Indianapolis in 1984. However, neither law remains in force. The mayor vetoed the Minneapolis law, and the Indianapolis ordinance was ruled unconstitutional in 1984 (Donnerstein, Linz, and Penrod, 1987, 137–145), a ruling that was upheld on appeal in 1985 (*American Booksellers Association, Inc. v. Hudnut*, 1985). The Indianapolis law failed to pass constitutional tests because the city's definitions of discriminatory pornography were considered to be too vague (*American Booksellers Association, Inc. v. Hudnut*, 1985, p. 324). They were stated as follows:

Pornography [is] the graphic sexually explicit subordination of women, whether in pictures or in words, that also includes one or more of the following:

1. Women are presented as sexual objects who enjoy pain or humiliation; or

2. Women are presented as sexual objects who experience sexual pleasure in being raped; or

3. Women are presented as sexual objects tied up or cut up or mutilated or bruised or physically hurt, or as dismembered or truncated or fragmented or severed into body parts; or

4. Women are presented as being penetrated by objects or animals; or

5. Women are presented in scenarios of degradation, injury, abasement, torture, shown as filthy or inferior, bleeding, bruised, or hurt in a context that makes these conditions sexual; or

6. Women are presented as sexual objects for domination, conquest, violation, exploitation, possession, or use, or through postures or positions of servility or submission or display.

In 1986, Andrea Dworkin testified before the Meese Commission, making a dramatic plea that pornography not be tolerated under the guise of free speech but that it be treated as a harmful exploitation of women. "Pornography is a civil rights issue for women because pornography sexualizes inequality, because it turns women into subhuman creatures. . . . Pornography creates bigotry and hostility and aggression toward all women, targets all women, without exception" (Dworkin 1995 in Stan, p. 34).

This passionate antipornography crusade in the 1980s provoked an equally passionate opposition from within the feminist movement. Free-speech feminists feared that efforts to suppress pornography would work against women's rights. Although many do not defend the violent and degrading images of women found in pornography produced for male audiences, they oppose empowering the government or courts to suppress it. They heed lessons from the fate of feminist arguments in the social-purity movement one hundred years ago. Although social-purity feminists, like the contemporary antipornography group, criticized male sexual dominance, efforts to control this dominance turned out to repress and regulate women. The free-speech feminists suggest that attempts to censor pornography could be used by moralists to reinforce traditional taboos and to silence women in their efforts to find their own ways of sexual expression. Such laws could be used to censor information books such as *Our Bodies, Ourselves*, women-centered erotica, or even information about contraception and abortion.

When antipornography feminists joined with Phyllis Schlafly and other moralists to promote the Indianapolis ordinance in 1984, some opponents formed FACT (Feminist Anti-Censorship Taskforce) and filed a brief against the Indianapolis ordinance in the *Hudnut* case. In their campaign, FACT activists pointed out that such ordinances would do the greatest harm not to pornographers but to feminists. They charged that antipornography feminists such as Dworkin and MacKinnon see sexuality in narrow terms as "unremitting, unequaled victimization for women. The ordinances' authors seek to impose their analysis by putting state power behind it. But this analysis is not the only feminist perspective on sexuality. . . . Women are agents, and not merely victims, who make decisions and act on them and who desire, seek out and enjoy sexuality" (Duggan and Hunter, 1995, p. 63).

Free-speech feminists and FACT activists argue that women have diverse interests in and reactions to pornographic images. Thus, women benefit the most from an atmosphere of freedom and tolerance of sexuality in order to be able to reach feminist goals of liberation. It is not pornography that keeps women subordinate, they argue, but lack of economic and educational opportunity. Women should seek to get control of some of the resources of the pornographers and change the images. They fear that once government has the power to determine whether sexual practices are acceptable or unacceptable, it will restrict women's efforts to explore and define their sexuality.

The pornography issue continues to provoke intense debate among feminists, although active consideration of pornography/civil rights legislation has subsided. There are periodic campaigns against companies that produce in music or video forms of speech that degrade women, such as gangsta rap. Meanwhile, moralists have turned their attention to the threats imposed by electronic communication media, which have the potential to put pornographic material on home computing and TV screens across the world. In 1996, as part of a massive overhaul of telecommunications law (PL104–104) Congress extended federal anti-obscenity regulations to cover the Internet. In public debate the question of indecency on the Internet was defined in conventional terms as that of moralists versus civil liberties advocates. Feminists have not yet staked out clear positions on this question.

Rape

What is *rape?* Consider the variety of images of rape in American culture: an act of uncontrollable male lust; an extension of male seduction and female submission; a fantasy of female sexual response; the stranger behind the bushes ready to attack a woman alone at night; a husband claiming conjugal rights (Rhett Butler carrying Scarlett O'Hara up those stairs in *Gone with the Wind*); the myth of the black rapist (See Davis, 1981, pp. 172–201); a date claiming "payment" for an evening of dinner and dancing; a hostile act to degrade women; the spoils of victory in war; the vile seduction of a chaste young virgin. Many of these examples contain some assumptions about the nature of female sexuality in relation to men. Yet, only recently have definitions of rape as a crime against women become an important part of the public policy debate.

All states and the District of Columbia have reformed their rape laws since 1970. All had statutes based on common law, modified by decades of practice and case law. Some states repealed these old laws and enacted new statutes based on contemporary debates. Others took their reforms piecemeal, without altering the basic common-law core. There are fifty-one different policy outcomes, products of the interaction between coalitions for reform and the political culture in fifty-one different jurisdictions. Presenting a clear and comprehensive description of U.S. public policy on rape is further stymied by the informal processes of the criminal justice system. The definition, prosecution, and punishment of rape often depends on the informal practices and relationships found among police officials, judges, lawyers, victims, and support groups in local jurisdictions. The following section is a general description of trends in the debate and policies related to rape in the United States. It is important to keep in mind that, in practice, the law will vary according to the elements of each case and the peculiarities of each jurisdiction.

Common-Law Definition of Rape

In the English society that spawned the common law, rape was considered a more serious crime than ordinary assault. In the United States, states assimilated the common-law definitions and penalties into their own law codes. For rape to be punished, the following three factors had to apply:

1. Carnal knowledge by a man of a woman.

2. Penile penetration of the woman's vagina.

3. Action by force and against the woman's will.

Rape carried serious penalties, up to death. Some states made rape a capital crime. But the conception of the type of sexual assault worthy of legal action was relatively narrow. In criminal rape, a man destroyed the chastity of a woman by force. The injured party was not the woman, but those men to whom her chastity had special value—her father and/or her husband or prospective suitors.

Lord Matthew Hale, the English judge credited with codifying rape law in the seventeenth century, generally viewed rape complaints and the women who made them with suspicion (Geis, 1978). Even if the elements of the crime were present, the assault might not be considered a rape if the woman was not chaste, that is, not a virgin or a faithful wife. According to common-law practice, an unchaste woman could not really be raped because, through her own promiscuity, she had lowered her value. Husbands and wives were exempt from law: "A husband cannot be guilty of a rape committed by himself upon his lawful wife, for by their mutual consent and contract the wife hath given up herself in this kind to her husband which she cannot retract" (Hale, 1678).

Despite the already-narrow definition of rape embodied in statutes based on English common law, the law in practice continued to narrow its definition even further. Conviction often depended on proof that the victim had not consented to the sexual advances. Since consent is a mental process, the only witness to its absence would be the victim. Basing the fate of a defendant solely on the word of the victim seemed to be too unreliable, so judges took special steps to erect safeguards for defendants. Some states adopted special jury instructions—also credited to seventeenth-century jurist Hale—that cautioned the jury not to accept a woman's testimony about her consent. The judge would instruct members of the jury as follows:

> A charge such as that made against the defendant in this case is one which is easily made and, once made, difficult to defend against, even if the person is innocent. Therefore, the law requires that you examine the testimony of the female person named in the information with caution. (Cary and Peratis, 1978, p. 130)

In trying rape cases, the courts developed tough standards of evidence. To prove she did not consent, a woman had to show that she resisted the sexual act, in fact, resisted "to the utmost" ("I'll never give in").

This usually meant evidence of physical injury and struggle. The assumption was that if a woman is really chaste, she will naturally fight hard, even risk her life, to protect her chastity. Men in charge of the legal system apparently believed that virginity was as important to a woman as to her father and that the chastity of a wife, because of its special value to her husband's self-worth, was more precious than her life.[4]

Twentieth-century changes in psychological and sociological information and attitudes about sexual behavior altered the legal conception of chastity and a woman's likely response to sexual assault. Knowledge that women were as capable as men of sexual desire and enjoyment seemed to change attitudes about the value of a woman's virginity. A woman who did not resist to the utmost might still not consent. This change helped reduce the resistance standard applied by the court to that which was reasonable "under the circumstances." However, new knowledge about female sexuality also produced other safeguards for defendants even more effective than the old resistance standard. Freud asserted that rape is a typical female sexual fantasy. This new psychology seemed to underscore the suspicion that women sometimes had difficulty knowing what they wanted from sex or even what had really happened in a sexual encounter. A woman who claimed she was raped may have dreamed it or been deluded; in any case, her testimony became even more suspect to judges and jurors than when she was considered vindictive. Some states, by statute, required corroboration of the victim's testimony to gain a conviction for rape. And most states permitted unlimited evidence about the victim's sexual history to be used to undermine her claim to lack of consent and her credibility as a witness. Meanwhile, the defendant's history was protected by Bill of Rights guarantees against self-incrimination and double jeopardy.

Rape-Law Reform

In the 1960s, there was a general movement to modernize all criminal laws and improve law enforcement. To promote uniform change across many states, the American Law Institute drafted a Model Penal Code. The code's primary purpose was to improve conviction rates. Since excessive penalties were seen as a barrier to conviction, the institute proposed graded penalties for different levels of assault. Despite its reform purpose, the code incorporated only a few changes in the definition of *rape* other than gender neutrality for minor offenses. The code even expanded the spousal exemption of common law to exclude cohabiting couples from

BOX 9.3

The More Things Change, the More They Remain the Same

The American Law Institute's Model Penal Code is an excellent example of what feminists find wrong with the so-called sexual revolution of the 1960s. Although nonmarital sex was now considered acceptable and even desirable, the value system of male dominance in marital gender roles (men possessing women) was merely extended to nonmarital gender roles. Male control of female sexuality remained undisturbed by the new mores.

prosecution. It retained corroboration requirements, and special language in the code even referred formally to "sexually promiscuous complainants."

Major changes in common-law–style rape laws waited for the arrival of feminists to the reform coalitions in various states. Early in the contemporary feminist movement, speakouts on rape were a consciousness-raising activity in which women broke codes of silence on sexual matters by publicly revealing their experiences. These speakouts led to workshops and study groups to help rape victims, as well as campaigns to seek the reform of rape laws. Feminist groups established help groups and hot lines for rape victims. These led to the establishment of rape crisis centers throughout the country, many funded by state and local governments (Matthews, 1995).

This activity was inspired by a feminist theory of rape as a political crime against women. Susan Griffin's essay "Rape: The All-American Crime" remains a definitive statement of feminist analysis of rape. "Rape is not an isolated act that can be rooted out from patriarchy without ending patriarchy itself" (reprinted in Chappell, Geis, and Geis, 1977, p. 66). Susan Brownmiller's *Against Our Will*, published in 1975, provided historical evidence to support her assertion that rape is an act of dominance over women, an integral part of patriarchal society. Although rape involves sex, she said, it is not a sex crime but a crime of power and aggression by one sex against another. Through rape or threat of rape, men control women: "Rape is not a crime of irrational, impulsive, uncontrollable lust, but is a deliberate, hostile, violent act of degradation and possession on the part of a would-be conqueror, designed to intimidate and inspire fear" (Brownmiller, 1975, p. 391). For the first time, feminists began a successful drive to replace ancient conceptions of rape as a crime against the male-valued chastity of individual women with a theory of rape as a crime against all women. Feminists organized to fight against this form of domination.

Liberal feminists, who are more likely than radical feminists to believe changes in the laws can improve women's status, joined the ongoing debate over the reform of rape laws. They had three major goals: to change the definition of the crime to eliminate all concepts of women as the sexual property of men; to protect victims' rights; and to increase the likelihood of the conviction of rapists. At the International Women's Year Conference held in Houston in 1977, they outlined a seven-point proposal for the new laws, as follows:

1. Provide for graduated degrees of the crime with graduated penalties, depending on the amount of force or coercion occurring with the activity.

2. Apply to assault by or upon both sexes, including spouses as victims.

3. Include all types of sexual assault against adults, including oral and anal contact and the use of objects.

4. Enlarge beyond traditional common-law concepts the circumstances under which the act will be considered to have occurred without the victim's consent.

5. Specify that past sexual conduct of the victim cannot be introduced into evidence.

6. Require no more corroborative evidence than is required in the prosecution of any other type of violent assault.

7. Prohibit the Hale instruction where it has been required by law or is customary. (Bird, 1979, p. 157)

The liberal feminists joined with lawyers and police officials interested in criminal-law reform to develop coalitions in nearly every state. Since that time, progress has been made in all of the demands made at the Houston conference. The Hale jury instruction and statutory requirements of corroboration have been removed in all jurisdictions. Reform coalitions have also been quite successful in gaining redefinitions of the crime. Only one-third of the states retain the common-law definition of rape (Searles and Berger, 1987). Some states have expunged the term *rape* altogether, in favor of terms such as *sexual assault, sexual battery, sexual abuse, criminal sexual conduct,* or *gross sexual imposition.* Three-fourths of the states use gender-neutral terms for both the victim and the offender. This last change was especially important to feminists because it undermines the official ideas of women as the sexual property of men and shifts the view of rape toward a form of assault. Nearly every state has enacted a *rape shield statute* to limit the right of defense attorneys to grill rape victims about their previous sexual conduct. Only a few states have eliminated all such evidence, however. Typical statutes set forth guidelines for the admissibility of testimony about a victim's sexual life, usually to show consent or lack of credibility in a trial. Judges frequently give liberal interpretation to these loopholes, allowing cross-examination about the victim's sex relations with other men to demonstrate a "pattern of conduct on the part of the woman that is arguably similar to her behavior with the defendant"(Kessler, 1992, p. 80).

In determining lack of consent, most reforms, following recommendations by the American Law Institute, have directed courts away from looking at the resistance behavior of the victim to determining the amount of force used by the assailant. For example, statutes may specify levels of force—such as use of weapons—which, if present, are evidence of lack of consent.[5] Some statutes have even eliminated the term *consent* altogether. Usually, degrees of force used in an assault are associated with graduated penalties—from a few years to life in prison.

The death penalty for the rape of an adult woman was declared unconstitutional by the Supreme Court in 1977 (*Coker v. Georgia*, 1977). The Court agreed that rape was a serious crime, "highly reprehensible both in a moral sense and in its total contempt for the personal integrity and autonomy of the female victim and for the latter's privilege of choosing those with whom intimate relationships are to be established" (p. 597). But rape is not as serious as murder, and the death penalty, which was in force in three states at the time, is "grossly disproportionate and excessive punishment" (p. 592).

The most recent reforms in rape laws have affected the spousal exemption. Before the 1970s, husbands were routinely exempted from prosecutions for rape. In practice, the exclusion also extended to spouses who were separated or divorced and to cohabiting couples. There is little disagreement among feminists on this issue. They consider the failure to prosecute husbands who rape their wives based on the assumptions that marriage vows imply consent to be an astonishing use of state power to abandon women to the use and abuse of men. For their part, many police officials and prosecutors have realized that the common-law concept that husbands had certain conjugal rights and that marriage implied consent made it extremely difficult to prosecute husbands and boyfriends who, at

BOX 9.4

The Criminal Justice System's Two Percent Response to Rape

From the perspective of the rape victim, there is less than a 2 percent chance that the attacker will be arrested, convicted, sentenced, and serve time in prison. The statistics prepared by the majority staff of the Senate Judiciary Committee conclude that a rape victim has a 2.5 percent chance of seeing the attacker convicted and a 1.9 percent chance of seeing the attacker incarcerated. The state-by-state survey showed that when arrests are made, conviction rates vary, as the following survey of rape conviction rates by state indicate (all data are for 1990):

State	Dispositions	Convictions	Rate
California	1,961	1,111	56%
Connecticut	311	87	29
Hawaii	561	240	43
New York	1,841	790	43
North Carolina	931	278	30
Oklahoma	275	141	51
Pennsylvania	452	211	47
South Carolina	911	235	26
Vermont	75	26	35

The average conviction rate for rape in these states is 43 percent. Compare that number with the average conviction rates for murder (69 percent) and robbery (61 percent).

Source: U.S. Senate. The Response to Rape: Detours on the Road to Equal Justice: A Majority Staff Report for the Committee on the Judiciary. Washington, D.C.: U.S. Government Printing Office, 1993.

times, went a "little too far" in their passion and injured their wives or girlfriends.

Nevertheless, there is ambivalence in the public debate on whether marital exemptions should be repealed. Some legislators continue to oppose changes in the spousal exemptions. Moralists see such reforms as an attack on the traditional family (and feminists would very likely agree). Others claim that permitting wives to bring complaints against their husbands will invite fraud and immerse the courts in the murky waters of marital sexual and emotional conflict. In many states, the long-standing reluctance to bring the government and the courts into the marriage relationship in any way has retarded the complete repeal of the marital exemption.

The current law on spousal exemption reflects this ambivalence in the public debate. Rape law reforms in the 1970s usually failed to mention the spousal exemption. Since 1978, when Oregon was the first state to repeal the exemption, spouses in about half the states have become liable for prosecution for rape on the same basis as any other individuals. The rest of the states retain some sort of limitation on rape prosecutions in marriages and in some cases in other types of close relations. For example, husbands may be exempt when spouses are living together but prosecuted if living separately or if the wife has filed for divorce. Some states exempt prosecution for simple rape and hold husbands liable for violent sexual assault. Still others allow prosecution only if the victim reports the crime within a certain period. A few states have even broadened the exemption to include couples who are acquaintances. The prohibitions that remain against the prosecution of husbands and boyfriends still severely limit efforts to prevent and punish woman battery (see Chapter 10).

The controversy over spousal exemptions illustrates feminist criticism of the current status of rape-law reforms in the criminal-justice system. Officials discount the credibility of rape claims by any victim who was even acquainted with her assailant. There is a separation between *stranger rape*, which is considered real, and *date rape* and *acquaintance rape*, which are considered simple and not serious. Most reforms have been effective only in prosecuting stranger rape. When the woman knows the offender at all, let alone is married to him, the assault is likely to go unprosecuted and unpunished (Estrich, 1987).

Estrich's book *Real Rape* and a 1985 survey by *MS* magazine showing that 25 percent of women in college had been victims of rape provoked a controversy among feminists over the issue. Katie Roiphe (1993) and others charged that campus feminists were turning impressionable women students into victims, afraid of men and afraid of sex. As evidence, these critics pointed to Antioch College's Sexual Offense policy, which required students to get verbal consent at every stage of an intimate sexual encounter. At the same time, however, feminists cited several high profile cases in which university administrators protected star athletes accused of rape; these cases, they argued, indicate that women who suffer assault are still unlikely to be taken seriously (Stan, 1995).

The changes in state rape laws have been in the direction of feminist demands, but the changes are incomplete. There has been a modest increase in the reports of rape since the law reforms, and offenders are now more likely to serve some time in prison (Bachman, 1995). However, rape law and its administration retain an antiwoman bias. The victim's testimony is still not adequately shielded, making rape prosecution excessively trying for many women. Although corroboration requirements are formally removed, prosecutors still want evidence beyond the victim's testimony. Many rape cases are not taken to court.

The change from resistance standards to degrees of force has not replaced reliance on proof of *lack of a victim's consent* to reach a conviction. Juries are still often persuaded that rape does not exist if the defendant *had reason to believe* the victim consented to the sexual advances. There is little evidence that rape law reform has improved the status of women or increased the number of convictions for simple rape. What constitutes force or lack of consent is still based on a male standard: the amount of force that a man would consider enough so that he would consent—for example, the use of a gun or knife; a physical beating with pain and injuries; or being tied up. These definitions exclude the coercion involved through the sex act itself.

Frustrated with the inadequacies of the criminal justice system in fighting back against rape, feminists in the national women's lobby have turned to Congress for additional resources. In 1994, Congress enacted the Violence Against Women Act. This law strengthens federal penalties for sex crimes, and authorizes funds for rape prevention education, training programs for professionals, and rape crisis centers. What is most interesting in this legislation is the extension of federal civil rights guarantees to victims of violent crimes, such as rape, when the crime is motivated by gender. Under this law, victims can sue perpetrators for damages in federal court.[6]

The state reforms of the rape law enacted in the 1970s redefined the common-law definition of rape from a crime against morality and the sexual property of men to a crime of violence. Rape became sexual assault, a gender-neutral crime that could happen to anyone, male or female. Brownmiller's claim that rape is not a crime of sex has been taken to mean that sex or gender is not particularly important: that, in fact, the amount of violence is the key. To counter the assumption that the gender of the victim does not matter, feminists have begun to redefine the term *rape* as a crime of sexual coercion and gender-based violence and to point out connections between rape, pornography, and the status of women in society. The concept of sexual coercion motivated by ideologies of gender relations is more inclusive than the idea of rape as a crime of violence.

This newer definition does not require evidence of injury or deadly weapons. Coercion may use psychological or physical means or combine elements of both. Thus, coerced sex is as possible between spouses, acquaintances, and dates as it is between strangers. The successful campaign for the Violence Against Women Act was an attempt to redefine the rape issue as a crime of violence and coercion against women and to counter the prevailing official definition of rape as a gender-neutral crime.

Sexual Harassment

While feminists have not been entirely successful in dominating the official definitions of the term *rape*, they have achieved remarkable success in defining the policy of sexual harassment. Sexual harassment is a relatively new name for an age-old practice: unwanted sexual advances by men to women in public places. One hundred years ago, a woman's virtue was central to her value. Women workers were considered vulnerable to male sexual advances, as the result of generalized male sexual aggression that could also lead to seduction, rape, or procurement for prostitution. If a man's public attention to a woman damaged her reputation for chastity, she might bring a civil suit for damages. For the most part, however, such sexual advances were not considered a matter for government interest but rather an area of private sexual choice.

In women's consciousness-raising groups in the early 1970s, feminists became aware of the pervasiveness of these sexual practices—at school, at work, and on the street—and of their effects on women's status. Some women found themselves faced with the "casting couch" in order to get or keep a job. Other women found their job or school environment made intolerable by constant teasing and sexual innuendos by their co-workers, their supervisors, or their professors. In 1975, feminists gave the problem a name: *sexual harassment.*[7] What happened next illustrates the importance of giving a name to a phenomenon. Once named, the hidden dirty little secrets were public, and the evidence mounted. Feminists argued that sexual harassment is sex discrimination against women and is thus prohibited by laws outlawing sex discrimination in employment (Title VII) and in education (Title IX) (MacKinnon, 1979). By naming it, feminists were able to define the issue and retain control of it.

Feminists made their case in articles and books, through complaints to the Equal Employment Opportunity Commission (EEOC), and in court. They claimed that since men dominate in economic, political, and educational institutions, men can use their positions to coerce women to submit to sexual advances in ways that men cannot be coerced. Beyond that, they claimed, a work or school environment that includes persistent and unwelcome sexual advances from supervisors and co-workers or professors limits opportunities for women in ways that it does not limit opportunities for men. Thus, employers and school administrators should be held responsible for sexual harassment.

The effort to bring sex-discrimination laws to bear on cases of sexual harassment began with litigation in the mid-1970s. At first, these cases were unsuccessful. Employers prevailed by arguing that any sexual relationships among employees were private matters and not their responsibility, that is, not an employment matter. They convinced judges that sexual relations were undertaken voluntarily by the women. And, they argued, even if adverse employment decisions resulted from such relationships, it was not because the victims were women, that is, because of their sex, but because of individuals' refusal to accede to sexual demands. Thus, employers would not be responsible under antidiscrimination statutes. If employers were successful in avoiding responsibility, feminists would have to seek new laws to protect women from sexual harassment (a formidable task).

In 1980, the EEOC adopted regulations defining sexual harassment as a form of prohibited sex discrimination under Title VII and holding employers responsible:

> Unwelcome sexual advances, requests for sexual favors, and other verbal or physical conduct of a sexual nature constitute sexual harassment when (1) submission to such conduct is made either explicitly or implicitly a term or condition of an individual's employment; (2) submission to or rejection of such conduct by an individual is used as a basis for employment decisions affecting such individual; or (3) such conduct has the purpose or effect of unreasonably interfering with an individual's work performance or creating an intimidating, hostile, or offensive working environment. (EEOC, 29 C.F.R. Chap. XIV, Part 1604.11)

Similarly, Title IX regulations prohibit sexual harassment and require federally funded educational institutions to have procedures for such grievances by students and faculty.

In 1986, the Supreme Court heard its first sexual-harassment case and generally reinforced the EEOC and feminist definitions of the issue

(*Meritor Savings Banks, FSB v. Vinson*, 1986). The Court decision covered both *quid pro quo* and *hostile environment* types of harassment.[8] The Court also ruled that the employer could be responsible for harassment carried out by the employer or his agents, especially if the employer has knowledge of the action but did not take immediate action to correct the situation. The message in both the *Meritor Savings* case and the subsequent EEOC regulations is that it is the employer's responsibility to prevent harassment by carefully selecting and educating supervisors, as well as to have adequate and nonthreatening procedures for handling grievance complaints.

There seems to be agreement on how to recognize and deal with the quid pro quo type of harassment—where there is evidence that a supervisor's sexual advances were connected to rewards or punishments for the employee. According to the *Meritor Savings* case, employers may not use the defense that a woman voluntarily participated in the sexual activities, but they can try to prove that the advances were "not unwelcome." In presenting such a defense, the employer can thus offer evidence about the plaintiff's behavior, clothing, and conversations. This may strike feminists as similar to the rape defense that women are "asking for it" by wearing provocative clothing. Women's rights advocates are wary of any tendency to blame the woman for the offender's behavior.

Consideration of the second type of sexual harassment—that leading to hostile working conditions—is more uncertain. A series of cases have considered what standards to use to determine when conditions become "hostile." In such cases, judges typically rely on what is known as the *reasonable person* standard, that is, the conditions most people would consider hostile or threatening. However, the gender-neutral term *reasonable person* was not so long ago called the *reasonable man* standard. And in cases dealing with gendered relations, like sexual harassment, men and women are likely to look at the same behavior quite differently. Thus, some courts have used a *reasonable woman* standard to determine whether what a man thinks is teasing and flirting makes the woman unable to do her work adequately (*Elison v. Brady*. 924 F.2d 872. 1991). Some advocates for women are concerned that the reasonable woman standard will introduce a formal gender hierarchy into the law. Employers will begin to think, once again, that women employees need special protection, setting them apart as a special work force and damaging efforts at equality in the work place.

The Supreme Court has not yet ruled on the reasonable woman standard, continuing to refer to the reasonable person standard. In 1993, however, in the case of *Harris v. Forklift Systems*, the Court tipped the rules of evidence in hostile environment cases in favor of the plaintiff. Prior to that case, lower court precedents were developing that required evidence of psychological damage to employees in order to prove that they were subject to a sex-discriminatory hostile environment; evidence of impairment of work or education was not sufficient. In *Harris*, the Court rejected this interpretation and recalled its definition in the *Meritor* case: "When the workplace is permeated with 'discriminatory intimidation, ridicule, and insult,' that is 'sufficiently severe or pervasive to alter the conditions of the victim's employment and create an abusive working environment,' Title VII is violated." (p. 370) This standard constitutes a middle ground between ruling any sexual comment as illegal harassment and requiring evidence that the victim has suffered a nervous breakdown.

The *Harris* case was decided in the wake of the televised testimony of law professor Anita Hill at the confirmation hearings for Clarence Thomas, appointed by President Bush to the Supreme Court in 1991. Hill testified that during the time she was an employee of Thomas, he had made unwelcome sexual advances toward her and had used language that was intimidating and threatening to her in her job. Hill's testimony, Thomas's response to it, and the conduct of the Senate Judiciary Committee drew nationwide attention to the issue of sexual harassment. Both Hill and Thomas were African Americans, and the Senate committee sitting in judgment on them was composed entirely of white males. The case therefore offered many examples of the complex intersection of gender, sexuality, and race in American society (Hill and Jordan, 1995; Morris, 1994; Morrison, 1992).

The gender-sexuality hierarchy was clear in the evidence Hill brought of her treatment by her male employer. She sought to make her case to a group of males who sat in judgment on her credibility and through their questions made it clear that they did not believe her, reinforcing the double edge of discrimination that black women face. Thomas's response was to charge that allowing Hill to present her evidence was an attempt to reinforce myths that black males were hypersexual predators and was an attempt by the white senators to "lynch" him. Americans watching the televised hearings or reading about them were divided over whether Thomas was suitable for the court, whether Hill was either lying or being used to deny a black man access to the Supreme Court or both, and whether the white male senators were sexist, racist, or both. The Hill-Thomas hearings brought national attention to sex discrimination and stimulated women to run for political office (see Chapter 2). The EEOC reported a 60 percent jump in sexual harassment complaints in the first nine months after the hearings (Ross, 1995).

In the wake of the hearings, sexual harassment law was strengthened. During the Hill-Thomas hearings, Congress was considering the Civil Rights Act of 1991 (a similar act had been vetoed by President Bush the previous year). The act, by allowing victims of sex discrimination under Title VII to sue for damages up to $300,000, convinced employers of the seriousness of sexual harassment to their "bottom line." In 1992, all nine Supreme Court justices (including Clarence Thomas) ruled in *Franklin v. Guinett* that victims of discrimination under Title IX (see Chapter 5) were also able to sue for monetary damages. In 1993, the Court then went on to strengthen the enforcement of the hostile working environment form of harassment in the *Harris* case (covered earlier in this chapter).

In the 1990s, public attention focused on the link between harassment and employment opportunity for women in the military. Although the official position has been to avoid recognizing it, U.S. Navy officials were apparently aware of the problem that harassment presented in denying women an opportunity to succeed in military careers. In the late 1980s, their surveys had revealed that 44 percent of enlisted women and 33 percent of women officers reported experiencing sexual harassment over a one-year period. Their Navy Equal Opportunity Sexual Harassment (NEOSH) surveys also showed a significant relationship between experiencing harassment and having a low perception of opportunity (Newell, Rosenfeld, and Culbertson, 1995). Nevertheless, when navy officers complained that sexual intimidation had occurred during a convention of the fliers association called the Tailhook Club, officers protected one another and the perpetrators suffered few consequences. Women of both parties in the Senate were especially critical of the navy's treatment of women (*CQ Almanac,* 1994, p. 445). While the navy leaders struggled to recover from the adverse publicity associated with Tailhook, public allegations about harassment and even rape in the army training facilities surfaced. Clearly, the sexual harassment issue is crucial to the success of women as they seek equality in the armed forces.

Lesbian Issues

Despite progress in the legislature and courts in defining sexuality issues in ways that improve the rights of women, some feminists see these gains as largely ineffective in battling male dominance over female sexuality. They contend that patriarchy is grounded in a heterosexual ideology and practice so pervasive that women are powerless to prevent their degradation unless they confront it directly. One way is to refuse to accept male-constructed compulsory heterosexuality by choosing woman-to-woman sexuality through lesbianism. Lesbianism as an expression of female sexuality has had an impact in feminist literature and art. As a public issue, however, female homosexuality is still at the margins; it is certainly not on many public agendas and is often overshadowed by male gay politics.

Of all aspects of female sexuality, lesbianism remained private the longest. No laws were enacted to regulate it in the nineteenth century. The constraints on female heterosexual expression in the Victorian era provided occasion for intimate relationships between women, but these were not seen as especially remarkable or dangerous. Female homosexuality did not pose the threat to traditional mores that male homosexuality did. Male homosexuality undermined patriarchal definitions of manliness, so closely related to male-dominated economic, political, and social institutions. Any overt sexual expression by women, whether toward women or men, was seen as a medical rather than a criminal or social problem, likely due to some inborn abnormality.[9] Unless overt, women loving women was labeled sisterly rather than sexual.

Oddly, it was when sexologists early in the twentieth century began to promote women's sexual fulfillment that lesbianism began to be noticed and labeled deviant. Sexologists declared that the real woman blossomed with the love of a man (officially, her husband). If lesbians could not be dismissed as weird feminist misfits, they were to be pitied as unfortunate deviants.[10] Psychiatry included homosexuality on the list of mental illnesses and disorders.

After World War II, with fresh data from the *Kinsey Reports* (1948, 1953), libertarians pushed for a definition of homosexual behavior as a matter of personal choice, making heterosexuality and homosexuality two alternatives available to human beings. The libertarians were successful in convincing the psychiatrists, who removed homosexuality from their list of pathologies in 1973. Lesbianism was no longer a disorder that needed curing. Soon, the feminists contributed another definition of lesbianism as a revolutionary political act against male dominance. More than specific acts of sexual conduct, that is, women making love to each other, to be a lesbian was to have an identity and an ideology that was founded on a life for, with, and of women (Rich, 1980).

Stimulated by social movements of the 1960s and 1970s, lesbian theory and politics expanded and became diverse. For example, in the 1970s, lesbian feminism flourished. "The core of lesbian feminism is the position that sexism and heterosexism are 'hopelessly intertwined,' that the oppression of women and lesbians is the 'prototype of all other oppressions, since the oppression of women and of lesbians crosses boundaries of race, class, and age'" (Phelan, 1989, p. 47). Lesbian feminists divided, however, over the relative significance of sexual acts and culture to the definition of *lesbian* and over whether to make alliances with kindred movements or to maintain separatism as a "lesbian nation."

A segment of lesbian politics focuses on equal rights strategies. While most lesbian writers worked for the development of a woman-centered culture, a few looked at laws. They found, as they openly declared their lesbian identity and lifestyle, that they were subject to discrimination similar in many ways to that suffered by male homosexuals. In over one-half of the states, forms of nonmarital or extramarital sexual activity, including adultery, fornication, sodomy, and oral sex are criminalized. The Supreme Court has upheld the constitutionality of sodomy laws but has not ruled on the others (*Bowers v. Hardwick*, 1986). The U.S. Immigration Service has barred homosexuals from entry visas and citizenship. Lesbians and gay men were excluded from military and other government jobs. Any discrimination against them by private employers or landlords has not been generally prohibited. Same-sex couples have not been permitted to marry, thus excluding them from rights based on family relationships in insurance, inheritance, guardianship, or adoption.

Lesbian equal-rights activists have been most critical of the fate of lesbian mothers in child-custody suits. The courts, often guided only by general admonitions to act in the best interest of the child, have great leeway in making child-custody decisions (see Chapter 6). Judges who consider lesbianism immoral or deviant have used it as a reason to deny mothers custody (sometimes giving the children not to the father but to the grandparents). Judges also have denied custody to mothers because they believe the arguments that exposure to lesbian lifestyles might have a detrimental effect on the normal development of the child and that the child should be raised in a heterosexual home.

Lesbian political activism dates from the 1950s but has been fragmented into small groups. Lesbian issues have been marginal in larger feminist organizations. Liberal-feminist activists have often been uneasy at identifying too closely with lesbian politics, wary of antifeminists using the lesbian label to undermine their demands on other issues, especially

BOX 9.5

Domestic Partnership Laws: Prelude to Legal Marriage?

In a few cities and counties, activists for gay and lesbian rights have gained for unmarried partners of employees legal recognition and benefits similar to those available to spouses. A San Francisco ordinance allows couples—two men, two women, or a man and a woman—to register formally as *domestic partners*. In Atlanta, a city employee may receive a Certificate of Domestic Partnership:

> The City of Atlanta recognizes domestic partners as a family relationship and not a marital relationship and shall provide sick leave, funeral leave, parental leave, health and dental benefits and any other employee benefit available to a City employee in a comparable manner for a domestic partner . . . as for a spouse. (Ordinance adopted August 9, 1993, reprinted in Newton, 1994, pp. 119–122)

The New York state Supreme Court has ruled that gay and lesbian couples have the same rights married couples have to inherit the lease of an apartment when the partner dies. In Florida, the Palm Beach County Commission has enacted a general law prohibiting discrimination in housing against gay and lesbian couples.

A state court in Hawaii took a further step in 1993. In applying the "sex is a suspect classification" test, the court ruled that denial of same-sex marriage is a violation of the equal rights provisions of the state constitution unless the state can show a compelling interest in keeping marriage exclusively heterosexual. On appeal, the state's lawyers argued unsuccessfully that such an interest was served because producing the next generation was the purpose of marriage, a function for which heterosexual couples are suited. Fierce opposition from moral conservatives across the country has driven state and federal legislators to seek their own protections against the effects of Hawaii's bold action.

on the Equal Rights Amendment (ERA). Organizations such as NOW usually support nondiscrimination laws and adopt civil-liberties–style endorsements of rights to privacy in sexual preference and behavior choice. Typical is the resolution from the International Women's Year Conference held in 1977:

> Congress, state, and local legislatures should enact legislation to eliminate discrimination on the basis of sexual and affectional preference

in areas including, but not limited to, employment, housing, public accommodations, credit, public facilities, government funding and the military. (Bird, 1979, p. 167)

This resolution goes on to advocate the decriminalization of private sexual behavior and the prohibition of discrimination against homosexuality in child-custody decisions. While sexual preference is on the agenda of moderate feminists, it does not have high priority.

Many lesbian activists consider that they have more in common with gay males than with liberal and radical feminist groups. Lesbians are a recognized part of the campaign to "mainstream" homosexuals in American politics and culture through legal reform, public education, and community organizing. Despite the appearance of unity in organizations such as the National Lesbian and Gay Task Force (NLGTF), there have been tensions over what some women perceive as a gender hierarchy in the lesbian/gay rights movement. Like their counterparts in the civil rights movement, women have often been relegated to secretarial and support roles, rather than leadership roles. Gay men may define their struggle as a civil liberties campaign against right-wing morality, and they often fail to recognize what many lesbian feminists consider to be problems deriving from their status as women within patriarchy. Gay male issues tend to focus more on sexual conduct than on culture and identity, questions heavily emphasized by some lesbian theorists.

The AIDS issue caused shifts and realignments in lesbian political strategies. Many lesbians joined in both conventional and militant campaigns that gave the AIDS issue high priority. Other lesbians lamented the emphasis on an issue that had little direct effect on their conduct or life. On the whole, however, the issue has tended to unite gay and lesbian activists to counter what they recognize as a right-wing political assault on both groups.

The effect of lesbian political activism has been mixed (Newton, 1994). Nearly half the states still criminalize homosexual conduct. However, a few states and 150 municipalities have included sexual orientation under antidiscrimination ordinances and laws. The Supreme Court in 1996 guaranteed the rights of homosexuals to seek such laws. In *Romer v. Evans* the court ruled that blanket prohibitions in Colorado's state constitution against a group's political rights to seek protection violated the Equal Protection Clause of the U.S. Constitution.[11] Some communities have enacted domestic partnership laws that allow nonmarital couples to qualify for family benefits. Some states have included attacks on homosexuals under hate crimes legislation, and the federal government now collects statistics on the incidence of such violence.

There continue to be some setbacks. Activists credit pressure from their opponents with their failure to secure equal rights for homosexuals in the armed forces. During the 1992 presidential campaign, Bill Clinton pledged to end the ban on homosexuals in the military. His efforts to carry out his pledge provoked intense opposition from the military brass and many members of Congress. The eventual "don't ask, don't tell" policy guarantees that no action will be taken to oust homosexuals from the military, or to investigate them, as long as they do not identify themselves. Lesbian activists see this policy as little improvement, making members of the armed forces still vulnerable to harassment and persecution. Thus, the armed forces continues to discriminate against its gay and lesbian members. Although stymied in efforts to ban gay rights ordinances, opponents pledge to fight any laws that give homosexuals protection from discrimination.

Legal solutions to discrimination against lesbians await further redefinition of the issue. Redefinition might take two directions. One direction would be toward social acceptance of the legitimacy of nonmarital and extramarital sexual behavior, both homosexual and heterosexual. Policies would further a variety of family forms rather than promoting the heterosexual nuclear family as the only ideal. To change these laws in the absence of a liberal activist Supreme Court will take state-by-state action, through state courts and legislatures. Civil liberties lawyers have advocated such reforms for decades, but there has not been enough organizational support. At times they face strong campaigns from ardent opponents of gay rights. Such reforms are unlikely as long as so many states retain policies criminalizing sexual behavior, and the issue of gay rights is caught up in so-called culture wars over morality.

A second direction for change might be toward using equal protection and antidiscrimination laws to include homosexuality as a classification due equal protection treatment. This change would require a redefinition of the public approach to homosexuality currently promoted by libertarians. The concept of *sexual preference* implies that homosexuality is a form of sexual behavior that individuals choose rather than an inherent characteristic, such as race or gender. Some reformers suggest, instead, a definition of homosexuality as a sexual identity characterized by emotions, affections, and self-concepts and not necessarily by forms of sexual conduct (Arriola, 1988). Such identities are very much a part of a person and not subject to rejection, change, or modification. That a person should not suffer unequal treatment because of his or her identity is the principle behind nondiscrimination due to religion or national origin already protected under the equal opportunity laws and the Fourteenth Amendment.

Conclusion

Contemporary feminist theories of sexuality link all issues with a sexual component to an overall critique of patriarchy. Yet, when these issues reach the arenas of public debate, they are treated separately, and the policy outcomes vary. The debates on prostitution and pornography are dominated by the moralist-libertarian axis. Compromises reached decades ago still endure: laws reflect moralist arguments, while enforcement permits a wide range of choice. Feminists argue that choice, to the extent that choice exists, is shaped by male dominance and male prerogative. They say women have had little power in the policy or practice of prostitution and pornography. But feminists are handicapped in exerting influence over this issue by their continuing disagreements over which policies will further women's rights and autonomy.

Feminists have been more successful in formulating a position on rape and influencing that debate. The idea, articulated by Brownmiller in the 1970s, that rape is a crime of violence has been taken up by lawyers and police officials to improve the effectiveness of laws in prosecuting offenders. The federal government codified the idea in the 1994 Violence Against Women Act. Despite this victory, few states have incorporated the idea at the level of prosecution. Sexual violence continues to be defined according to male standards, making it difficult to use the new rape laws to prosecute date and acquaintance rape. The motives for statutory reforms often are different from the motives of juries who must apply rape laws. Traditional attitudes about male and female sexuality are still widespread in the population. Jurors may personally believe that women tease men by saying no to sexual advances when they mean yes, that they "ask for sex" by wearing provocative clothing, and that, unless an attacker has a gun or knife, a woman who really doesn't want sex can always scream or get away.

For a time, traditional attitudes also made it difficult to convince employers that they had some responsibility for the sexual harassment of their employees. But feminists were quite successful in persuading the

EEOC and the courts that harassment constituted sex discrimination in employment and education. Remedies for victims have been strengthened. Because the behavior occurs within the confines of an organization, someone can be held responsible. Most of the places where males use sexuality to dominate women are not so confined. Still, it is often difficult to prove cases of sexual harassment, as well as cases of rape.

Lesbian issues remain marginal to the policy agenda of most feminist organizations. Some attention to lesbian rights has arisen in the area of child custody, and this matter must be resolved on a case-by-case basis. Lesbians gain resources through their alliances with male gay activists. Still, they are often subject to male-dominated hierarchies in that movement. Discrimination against lesbians as a group separate from women or gay men in employment, education, and housing is not well documented. For lesbians, as for African Americans, Hispanic/Latina Americans, Native Americans, older women, poor women, and other subgroups of women, the agenda of moderate feminist organizations such as NOW is of general help at best. Lesbians are among the women who face problems reconciling their gender interests with the interests of the subgroups they share with men.

Taken together, public policies on sexuality issues reveal serious limits to the status and rights of women in the United States. One way to evaluate the impact of the laws pertaining to prostitution, pornography, rape, sexual harassment, and lesbianism is to consider the extent to which they foster dignity and empower women to fight against sexual coercion by men. Using this standard, only sexual harassment law gives women legal tools to challenge men's sexual use and abuse of them. Without such dignity and empowerment it is difficult to argue that women enjoy equal rights. In fact, according to international feminist definitions of women's human rights, laws such as those in force in the United States have failed to guarantee essential rights of citizenship (Stetson, 1995).

Notes

1. Enforcement of laws is variable. Streetwalkers make up 10 to 20 percent of all prostitutes but constitute 85 to 90 percent of the arrests for prostitution (Miller, Romenesko, and Wondolkowski, 1993).
2. A study commissioned by the Supreme Court of Florida came down solidly in support of WHISPER's position. The Gender Bias Study Commission of 1990 (Florida, 1990) recommended against decriminalization of prostitution.
3. In 1976, the American Bar Association came close to passing a resolution recommending that the states repeal laws that prohibit commercial sexual

transactions between consenting adults. This situation occurred at the height of the debate for reform, and the proposal has received little attention outside legal circles since.

4. There is a long romantic tradition in literature and opera of men using violence to avenge attacks on their honor, even to killing their wives and children. Those influenced by such a tradition might be expected to believe that a man's wife and children would feel as he would.

5. A few states now accept the absence of a woman's verbal consent as sufficient evidence of lack of consent.

6. The first case was filed under this law in 1996. It was a case of campus acquaintance rape, and the defendants included the alleged rapist (a football player) and the university administration that refused to punish him.

7. Letty Cottin Pogrebin is credited with giving the problem a name in a 1976 column in the *Ladies Home Journal* (Reprinted in Stan, 1995, pp. 3–9).

8. *Quid pro quo* refers to an exchange of sexual favors for job advantages; *hostile environment* refers to more generalized unwelcome sexual advances.

9. Women who were sexually involved exclusively with other women were believed to have, for example, too many male hormones or an abnormally large clitoris.

10. Radclyffe Hall's *The Well of Loneliness*, which caused a bit of a scandal in the 1920s as the first lesbian novel, is really a tale of the torment manly women endured.

11. The amendment reads: "Neither the State of Colorado, through any of its branches or departments, nor any of its agencies, political subdivisions, municipalities or school districts, shall enact, adopt or enforce any statute, regulation, ordinance or policy whereby homosexual, lesbian or bisexual orientation, conduct, practices or relationships shall constitute or otherwise be the basis of or entitle any person or class of persons to have or claim any minority status, quota preferences, protected status or claim of discrimination."

References

American Booksellers Association, Inc. v. Hudnut. 771 F. 2d 323. 1985.

Arriola, Elvia Rosales. "Sexual Identity and the Constitution: Homosexual Persons as a Discrete and Insular Minority." *Women's Rights Law Reporter* 10 (Winter 1988): 143–176.

Bachman, Ronet. "Is the Glass Half Empty or Half Full? A Response to Pollard." *Criminal Justice and Behavior* 22 (March 1995): 81–85.

Barry, Kathleen. *Female Sexual Slavery.* Englewood Cliffs, N.J.: Prentice-Hall, 1979.

Barry, Kathleen. *The Prostitution of Sexuality.* New York: New York University Press, 1995.

Beckman, Marlene. "The White Slave Traffic Act: The Historical Impact of a Criminal Law Policy on Women." *Georgetown Law Journal* 72 (Fall 1984): 111–142.

Beinen, Leigh. "Rape III: National Developments in Rape Reform Legislation." *Women's Rights Law Reporter* 6 (1980): 170–214.

Bennett-Alexander, Dawn D. "The Supreme Court Finally Speaks on the Issue of Sexual Harassment—What Did It Say?" *Women's Rights Law Reporter* (Spring 1987): 65–78.

Bird, Caroline. *What Women Want.* New York: Simon & Schuster, 1979.

Bowers v. Hardwick. 106 S.Ct. 2841. 1986.

Brown, Barbara A., Freedman, Ann E., Kate, Harriet N., and Price, Alice M. *Women's Rights and the Law.* New York: Praeger, 1977.

Brownmiller, Susan. *Against Our Will*. New York: Simon & Schuster, 1975.

Cary, Eve, and Peratis, Kathleen W. *Women and the Law*. Skokie, Ill.: National Textbook Company, 1978.

Chappell, Duncan, Geis, Robley, and Geis, Gilbert, eds. *Forcible Rape: The Crime, the Victim, the Offender*. New York: Columbia University Press, 1977.

Coker v. Georgia. 433 U.S. 584. 1977.

Congressional Quarterly Almanac. Washington, D.C.: Congressional Quarterly News Features, 1948–.

Davis, Angela. *Women, Race, and Class*. New York: Vintage, 1981.

Delacoste, B. Frédérique, and Alexander, Priscilla, eds. *Sex Work: Writings by Women in the Sex Industry*. Pittsburgh: Cleis Press, 1987.

Donnerstein, Edward, Linz, Daniel, and Penrod, Steven. *The Question of Pornography*. New York: Free Press, 1987.

Duggan, Lisa, and Hunter, Nan D., eds. *Sex Wars: Sexual Dissent and Political Culture*. New York: Routledge, 1995.

Dworkin, Andrea. *Pornography: Men Possessing Women*. New York: Perigee Books, 1981.

Dworkin, Andrea. "Pornography Is a Civil Rights Issue." In *Debating Sexual Correctness*, edited by Adele M. Stan, pp. 26–40. New York: Delta, 1995.

Espin, Oliva M. "Cultural and Historical Influence on Sexuality in Hispanic/Latin Women." In *All American Women: Lines That Divide, Ties That Bind*, edited by Johnnetta B. Cole, pp. 272–284. New York: Free Press, 1986.

Estrich, Susan. *Real Rape*. Cambridge: Harvard University Press, 1987.

Faderman, Lillian. *Odd Girls and Twilight Lovers: A History of Lesbian Life in Twentieth-Century America*. New York: Columbia University Press, 1991.

Ferguson, Ann, Philipson, Ilene, Diamond, Irene, Quimby, Lee, Vance, Carol S., and Snitow, Ann Barr. "Forum: The Feminist Sexuality Debates." *Signs* 10 (Autumn 1984): 106–135.

Florida, State of. *Report of the Florida Supreme Court Gender Bias Study Commission*. Tallahassee: Florida Supreme Court, 1990.

Flowers, R. Barri. *The Victimization and Exploitation of Women and Children*. Jefferson, N.C.: McFarland & Co., 1994.

Franklin v. Guinett Cty. Public Schools. 503 U.S. 60. 1992.

Frazer, James George. *The Golden Bough*. New York: Macmillan, 1922.

Geis, G. "Lord Hale, Witches, and Rape." *British Journal of Law and Society* 5 (Summer 1978), pp. 26–44.

Goldberg-Ambrose, Carole. "Unfinished Business in Rape Law Reform." *Journal of Social Issues* 48 (1992): 173–185.

Griffin, Susan. *Pornography and Silence: Culture's Revenge Against Nature*. New York: Harper & Row, 1981.

Grittner, Frederick K. *White Slavery: Myth, Ideology, and American Law*. New York: Garland Publishing, 1990.

Hale, Matthew. *Pleas of the Crown, or, A Methodological Summary of Principal Matters Relating to That Subject*. London: Printed by the assigns of Richard Atkyns and Edward Atkins, Esquires for William Schrewsbury . . . and John Leigh . . . 1678.

Harris v. Forklift Systems. 114 S.Ct. 367. 1993.

Hill, Anita Faye, and Jordan, Emma Coleman, eds. *Race, Gender, and Power in America: The Legacy of the Hill-Thomas Hearings*. New York: Oxford University Press, 1995.

Hobson, Barbara Meil. *Uneasy Virtue: The Politics of Prostitution and the American Reform Tradition*. New York: Basic Books, 1987.

Itzin, Catherine, ed. *Pornography: Women, Violence, and Civil Liberties*. New York: Oxford University Press, 1992.

Kessler, Elizabeth. "Patterns of Sexual Conduct Evidence and Present Consent: Limiting the Admissibility of Sexual History Evidence in Rape Prosecutions." *Women's Rights Law Reporter* 14 (Winter 1992): pp. 79–96.

Kinsey, Alfred C., Pomeroy, Wardell B., and Martin, Clyde G. *Sexual Behavior in the Human Male*. Philadelphia: Saunders, 1948.

Kinsey, Alfred C. et al., *Sexual Behavior in the Human Female*. Philadelphia: Saunders, 1953.

Kitzinger, Celia. *The Social Construction of Lesbianism.* London: Sage, 1987.

Klaich, Delores. *Woman + Woman: Attitudes Toward Lesbianism.* New York: Simon & Schuster, 1974.

Langum, David J. *Crossing over the Line: Legislating Morality and the Mann Act.* Chicago: University of Chicago Press, 1994.

Lederer, Laura. *Take Back the Night: Women on Pornography.* New York: Morrow, 1980.

MacKinnon, Catharine A. "Feminism, Marxism, Method, and the State: An Agenda for Theory." *Signs* 7 (1982): 515–554.

MacKinnon, Catharine A. "Feminism, Marxism, Method, and the State: Toward Feminist Jurisprudence." *Signs* 8 (1983): 635–658.

MacKinnon, Catharine A. *Feminism Unmodified.* Cambridge: Harvard University Press, 1987.

MacKinnon, Catharine A. *Only Words.* Cambridge: Harvard University Press, 1993.

MacKinnon, Catharine A. *Sexual Harassment of Working Women.* New Haven: Yale University Press, 1979.

Matthews, Nancy. "Feminist Clashes with the State: Tactical Choices by State-Funded Rape Crisis Centers." In *Feminist Organizations*, edited by Myra Marx Ferree and Patricia Yancey Martin, pp. 291–305. Philadelphia: Temple University Press, 1995.

Meritor Savings Banks, FSB v. Vinson. 106 S. Ct. 2399. 1986.

Miller, Eleanor M., Romenesko, Kim, and Wondolkowski, Lisa. "The United States." In *Prostitution: An International Handbook on Trends, Problems, and Policies*, edited by Nanette J. Davis, pp. 300–326. Westport, Conn.: Greenwood Press, 1993.

Miller v. California. 413 U.S. 15. 1973.

Morgan, Robin. *Going Too Far.* New York: Random House, 1977.

Morris, Celia. *Bearing Witness: Sexual Harassment and Beyond—Everywoman's Story.* Boston: Little, Brown, 1994.

Morrison, Toni, ed. *Race-ing Justice, En-gendering Power.* New York: Pantheon, 1992.

Newell, Carole E., Rosenfeld, Paul, and Culbertson, Amy L., "Sexual Harassment Experiences and Equal Opportunity Perceptions of Navy Women." *Sex Roles* 32 (Nos. 3/4, 1995): pp. 159–168.

Newton, David E. *Gay and Lesbian Rights.* Santa Barbara: ABC-CLIO, 1994.

Paris Adult Theatre 1 v. Slaton. 413 U.S. 49. 1973.

Parnas, Raymond. "Legislative Reform of Prostitution Laws: Keeping Commercial Sex Out of Sight and Out of Mind." *Santa Clara Law Review* 21 (1981): 669–696.

Petrie, Glen. *A Singular Iniquity: The Campaigns of Josephine Butler.* New York: Viking Press, 1971.

Phelan, Shane. *Identity Politics: Lesbian Feminism and the Limits of Community.* Philadelphia: Temple University Press, 1989.

Pivar, David J. *Purity Crusade: Sexual Morality and Social Control, 1868–1900.* Westport, Conn.: Greenwood Press, 1973.

Rich, Adrienne. "Compulsory Heterosexuality and Lesbian Existence." 1980. Reprinted in *The Signs Reader: Women, Gender, and Scholarship*, edited by Elizabeth Abel and Emily K. Abel, pp. 139–168. Chicago: University of Chicago Press, 1983.

Roiphe, Katie. *The Morning After: Sex, Fear, and Feminism.* Boston: Little, Brown, 1993.

Romer v. Evans. 116 S.Ct. 1620. 1996.

Ross, Susan Deller. "Sexual Harassment Law in the Aftermath of the Hill-Thomas Hearings." In *Race, Gender, and Power in America: The Legacy of the Hill-Thomas Hearings*, edited by A. F. Hill and E. C. Jordan, pp. 228–241. New York: Oxford University Press, 1995.

Roth v. United States. 354 U.S. 476. 1957.

Searles, Patricia, and Berger, Ronald. "The Current Status of Rape Reform Legislation: An Examination of State Statutes." *Women's Rights Law Reporter* 10 (1987): 25–43.

Sheppard, Annamay T. "Lesbian Mothers II: Long Night's Journey into Day." *Women's Rights Law Reporter* 8 (Fall 1985): 219–246.

Stan, Adele, ed. *Debating Sexual Correctness: Pornography, Sexual Harassment, Date Rape, and the Politics of Sexual Equality.* New York: Delta, 1995.

Steinem, Gloria. "Erotica and Pornography: The Clear and Present Difference." *Ms.* (November 1978): 53ff.

Stetson, Dorothy McBride. "Human Rights for Women: International Compliance with a Feminist Standard." *Women and Politics* 15, no. 3 (1995): 71–95.

Symanski, Richard. "Prostitution in Nevada." *Annals of the Association of American Geographers* 64 (September 1974): 357–377.

Tong, Rosemarie. *Feminist Thought.* Boulder: Westview Press, 1989.

Tong, Rosemarie. *Women, Sex, and the Law.* Totowa, N.J.: Rowman & Littlefield, 1984.

U.S. Commission on Obscenity and Pornography. *Report of the Commission.* Washington, D.C.: Government Printing Office, 1970.

U.S. Department of Justice. *Attorney General's Commission on Pornography.* Washington, D.C.: Government Printing Office, 1986.

Vaid, Urvashi. *Virtual Equality.* New York: Anchor/Doubleday, 1994.

Weitzer, Ronald. "Prostitutes' Rights in the United States." *Sociological Quarterly* 32, no. 1 (1991): 23–41.

Wynter, Sarah. "WHISPER: Women Hurt in Systems of Prostitution Engaged in Revolt." In *Sex Work*, edited by B. Frédérique Delacorte and Priscilla Alexander, pp. 266–270. Pittsburgh: Cleis Press, 1987.

CHAPTER 10

Economic Status

> "We burst out in scorn at the reprehensible poverty of our sex. What
> had our mothers been doing that they had no wealth to leave us?"
> Virginia Woolf, *A Room of One's Own* (1929)

Virginia Woolf provided her own answer to the question of why women
are poorer than men: "They were having children." A woman with children lacked the conditions to be a writer—money and privacy. When
Woolf wrote these thoughts in the 1920s, she stood apart from her con-
temporaries by considering the economic status of women as a group
separate from their husbands, fathers, and brothers. By the late 1970s, evidence showed that more and more women were classified as poor, defined as receiving income in an amount below government-set limits.[1]
The disproportionate number of women found among the poor is just
one facet of a consistent pattern of inequality revealed in comparisons of
men and women according to any indicator of economic status. Women
earn less than men for the same work; their share of national income is
less. Income is stratified by both ethnicity and gender with African
American and Hispanic/Latina women at the bottom. In any group or
class, women's job status is lower than men's. If married, they earn less
than their husbands. If single and the head of a family, their family income is lower than that of comparable families headed by men.

The Feminization of Poverty

A new concept, the *feminization of poverty*, entered the political debate in the 1970s.[2] The idea of feminized poverty offered two new ways of looking at economic status. First, this concept described the poor in terms of the composition by sex: women are a majority of adults in poverty. Second, this concept implied that poverty is a different condition for women than for men and that policy makers should take these differences into account. Poverty continued to show a female face into the 1990s as women's share of poverty increased (Pearce, 1989; Thomas, 1994). The economic plight is especially severe for African American and Hispanic/ Latina women, young single mothers, and those over sixty-five.

With evidence of women's inferior status mounting, Woolf's question has increasingly occupied the attention of feminists and policy makers. The concept of the feminization of poverty offered a new framework for explaining poverty and promised a more global attack on it. According to this concept, women are poor because of the effect of traditional gender roles on their ability to accumulate economic resources. The economic dependency of women, an integral part of the common-law marriage contract, is reinforced by many social and economic institutions. Social science and religion sustain beliefs that the natural and best way to rear children is in the nuclear family. In this view, the family works most comfortably if the mother is the primary caregiver to the children. To play this role, the mother must depend on the father for economic support. It is this economic dependency in the family that has made women vulnerable to poverty. Those women who are poor are those who have not achieved the preferred family goal: they are single mothers, whose numbers increase because of divorce and teen pregnancies, or women over age sixty-five, four-fifths of whom are single, divorced, or widowed. And the economic vulnerability of women in families is exacerbated by disadvantages in employment: concentration in low-paying jobs, and limited access to health and pension plans.

Comparative studies of women's economic status show that the feminization of poverty is not unique to the United States: women are at the bottom of the economic ladder in many countries (United Nations, 1995). These studies suggest that systemic factors are responsible and that the solutions that rely on the individual clawing her way out of poverty ("Mama scrubbed floors so I could become a doctor") will not be effective. The feminization of poverty requires a critical look at all the social and political institutions and practices that sustain and reinforce

BOX   10.1

"Reprehensible Poverty of Our Sex": Indicators of Economic Status

11.6 percent of all U.S. families are poor according to U.S. government definitions. But families headed by women are poorer: 34.5 percent of families headed by women are below poverty levels and 52.6 percent of all poor families are headed by women.

Weekly median earnings, 1994

White men	$547	Black men	$400	Hispanic men	$343
White women	$408	Black women	$346	Hispanic women	$305

Ratio of wives' median salary to husbands' median salary

1981	.41
1987	.45
1995	.40

Percent of workers in low wage jobs (less than $12,000 per year) by sex

Year	Women	Men
1979	14.4%	4.9%
1989	15.3	7.7

Median household income, 1993

Married couple	$43,129
Male-headed household	$29,849
Female-headed household	$18,545

Distribution of income, 1993

Income	Women	Men
$1,000 per week	5.0%	13.9%
Less than $300 per week	28.9	17.4

Mean earnings of workers with advanced degrees, 1992

Women	Men
$33,814	$58,324

Sources: U.S. Department of Labor, Bureau of Labor Statistics. *Employment in Perspective: Women in the Labor Force, 1993–1994.* Washington, D.C.: GPO, 1995; Paul Ryscavage. "Distribution of Wages, by Gender." *Monthly Labor Review* 117 (July 1994): 3–15; Bureau of the Census, "Women in the United States: A Profile." Washington, D.C.: GPO, July 1995; Taeuber, Cynthia M., ed. *Statistical Handbook on Women in America.* 2nd. ed. Phoenix, Ariz.: Oryx Press, 1991, p. 94; U.S. Bureau of the Census, *CPS Annual Demographic Survey (P60), Detailed Family Income.* March 1996. (Data ferret Homepage).

women's low economic status. In the area of public policy, this critical look requires scrutinizing programs "through the feminist lens" and being especially alert to the ways these programs may reinforce women's economic dependency or increase their economic vulnerability. Women's rights advocates lobby for specific policies that will help single mothers and elderly women to escape poverty. Such efforts are difficult. Feminists are not united behind an agenda on behalf of poor women. Even if they were, the magnitude of the problem is daunting, not only in its scope but also in the depth of its foundations in society and culture. Belief in the nuclear-family ideal remains entrenched in social myths, expectations, and discourse. Solutions to the economic disadvantages women face will require the official acceptance of a new ideology of family formation based on female autonomy as a legitimate alternative to the nuclear family. At the same time, women will not have equal economic status without confronting racist and ethnic bias deep in the U.S. culture.

What Causes Women's Poverty?

When people accept the idea of the feminization of poverty, they recognize that women's poverty is different from men's poverty and won't respond to the same policy solutions. Just what policies will effectively address women's low economic status is the subject of disagreement among social workers, advocates for women's rights, and policy makers. Groups disagree over the solutions because they disagree over the causes of women's poverty. A brief review of some of these explanations will provide an introduction to the debates on a specific topic.

Capitalist Structures

Some feminists look to the capitalist system to account for persistent economic oppression of women. They recognize, of course, that capitalism exploits men as well, but when combined with the demands of patriarchy, capitalism maintains an inferior status for women that is lower even than that of men. For African Americans, the economic plight of men, unable to find jobs that pay a family wage, has deprived many women of the opportunity to succeed in a nuclear family. Agribusiness cultivates a pool of Hispanic/Latino men. These men must work in migrant and seasonal jobs and their wives and children must follow them. The capitalist economy requires women to provide free reproductive and household services and relegates them to menial low-wage jobs; in the end, the patriarchal capitalist system benefits from these sources of cheap labor. Without fundamental change in these twin systems of domination, women will remain at the bottom of the social ladder.

Family Gender Roles

A second set of explanations focuses directly on the family and its system of gender roles. According to these views, women's assignment to child rearing and care of family members is basic to society. For women to achieve economic security and fulfill their role assignment, they must find and stay married to husbands who can support them—Male Breadwinners. Many women are influenced by the persistent myth that they can safely choose between a career in waged work and a career as a full-time wife and mother. Women fall into economic trouble because of the failure of the ideal: they become pregnant out of wedlock, their marriages break up, or their husbands are unable to support them. Then they must join the work force but retain their duties in the family, carrying a dual burden that depresses their earning power and standard of living. Some analysts connect women's economic fate to critical life cycle events: teenage pregnancy and childbearing; divorce; and widowhood (Ozawa, 1989).

Segregated Labor Markets

A third explanation for women's economic status focuses on the inadequacy of the waged labor market for women. Gender bias in socialization and education produces adult women with poor training and skills and relegates them to low-paying jobs. In the segregated work force, they are not able to compete in the dominant labor market where men find better paying "breadwinner" jobs. Instead, women are assigned to the marginal labor market, marked by contingency jobs and little income security.

Failure of Government Policy

Finally, some feminists look to inadequacies of government policies to explain the feminization of poverty. One approach is to criticize the failure of the courts to award sufficient alimony to compensate for the economic effects of divorce. Along with inadequate alimony are low levels of child support and ragged enforcement of support orders. They charge that government leaders, mostly male, refuse to provide adequate services that would enable working women to gain job training and assume full-time jobs that would pay a decent wage.

Multiple Interacting Forces

Efforts to explain the special plight of women of color show the interaction of capitalist structures, family gender roles, segregated labor markets, and the failure of government policy. The restructuring and deindustrialization of the U.S. economy has contributed to increases in joblessness, especially among young African American men. With men increasingly unable to support families, the number of households headed by African American women has risen dramatically. These women seek income through jobs and welfare. Their education and skills, limited due to gender bias in vocational education and gender segregation in the job market, relegates them to low-wage jobs. And since the 1980s, antipoverty and welfare funds have declined sharply (Zinn, 1989; Amott, 1990).

Personal and Cultural Factors

Many participants in policy debates over poverty and welfare refuse to recognize explanations based on gender and race discrimination. Rather, they look at personal and cultural factors, asserting that poverty itself sustains a culture of dependency, low aspirations, and family pathology.[3] Conservative critics assert that the government promotes this culture: welfare policy itself encourages dependency. By providing support to poor families, this argument goes, the government is rewarding the very behavior that has brought about the poverty in the first place: illegitimate pregnancy, laziness, family breakup.

In the discussion of policies and debates in the following sections, many of these themes will recur as we examine issue areas related to government's efforts to provide economic security for the poor who are predominantly women.

Government Programs for Income Security

A central feature of the twentieth century has been the expansion of government programs to provide citizens with income security. In the United States, these policies may be classified in two categories. Programs in the first category are directed at dependent mothers and children and the very poor and destitute; they include transfer payments from the tax revenues to the needy. Many analysts have noted that this categorization is gendered (Nelson, 1990). Transfer payments are designed to provide for dependent women and children and are considered a sort of dole, charity, or "welfare" (Gordon, 1990). In the second category are social insurance programs to help waged workers at times when they are unable to work and provide for families. Social insurance programs were designed to sustain the male breadwinner—a full-time worker—and are considered an essential right for workers. This section examines the process and content of these gendered policies, beginning with those directed at dependent mothers, followed by an examination of the effect of the reforms in social insurance programs.

Single Mothers and Welfare

The public image of a poor family is usually represented by a mother and her children living on welfare. This public image and concept of the feminization of poverty coincide. As far as federal policy is concerned, the image is not a new one; mothers and children have always figured prominently in official definitions of poverty. But policy makers have tended to divide them into two standard categories: those who are deserving of government help and those who are undeserving of that help.

There was a time when all poor people were considered more or less undeserving—treated miserably, exploited, and indentured. Children of the poor perished at high rates under the English-style poor laws. Public authorities dispensed little charity and feared that direct financial assistance would destroy poor people's will to work. Thus, the poor and destitute, who could not be cared for by their families as poor relations, were sent to almshouses and orphanages.

Early in this century, progressives and other reformers were alarmed at the high infant-mortality rate among the poor, and they praised the family home as the proper milieu for rearing children. Through the

White House Conference on Children in 1909, they argued for direct help to mothers who had to raise children alone. They were careful to argue in favor of "suitable" homes and to insist that money should go to deserving, moral women. Starting in 1911, states began to adopt mothers' pension plans to help women to raise their children at home. These plans included requirements that mothers be investigated and deemed competent to provide suitable, moral homes for children. Those most likely to qualify were widows whose single-parent status was due to fate, not their own inability to keep their husbands. Needless to say, unmarried mothers had already demonstrated immorality, excluding them from public aid.

Aid to Families with Dependent Children (AFDC)

It was in this cultural environment that Congress delivered a federal welfare program in 1935 as part of the Social Security Act. The Aid to Dependent Children (ADC) program established basic outlines and definitions of the aid to poor families. This program was "designed to release from the wage earning role the person whose natural function is to give her children the physical and affectionate guardianship necessary not alone to keep them from falling into social misfortune, but more affirmatively to rear them into citizens capable of contributing to society" (quoted in Kamerman and Kahn, 1988, p. 51). The program started as matching grants to help states provide help to their needy children who had lost one parent's support through death, incapacitation, or desertion.

For sixty years, welfare formulas gave states the primary responsibility to determine the eligibility of clients and to define benefit levels. While the federal administration could set general rules for the use of its funds, congressional amendments to ADC were for the most part permissive, serving primarily as suggestions or recommendations to states. Thus, welfare standards and services have always varied greatly by state. At first, the states by and large continued their practice, begun under mothers' pensions, of limiting aid to the families they deemed suitable. Those children who received ADC help were, overwhelmingly, the children of white widows. In 1950, amendments to the federal act extended aid to the mothers also, and the program got a new name: Aid to Families with Dependent Children (AFDC). In 1961, the states were permitted to give AFDC to families with both parents present, called AFDC-Unemployed Parent (AFDC-UP), but only half the states accepted this AFDC-UP option.

In the 1950s, the welfare system was changed to aid fewer widows and more divorced, separated, and unmarried mothers, including a greater proportion of African Americans and Hispanic/Latino Americans. Advocacy groups organized, responding to the demands of welfare recipients, civil rights groups, and anti-poverty campaigns. These advocacy groups considered public assistance to be a right, and they rejected the idea of a moral test of suitability. They complained about the inadequacy of the typical cash payments, which were automatically set below the minimum survival standards in every state but Alaska. They especially protested "man in the house" rules that made women ineligible for benefits if a man was living in their home. The Supreme Court declared the "man in the house" rule invalid in 1968 in *King v. Smith*. In the 1970s, welfare-rights groups sought to replace the concept of aid to children, which they saw as a perpetuation of a state of dependency tending to keep people in poverty. They proposed instead the idea of a minimum guaranteed income that would not be dependent on the characteristics of the house, the living arrangements, or the work habits. Such a concept would lay to rest the age-old dichotomy of the deserving and undeserving poor by abolishing poverty assistance as a public responsibility. The social democratic idea of minimum income as a social right would have meant a dramatic shift in American ideologies of government's role in people's lives. Before politicians could digest such a new idea, however, the proposal died during the economic crises of the later 1970s and early 1980s.

The welfare-rights movement pushed successfully for increased AFDC benefits, along with congruent programs such as Food Stamps and Medicaid. Welfare rolls seemed to be on a perpetual upward track. As more and more women with children entered the job market, the idea that government should support some women to stay home with their children began to seem unfair and incongruous. Coupled with increases in welfare costs, this change in attitudes produced counterefforts to reduce the number of welfare recipients.

Since the 1950s, the solution to excessive welfare costs and poverty has been framed in two ways: (1) to improve the employability of welfare recipients, and (2) to coerce fathers to assume responsibility for support of their children. Increasingly, the standard for differentiating between the deserving and undeserving poor has shifted from morality to employability: those able to work and those unable to work. Those able to work should be put to work, and any public assistance should be temporary. At the same time, more and more policy makers have become willing to shift mothers with children from the "unable" category to the "able" category.

BOX   10.2

A Sampling of AFDC Payments: The Erosion of a Safety Net

Monthly payments for AFDC families of one needy adult and two children, in selected states for October 1987 and January 1994 show the following distribution. Note that the proportion of the need standard actually paid has declined in most states.

State	Need Standard*		Payment	
	1987	1994	1987	1994
Alabama	$354	$118	$673	$164
Alaska	749	749	975	923
Arizona	621	293	964	327
California	633	633	715	607
Connecticut	514	514	680	680
Delaware	319	319	338	338
Florida	775	264	991	303
Georgia	366	263	424	280
Idaho	554	304	991	317
Indiana	320	288	320	288
Maine	558	405	553	418
Montana	434	359	511	401
New York (City)	497	497	577	577
North Carolina	518	259	544	272
Ohio	685	309	879	341
South Dakota	366	366	491	417
Washington State	800	492	1158	546
Wisconsin	647	517	647	517

*Need standard is set by each state. Nearly all states include costs of food, clothing, shelter, utilities, and personal care items, but a few include a variety of other costs, which accounts for the variation in the standard. States vary also in the percentage of the standard they actually pay to recipient families.

Sources: U.S. Department of Health and Human Services, Family Support Administration. *Characteristics of State Plans for Aid to Families with Dependent Children.* Washington, D.C.: GPO, 1989, p. 373; U.S. House of Representatives, Committee on Ways and Means. *Overview of Entitlement Programs.* Washington, D.C.: GPO, 1995, pp. 311–312.

Welfare Reform

Debate on AFDC has been so continuous since the 1940s that *welfare reform* has become a formal subject heading in Congress, the states, and the academic community. In the 1980s, the struggle over this major income-transfer program yielded both a new definition of the economic status of poor women with children and a welfare reform act: the Family Support Act (FSA) of 1988. The definitional shift came about because of the gradual erosion of the expectation that mothers with small children are inevitably dependent and because of the buildup of a belief in the right and responsibility of mothers to be economically self-sufficient, not dependent on government for support. The necessary means to self-sufficiency is a job providing an adequate income. The Family Support Act essentially revised the agreement between the federal government and the states and redirected welfare policy to the goal of self-sufficiency. But rather than settling the conflict over welfare policy, the effect of the FSA was to expand it to encompass an ideological rift over whether the federal government should guarantee a safety net to the poor or return this policy entirely to the individual states. Then in 1996, the Personal Responsibility and Work Opportunity Reconciliation Act ended the contract between the federal and state governments and shifted all but the financial burden almost entirely to the states.

Welfare reform debates in the 1990s are the product of policy activities begun in the early 1960s. At first, Congress responded to concerns about the cost of welfare and to criticisms of welfare "queens" getting wealthy living off public assistance. The key response to this criticism was "Let's put the loafers to work." Despite the rhetoric, the motive of these policies was to answer the critics rather than to put women permanently in the work force. In 1962, Congress offered *workfare* to the states. The Community Work and Training Program allowed states to make unpaid community work a condition for receiving welfare. Proponents hoped that welfare recipients would be seen as giving something back to the community in return for its support. Thus, the 1935 idea that the work of raising children was return enough for support had already begun to fade by 1962. In 1967, the Work Incentive (WIN) programs replaced workfare as the preferred way to lower welfare costs. The WIN programs made enrollment in work-related programs a condition for receiving aid, but a certain amount of income was forgiven before a person's welfare benefits were reduced. In practice, most AFDC recipients were exempt from the WIN programs because these programs excluded from work requirements mothers with children under age six. Men in two-parent households with children under age six were not exempt, however, which meant that the people most likely to get job assistance from the WIN programs were men in states with the AFDC-UP option. Thus, despite the criticisms of excessive welfare costs and idleness, traditional gender roles prevailed to exempt two-thirds of AFDC recipients—mothers with small children (U.S. Congress, 1987).

Welfare-rights advocates were critical of both workfare and WIN. To them, the workfare jobs were degrading "make-work" and exploited the poor. Although the WIN programs were supported by the rhetoric that they would "foster a sense of dignity, self-worth and confidence" from being a wage earner, their critics claimed they were based on the conception that the poor needed to be forced to work. Most of the time, the WIN programs put women only in low-paid dead-end jobs, with pay barely above the welfare level itself, and threatened them with loss of health-care coverage as well. Also, their work costs often overwhelmed their meager pay. In addition, the WIN programs provided little help to women in gaining the necessary experience and education to increase their job skills and earning power.

The welfare-reform debate intensified in the 1980s, especially in response to the Omnibus Budget Reconciliation Act (OBRA) of 1981. OBRA resuscitated workfare and sharply reduced the eligibility levels for AFDC assistance. The idea was to force all but the truly deserving (or "needy") mothers to work. This solution led to graphic evidence of the persistence of dependency among the welfare population. Poverty levels increased in the midst of the "Reagan revolution." Arguments about the feminization of poverty grew, making it clear that children would remain hungry unless women could find self-sufficiency through work (U.S. House of Representatives, 1985). And evidence also mounted that putting women to work involved more than arranging for unpaid community make-work or "job-search clubs." It meant providing a full range of options—including job training and the support services of child care, health care, and transportation—to respond to the diversity of the population. At the same time, fears about costs of such supports remained. Conservatives and liberals finally found a way to compromise: liberals accepted work as a condition of welfare assistance, and conservatives accepted the need to provide support services. Each side contended this approach would reduce costs in the long run.

Family Support Act and the Aftermath

The Family Support Act of 1988 (FSA) marked a major step toward a new national policy for the poor. FSA required all states to make two-parent families eligible for welfare assistance. In addition, the states were to establish education, training, and employment programs to move families off welfare into jobs and require that welfare recipients enroll in these programs. The states were obliged, as well, to offer child care and other support services to ease the transition to self-sufficiency. There was also a whole set of provisions to improve child-support contributions (see Chapter 6).

While FSA marked a new national standard for AFDC, the act contained seeds of the disintegration of the very concept of a national welfare policy. Even more important than the specific requirements set for the states in the FSA was the provision that encouraged states to launch experimental programs. As a result of these experiments, political support grew for a transformation of welfare, as President Clinton noted in his 1992 campaign: "to end welfare as we know it." Conservative activists, inspired by such books as *The Underclass* (Auletta, 1982) and *Losing Ground* (Murray, 1984), took advantage of this opening to push for drastic cutbacks in government support of mothers and children. The themes of their reform effort were based on the assumptions that welfare programs cause poverty rather than alleviating it. The government should encourage individual responsibility, not "welfare dependency." As it stands, these critics argued, AFDC undermines work incentives while it pays people for not working, for not getting married, and for not being responsible for their children. As the federal debt and deficit spending became a major policy issue, conservatives turned to welfare spending as an area where cuts could be made. Such cuts not only would be feasible but would be popular with workers who resented having their taxes used to support people they saw as freeloaders.

In August 1996, President Clinton and Congress agreed to a welfare statute that leaders claimed would "end welfare as we know it." Its provisions include:

1. Formal elimination of AFDC and replacement with federal block grants to states, to be called Temporary Assistance for Needy Families

2. Eligibility for receipt of assistance to be determined entirely by the states, thus ending the federal guarantee of assistance to those who meet general criteria

3. Requirement that adult recipients take waged jobs within two years of receiving assistance

4. Requirement that federal funds not be used for adults who have received assistance for more than five years

5. A state's right to deny food stamps and Supplemental Security Income to legal immigrants

6. Financial incentives to states who reduce their rate of out-of-wedlock births

This legislation takes welfare policy in a new direction, increasing states' discretionary powers and creating a decentralized system, with benefits and regulations varying from state to state. This is not an overnight shift, however, since nearly all states have experimented with these changes since the Family Support Act. The effects on poor women, teenage girls, and children will be closely watched by advocacy groups.

Thus far, advocates for women's rights have been marginal to the debates over welfare reform. While they have supported the idea of self-sufficiency for mothers through job training and employment, feminist policy analysts present evidence that the work requirements in the new act are unrealistic. There are not enough jobs available to enable all needy mothers to support their children, nor is there adequate child care or health insurance to replace Medicaid. Many feminists warn that the conservative welfare reform argument places too much emphasis on the traditional nuclear male-breadwinner family as the ideal, an ideal that has contributed greatly to the low economic status of women. In general, women's rights advocates have tried to convince policy makers not to remove the social support for poor mothers and children and cast them into the labor market without a life raft. Rather than punitive regulations and drastic cuts in financial support for the poor, they advocate more flexibility to allow welfare mothers to combine income from available work, child-support payments, and public programs such as Medicaid and public cash assistance (Spalter-Roth and Hartmann, 1995). It is important to note, however, that feminist analysts do not believe that women's economic plight can be resolved with a better welfare program. Since women's status is due to the combination of social, economic, and cultural factors, including class and race discrimination, it will be raised only by changes throughout society. The conclusion of this chapter summarizes the major proposals for such changes.

Welfare for Waged Workers: Women's Share

Unemployment Insurance and Job Training

An array of government programs is in place to help workers whose income is threatened by the forces of the market. One of the major accomplishments of U.S. national labor policy was the expansion, in the 1930s, of unemployment insurance to nearly all waged workers. Under this program, states are required to provide cash payments to workers who lose their jobs and who are available and ready to work. Of course, women are eligible for these benefits on the same basis as men. However, the program is based on a model of the full-time year-round worker that fits more men than women. Part-time contingency workers—more likely to be female—are not covered. Even among full-time workers, women are less likely to qualify for the assistance because workers who "voluntarily" terminate their work cannot collect. Sexual harassment drives some women to quit their jobs. Women with family responsibilities often find they must leave jobs for pregnancy and because they have difficulty in finding day care. If so, they are likely to find it difficult to qualify. Although the federal regulations limit the ability of states to disqualify a person solely on the basis of pregnancy, a worker who quits when pregnant usually becomes ineligible for benefits.

Another way the government tries to help workers who are unemployed is through job-training programs. Public attention to job training for the young first developed in the form of vocational-education courses in high school and later in junior colleges. Federal aid to vocational-education programs dates from the nineteenth century, and there have been periodic reviews of these aid packages to respond to changes in labor-force needs. Until the 1970s, this aid was focused primarily on training men. When these programs were established, they were influenced by traditional gender-role attitudes that associated job preparation with the male-breadwinner role. A woman's primary adult career was to be as a homemaker, wife, and mother: girls were enrolled in home economics and nursing, and later in commercial courses and cosmetology.

Sex segregation has persisted even though Title IX removed the formal barriers to vocational-educational classes. Feminist groups have advocated special government efforts to overcome the tracking of women into dead-end jobs and have frequently found a response in Congress. In 1976, the Vocational Education Act authorized states to appoint full-time sex-equity coordinators (VEECs) to oversee efforts at sex integration, especially those aimed at bringing women into traditionally male fields. The Carl Perkins Vocational Education Act of 1984 provided "set-aside" funds to assist women (3.5 percent) and single parents (8.5 percent) to acquire marketable job skills. It also authorized vocational-education funds to be used for child care, transportation, and other support services. Women's rights advocates believed that these special efforts should be continued, and that young women must expect to support themselves: "Although vocational education improves future incomes, occupational segregation keeps women's incomes below men's. Young women will have to work to support their families and need to be prepared to do so" (American Association of University Women, 1989).

Federal job-training programs for adults respond to several debates: to the welfare debate, of course, but also to concerns about unemployment, economic growth, and the competitiveness of U.S. business in world markets. There have been frequent demands to provide more job training for poor women and to end, once and for all, the pattern of "jobs for men, welfare for women." For the most part, job-training programs have not been directed to women specifically; in fact, the opposite has been true. The Manpower Development and Training Act of 1962 specifically helped "adult family heads" receive on-the-job training. The Comprehensive Employment and Training Act (CETA) enacted in 1973 targeted low-income and welfare recipients, but it was primarily a job-creation scheme rather than a job-training program. In 1979, fewer than 20 percent of the CETA enrollees were welfare recipients, and many of them were males in the states with the AFDC-UP option. The CETA program was heavily criticized as a wasteful approach to the problem of jobs. The Job Training Partnership Act (JTPA) of 1982 eliminated public job creation. This act focuses on job training by the private sector. It specifically targets welfare recipients, but participation is voluntary. The Nontraditional Employment for Women Act (NEW) of 1991, an amendment to JTPA, ordered states to set aside a small portion of funds to bring women into training programs for nontraditional occupations. The Family Support Act of 1988 created the Job Opportunities and Basic Skills (JOBS) Training Program and requires nonexempt AFDC recipients to enroll as a condition of aid. The JTPA and JOBS programs both include child care and other support services, which were missing from earlier training and job-creation legislation.[4]

In the 1970s, women's rights lobbyists advocated help for displaced homemakers—a special group of women who were, in a way, casualties of divorce. Kamerman and Kahn find the following definition useful in describing the displaced homemaker: a person "over 35 years of age [who] has worked without pay as a homemaker for his or her family, is not gainfully employed, has had or would have difficulty finding employment, has depended on the income of a family member and has lost that income or has depended on government assistance as the parent of dependent children but is no longer eligible" (Kamerman and Kahn, 1988, p. 141). Displaced homemakers are usually not eligible for AFDC because their children are too old. And they need a range of services—including counseling, training, and job referral—to help make them economically self-sufficient. They were included as a special category for job grants in the CETA legislation. Local activists helped start displaced-homemaker services at community centers and junior colleges.

A person's economic status is closely related to his or her earning power and employability. For women, employability has been limited not only by inadequate vocational and job training, child-care responsibilities, and family dependence but also by the culture, which has not defined women's roles in terms of autonomy and self-sufficiency. Being economically responsible for oneself and one's family has been officially defined as the exception for women but the rule for men. Public policy debates prompted by chronic failures of programs to help the poor have begun to associate poverty with aspects of traditional expectations of girls and women for themselves and by others. The goal of economic self-sufficiency for single mothers has entered the debate. The extension of that concept to full female autonomy is incomplete; it is usually reserved for poor single women, not for women across the board. Meanwhile, more generations of elderly women are likely to be part of the feminized poverty.

Still, to promote autonomy for mothers will require continuing change in conceptions and policies. Some feminists contend that policy should focus on child support through family allowances and free medical care for children to aid all families, as in the European social democracy model. This would mean the end of the "pseudo-housewife" status of single mothers once and for all (Bergmann, 1986). Instead, single mothers could be officially defined as workers, thereby promoting their autonomy and independence. They would have access to job training, health insurance, child care, and parental leave, as would two-parent working families. When single mothers are unemployed, they should be eligible for unemployment insurance. Such a policy would depend on three major redefinitions of poverty: (1) it would abolish the age-old dichotomy between the deserving and the undeserving poor: (2) it would recognize the autonomy and responsibility of the single mother and her minor children; and (3) it would officially define the single-parent family as a legitimate family form and remove the assumption that female dependency is inevitable or desirable.

While support services remain a key part of policies designed to help women with family responsibilities, the major condition that contributes to the low economic status of women is their low earning power, resulting from inadequate job preparation and training. This leads to the earnings gap between men and women, the welfare status of many women with families, and poverty among older women. From segregation in vocational education and job-training programs develops segregation in jobs. Just how much of this segregation is the result of the preferences of women and how much is the result of sex discrimination and traditional sex-role definitions is still an ongoing debate. Most observers would agree, however, that access to training for jobs and decent pay remains an exceptional option for most women.

Retirement, Social Security, and Insurance

In 1935 the Social Security Act established a federal pension plan to cover all workers, and that plan has greatly improved the economic and social condition of the elderly in the United States. Nevertheless, women over age sixty-five are more likely to be alone and poor than are men of that age. By some accounts, these women comprise the fastest-growing segment of the population, and one-third to one-half of them are in poverty (Sidel, 1986; U.S. House of Representatives, 1992). Ideally, an adequate retirement income should be a combination of Old Age and Survivors Insurance (OASI) provided under the Social Security Act of 1935, private pensions, and savings. However, women are less likely than men to have savings, property, or private pensions, and they frequently must rely only on OASI. An elderly women by herself is more likely to be in poverty than is a married couple. Hispanic/Latina and African American women are especially vulnerable, and their Social Security benefits are the lowest of all (Ozawa, 1995). The plight of those people who depend only on Social Security reveals that program's inadequacy for women.

From its inception, the OASI portion of the Social Security Act was designed to serve the traditional single-earner family. The worker contributes through payroll taxes, and after ten years of equivalent contributions by the employer, the worker is covered. Such coverage includes a pension, based on the worker's earnings levels, as well as benefits for dependents and survivors. A dependent wife's pension is one-half that of her husband. Of course, a wife may obtain pension rights as a covered worker through her own employment. She cannot, however, receive two pensions; she receives her own or her spouse's benefits, whichever is larger. In either case, she may face problems. An astonishing number of women, many who have been in the labor force for decades, find that their own pensions are worth less than one-half of their husband's: such is the impact of the earnings gap and sex segregation in the work force. The wife who is dependent on her husband's pension faces other barriers. She cannot receive anything until her husband retires. If the couple divorces, she receives the wife's benefits only if the marriage lasted at least ten years.[5]

The cumulative effect of the OASI policy is that a woman may be employed and contribute to the costs of raising children and yet not receive a retirement pension proportionate to her contribution to the family. A homemaker cannot get pension rights in her own name. The single parent at low wage levels has difficulty accumulating adequate qualifying contributions to Social Security.

The status of women is especially grim in the area of private pensions. Fewer than one-half of all U.S. workers are covered by private pension plans, and it is again the low-paying, low-status jobs—dominated by women—that are usually left out. Even when covered by a private pension plan, women who shift jobs frequently to accommodate their family responsibilities fail to have the years of continuous service required for vesting. Employees' private pension plans usually have dependents' benefits built in, but coverage for the homemaker may be an option. Since pension contributions reduce a family's immediate income, husbands have been known to decline coverage for their wives, without informing them. Divorce can also cut a dependent spouse adrift from a private pension plan, unless her rights are guaranteed in the property settlement.

Savings and property available in old age are a product of earnings and expenses during the productive years. Again, the double whammy of employment status and marital status puts women at a disadvantage. A homemaker must depend on the savings decisions of the breadwinner. A working wife is often a secondary earner whose salary goes for home and children. Pay levels and work costs (such as child care and transportation) mean there is little left over for purchasing stocks and bonds and real estate. In divorce, wives depend on a decent property settlement and then usually must get back into the work force or receive permanent alimony. For women who *are* self-sufficient and able to earn a living, their pay levels may not be high enough to permit any significant accumulation of capital for old-age income.

In the 1980s, the national feminist coalition and the Congressional Caucus on Women's Issues joined together to try to improve the economic status of women, especially older women, with an omnibus legislative package entitled the Economic Equity Act (EEA). This act was a series of bills promoted in Congress between 1982 and 1986 to address pensions, insurance, child support, day care, and tax reforms. The coalition was most successful in the area of pensions and child support (see Chapter 6), while other proposals were deferred or defeated. The bill to rid individual insurance contracts of sex and race classifications was built on Supreme Court decisions that required group plans to be unisex (*Los Angeles Department of Water and Power v. Manhart*, 1978; *Arizona Governing Committee v. Norris*, 1983). The insurance industry, however, blocked the bill by successfully using a public-relations campaign to warn women that they would pay higher rates for life insurance and car insurance.[6]

The main victory for the EEA was the Retirement Equity Act (REA) of 1984. In contrast to the insurance bill, there was little controversy on this measure, which mainly involved tinkering with pension rules. It did not extend any new pension rights to women workers. For those who are covered, however, a series of rule changes allow women to retain pension credits they had been losing when they left the work force to have children. Workers must be enrolled in pension plans at age twenty-one rather than age twenty-five; women can take maternity leave and parental leave without sacrificing their pension credit. Employers must now get a spouse's approval before a worker can waive spousal benefits. The REA also permits the courts to include pensions as part of marital property in a divorce.[7]

Feminists have been proposing changes in Social Security laws for decades, but they have not come up with a feasible reform. Many of the inadequacies of OASI result from the earnings gap and sex segregation in the labor force and await changes in job markets, education, and attitudes. But there should be something that could be done to improve the economic status and independence of the homemaker. The National Organization for Women's Bill of Rights for Homemakers includes some recommendations:

> Homemakers should be granted the recognitions and rights of paid, skilled workers . . . through independent Social Security [the home-

BOX 10.3

Confused? Some Federal Programs and Their Acronyms

Acronym	Program	Start-up Date
AFDC	Aid to Families with Dependent Children	1935, 1950
AFDC-UP	Aid to Families with Dependent Children— Unemployed Parent	1961
CETA	Comprehensive Employment and Training Act	1973
EEA	Economic Equity Act	1982–1986
FSA	Family Support Act	1988
JOBS	Job Opportunities and Basic Skills Training Program	1988
JTPA	Job Training Partnership Act	1982
OASI	Old Age and Survivors Insurance	1935
OBRA	Omnibus Budget Reconciliation Act	1981
REA	Retirement Equity Act	1984
SSI	Supplemental Security Income	1935
WIN	Work Incentive Program	1967
VAW	Violence Against Women Act	1994

maker should receive] coverage in her own name, portable into and out of marriage and continuing as the homemaker leaves and re-enters the paid workforce, containing provision for disability and retirement benefits adequate to maintain a decent standard of living. (Reprinted in McGlen and O'Connor, 1983, pp. 395–396)

Proposed solutions to the dependency of homemakers usually involve some scheme whereby homemakers can get OASI coverage, based on their work caring for home and children. One solution might be to allow homemakers to gain credits in their own names. For this to occur, however, policy makers would have to recognize, explicitly, the economic and labor value of housework. This step would be akin to accepting the concept of wages for housework or including the value of unpaid labor in the home in calculations of the gross national product (GNP). As for who would pay for these workers, the cost would be shared among the entire paid labor force. However, given public distaste for the AFDC programs that paid women to stay home and take care of their children, such payment to homemakers might jeopardize support for Social Security by making Social Security look like welfare. One of the reasons Social Security is so politically popular is because it is viewed as an insurance scheme, paid for by the recipients, and not a dole. An alternative would be to have the breadwinner pay taxes on behalf of his or her spouse, but unless this provision is mandatory, it would continue the spouse's dependency.

Another proposal more frequently made is a system of shared earnings: a married couple would combine the contributions of both spouses and would split the benefits equally, based on the number of years the couple is married. At divorce, each spouse would be left with equal credits. This approach would make OASI a form of marital property.

A third proposal is modeled after some European public-pension schemes. It would provide a universal minimum benefit to all persons over age sixty-two or age sixty-five and then increase each person's benefit based on variations in his or her lifetime earnings. This proposal would make OASI a form of guaranteed minimum income. The current eligibility requirements for a guaranteed income under Supplemental Security Income (SSI), state that a person must have no assets or income.[8] The political and economic barriers to any of these reforms are considerable. They require not only increased costs to OASI but also a shift in the definition of the basis for Social Security pensions and a shift in the value accorded to homemaking.

Battered Women and Dependency

At first glance, the problem of battered women does not seem to belong with other policy issues in this chapter on economic status. Women of all economic backgrounds are victims of violence from husbands, ex-husbands, boyfriends, and ex-boyfriends. Abuse of women is closely related to sexuality and family issues. However, the subject is included here because the policy definition of violence directed against women has been affected by more general questions of economic dependence and gender roles. Regardless of improved criminal laws, police protection, and social services, the best remedy for victims of domestic abuse remains achieving economic and psychological independence.

The public's main concerns about family relationships, gender roles, and social problems at any particular moment will determine the way the problem of woman battery is defined. In the past, age-old interpretations of family relations accepted violence as a legitimate form of punishment. Legend has it that common-law courts operated according to the rule of thumb: a husband's legitimate authority to use violence to control his wife, children, and other family members was limited to the use of a stick no larger than his thumb. Blackstone, too, recognized the historic legitimacy of such beatings: "The husband also by the old law might give his wife moderate correction. For, as he is to answer for her misbehavior, the law thought it reasonable to intrust him with his power of restraining her, by domestic chastisement, in the same moderation that a man is allowed to correct his servants or children; for whom the master or parent is also liable in some cases to answer" (Blackstone, 1803, p. 445). Physical encounters, especially for the purpose of ensuring proper behavior and punishing wrong, have long been accepted as a legitimate use of authority; when the authority is fixed on the male family head, he has its legitimate use to carry out his responsibilities.

At least three times in American politics—1640 to 1680, 1874 to 1890, and 1970 to the present—political leaders have disturbed public complacency and called woman battery an unacceptable practice warranting public attention (Pleck, 1987).[9] In each of these periods, social perceptions of violence have varied. In colonial New England, wife abuse had the aroma of sin and wickedness. After the Civil War, drunkenness among lower-class males seemed to explain excessive abuse of unfortunate women and children. In the 1970s, the concept of *domestic violence* signaled an appreciation of increasing tensions in family relationships. Feminists were prominent in policy debates of both the 1880s and 1970s. They have injected feminist interpretations into the controversies and participated in coalitions promoting changes in the law. In the 1970s, because of the growing attention to economic issues, feminists linked wife battery to women's economic status. Women's dependency on men for support has made them more vulnerable to abuse and more likely to stay in abusive relationships.

In the 1870s, wife-abuse problems were closely associated with problems related to the welfare of children. Still, feminists saw the wife-abuse issue as a sexuality question—another example of the male brutishness that also accounted for rape, prostitution, and pornography. They concluded that the social solution was to restrain male power, but the immediate policy response feminists endorsed was to amend family laws to allow separation and divorce on grounds of physical cruelty. With adequate maintenance, alimony, and child support, women would not face destitution. Since the public debate often linked violence with drunkenness, feminists also decided to get involved in temperance activities as a way of protecting women. Their enemy eventually became not husbands but bartenders and whisky peddlers. In this period, feminist leaders were often critical of male behavior among the poor, probably because they considered violence, drunkenness, and child abuse to be characteristics of loutish lower-class men. Proposals surfaced at one point to bring back the stocks and whipping posts to punish wife and child beaters. It is unlikely that these were to be used to punish wealthy businessmen and merchants.

Between 1900 and 1960, family violence fell back to the private sphere and was not a matter of policy discussion. Psychologists, psychiatrists, and social workers took up the question, with little attention from feminists. Some of these practitioners believed that women often provoked abuse because they were unable to adapt to their marital responsibilities. In any event, according to these counselors, if there were a problem, it was best left to counselors. Meanwhile, it seemed that there was popular acceptance that violence in male-female intimate relations was inevitable, even desirable.[10]

Woman battery came back to the public agenda as a problem of women's rights in the early 1970s. It was, in fact, partially a product of the feminist movement. During this period, the scope of the suffering of women at the hands of their husbands and lovers first rose to public attention through community centers and rape hotlines: a high percentage of calls for help were from abused women.[11] Some communities responded by establishing special shelters for battered women. At the national level, the National Organization for Women formed the National Coalition Against Domestic Violence to press for aid for shelters and information programs. Women's rights advocates joined with lawyers and social activists to reform state laws and improve police assistance. The groups in these coalitions were similar to earlier ones in the nineteenth century, but the definitions of the issue were somewhat different because they had been affected by changes in women's status and in public perceptions of women's roles. In the nineteenth century, the coalitions fought for divorce as a solution to wife battery. Feminists in the 1970s found themselves defending women and explaining why women did *not* get divorces, that is, why they stayed with abusive men. The assumption they confronted was that there was something wrong with women. The belief that women brought beatings on themselves by provoking their men to violence led to putting blame on women for not doing something about the abuse they received.

Looking for reasons why women stay with abusive men produced new definitions and policy proposals. They focused on the persistence of patriarchal gender roles and machismo and the inadequacy of laws and police protection. Women's subordination in marriage, their emotional dependency, and their lack of economic autonomy tied many women to their tormentors. Women live in fear, petrified in a *battered-wife syndrome* that is analogous to the battered-child syndrome analyzed by psychologists in the 1960s. Psychological damage from abuse robs a woman of the power to save herself. Men use violence to maintain dominance over women and to punish them for transgressions usually associated with their efforts to become more independent.

Some people also blamed law enforcement and the courts. Police officials refused to interfere in "domestic disturbances." They were not trained, they said, to understand the dynamics involved in intimate violence, which was so different from stranger violence, such as kidnapping or armed robbery, which they were trained to handle. In addition, they often identified with the husband and believed the wife had provoked him. Assault laws were designed to regulate strangers, not lovers, and were inadequate. Typical arrests and jail punishment were not enough to protect battered women; these might provoke even further violence. During this debate in the 1970s, the definition of the issue became more comprehensive—from wife abuse to woman battery (including ex-wives and cohabitants) and then, finally, to *domestic violence* (to include child abuse). The concept of domestic violence, although it does not point exclusively to female victims, permits criticism of gender-role relationships and the economic dependency of women in the family. This definition of the issue resulted in a coalition of activists that has been successful in gaining attention to the issue. It started a process that has led to more legal reforms to deal with woman battery than have ever before been enacted in the United States.

Most of this activity has been at the state and local levels. Almost every state has amended its assault laws to increase the powers of police to remove an abusive man from his victim's home. Provisions for warrantless arrests, cooling-off periods, restraining orders, and special-protection orders are among the reforms enacted since the mid-1970s (Fagan, 1996; Lerman, 1980; NOW-LDEF, 1987; Wolfe, 1994). Some states place surcharges on marriage licenses to pay for shelters. Others have special statutes making domestic violence a separate criminal offense including, in some cases, special domestic violence courts. Anti-stalking laws enable police to intervene to protect women in situations where violence is probable. Prosecutors may have separate units to aid victims in prosecuting their attackers. Pressure has increased on police, and some victims have prosecuted police departments for failing to respond to their calls for help. Special training for police has occasionally been part of the reforms, along with improved reporting procedures and response times to calls for help. Some states have enacted laws providing for mandatory arrests at the scene of the complaint. Whether such tough laws restrain abusers or anger them to further violence remains controversial (Fagan, 1996).

There are over one thousand shelters for battered women in the country, reflecting some interest in the physical well-being of battered women and support services for them. Shelter staff recognize that the plight of the victims results more from economic dependency and isolation than from anything else. Many of these shelters are under private auspices funded by donations and a combination of state and federal grants. Although the number of shelters has grown, these facilities are not adequate to meet local needs.

The national feminist coalition has successfully lobbied Congress to bring the federal government into the battle against domestic abuse of women. The passage of the Violence Against Women Act of 1994 (VAW) pledged federal legal and administrative resources to the states and social service providers in a variety of ways. Domestic assault may be considered a gender-based crime, enabling victims to sue batterers in federal court (see Chapter 9 for similar provision for rape victims). The act authorizes grants to train judges and courts in domestic violence cases and to subsidize shelters. Federal authorities may prosecute abusers who cross state lines to harass or attack others or to avoid punishment for violating a protection order. The act charges the Justice Department with responsibility for collecting data on domestic violence and stalking prosecutions nationwide and for providing an assessment of the use of the battered-woman syndrome as a defense (see Box 10.4).

Sustained pressure by feminists and other groups on lawmakers in states and Congress has yielded many improvements in criminal laws, enforcement, and services for victims of domestic abuse. Nevertheless, data on "femicide" shows the limited effectiveness of reforms to protect women from husbands or boyfriends determined to kill them (Radford and Russell, 1992). In cases that have drawn national attention, women have been murdered even though they used the available resources to get away from their abusers: getting a divorce, establishing a new life, prosecuting the offender, and even seeing him convicted and imprisoned.

BOX 10.4

The Violence Gender Gap

♀ ♂ In 1977, 54 percent of all murder victims killed by intimates were female. By 1992, the ratio of female to male victims had changed, and 70 percent of the victims were female.

♀ ♂ Compared with males, females experienced more than ten times as many incidents of violence by an intimate. On average each year between 1987 and 1991, women were the victims in more than 572,000 violent incidents at the hands of an intimate, compared with approximately 49,000 incidents in which men were the victims.

♀ ♂ Women are much less likely than men to become victims of violent crime in general, but they are more likely than men to be victimized by intimates, such as husbands or boyfriends. Men are more likely than women to be victims of violence perpetrated by acquaintances or strangers.

♀ ♂ In large urban counties in 1988, a spousal murder case was more likely to be diverted, rejected, or dismissed if the defendant was a woman (12 percent) than if the defendant was a man (9 percent). Similarly, a woman defendant's case was more likely to result in an acquittal (13 percent versus 1 percent).

♀ ♂ Of those accused of killing their spouses, 41 percent of the men and 31 percent of the women were convicted at trial; 46 percent of the men and 38 percent of the women entered guilty pleas. Of the men convicted of killing their wives, 94 percent were sentenced to prison, including 15 percent who were sentenced to life terms. Women who killed their husbands were less likely to receive a prison sentence: 81 percent were sentenced to prison, including 8 percent who received a life term.

Source: U.S. Justice Department, Bureau of Justice Statistics. "Domestic Violence: Violence Between Intimates." *Selected Findings.* Washington, D.C.: Government Printing Office, November 1994.

Some battered women, unable to escape their attackers, have killed their tormentors and offered their own battered-wife syndrome as a defense (Ewing, 1987). This is a gendered variant of the argument that a person killed another in self-defense. U.S. criminal law has accepted a person's right to defend himself against another as long as he meets the following criteria: he has reason to believe that he is in imminent danger of death or serious bodily harm at the time of the killing, and he used force proportionate to that directed at him. This is called the "reasonable man" defense.

The circumstances under which women kill their abusers may not meet these criteria because their action is usually not in immediate response to an attack. These women often explain that they killed because they feared their abusers would kill them. Their advocates claim that they meet a "reasonable woman" standard. This standard asks juries to recognize that the psychological effects of abuse may have left a woman unable to fight back as a man might. Yet, she may resort to self-defensive acts that are appropriate to her situation as a battered woman.[12]

Conclusion

The political debates over the problem of the low economic status of women typically break down the question by centering on separate groups of women: teen mothers, divorced and widowed mothers, and elderly widows. Interested participants in the debate then tailor their explanations and policy solutions to respond to the perceived needs of a specific group. Not only are these policy debates often marginal to the business of legislatures and bureaucrats, they are also frequently ungendered, that is, they do not question the underlying assumptions about gender roles in private and public life.

What makes feminist analyses of public policy issues unique is that they place the question of gender—how a particular situation affects women and men differently—at the center of the debate. Thus, feminist approaches to questions of the economic status of women (as compared with that of men) look beyond the specific circumstances of a group of welfare mothers or elderly women to the gender dimensions of social structures and cultural patterns that produce and sustain specific instances of subordination of women. These larger gender frameworks interact with policy and practice to produce and maintain a lower economic status of women in all groups in society.

In American politics, sweeping reforms that overhaul segments of social life are extremely rare. The descriptions of policies in the chapters of this book demonstrate that laws tend to change in incremental ways and in response to specific needs. Looking at the results of this incremental decision making across the various issue areas pertaining to women's rights shows a pattern of contradictions and tensions over gender that illustrates as well as anything the conflict in society over the relations between women and men. While this is certainly a general social phenomenon, individual women find themselves caught in the cross-pressures of what is expected and rewarded in the family, at work, in politics, in intimate relations. Many women confront situations of great economic insecurity and dependency as a result.

Family law, for example, conveys mixed messages of self-sufficiency and dependency. For the most part, family laws have substituted assumptions of a division of labor in the home with assumptions that marriages are shared partnerships where men and women can share equally in caregiving and breadwinning. Divorce statutes encourage judges to end financial obligations between the spouses as soon as possible and to make their decisions about child custody and support in a neutral way. These laws can work fairly for those couples who have a marriage of shared roles and fairly equal responsibilities. However, in most marriages, division of labor remains separate. Wives have greater responsibility for home and family and have lower earning capacity than their husbands. For these women, the operation of family law can reinforce and increase their inferior economic position.

When we consider education and work policies, the double bind that faces women becomes clearer. Whereas family law is increasingly based on the assumption of interchangeable gender roles in families, education and work policies are most compatible with a separation of gender roles and responsibilities. Despite antidiscrimination legislation such as Title IX, gender bias remains in the education system. Boys and girls have formal equal opportunity in schools, but the effect of their education is to track them into different skills and occupations. An examination of the jobs that women hold reveals that they are the ones that fit most comfortably with expanded family duties based on the separate spheres ideology.

Laws relating to employment attack sex discrimination in favor of a policy of gender neutrality with respect to hiring and compensation. This means that women can succeed equally with men to the extent that their lives are like men's. Competing with men on an equal basis requires the ability to meet the demands of the workplace, which is usually structured according to assumptions of a separate-spheres ideology. Higher-wage jobs with benefits and status go to those who either have no families to care for or have someone else to do the caregiving. Women have the option, apparently, to choose between providing caregiving so their husbands can succeed in the better jobs or taking the jobs themselves and employing someone else to care for their children. The economic status of those who choose to follow the separate spheres model is secure as long as the marriage holds together. Divorce is a threat because, as we have seen, divorce courts are most friendly to those who followed a shared model of marriage.

Policies in areas of sexuality and reproductive rights reflect the same ambivalence over gender roles. Laws governing contraceptives and abortion are grounded in the legal doctrine of privacy. This leaves women alone to cope with the intense conflict over birth control and abortion that has dominated public debate for more than twenty-five years. This burden falls most heavily on poor girls and women. While welfare reformers blame poverty on the sexual promiscuity of teenage girls and welfare mothers, right-to-life advocates warn against sex education and contraceptive services and harass doctors who perform abortions.

Feminists link economic status and self-sufficiency to women's dignity and personal autonomy in matters relating to their sexuality; policy makers rarely make this connection. Surprisingly, the dignity and personal autonomy of women are not central to conventional policy debates and reforms relating to prostitution, rape, lesbianism, and pornography. Only feminist voices raise these issues. In one area they have had some success: sexual harassment law. What stands out about the debate and the resulting laws on sexual harassment is the linkage of men's sexual use of women to women's rights to education and employment opportunity. How many women have had to quit jobs (and find themselves ineligible for unemployment insurance as a result) because sexual harassment made their jobs too uncomfortable?

By looking at the interconnections among policy areas and women's economic status we can readily see that no one policy reform will succeed in attacking the feminization of poverty nor increase women's share of income and wealth in the United States. Advocates for women, both in Washington and in the fifty states, are aware of these interrelations and seek a range of policy reforms that cut across the work-family divide. Nancy Fraser (1994) identifies two models of reform: the universal breadwinner model and the caregiver parity model.

The universal breadwinner model advocates a set of policies to improve women's self-sufficiency through access to jobs that pay enough to support their families. Policy needs include bias-free education; better enforcement of equal-opportunity legislation; affirmative action for job training, hiring, and promotion; services for workers, such as paid family leave, child care, and elder care; eliminating sexist and racist stereotypes in education and the workplace; enforcement of anti–sexual harassment policies; knocking out the glass ceiling; and creating high-paying jobs for women.

The caregiver parity model reflects an attack on inferior economic status by increasing caregivers' access to income. This means policies to support mothers who care for children through more part-time work, flexible hours, family allowances, and paid family leave; generous alimony and child-support awards, vigorously enforced through the courts; and inclusion of homemakers and caregivers in insurance schemes now reserved for waged workers, such as pensions and health insurance.

Women's economic status would improve under both models (in the unlikely event that policies were adopted). Yet, comprehensive as these models are, they remain incomplete vehicles for achieving economic equality for men and women. As Fraser demonstrates, both models leave men's lives and roles largely untouched. Both also fail to draw connections between racism and ethnic bias and gender role inequities. Although some of the policies, such as affirmative action and improved alimony and child-support laws require some redistribution of resources from men to women, they do not change gender roles or relations. Equitable sharing of income and wealth will ultimately depend not only on a shift in gender-role assumptions underlying policy but also on changes in gender-role values and habits in society. In short, they depend on changes in men's responsibilities to make their lives more like women's by achieving shared contribution to caregiving. "The key to achieving gender equity in a postindustrial welfare state then is to make women's current life patterns the norm" (Fraser, 1994, p. 611).

Dismantling and reconstructing the gender-role system sounds revolutionary. However, the stories of women's rights policy debates in this book suggest that such a journey is well under way. Nineteenth-century leaders of the Woman Movement might disagree. Compare their demands in the 1848 Seneca Fall Declaration with contemporary demands of the women's lobby and you will find the agendas are similar in some ways. But unlike their ancestors, feminists of the twentieth and twenty-first centuries have not only challenged the inequities in law (and removed most of them), they have gone on to take on the assumptions of gender roles that sustain them, a campaign that promises to keep advocates for women's rights in the United States occupied for many years to come.

Notes

1. The federal government defines the level of income that marks the poverty level for various groups in the population. It is derived from data about the consumer price index and other living costs. The poverty level for 1995 for a family of four (two parents, two children under age eighteen) was $15,455 (U.S. Census Bureau. "Income and Poverty: 1995 Poverty Thresholds." U.S. Census Bureau Home Page, *The Official Statistics*, July 11, 1996.)

2. Sidel (1986, p. 15) credits Diana Pearce (1978) with coining the phrase *feminization of poverty*.

3. Senator Daniel Patrick Moynihan's work has been frequently cited to support this argument. His 1965 study "The Negro Family, the Case for National Action" described the black family as a "tangle of pathology," and he lamented the "reversal of roles of husband and wife" (Moynihan, 1967, pp. 29–30). The report caused a furor among civil rights activists, and a generation of black feminist scholars has provided evidence of the roots of black poverty in the economic structure and systems of racism and sexism. When Moynihan had opportunity to present a sequel in 1985 in *Family and Nation*, he extended his analysis of family breakdown and poverty to all races and cultures.

4. Efforts to cut spending in federal budgets have undermined financial support for job-training programs (see Chapter 7).

5. Before 1977, the minimum requirement was twenty years.

6. Some states require unisex insurance policies.

7. In 1989, the Supreme Court allowed retired military personnel to exclude their disability retirement pay from their divorce settlements (*Mansell v. Mansell*, 1989).

8. Some elderly women divest themselves ("spend down") to destitution because Supplemental Security Income comes with Medicaid, which covers long-term health care. Seventy-five percent of all aged recipients of SSI are women.

9. The issue has not left the public policy agenda since the 1970s, although it has not always been prominent at the national level. The 1995 trial of O. J. Simpson for the murder of his former wife, Nicole Simpson, gave the issue media attention.

10. Images of violence as inevitable, even desirable, were found in movies of the period. In *Gone with the Wind*, (1939), Rhett Butler, a dashing romantic hero, spends his time trying to force Scarlett O'Hara to love him. She realizes too late that she has been wrong to resist. *Carousel* (1954) shows leading man Billy Bigelow slapping his wife and his daughter; both agree that it "doesn't hurt at all." In *Streetcar Named Desire* (1951), Blanche is shocked to see her sister fall into the arms of her ardent husband moments after he has beaten her.

11. A key consciousness-raising book by Erin Pizzey came from England in 1974 with startling accounts from the Chiswick Women's Aid Centre.

12. The National Coalition Against Domestic Violence reports that a woman who kills her abuser is likely to spend more time in jail than an abusive man who is convicted of killing his partner (Lindgren and Taub, 1993, p. 349). The Justice Department reports that women are less likely to receive a prison sentence for spousal murder (U.S. Justice Department, Bureau of Justice Statistics, 1994).

References

American Association of University Women. *Women in Vocational Education.* 1989.

Amott, Teresa L. "Black Women and AFDC." In *Women, the State, and Welfare,* edited by Linda Gordon, pp. 280–298. Madison: University of Wisconsin Press, 1990.

Arizona Governing Committee v. Norris. 463 U.S. 1073. 1983.

Auletta, Ken. *The Underclass.* New York: Vintage Books, 1982.

Barusch, Amanda S. *Older Women in Poverty.* New York: Springer Publishing, 1994.

Bell, Marilyn J., ed. "Women As Elders: Images, Visions, and Issues." *Women and Politics* 6 (Summer 1986): entire issue.

Bergmann, Barbara. *The Economic Emergence of Women.* New York: Basic Books, 1986.

Blackstone, William. *Commentaries on the Laws of England,* Book 1, 14th ed. London: Strahan, 1803.

Clifford, Geraldine J. "'Marry, Stitch, Die, or Do Worse,' Educating Women for Work." In *Work, Youth, and Schooling: Historical Perspectives on Vocationalism in American Education,* edited by Harvey Kantor and David B. Tyak, pp. 223–268. Stanford, Calif.: Stanford University Press, 1982.

Erie, Steven P., Rein, Martin, and Wiget, Barbara. "Women and the Reagan Revolution: Thermidor for the Social Welfare Economy." In *Families, Politics, and Public Policy,* edited by Irene Diamond, pp. 94–119. New York: Longman, 1983.

Ewing, Charles Patrick. *Battered Women Who Kill.* Lexington, Mass.: Lexington Books, 1987.

Fagan, Jeffrey. *The Criminalization of Domestic Violence: Promises and Limits.* Washington, D.C.: National Institute of Justice, 1996.

Fraser, Nancy. "After the Family Wage: Gender Equity and the Welfare State." *Political Theory* 22 (November 1994): 591–618.

Funiciello, Theresa. *Tyranny of Kindness: Dismantling the Welfare System to End Poverty in America.* New York: Atlantic Monthly Press, 1993.

Gelb, Joyce. "The Politics of Wife Abuse." In *Families, Politics, and Public Policy,* edited by Irene Diamond, pp. 250–262. New York: Longman, 1983.

Gelb, Joyce, and Palley, Marian. *Women and Public Policies,* rev. ed. Princeton: Princeton University Press, 1987.

Gelpi, Barbara C., Hartsock, Nancy C. M., Novak, Clare C., and Strober, Myra H., eds. *Women and Poverty.* Chicago: University of Chicago Press, 1986.

Gordon, Linda, ed. *Women, the State, and Welfare.* Madison: University of Wisconsin Press, 1990.

Kamerman, Sheila B., and Kahn, Alfred J. *Mothers Alone: Strategies for a Time of Change.* Dover, Mass.: Auburn House, 1988.

King v. Smith. 392 U.S. 309. 1968.

Leader, Shela Gilbert. "Fiscal Policy and Family Structure." In *Families, Politics, and Public Policy,* edited by Irene Diamond, pp. 139–147. New York: Longman, 1983.

Lerman, Lisa. "Protection of Battered Women: A Survey of State Legislation." *Women's Rights Law Reporter* 6 (Summer 1980): 271–284.

Lindgren, J. Ralph, and Taub, Nadine. *The Law of Sex Discrimination,* 2nd. ed. Boulder: West Publishing, 1993.

Los Angeles Department of Water and Power v. Manhart. 435 U.S. 702. 1978.

McGlen, Nancy E., and O'Connor, Karen. *Women's Rights: The Struggle for Equality in the Nineteenth and Twentieth Centuries.* New York: Praeger, 1983.

Mansell v. Mansell. 109 S. Ct. 2023. 1989.

Miller, Dorothy C. *Women and Social Welfare: A Feminist Analysis.* New York: Praeger, 1990.

Moynihan, Daniel Patrick. *Family and Nation.* San Diego: Harcourt Brace, 1986.

Moynihan, Daniel Patrick. "The Negro Family: The Case for National Action." In *The Moynihan Report and the Politics of Controversy,* edited by Lee Rainwater and William L. Yancey, pp. 39–124. Cambridge: M.I.T. Press, 1967.

Murray, Charles. *Losing Ground.* New York: Basic Books, 1984.

National Coalition on Women, Work and Welfare Reform. "Perspectives on Women and Welfare Employment." In *Welfare Reform*, U.S. House of Representatives. Committee on Ways and Means. Subcommittee on Public Assistance and Unemployment Compensation, pp. 50–57. Washington, D.C.: GPO, January–March 1987.

Nelson, Barbara. "The Origins of the Two Channel Welfare State: Workmen's Compensation and Mothers' Aid." In *Women, the State and Welfare*, edited by Linda Gordon, pp. 123–151. Madison: University of Wisconsin Press, 1990.

Norris, Donald F., and Thompson, Lyke, eds. *The Politics of Welfare Reform*. Thousand Oaks, Calif.: Sage Publications, 1995.

NOW-Legal Defense Education Fund, and O'Leary, Renee Cherow. *State-by-State Guide to Women's Rights*. New York: McGraw-Hill, 1987.

Ozawa, Martha N. "The Economic Status of Vulnerable Older Women." *Social Work* 40 (May 1995): 323–331.

Ozawa, Martha N., ed. *Women's Life Cycle and Economic Insecurity: Problems and Proposals*. New York: Greenwood Press, 1989.

Pearce, Diana M. "The Feminization of Poverty: A Second Look." Paper presented at the annual meeting of the American Sociological Assocation, 1989.

Pearce, Diana M. "The Feminization of Poverty: Women, Work, and Welfare." *Urban and Social Change Review* 2 (February 1978): 28–36.

Pizzey, Erin. *Scream Quietly or the Neighbours Will Hear*. Harmondsworth, England: Penguin, 1974.

Pleck, Elizabeth. *Domestic Tyranny*. New York: Oxford University Press, 1987.

Radford, Jill, and Russell, Diana E. H., eds. *Femicide*. New York: Twayne, 1992.

Schaffer, Diane M. "The Feminization of Poverty: Prospects for an International Feminist Agenda." In *Women, Power, and Policy*, edited by Ellen Boneparth and Emily Stoper, pp. 223–246. New York: Pergamon, 1988.

Sidel, Ruth. *Women and Children Last*. New York: Penguin, 1986.

Skocpol, Theda. *Protecting Soldiers and Mothers: The Political Origins of Social Policy in the United States*. Cambridge: Belknap/Harvard University Press, 1992.

Spalter-Roth, Roberta, and Hartmann, Heidi. "Dependency on Men, the Market, or the State: The Rhetoric and Reality of Welfare Reform." *IWPR Report*, Washington, D.C., 1995.

Thomas, Susan. *Gender and Poverty*. New York: Garland Publishing, 1994.

United Nations. *The World's Women, 1995: Trends and Statistics*. New York: United Nations, 1995.

U.S. Census Bureau. "Income and Poverty: 1995 Poverty Thresholds." U.S. Census Bureau Home Page, *The Official Statistics*, July 11, 1996.

U.S. Congress. Congressional Budget Office. *Work-Related Programs for Welfare Recipients*. Washington, D.C.: GPO, April 1987.

U.S. House of Representatives. Committee on Governmental Operations. *Barriers to Self-Sufficiency for Single Female Heads of Families*. Washington, D.C.: GPO, July 9 and 10, 1985.

U.S. House of Representatives. Committee on Ways and Means. Subcommittee on Public Assistance and Unemployment Compensation. *Welfare Reform*. Washington, D.C.: GPO, January–March 1987.

U.S. House of Representatives. Select Committee on Aging. "Living in the Shadows: Older Women and the Roots of Poverty." Washington, D.C.: GPO, 1992.

U.S. Justice Department. Bureau of Justice Statistics. "Domestic Violence: Violence Between Intimates." *Selected Findings*. Washington, D.C.: GPO, November 1994.

Warlick, Jennifer L. "Aged Women in Poverty: A Problem Without a Solution." In *Aging and Public Policy*, edited by William P. Browne and Laura Katz Olson, pp. 35–66. Westport, Conn.: Greenwood Press, 1983.

West, Guida. *The National Welfare Rights Movement*. New York: Praeger, 1981.

Wolfe, Leslie, and Copeland, Lois. "Violence Against Women as Bias-Motivated Hate Crime: Defining the Issues in the USA." In *Women and Violence*, edited by Miranda Davies, pp. 200–213. London: Zed Books, 1994.

Woolf, Virginia. *A Room of One's Own*. San Diego: Harcourt Brace, 1989. Originally
    published in 1929.
Zinn, Maxine Baca. "Family, Race, and Poverty in the Eighties." *Signs* 14 (1989): 856–
    874.

Index

Abolitionist position on prostitution, 298–300

Abortion, 109–131
    contemporary debate about, 125–127
    clinic access, 123
    criminalization of, 109–110
    husband's consent to, 119–120
    Medicaid payments for, 114–115
    parental consent to, 120
    provision in Pregnancy Discrimination Act, 267
    public opinion on, 126
    rates in the United States, 118

Abortion law(s)
    administrative hurdles in, 119–121
    reform/repeal of, 110–112
    Planned Parenthood v. Casey, 121–123, 124–125
    Roe v. Wade, 112–114, 124–125

Abortion rights organizations, 111, 121

Abzug, Bella, 78

Acquaintance rape, 314

Act for Better Child Care (ABC), 281–282

Act for Suppression of Trade in and Circulation of Obscene Literature and Articles of Immoral Use, 301–302

Adams, Abigail, 62–63

Adarand Constructors v. Pena, 242

Adkins v. Children's Hospital, 222

Admission policy, under Title IX, 147–148

Adolescent Family Life Act, 117

Affirmative action, 233–235, 240–242, 244–245. *See also* Positive discrimination; Reverse discrimination

African American women, 105, 179, 291, 350. *See also* Black women, Women of color
    economic status of, 334, 336
    political participation of, 86–87, 89
    and sterilization, 108
    work status of, 224, 250–251

Against Our Will, 310

Age laws
    constitutionality of, 38, 39–40
    marriage, 184
    sexual consent, 294

Agenda for public policy. *See* Public agenda

Aid to Dependent Children (ADC), 340

Aid to Families with Dependent Children (AFDC), 340–346. *See also* Welfare reform, Family Support Act, and Personal Responsibility and Work Opportunity Reconciliation Act
    as child care measure, 275–276
    unemployed parent option, 340

AIDS, 300, 324

Akron v. Akron Center for Reproductive Health, 120

Alaska, 47–48

Albright, Madeleine K., 75, 76

Alimony, 197–198

Alliance of equals in marriage, 193–194

American Association of Retired Persons (AARP), 274–275

American Association of University Women
    (AAUW), 158, 223
American Birth Control League (ABCL), 100
American Booksellers Association, Inc. v.
    Hudnut, 304–305
American Civil Liberties Union (ACLU), 34–
    35, 297
American Federation of Labor (AFL), 225
American Federation of State, County and
    Municipal Employees (AFSCME), 268
American Law Institute (ALI), 111–112, 297,
    309, 310, 312
American Medical Association (AMA), 109,
    263
Anderson, Marie, 78
Antenuptial marriage settlements, 179
Anthony, Susan B., 25, 63, 65, 73, 143
Antioch College, 314
Antipornography feminists, 304–306
Appointments of women, 74–79
Arena of public policy debate, 3–4
Arizona, 192
Arizona Governing Committee v. Norris, 352
Article III, 213 (note 1)
Artificial insemination, 127, 134 (note 19)
Athletics, 150–155
Atlanta, 323
Attorney General's Commission on
    Pornography, 302, 303

Baby "M", 130
Baird, Zoe, 283
Battered wife syndrome, 357
Battered women, 354–360. *See also* Domestic
    violence
    interspousal immunity and, 187
Bayh, Senator Birch, 37
Beal v. Doe, 133 (note 13)
Belotti v. Baird, 120
Bennett, Senator Wallace, 242
Bennett Amendment, 242, 248
Best interests of the child, 202
BFOQ (Bonafide occupational qualification),
    236–238
Bill of Rights for Homemakers, 193, 213 (note
    4)
Birth control campaign, 100–101
Blackmun, Justice Harry, 38–39, 40, 113

Black women. *See also* African American
    women, Women of color
    on ERA, 31
    prostitution arrests of, 299
    sexual exploitation of, 291
    support for suffrage, 66
Blackstone, William, 355
Blackstone's commentaries, 179, 188. *See also*
    Common law
Bolling v. Sharpe, 56 n 6
Borshevsky, Charlene, 76
Bowers v. Hardwick, 322
Bradley, Justice, 25
Bradwell, Myra Colby, 25, 26
Bradwell v. Illinois, 25–26
Brandeis, Louis, 221
Brandeis brief, 221
Breckrinridge, Sophonisba, 71
Brennan, Justice William, 40, 56 (note 7), 121
Breyer, Justice Steven, 286 (note 6)
Brown University, 154–155
Brown v. Board of Education, 145, 162, 229
Browner, Carol, 76
Brownmiller, Susan, 304, 310
Burden of proof, 239–240
Burn, Harry T., 90 (note 5)
Bush, President George, 75, 76, 119, 121, 122,
    271–272, 282
Business and Professional Women's Clubs,
    National Federation of, 30, 234
Business necessity, 237, 239
Burger, Chief Justice Warren, 34, 40
Butler, Josephine, 294

Caban v. Mohammad, 210
Cable Act, 85
Califano v. Goldfarb, 39
California, 43, 111, 192, 196, 267, 269–270
California Federal Savings and Loan v. Guerra,
    269–270
Campaign to End Discrimination Against
    Pregnant Workers, 266–267
Cannon v. University of Chicago, 155
Capitalism, 336–337
Capital punishment, 308, 312
Caregiver parity model, 363
Carey v. Population Services International, 104

Carl Perkins Vocational Education Act (1984), 160, 348
Carlson v. Carlson, 186
Carter, President Jimmy, 75, 76, 77–78
Carter, Rosalyn, 75
Catholic church, 100, 102, 132–133 (note 6)
Cellar, Rep. Emanuel, 37
"Chastity clinics", 117
Childbirth and work, 260–275
Child-Care and Dependent-Care Tax Credit, 282
Child Care and Development Block Grant (1990), 282
Child-care policy, 275–284
   in vocational/job training acts, 348
   in welfare policy, 275–276
Child development, 276
Child Development Act (1971), 276–279
Child custody
   feminist views of, 206–207
   in divorce, 202–203
   lesbian rights in, 322
   out of wedlock, 209–211
Child Custody Jurisdiction Act, 214 n 15
Child Support, Office of, 204–205
Child support laws, 203–205, 209–210
Child Support Recovery Act, 204–205
Chilly climate, 160
Choice in family planning, 102–104
Citizens' Advisory Council on the Status of Women (CACSW)
   endorses ERA, 36
   established, 77
   on Executive Order 11375, 234
   proposes pregnancy as disability, 264–265
Citizenship rights, 85. *See also Minor v. Happersett*
Civil liberties. *See* American Civil Liberties Union; Libertarian Views
Civil Rights Act (1964). *See also* Title VII; Equal Employment Opportunity Commission
   affirmative action under, 233–234
   enactment of, 229
Civil Rights Act (1991), 233, 240, 320
   creates Glass Ceiling Commission, 245
Civil rights movement, 145–146, 229, 230
Civil Rights Restoration Act (1988), 157–158

Clarke, Edward H., 144
Clay, Rep. William, 271
Cleveland Board of Education v. LaFleur, 266
Clinton, Hillary Rodham, 75, 76
Clinton, President Bill, 75, 76, 79, 123, 272, 325, 345
Coeducation, 140–145
Cohabitation laws, 208
Cohen v. Brown University, 154
Coker v. Georgia, 312
Colorado, 47–48, 111, 328 (note 11)
Commission on Obscenity and Pornography (1970), 302–303
Commission on Population and Family Planning, 104
Commissions on the status of women, State, 77–79, 230, 231–232
Common law
   abortion under, 109
   age at marriage under, 184
   cohabitation under, 208
   divorce under, 194
   of marital property, 191
   of marriage, 178–181
   on out-of-wedlock child, 209
   parental rights under, 201–202
   of rape, 307–309
   wife abuse under, 355
Common-law marriage, 214 (note 16)
Common schools, 140
Community Facilities Act (1941), 275
Community-property regimes
   in divorce, 198
   Kirchberg v. Feenstra, 39
   in marriage, 192–193
Community Work and Training Program, 343
Comparable work, 228
Comparable worth, 245–248
Comprehensive Employment and Training Act (CETA) (1973), 348
Comstock, Anthony, 98–99,
Comstock Act (1873), 98–99, 104, 301–302
Conceptual framework, 6–8, 113
Congress of Industrial Organization (CIO), 225
Congressional Caucus on Women's Issues, 71–72, 352

Connecticut, 47, 102–103, 286 (note 4), 247, 269
Consent in rape cases, 308–309, 312
Consortium, 190–191
Constitution, Amendment process of, 44–45
Constitutionality, Tests of, 27, 35–36
Contact sports, 149, 152
    definition of, 170 (note 5)
Contagious Diseases Acts, 294
Contingent work force, 286 (note 7)
Contraception, 97–108
Contract, marriage, 178
Contract compliance, federal, 233–235
Contract law
    for cohabiting couples, 208
    and protective labor legislation, 220
    surrogacy under, 127–130
Contract With America, 106–161
Cornelia Whitner v. South Carolina, 130–131
Corroboration in rape cases, 309, 311
Counseling, sex specific, 149
County of Washington v. Gunther, 248
Coverture, 178–81
COYOTE (Call Off Your Old Tired Ethics), 299–300
Craig v. Boren, 39–42
Crawford v. Cushman, 266
Credit, equal rights to, 200
Criminal conversation, 191
Criminalization
    of abortion, 109–110
    of prostitution, 295–297

Dalkon shield, 106
Date rape, 314
Day care. *See* Definition of issues, Child-care policy
Death penalty, 308, 312
Debates. *See* Definition of issues; Public debates
Declaration of Sentiments (Seneca Falls Declaration), 63–64, 173
Decriminalization of prostitution, 298–300
Defense Advisory Committee on Women in the Service (DACOWITS), 79
Definition of issues, 3
    abortion, 109–110, 113, 115–116, 117–118, 131–132

child care, 277–279, 280–283
contraception, 97–105
education, 138–139, 143–145, 145–146
Equal Rights Amendment, 55
family law, 174–177
lesbian rights, 320–326
pornography, 301, 303–304
poverty, 334–338
pregnancy, 264–266, 270–271
prostitution, 292–295, 295–296, 298–299
rape, 307–316
reproductive policy, 96–97
sexual harassment, 316–320
sexuality, 290–292
surrogate motherhood, 127–130
voting rights for women, 62–69
woman battery, 354–360
work and women, 217–219
work and family, 258–260
Democratic party, 31, 73, 82–83
Democratic theory, 87–89
Dependent care, 273–275
Dependent-Care Assistance Program, 282
Dependent Care Planning and Development Grant, 274
Diaz v. Pan American, 236–237
Differences, sex and gender. *See* Equality/ difference debate
Disability, pregnancy as, 264–268
Disparate impact, 42, 238–240
Disparate treatment, 238
Displaced homemakers, 348–349
Divorce, 194–200
Doctrine of necessaries, 188–190
Doe v. Bolton, 114
Dole, Elizabeth H., 76
Domestic partners, 323
Domestic violence, 355, 357–360. *See also* Battered women
Domicile laws, 85, 185–186
"Don't ask, don't tell" policy, 325
Douglas, Justice William O., 38, 39, 40, 103
Draft, registration for, 43–44
Dual labor market, 247, 337
Due Process Clause, 24
Dukakis, Michael, 282
Dworkin, Andrea, 304–305

Economic dependency, 339–354
  battered women and, 354–360
  of homemakers, 350–354
  no-fault divorce and, 199–201
  women's rights and, 360–363
Economic Equity Act (EEA) (1982–1986), 353
Economic Recovery Act (1981), 274
Egalitarian feminism, 12, 30, 224, 262–263
Eisenhower, President Dwight, 75, 76, 102
Eisenstadt v. Baird, 103–104
Elderly people, 273–275, 350–354
Election laws, 86
Elementary education, 140
Elementary and Secondary Education Act
  (ESEA) (1994), 160
Elison v. Brady, 318
EMILY'S List, 74
Emotive-symbolic issues, 96
Enforcement
  child-support laws, 203–205
  domestic-violence laws, 357–360
  equal opportunity laws, 235–243
  Equal Pay Act, 242–243
  Executive Order 11375, 234–235
  marital-support laws, 188–190
  power of EEOC, 232–233
  prostitution laws, 298–299
  Title IX, 155–158
Equal Credit Opportunity Act (1974), 200
Equal distribution of property in divorce, 198
Equal Employment Opportunity
  Commission (EEOC) 231–233, 317
Equal employment opportunity policy
  (EEO), 226–248
Equal Pay Act (1963), 226–229, 242–243
Equal pay legislation, 226–229, 242–243
Equal Protection Clause, 21, 25
  illegitimacy under, 209
  and lesbian rights, 324–325
  litigation of 1973–1982, 38–44
  and pregnancy leave, 265–266
  race discrimination, effect on, 26
  and single sex schools, 164–167
  tests of constitutionality under, 35–36
Equal Rights Amendment (ERA), 29–33,
  44–47
  campaign and family law, 193

  effect of, on Supreme Court, 36
  efforts to reintroduce, 49
  in state constitutions, 47–48
  and support obligation, 188
Equal rights ideology, 33
Equal Status Bill, 31–32
Equal work, 228–229
Equality/difference debate
  in athletics, 152
  on constitutional law, 21–24, 44, 48–52
  and family law, 212–213
  feminist deconstruction of, 89
  and women's political rights, 61–62
  and work/family policy, 270
Equality legislation, 224–248
Erotica, 304
Ervin, Senator Sam, 37
Estrich, Susan, 314
Eugenics issue, 100–101
Executive Orders 11246 and 11375, 146, 233–
  235
  and child care, 279

Facially neutral job qualifications, 242–243
FACT (Feminist Anti-Censorship Task Force),
  306
Fair Labor Standards Act (1938), 227, 228
Families without marriage, 207–212
Family and Medical Leave Act (FMLA)
  (1993), 271–273, 274–275
Family expense statutes, 188
Family law. *See also* Divorce; Marriage law;
  Parental rights and responsibilities
  and economic status of women, 198–201,
  249–250
  and political opportunity, 84–85
Family Leave Tax Credit Act, 272
Family planning, 101–105
Family Planning Services and Population
  Research Act (1970), 104
Family Support Act (1988), 209, 276, 343–
  345, 348
Family values ideology, 283
Family wage, 227
Fathers' rights
  to child custody, 202–203
  in marriage, 201–202
  out of wedlock, 208–211

Fault
   in alimony settlements, 197–198
   in property distribution, 198
Federal Council on Women (FCW), 79
Feeney. See *Personnel Administrator of
   Massachusetts v. Feeney*
Femicide, 358
Feminism, 10–11. *See also* Feminist debates;
   Feminist demands
   antipornography, 303–306
   egalitarian, 30, 224, 262–263
   free speech, 305–306
   liberal, 12, 51–52, 290–292, 298–301, 311–
     312
   radical, 12, 111–112, 291, 303–306
   social, 12, 30, 224, 261–263
   women of color, 13
Feminist debates
   constitutional equality, 48–54
   divorce, 194–195, 198–201
   family law, 175, 177
   general description of, 11–13
   homemakers, 199–201
   joint custody, 205–206
   marriage law, 193–194
   maternity/parental leave, 268–269
   motherhood, 260–261
   new reproductive technology, 129, 130–131
   non-marital parents, 211
   parental rights laws, 205–207
   pornography, 303–306
   poverty, 336
   prostitution, 298–300
   protective laws, 223–224
   rape laws, 310–312
   sexuality, 290–292, 320–321
   single-sex schools, 162–164
   surrogacy, 128
   woman battery, 355–356
   women's political participation, 88–89
Feminist demands
   abortion, 116
   athletics, 105–155
   birth-control campaign, 101
   child care, 277–278
   comparable worth, 245–246
   contraceptives, 99–100
   displaced homemakers, 348–349

   divorce reform, 198–202
   equal credit, 200
   equal education, 145–148
   equal pay, 226–229
   family law reform, 175–177, 212–213
   job training, 348–350
   lesbian rights, 322–324
   married women's rights, 179–181
   older women, 350–354
   prostitution, 293–295, 298–299
   rape law reform, 310–312
   sexual harassment, 316–320
   Violence Against Women Act, 358–359
   unmarried mothers, 211
   welfare reform, 346
   woman battery, 356–357
Feminist lobby, 71–72
Feminist Press, 169
Feminization of poverty, 4, 334–336, 336–338
Femme couverte, 179
Ferraro, Geraldine, 73, 83
Fetal-protection policies, 251–252
Fetal rights, 112–113, 130
Fetal viability, 113, 119–120, 122
Fifty-fifty laws, 72–73, 77
Financial aid, 149
Finkbine, Sherri, 111
Florida, 28, 48, 77, 130, 323
Florida v. Johnson, 130
Forbush v. Wallace, 185
Ford, President Gerald, 75, 76, 77
Fourteenth Amendment, 24, 65, 164–167. *See
   also* Equal Protection Clause; Due
   Process Clause
   judicial interpretation (1868–1963), 24–29
   judicial interpretation (1970–1973), 34–38
   judicial interpretation (1973–1982), 38–44
Frankfurter, Justice Felix, 27
Franklin, Barbara, 76
Franklin v. Guinnett Cty. Public Schools, 155–
   156, 320
Fraser, Nancy, 362, 363
Fraternities, 150
Free dealer statutes, 191, 213 n 6
Free speech advocates, 99. *See also* Libertarian
   views, American Civil Liberties Union
Free speech feminists, 305–306

Freedom of Access to Clinic Entrances (FACE) Act (1994), 123
Freedom of Choice Act, 122
Freeman, Jo, 80
Friedan, Betty, 268–269, 270
Frontiero v. Richardson, 35–36
Fruits of Philosophy, 98

Gay rights movement, 324
Gay rights ordinances, 324–325
Geduldig v. Aiello, 265–266
Gender, definition of, 10
Gender balance bills, 77
Gender-based job segregation, 243–248
Gender Bias Study Commission (Florida), 327 (note 2)
Gender equity in education, 145–162
Gender gap, 79–84
Gender neutrality, 7, 50–51
Gender roles
  definition of, 10
  family, 175–177, 178–179
  marriage, 178–83, 193–194
  poverty, 334–336, 337
  race and sexuality, 319–320
  work, 217–219
Gender role system, 362–363
General Electric v. Gilbert, 265–266
Georgia, 43
Ginsburg, Justice Ruth Bader, 39, 44, 49,
  opinion in *U.S. v. Virginia*, 166
  and Women's Rights Project, 35
Girls' schools, 142, 147, 162–167
Glass ceiling, 244–245
Glass Ceiling Commission, 79, 245
Goesaert v. Cleary, 27
Goldmark, Josephine, 221
Green, Edith, 146–147
Griffin, Susan, 310
Griffiths, Martha, 37
Griggs v. Duke Power Co., 239–240
Griswold v. Connecticut, 102–103
Grove City College v. Bell, 156–157
Gyno-thanatica, 304

Hale, Lord Matthew, 308
Hale jury instruction, 308, 311
Hall, Radclyffe, 328 (note 10)

Harlan, Justice, 56 (note 4)
Harris, Patricia Roberts, 76
Harris v. Forklift Systems, 319
Harris v. McRae, 115, 133 (note 13)
Hawaii, 45, 47, 267, 323
Hayden, Senator Carl, 32
Hayden Amendment, 32
Head Start Program, 276
Heckler, Margaret M., 76
Heightened scrutiny. *See* Middle-level scrutiny
Herman, Alexis, 76
Higher education, 142–143
Hill, Anita, 319–320
Hills, Carla, 75, 76
Hispanic/Latina women
  capitalism and, 336
  elderly, 350
  EEO policy effects on, 251
  poverty status of, 334
  sexuality and, 291
  sterilization and, 108
Homemakers, 199–201. *See also* Displaced homemakers
Homemakers Bill of Rights (NOW), 352–353
Homosexuality, 321. *See also* Lesbian issues; Gay rights movement
Hostile environment, 318, 319, 328 (note 8)
Howe, Florence, 169
Hoyt v. Florida, 28
Hufstedler, Shirley, 76
Human Life Amendment, 118
Hurston, Zora Neale, 218
Husband and wife. *See* Wife and husband
Hyde, Representative Henry, 114
Hyde Amendment, 114–115

Idaho, 34, 192
Illegitimacy, 209
Illinois, 26, 47, 68, 77
Immer v. Risko, 187
Immigrant women, 283
Income security policies, 339–354
Indianapolis, 304–305
Insurance, 350–354
Interest groups, 70–72
International Women's Year (IWY) Conference (Houston), 45, 77, 78, 182–183, 311, 323–324

Internet, 306
Interspousal immunity, 186–187
Iowa, 48, 77, 247
Irving, John, 141
Issues, definition of, 3. *See also* Definition of issues; Public debates

J.E.B. v. Alabama ex rel T.B., 41, 50, 86
Job-evaluation plans, 246
Job Opportunities and Basic Skills (JOBS) Act (1988), 348
Job segregation, 243–248
Job training, 347–350
Job Training Partnership Act (JTPA) (1982), 245, 348
Johnson, President Lyndon B., 104, 148, 234, 302, 303
Johnson v. Transportation Agency of Santa Clara County, 240–242
Joint custody, 203, 205–206
Joyce, Teresa, 240–241
Judicial review, 23, 38–42
Jury duty, 27–28, 85–86
Jury instructions, 308

Kahn v. Shevin, 39
Kennedy, Justice Anthony M., 120
Kennedy, President John F., 75
Kentucky, 60
King v. Smith, 341
Kinsey reports, 102, 321
Kirchberg v. Feenstra, 39
Kirkpatrick, Jean J., 76
Kirstein v. University of Virginia, 164–165
Klein, Viola, 259
Knowlton, Charles, 98
Korematsu v. U.S., 56 (note 6)
Kreps, Juanita M., 76

Labor markets, 247, 337
Land-grant colleges, 143
Lanham Act (1941), 275
League of Women Voters (LWV), 68–69, 80, 223, 269
Lehr v. Robertson, 210
Lesbian feminism, 322
Lesbian issues, 320–326
Levy v. Louisiana, 209

Liberal feminism. *See also* Reform feminism
definition of, 12
gender neutrality, 51–52
lesbian issues, 322–323
prostitution, 298–300
rape-law reform, 311–312
sexuality, 290–292
Liberalism, 286 (note 1)
Libertarian views
antipornography feminists, 304
homosexuality, 321
pornography, 301
sexuality, 290–292
Living together, 207–212
Los Angeles Department of Water and Power v. Manhart, 352
Louisiana, 192, 213 (note 7)
Loving v. Virginia, 183, 213 (note 5)
Lucas, Rita C., 214 (note 11)
Lump sum alimony, 197

MacKinnon, Catharine, 304–305
Maher v. Roe, 114–115
Maine, 48
Malthusians, 97–98
"Man in the house" rules, 341
Mann Act, 295–296
Manpower Development and Training Act, 348
Mansell v. Mansell, 214 (note 10)
Marital breakdown, 196–197
Marital property systems, 191–193
Marital rape, 308, 312–314
Marital services, 190–191
Marital support, 187–190
Marriage contracts, 178
Marriage law, 178–194
Married women's citizenship rights, 85
Married women's legal disabilities, 179
Married Women's Property Acts (MWPA), 179–181, 185–187
Marshall, Justice Thurgood, 40, 269–270
Martin, Lynn, 76
Marvin, Lee and Michele, 214 (note 17)
Maryland, 47, 179
Massachusetts, 42, 47, 103–104, 221, 269
Maternal health policy, 262–263
Maternal thinking, 261

Maternity/parental leave, 268–273
Maternity protection, 261–264
Maynard v. Hill, 178
McCorvey, Norma, 112, 133 (note 9)
McGuire v. McGuire, 188
McLaughlin, Ann Dore, 76
Medicaid, 133 (note 12)
    funds for abortion, 114–116
Medicalization of issues, 100, 105
    abortion, 109–110, 115–116
    pregnancy, 130, 132
Meese Commission, 302, 303
Men, 10. *See also* Fathers' rights; Wife and
    husband
Men's sports, 154–155
Men's voting bloc, 84
Meritor Savings Bank, FSB v. Vinson, 317–318
Michael H. v. Gerald D., 211
Michael M. v. Superior Court of Sonoma
    County, California, 8–9, 43, 43–44
Michigan, 27, 47
Middle-level scrutiny, 39–42, 50
Military
    lesbians in, 322, 325
    pensions, 199
    schools, 147, 163–64, 165–67
    sexual harassment in, 320
    status of women and men in, 43–44, 24
Miller, Frieda, 31
Miller, Rep. George, 280
Miller test of obscenity, 301–302
Miller v. California, 301–302
Miller-Wohl v. Commissioner of Labor and
    Industry, State of Montana, 269
Millington v. Southeastern Elevator Co., 190
Minimum guaranteed income, 341
Minimum wage laws, 221–222
Minneapolis antipornography ordinance,
    304–305
Minnesota, 247
Minor, Virginia, 25
Minor v. Happersett, 65
Minors, 104
Mississippi, 179
Mississippi University for Women, 165
Mississippi v. Hogan, 41, 42, 165
Missouri, 120–121
Model Penal code, 309–310

"Mommy" track, 286 (note 8)
Mondale, Senator Walter, 73, 83, 278–279
Montana, 47–48, 77, 182, 269
Montana Maternity Leave Act (MMLA), 269
Montana School of Mines, 170 (note 2)
Moralist-libertarian debate, 290–292
    homosexuality, 321
    pornography, 301
    sexuality issues, 290
Morgan, Robin, 303–304
Motherhood, 260–261
Mothers' pension plans, 340
Mothers' rights, 201–202
    to child custody in divorce, 202–203
    feminist demands for, 205–207, 211
    lesbian, 322
    to out-of-wedlock children, 208–211
Motor voter laws, 87
Moynihan, Senator Daniel P., 364 (note 3)
Muller v. Oregon, 27, 221, 261–262
Multiple consciousness, 88–89
Murray, Pauli, 28, 29
Myrdal, Alva, 259

Name
    of child, 202
    in marriage, 184–185
"Nannygate", 286 (note 6)
Nashville Gas Co. v. Satty, 266
National Abortion Rights Action League
    (NARAL), 121
National Advisory Committee for Women,
    77–78
National Advisory Council on Women's
    Educational Programs, 79, 158
National Coalition Against Domestic
    Violence, 356
National Coalition for Women and Girls in
    Education (NCWGE), 1, 148, 152, 158,
    160
National Collegiate Athletics Association
    (NCAA), 150–152
National Committee to Defeat the Unequal
    Rights Amendment (NCDURA), 31–32
National Conference of Commissioners on
    Uniform State Laws, 174
National Consumers' League (NCL), 221, 223,
    261

National Lesbian and Gay Task Force (NLGTF), 324
National Organization for Women (NOW), 182
  abortion reform, 111
  athletics, 152
  Bill of Rights for Homemakers, 352–353
  brief in *Calfed* case, 269
  child-care proposals, 277–278
  education, 146
  Equal Rights Amendment campaign, 36–37, 46–47
  Executive Order 11375, 233–235
  founded in 1966, 231
  goals for men as parents, 206–207
  homemakers, 193
  lesbian issues, 323
National Woman's Party (NWP), 72, 80
  equality for women workers, 223–224
  ERA, 29–31
  Executive Order 11375, 234
  Sheppard-Towner Act, 263
  state ERAs, 47
  Title VII, 229–230
National Women's Political Caucus (NWPC), 81
National Women's Suffrage Association, 67
Native American women, 126. *See also* Women of color
Nebraska, 188
Necessaries, Doctrine of, 188–189
Nevada, 192, 298
Newbury v. Board of Public Education, 170 (note 8)
New Hampshire, 47
New Jersey, 60, 90 (note 6), 267
New Mexico, 47, 192
New reproductive technology, 127–131
New York, 112, 180, 247, 267, 323
Nineteenth Amendment, 66–69, 90 (note 5)
Nixon, President Richard, 77, 78, 277, 278, 279
No-fault divorce, 195–197
Nontraditional Employment for Women (NEW) Act (1991), 348
Normal schools, 143
Norplant, 106
North Carolina, 111

North Dakota, 77
North Haven v. Bell, 156
Norton, Eleanor Holmes, 253 (note 7)

Obscenity, pornography as, 301–303
Obscenity laws, 97–100
O'Connor, Justice Sandra Day, 38, 120, 154, 155–156
Office of Federal Contract Compliance (OFCC), 234
Ohio, 220
Oklahoma, 39–42
Old Age and Survivors Insurance (OASI), 350–354
Older Americans, 273–275
Older women, 350–354
O'Leary, Hazel Rollins, 76
Omnibus Budget Reconciliation Act (OBRA) (1981), 344
Operation Rescue, 123
Opportunity structure, 60–61, 84–87
Ordinary scrutiny, 28, 35–36, 40–42
Oregon, 221, 247, 314
Orr v. Orr, 39, 56 (note 7), 197
Out-of-wedlock children, 43, 208–211

PACs (Political Action Committees), 74
Palimony, 214 (note 17)
Parental consent
  for abortion, 120, 121–123
  for marriage, 184
Parental leave, 268–273
Parent Locator Services, 204
Parental rights and responsibilities, 201–205, 208–211
Paris Adult Theater 1 v. Slaton, 302
Parity, 89
Parnham v. Hughes, 43, 209
Paternity suits, 209–210
Paul, Alice, 29–31
Pennsylvania, 47, 48, 77, 121, 165, 182
Pensions, 350–354
Perkins Vocational Education Act, 160, 348
Permanent alimony, 197
Personal Responsibility and Work Opportunity Reconciliation Act (1996), 343

Personnel Administrator of Massachusetts v. Feeney, 42, 239
Peterson, Esther, 32–33, 228, 264
Philadelphia, 165
Pizzey, Erin, 364 (note 11)
Planned Parenthood Federation of America (PPFA), 101–105, 269
Planned Parenthood v. Casey, 121–123, 124–125
Planned Parenthood v. Danforth, 119–120
Plessy v. Ferguson, 26, 56 (note 4)
Poelker v. Doe, 133 (note 13)
Pogrebin, Letty Cottin, 328 (note 7)
Policy communities, 5–6, 223
Policy-making process, 2–9
Political opportunity structure, 84–87
Political parties, 72–74, 83–84
Pornography, 300–306
Positive discrimination, 39, 42, 56 (note 7)
Poverty level, 364 (note 1)
Powell, Justice Lewis, 40
Pregnancy, 260–275
Pregnancy Discrimination Act (PDA) (1978), 267–268, 269–270
Prenuptial contracts, 178
President's Advisory Commission for Women (President Carter), 78
President's Commission on the Status of Women (President Kennedy)(PCSW), 14, 77
　compromise on ERA, 23,33
　endorses equal pay law, 228
　on education, 145
　on pregnancy leave, 264
President's Interagency Council on Women (President Clinton), 79
President's Task Force on Women's Rights and Responsibilities (President Nixon), 14, 36, 77, 78, 146
Price Waterhouse v. Hopkins, 245
Primary-caregiver laws, 203
Privacy, 103–104, 237. See also *Roe v. Wade*
Privileges and Immunities Clause, 24, 65, 90 (note 4)
Pro-choice/Pro-life debate, 116–119, 121–123
Pro-life activists, 114, 116–121
Pronatalism, 96, 132 (note 1), 259
Property division in divorce, 198
Prostitutes, 299–300

Prostitution, 292–300
Protective labor laws, 30, 31, 219–224, 231–232, 261–263
Public agenda, 4–5
Public arena, 3–4
Public debates. *See also* Definition of issues
　abortion, 116–119, 121–123
　affirmative action, 240–242
　birth control, 100–102
　child care, 276–84
　comparable worth policy, 246–47
　contraception, 97–107
　definition of, 3
　family law, 175–176
　job segregation, 243–248
　pornography, 301–306
　poverty, 336–338
　pregnancy leave, 265–267
　rape, 307–16
　sexual harassment, 316–320
　sexuality, 290–292
　single-sex schools, 162–164
　spousal exemption for rape, 312–314
　woman battery, 354–360
　work and welfare, 341–346
Public funding of abortion, 121. *See also* Medicaid
Public opinion on abortion, 126
Public school movement, 140
Putative fathers, 210–11

Quickening, 109, 132 (note 6)
Quid pro quo, 318, 328 (note 8)
Quotas, 70, 72–73, 77, 89, 154

Race and poverty, 4
Race and sex discrimination, 50, 64–65, 145–146, 166–167, 230
Race and sexuality, 319–320
Radical feminism
　abortion, 111–112
　antipornography, 303–306
　defined, 12
　sexuality, 291
Rape-law reform, 309–316
Rape shield statutes, 312
Rationality test, 103–104. *See also* Ordinary scrutiny; *Reed v. Reed*

Reagan, President Ronald, 75, 76, 78–79, 83–
    84, 119, 302, 303
Real Rape, 314
Reasonable man defense, 359–360
Reasonable person standard, 318–319
Redistributive issues, 152, 155
Reed v. Reed, 34–35
Reform
    abortion law, 110–112
    marital property law, 191–193
    prostitution law, 297–300
    rape law, 309–316
Reform feminism, 265, 270–273. *See also*
    Liberal feminism
Regulated prostitution, 297–299, 300
Rehabilitative alimony, 197–198, 199
Rehnquist, Justice William, 40, 43, 44, 286
    (note 3)
Religious schools, 147
Reno, Janet, 76
Representation of women, 59–62
Reproductive hazards in the work place, 251–
    252
Republican party, 30, 31, 46–47, 73, 83–84,
    160
Resistance standards, 308–309, 312
Responsible parenthood, 102
Restricted hours legislation, 221
Retirement, 350–354
Retirement Equity Act (REA) (1984), 352
Reverse discrimination, 240–242
Rhode Island, 77, 267
Rights. *See* Women's rights
Right to privacy, 103–104
Right to choose. *See* Abortion; Pro-choice/
    Pro-life debate
Right to life. *See* Pro-choice/Pro-life debate
Right to sue letter, 232–233
Roe v. Wade, 112–114, 124–125
Roiphe, Katie, 314
Romer v. Evans, 324
Rossi, Alice, 277
Rostker v. Goldberg, 43–44
Roth v. United States, 301
Rucci v. Rucci, 190
Ruddick, Sara, 261
Rule of thumb, 355

Salmon, Marylynn, 196
Same-sex marriage, 323
Sandler, Bernice, 146
Sandwich generation, 273–275
San Francisco, 323
Sanger, Margaret, 100
Scalia, Justice Antonin, 120
Schlafly, Phyllis, 10, 37, 57 (note 13), 247
Schlesinger v. Ballard, 39
Schroeder, Rep. Patricia, 271
Schwartz, Felice, 286 (note 8)
Secondary family income, 193
Secondary school, 140–141
Seneca Falls Declaration, 63–64, 173. *See also*
    Declaration of Sentiments
Separate property, 191–192, 198
Separate spheres ideology, 25–26, 38–39
    and education, 143–145
    and parental rights, 201–202
    and poverty, 334
    as argument for votes for women, 65–66
    reinforced by FMLA, 272–273
    roles in marriage, 181
    and work, 219–220, 257–260
Separation as ground for divorce, 197
Services in marriage, 187–191
Service Workers International, 268
Set-asides, 160
Sex, definition of, 9–10
Sex as a BFOQ, 236–238
Sex as a suspect classification, 42
Sex differences, 21–22. *See also* Equality/
    difference debate
Sex discrimination
    analogy to race discrimination, 50, 64–65,
        230
    in education, 149–166
    pornography defined as, 304–305
    sexual harassment as, 317–320
    under Title VII, 238–240
Sex equity coordinators, 347–348
Sex-plus hiring policy, 237–238
Sexist materials in classroom
    Title IX regulations, 149
    WEEA program, 158
Sexual harassment, 316–320
Sexual history of the victim, 309, 312
Sexual Offense Policy (Antioch College), 314

Shalala, Donna, 76
Shared parental responsibility, 203
Shared partnership, 181–182, 202
Sheppard-Towner Act (1921), 262, 263
The Silent Scream, 133 (note 16)
Simpson, O.J. and Nicole, 364 (note 9)
Single-axis framework, 53
Single-sex schools, 147, 162–167
Slave women, 218
Smith, Rep. Howard, 230
Social feminism, 12, 30, 224, 261–263
Social purity movement, 99, 294–295, 305–306
Social Security Act (1935), 275–276
Social security laws, 350–354
Sororities, 150
Souter, Justice David, 121
South Carolina, 130–131, 165, 196
Spousal consent to abortion, 120
Spousal exemption in rape, 308, 309, 312–314
Spousal notification, 121–123
Stanley v. Illinois, 210
Stanton, Elizabeth Cady, 25, 65, 143
Stanton v. Stanton, 38–39, 182, 184
State laws
    child care, 279
    comparable worth, 247
    domestic violence, 357–358
    education equity, 161–162
    equal pay, 228
    ERAs, 47–48
    maternity leave, 268–270
    prostitution, 297–298
    rape law reform, 311–316
States' rights issues, 65, 138, 148
Statutory rape laws, 43, 294
Sterilization, 107–108
Stevens, Justice Paul, 38, 40
Stewart, Justice Potter, 40
St.James, Margo, 299
STOP-ERA, 37, 46–47, 188, 193
Stranger rape, 314
Strict scrutiny, 28–29, 41. See also Suspect classification
Student organizations, 149–150
Suffrage movement, 62–69
Supplementary Security Income (SSI), 364 (note 8)

Support/services marriage contract, 187–191
Surname, 184–185, 202
Surrogacy contracts, 127–130
Suspect classification, 28–29, 35–36, 41, 56 (note 6)

Tailhook Club, 320
Take Back the Night rallies, 303
Task Force on Legal Equality, 78–79
Task Force on Women, Minorities, and the Handicapped in Science and Technology, 79
Tax laws, 279, 282
Taylor v. Louisiana, 38
Telecommunications law, 306
Temporary alimony, 197–198
Temporary Disability Insurance (TDI), 267–268
Tender years principle, 202
Tennessee, 90
Tests of constitutionality, 27, 35–36
    before 1963, 24–29
    middle-level scrutiny, 39–42, 50
    ordinary scrutiny, 28, 35–36, 40–42
    strict scrutiny, 28–29, 41
    weak, 27–28
Texas, 47, 112, 192
Texas Department of Community Affairs v. Burdine, 238
Textbooks, 149, 158, 170 (note 4)
Thomas, Clarence, 253 (note 7), 319–320
Thompson v. Thompson, 187
Thornburgh v. American College of Obstetricians and Gynecologists, 120
Title VII, 229–233. See also Equal Employment Opportunity Commission
    affirmative action under, 242
    Bennett Amendment, 242, 248
    comparable worth, 248
    effect on maternity leave in the states, 269–270
    pregnancy discrimination, 266, 267–268
    sexual harassment under, 317–319
Title IX, 146–158
    admissions, 163–164
    athletics, 1–2, 150–155
    enforcement, 155–158
    regulations, 148–149
    sexual harassment under, 317

Title XX, 276
Tower, Senator John, 152
Traffic in women, 295–296
Truman, President Harry S, 75
Turandot, 90–91 (note 12)
Twenty-Sixth amendment, 184

U.A.W. v. Johnson Controls, 252
Unemployment insurance, 347
Uniform Child Custody Jurisdiction Act, 214
    (note 15)
Uniform Marriage and Divorce Act (UMDA),
    182, 196–197, 198
Uniform Premarital Agreement Act, 178
Uniform Putative and Unknown Fathers Act,
    211
Uniform Reciprocal Enforcement of Support
    Act (URESA), 204
Uniform state laws, 174
United Steelworkers v. Weber, 242
Unity theory of gender roles, 201–202
Universal breadwinner model, 362–363
U.S. v. Virginia, 38, 39, 169–171, 182

Vermont, 48
Veterans' preference laws, 42, 243
Viability. *See* Fetal viability
Violence Against Women Act (1994), 315–
    316, 358
Virginia, 47
Virginia Military Institute (VMI), 166. See
    also *U.S. v. Virginia*
Virginia Military Institute for Leadership
    (VMIL), 160
Vocational education, 142, 159, 160, 347–348
Vocational Education Act (1976), 347–348.
    See also Perkins Vocational Education
    Act
Vocational Education Equity Coordinators
    (VEECs), 347–348
Voluntary motherhood, 99–100
Vorchheimer v. School District of Philadelphia,
    165
Voter turnout, 81
Voting bloc
    men's, 84
    women's, 79–84
Voting Rights Act (1965), 87
Voting rights of women, 60, 62–69

Wage gap, 243–248, 255
Wards Cove Packing v. Atonio, 240
Washington (state), 47, 48, 192, 246, 247
Weak test of constitutionality, 27–28
Weber test, 242
Webster v. Reproductive Health Services, 120–
    121
Weinberger, Caspar, 149
Weinberger v. Wiesenfeld, 39
Welfare policy, social, 339–346
    child care and, 275–276, 349–350
Welfare reform, 342–346
Welfare rights movement, 341–344
WHISPER, 299–300
White, Justice Byron, 40
White House Conference on Children (1909),
    339–340
White Slave Traffic Act, 295–296
Wife and husband
    alimony, 197–198
    earnings gap, 214 (note 9), 335
    legal rights and responsibilities, 185–191
    parental rights and reponsibilities, 201–205
    property rights in marriage, 191–193
    property settlements in divorce, 198
    support/services contract, 187–191
    surname, 184–185
Williams v. McNair, 165
Wilson, President Woodrow, 66–67
Winthrop College, 165, 170 (note 7)
Wisconsin, 192, 247
Wisconsin Marital Property Act, 192
WISH (Women in the Senate and House), 74
Wollstonecraft, Mary, 141
Women
    definition of, 10
    representation of, 59–62
    in the military, 249
    workers, 226
Women Against Pornography (WAP), 303
Women Against Violence Against Women
    (WAVAW), 303
Women Against Violence in Pornography and
    Media (WAVPM), 303
Women of color. *See also* African American
    women; Hispanic/Latina women; Native
    American women

equality/difference debate, 12–13
ERA, 47
gender roles in marriage, 179
poverty issue, 4
on sexuality, 291–292
vulnerable to prostitution, 299
workers, 224, 250–251
Women's Bureau, 6, 219
  clearing house on child care, 286 (note 5)
  defense of protective laws, 222–224
  Executive Order 11375 and, 234
  on maternity protection, 262–263
  opposition to ERA, 31
  opposition to sex in Title VII, 230
  pregnancy leave issue and, 264–265
  support for Equal Pay Act, 228
Women's colleges, 144, 147–148
Women's commissions, 74–79
Women's Educational Equity Act (WEEA)
  (1974), 158, 168
Women's Equity Action League (WEAL), 145,
  146, 152, 234
Women's Health Movement, 105–107
Women's jobs, 253 (note 13)
Women's Joint Congressional Coordinating
  Committee, 71, 262
Women's Legal Defense Fund (WLDF), 269,
  272
Women's movement, 230–232
Women's representation, 70

Women's rights
  agendas, 13–15
  definition of, 1
  feminism and, 9–13
  historical context, 8–9
  movement, 230–232
Women's rights convention
  Houston, 13
  Seneca Falls, 13
Women's Rights Project, 34–35
Women's role in the family, 176–177
Women's sports, 153–155
Women's studies, 167–168
Women's Studies Act, 168
Women's suffrage campaign, 62–69
Women's Trade Union League (WTUL), 223,
  225
Women's two roles, 259–260, 268–270
Women's voting bloc, 67–68, 79–84. *See also*
  Gender gap
Women's voting rights, 60
Wood, Kimba, 286 (note 6)
Woodwork feminists, 80
Woolf, Virginia, 333
Work, 217–219
Workfare, 343–344
Work Incentive (WIN) programs, 276, 343–
  344
Wyoming, 47, 56 (note 10), 68, 90 (note 6)

Young Women's Christian Association
  (YWCA), 223